Reading STREET

Program Authors

Peter Afflerbach	P. David Pearson
Camille Blachowicz	Sam Sebesta
Candy Dawson Boyd	Deborah Simmons
Elena Izquierdo	Alfred Tatum
Connie Juel	Sharon Vaughn
Edward Kame'enui	Susan Watts Taffe
Donald Leu	Karen Kring Wixson
Jeanne R. Paratore	

PEARSON

Glenview, Illinois • Boston, Massachusetts
Chandler, Arizona • Upper Saddle River, New Jersey

We dedicate Reading Street to
Peter Jovanovich.

His wisdom, courage,
and passion for education
are an inspiration to us all.

Accelerated Reader

PEARSON

ISBN-13: 978-0-328-47055-6
ISBN-10:   0-328-47055-4
4 5 6 7 8 9 10 V003 14 13 12 11
CC1

Any Path, Any Pace

"Welcome to Reading Street! Bienvenidos too."

PEARSON

Find Your Place on Reading Street!

Who said so?

The Leading Researchers,

Program Authors

Peter Afflerbach, Ph.D.
Professor
Department of Curriculum
and Instruction
University of Maryland
at College Park

Camille L. Z. Blachowicz, Ph.D.
Professor of Education
National-Louis University

Candy Dawson Boyd, Ph.D.
Professor
School of Education
Saint Mary's College of California

Elena Izquierdo, Ph.D.
Associate Professor
University of Texas at El Paso

Connie Juel, Ph.D.
Professor of Education
School of Education
Stanford University

Edward J. Kame'enui, Ph.D.
*Dean-Knight Professor of
Education and Director*
Institute for the Development of
Educational Achievement and
the Center on Teaching and Learning
College of Education
University of Oregon

Donald J. Leu, Ph.D.
*John and Maria Neag Endowed
Chair in Literacy and Technology
Director, The New Literacies
Research Lab*
University of Connecticut

Jeanne R. Paratore, Ed.D.
Associate Professor of Education
Department of Literacy and
Language Development
Boston University

P. David Pearson, Ph.D.
Professor and Dean
Graduate School of Education
University of California, Berkeley

Sam L. Sebesta, Ed.D.
Professor Emeritus
College of Education
University of Washington, Seattle

Deborah Simmons, Ph.D.
Professor
College of Education and
Human Development
Texas A&M University

Alfred W. Tatum, Ph.D.
*Associate Professor and Director
of the UIC Reading Clinic*
University of Illinois at Chicago

Sharon Vaughn, Ph.D.
*H. E. Hartfelder/Southland
Corporation Regents Professor
Director, Meadows Center for
Preventing Educational Risk*
University of Texas

Susan Watts Taffe, Ph.D.
Associate Professor in Literacy
Division of Teacher Education
University of Cincinnati

Karen Kring Wixson, Ph.D.
Professor of Education
University of Michigan

Consulting Authors

Jeff Anderson, M.Ed.
Author and Consultant
San Antonio, Texas

Jim Cummins, Ph.D.
Professor
Department of Curriculum,
Teaching and Learning
University of Toronto

Lily Wong Fillmore, Ph.D.
Professor Emerita
Graduate School of Education
University of California, Berkeley

Georgia Earnest García, Ph.D.
Professor
Language and Literacy Division
Department of Curriculum
and Instruction
University of Illinois at
Urbana-Champaign

George A. González, Ph.D.
Professor (Retired)
School of Education
University of Texas-Pan American,
Edinburg

Valerie Ooka Pang, Ph.D.
Professor
School of Teacher Education
San Diego State University

Sally M. Reis, Ph.D.
*Board of Trustees Distinguished
Professor*
Department of Educational
Psychology
University of Connecticut

Jon Scieszka, M.F.A.
*Children's Book Author
Founder of GUYS READ
Named First National Ambassador
for Young People's Literature 2008*

Grant Wiggins, Ed.D.
Educational Consultant
Authentic Education
Concept Development

Lee Wright, M.Ed.
Pearland, Texas

Practitioners, and Authors.

Consultant

Sharroky Hollie, Ph.D.
Assistant Professor
California State University
Dominguez Hills, CA

Teacher Reviewers

Dr. Bettyann Brugger
Educational Support Coordinator–
Reading Office
Milwaukee Public Schools
Milwaukee, WI

Kathleen Burke
K–12 Reading Coordinator
Peoria Public Schools, Peoria, IL

Darci Burns, M.S.Ed.
University of Oregon

Bridget Cantrell
District Intervention Specialist
Blackburn Elementary School
Independence, MO

**Tahira DuPree Chase,
M.A., M.S.Ed.**
Administrator of Elementary
English Language Arts
Mount Vernon City School District
Mount Vernon, NY

Michele Conner
Director, Elementary Education
Aiken County School District
Aiken, SC

Georgia Coulombe
K–6 Regional Trainer/
Literacy Specialist
Regional Center for Training and
Learning (RCTL), Reno, NV

Kelly Dalmas
Third Grade Teacher
Avery's Creek Elementary, Arden, NC

Seely Dillard
First Grade Teacher
Laurel Hill Primary School
Mt. Pleasant, SC

Jodi Dodds-Kinner
Director of Elementary Reading
Chicago Public Schools, Chicago, IL

Dr. Ann Wild Evenson
District Instructional Coach
Osseo Area Schools, Maple Grove, MN

Stephanie Fascitelli
Principal
Apache Elementary, Albuquerque
Public Schools, Albuquerque, NM

Alice Franklin
Elementary Coordinator, Language
Arts & Reading
Spokane Public Schools, Spokane, WA

Laureen Fromberg
Assistant Principal
PS 100 Queens, NY

Kimberly Gibson
First Grade Teacher
Edgar B. Davis Community School
Brockton, MA

Kristen Gray
Lead Teacher
A.T. Allen Elementary School
Concord, NC

Mary Ellen Hazen
State Pre-K Teacher
Rockford Public Schools #205
Rockford, IL

Patrick M. Johnson
Elementary Instructional Director
Seattle Public Schools, Seattle, WA

Theresa Jaramillo Jones
Principal
Highland Elementary School
Las Cruces, NM

Sophie Kowzun
Program Supervisor, Reading/
Language Arts, PreK-5
Montgomery County Public Schools
Rockville, MD

David W. Matthews
Sixth Grade Teacher
Easton Area Middle School
Easton, PA

Ana Nuncio
Editor and Independent Publisher
Salem, MA

Joseph Peila
Principal
Chappell Elementary School
Chicago, IL

Ivana Reimer
Literacy Coordinator
PS 100 Queens, NY

Sally Riley
Curriculum Coordinator
Rochester Public Schools
Rochester, NH

Dyan M. Smiley
Independent Educational Consultant

Michael J. Swiatowiec
Lead Literacy Teacher
Graham Elementary School
Chicago, IL

Dr. Helen Taylor
Director of English Education
Portsmouth City Public Schools
Portsmouth, VA

Carol Thompson
Teaching and Learning Coach
Independence School District
Independence, MO

Erinn Zeitlin
Kindergarten Teacher
Carderock Springs Elementary School
Bethesda, MD

Any Path, Any Pace

UNIT 6

The Unexpected

In this Teacher's Edition Unit 6, Volume 1

In the **First Stop** on Reading Street

- **Dear Fifth Grade Teacher**

- **Research into Practice on Reading Street**

- **Guide to Reading Street**

- **Assessment on Reading Street**

- **Customize Writing on Reading Street**

- **Differentiate Instruction on Reading Street**

- **ELL on Reading Street**

- **Customize Literacy on Reading Street**

- **Digital Products on Reading Street**

- **Teacher Resources for Grade 5**

- **Index**

GO Digital!

See It!
- Big Question Video
- Concept Talk Video
- Envision It! Animations

Hear It!
- eSelections
- eReaders
- Grammar Jammer
- Leveled Reader Database

Do It!
- Vocabulary Activities
- Story Sort
- 21st Century Skills
- Online Assessment
- Letter Tile Drag and Drop

UNIT 1

Meeting Challenges

Volume 1

Volume 2

UNIT 2

Doing the Right Thing

Volume 1

Volume 2

Inventors and Artists

Volume 1

Volume 2

What do people gain from the work of inventors and artists?

UNIT 4

Adapting

Volume 1

Volume 2

UNIT 5

Adventurers

Volume 1

WEEK 1 • The Skunk Ladder

WEEK 2 • The Unsinkable Wreck of the R.M.S. Titanic   Expository Text

WEEK 3 • Talk with an Astronaut

Volume 2

WEEK 4 • Journey to the Center of the Earth

WEEK 5 • Ghost Towns of the American West

WEEK 6 • Interactive Review

Who goes seeking adventure and why?

UNIT 6

The Unexpected

Volume 1

WEEK 1 • The Truth About Austin's Amazing Bats   Expository Text
The Animals in My Life Autobiography

WEEK 2 • The Mystery of St. Matthew Island
Expository Text
City Hawks Expository Text

WEEK 3 • King Midas and the Golden Touch
Myth
Prometheus, the Fire-Bringer Myth

Volume 2

WEEK 4 • The *Hindenburg*   Expository Text
The Mystery of the *Hindenburg* Disaster Web Site

WEEK 5 • Sweet Music in Harlem
Realistic Fiction
Author's Note Expository Text

WEEK 6 • Interactive Review

What can we learn from encounters with the unexpected?

UNIT 6

Skills Overview

	WEEK 1 	**WEEK 2** 
	The Truth About Austin's Amazing Bats Expository Text pp. 324–335 **The Animals in My Life** Autobiography pp. 340–341	**The Mystery of St. Matthew Island** Expository Text pp. 350–359 **City Hawks** Expository Text pp. 364–367
Get Ready to Read		
Question of the Week	How can unplanned situations have positive outcomes?	What unexpected effects can humans have on nature?
Amazing Words	*unintended, fortuitous, advantageous, potential, spontaneous, perspective, happenstance, occurrences, perceptive, unaware*	*accommodates, refuge, domesticated, contaminated, grandiose, prune, composition, depletion, natural resources, aggravate*
Word Analysis	Compound Words	Russian Word Origins
Literary Terms	Sensory Details	Word Choice
Story Structure/Text Features	Cause and Effect	Maps
Read and Comprehend		
Comprehension	T 🔄 **Skill** Draw Conclusions 🔄 **Strategy** Important Ideas **Review Skill** Generalize	T 🔄 **Skill** Main Idea and Details 🔄 **Strategy** Text Structure **Review Skill** Sequence
Vocabulary	T 🔄 **Skill** Unknown Words bizarre, breathtaking, headline, high-pitched, roost, vital	T 🔄 **Skill** Endings -*s* and -*es* bleached, carcasses, decay, parasites, scrawny, starvation, suspicions, tundra
Fluency	Accuracy	Appropriate Phrasing
Language Arts		
Writing	Journal Entry Trait: Voice	Mystery Trait: Focus/Ideas
Conventions	Modifiers	Conjunctions
Spelling	Suffixes -*ous*, -*sion*, -*ion*, -*ation*	Final Syllable -*ant*, -*ent*, -*ance*, -*ence*
Speaking/Listening	Debate	Interview
Research Skills	Follow and Clarify Directions	Time Line

The Big Question

What can we learn from encounters with the unexpected?

WEEK 3	WEEK 4	WEEK 5	WEEK 6
King Midas and the Golden Touch Myth pp. 376–393 **Prometheus the Fire-Bringer** Myth pp. 398–399	**The *Hindeburg*** Expository Text pp. 408–423 **The Mystery of the *Hindenburg* Disaster** Web Site pp. 428–431	**Sweet Music in Harlem** Realistic Fiction pp. 440–457 **Author's Note** Expository Text pp. 462–465	**Interactive Review**
How can we learn from the results of our actions?	How can unexpected encounters reveal hidden dangers?	What unexpected influence do we have on those around us?	Connect the Question of the Week to the Big Question
specimen, valuable, geologist, rare, deplorable, outcome, victor, unforeseen, repercussion, penitence	*updrafts, waterlogged, destination, calamity, suitable, locale, traction, prudent, passport, augment*	*career, inspired, wealth, celebrity, fervor, malevolent, foster, renown, coerce, predispose*	**Review** Amazing Words for Unit 6
Complex Spelling Patterns: ci=/sh/, ti=/sh/, ous=/us/	Word Families	Compound Words	
Foreshadowing	Symbolism	Point of View	
Conflict and Resolution	Illustrations/Captions	Sequence	
T **Skill** Compare and Contrast **Strategy** Story Structure **Review Skill** Draw Conclusions	T **Skill** Fact and Opinion **Strategy** Predict and Set Purpose **Review Skill** Main Idea and Details	T **Skill** Sequence **Strategy** Background Knowledge **Review Skill** Draw Conclusions	**Review** Draw Conclusions, Main Idea and Details, Compare and Contrast, Fact and Opinion, Sequence
T **Skill** Suffixes *-less* and *-ful* adorn, cleanse, lifeless, precious, realm, spoonful	T **Skill** Unfamiliar Words criticizing, cruised, drenching, era, explosion, hydrogen	T **Skill** Homographs bass, clarinet, fidgety, forgetful, jammed, nighttime, secondhand	**Review** Endings *-s, -es,* Unknown Words, Unfamiliar Words, Homographs, Suffixes *-less, -ful*
Rate	Appropriate Phrasing	Expression	**Review** Expression, Accuracy, Appropriate Phrasing, and Rate
Parody Trait: Voice	Review Trait: Organization/Paragraphs	Personal Narrative Trait: Voice	Quick Write for Fluency
Commas	Quotations and Quotation Marks	Semicolons, Colons, Periods, Hyphens	**Review** Conventions covered in Unit 6.
Latin Roots	Related Words	Easily Confused Words	**Review** Spelling patterns covered in Unit 6.
Storytelling	Media Literacy: Newscast	Readers' Theater	
Order Form/Application	Map/Globe/Atlas	Poster/Announcement	

UNIT 6 Monitor Progress

SUCCESS PREDICTOR	WEEK 1	WEEK 2	WEEK 3	WEEK 4
Fluency (WCPM)	Accuracy 130–140 WCPM	Appropriate Phrasing 130–140 WCPM	Rate 130–140 WCPM	Appropriate Phrasing 130–140 WCPM
Oral Vocabulary/ Concept Development (assessed informally) (Vocabulary)	unintended fortuitous advantageous potential spontaneous perspective happenstance occurrences perceptive unaware	accommodates refuge domesticated contaminated grandiose prune composition depletion natural resources aggravate	specimen valuable geologist rare deplorable outcome victor unforeseen repercussion penitence	updrafts waterlogged destination calamity suitable locale traction prudent passport augment
Lesson Vocabulary	T bizarre T breathtaking T headline T high-pitched T roost T vital	T bleached T carcasses T decay T parasites T scrawny T starvation T suspicions T tundra	T adorn T cleanse T lifeless T precious T realm T spoonful	T criticizing T cruised T drenching T era T explosion T hydrogen
Text Comprehension (Retelling)	T Skill Draw Conclusions Strategy Important Ideas	T Skill Main Idea and Details Strategy Text Structure	T Skill Compare and Contrast Strategy Story Structure	T Skill Fact and Opinion Strategy Predict and Set Purpose

Key

T	Tested Skill
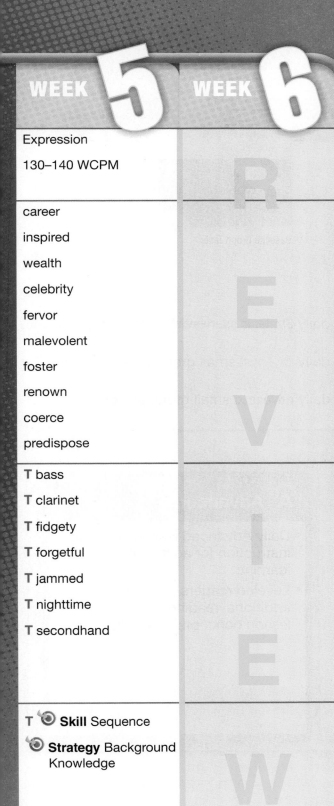	Target Skill

WEEK **5**	WEEK **6**
Expression 130–140 WCPM	R E V I E W
career inspired wealth celebrity fervor malevolent foster renown coerce predispose	
T bass **T** clarinet **T** fidgety **T** forgetful **T** jammed **T** nighttime **T** secondhand	
T **Skill** Sequence **Strategy** Background Knowledge	

Online ASSESSMENT
ReadingStreet.com

Online Classroom

Manage Data

- Assign the Unit 6 Benchmark Test for students to take online.

- Online Assessment records results and generates reports by school, grade, classroom, or student.

- Use reports to disaggregate and aggregate Unit 6 skills and standards data to monitor progress.

- Based on class lists created to support the categories important for AYP (gender, ethnicity, migrant education, English proficiency, disabilities, economic status), reports let you track adequate yearly progress every six weeks.

Group

- Use results from Unit 6 Benchmark Tests taken online through Online Assessment to measure whether students have mastered the English-Language Arts Content Standards taught in this unit.

- Reports in Online Assessment suggest whether students need Extra Support or Intervention.

Individualized Instruction

- Assessments are correlated to Unit 6 tested skills and standards so that prescriptions for individual teaching and learning plans can be created.

- Individualized prescriptions target instruction and accelerate student progress toward learning outcome goals.

- Prescriptions include remediation activities and resources to reteach Unit 6 skills and standards.

Assessment and Grouping
for Data-Driven Instruction

4-Step Plan for Assessment
1 Diagnose and Differentiate
2 Monitor Progress
3 Assess and Regroup
4 Summative Assessment

STEP 1 **Diagnose and Differentiate**

Diagnose

To make initial grouping decisions, use the Baseline Group Test, the *Texas Primary Reading Inventory (TPRI),* or another initial placement test. Depending on student's ability levels, you may have more than one of each group.

Baseline Group Tests

Differentiate

If... student performance is **then...** use the regular instruction and the daily **Strategic Intervention** small group lessons.

If... student performance is **OL** **then...** use the regular instruction and the daily **On-Level** small group lessons.

If... student performance is **A** **then...** use the regular instruction and the daily **Advanced** small group lessons.

Small Group Time

SI Strategic Intervention

- Daily small group lessons provide more intensive instruction, more scaffolding, more practice, and more opportunities to respond.
- Reteach lessons in the *First Stop on Reading Street* provide more instruction with target skills.
- Leveled readers build background and provide practice for target skills and vocabulary.

OL On-Level

- Explicit instructional routines teach core skills and strategies.
- Daily On-Level lessons provide more practice and more opportunities to respond.
- Independent activities provide practice for core skills and extension and enrichment options.
- Leveled readers provide additional reading and practice for core skills and vocabulary.

A Advanced

- Daily Advanced lessons provide instruction for accelerated learning.
- Leveled readers provide additional reading tied to lesson concepts and skills.

Additional Differentiated Learning Options

Reading Street Response to Intervention Kit

- Focused intervention lessons on the five critical areas of reading: phonemic awareness, phonics, vocabulary, comprehension, and fluency

My Sidewalks on Reading Street

- Intensive intervention for struggling readers

STEP 2 Monitor Progress

Weekly Tests

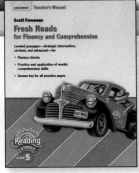
Fresh Reads for Fluency and Comprehension

Use these tools during lesson teaching to **monitor student progress.**

- **Skill and Strategy** instruction during reading
- **Don't Wait Until Friday** boxes to check retelling, fluency, and oral vocabulary
- **Weekly Assessment** on Day 5 checks comprehension and fluency
- **Reader's and Writer's Notebook** pages at point of use
- **Weekly Tests** assess target skills for the week
- **Fresh Reads** for Fluency and Comprehension

STEP 3 Assess and Regroup

Unit Assessment Charts in First Stop

Use these tools during lesson teaching to **assess and regroup.**

- **Weekly Assessments** Record results of weekly assessments in retelling, comprehension, and fluency to track student progress.
- **Unit Benchmark Test** Administer this assessment to check mastery of unit skills.
- **Regroup** We recommend the first regrouping to be at the end of Unit 2. Use weekly assessment information and Unit Benchmark Test performance to inform regrouping decisions. Then regroup at the end of each subsequent unit.

Group

Baseline Group Test	→ Regroup Units 1 and 2	→ Regroup Unit 3	→ Regroup Unit 4	→ Regroup Unit 5	→ End of Year
Weeks 1-6	Weeks 7-12	Weeks 13-18	Weeks 19-24	Weeks 25-30	Weeks 31-36

Outside assessments, such as *DRA, TPRI,* and *DIBELS,* may recommend regrouping at other times during the year.

STEP 4 Summative Assessment

Unit and End-of-Year Benchmark Tests

Use these tools after lesson teaching to **assess students.**

- **Unit Benchmark Tests** Use to measure a student's mastery of each unit's skills.
- **End-of-Year Benchmark Test** Use to measure a student's mastery of program skills covered in all six units.

Concept Launch

The Unexpected

Understanding By Design

Grant Wiggins, Ed. D.
Reading Street Author

"The best questions point to and highlight the big ideas. They serve as doorways through which learners explore the key concepts, themes, theories, issues, and problems that reside within the content, perhaps as yet unseen: it is through the process of actively 'interrogating' the content through provocative questions that students deepen their understanding."

Reading Street Online

www.ReadingStreet.com

• Big Question Video
• eSelections
• Envision It! Animations
• Story Sort

What can we learn from encounters with the unexpected?

Theme Launch xxi

UNIT 6

Small Group Time
Flexible Pacing Plans

Key
- **SI** Strategic Intervention
- **OL** On-Level
- **A** Advanced
- **ELL** ELL

SI   OL   A

5 Day Plan

DAY 1	• Reinforce the Concept
	• Read Leveled Readers
	  Concept Literacy
	  Below-Level

DAY 2	• Comprehension Skill • Comprehension Strategy • Revisit Main Selection
DAY 3	• Vocabulary Skill • Revisit Main Selection
DAY 4	• Practice Retelling • Read/Revisit Paired Selection
DAY 5	• Reread for Fluency • Reread Leveled Readers

4 Day Plan

DAY 1	• Reinforce the Concept
	• Read Leveled Readers
	  Concept Literacy
	  Below-Level

DAY 2	• Comprehension Skill • Comprehension Strategy • Revisit Main Selection
DAY 3	• Vocabulary Skill • Revisit Main Selection
DAY 4	• Practice Retelling • Read/Revisit Paired Selection • Reread for Fluency • Reread Leveled Readers

3 Day Plan

DAY 1	• Reinforce the Concept
	• Read Leveled Readers
	  Concept Literacy
	  Below-Level

DAY 2	• Comprehension Skill • Comprehension Strategy • Revisit Main Selection

DAY 3	• Practice Retelling
	• Read/Revisit Paired
	  Selection
	• Reread for Fluency
	• Reread Leveled
	  Readers

ELL

5 Day Plan

DAY 1	• Frontload Concept • Preteach Skills • Conventions/Writing
DAY 2	• Review Concept/Skills • Frontload and Read Main Selection • Conventions/Writing
DAY 3	• Review Concept/Skills • Reread Main Selection • Conventions/Writing
DAY 4	• Review Concept/Skills • Read ELL or ELD Reader • Conventions/Writing
DAY 5	• Review Concept/Skills • Reread ELL or ELD Reader • Conventions/Writing

4 Day Plan

DAY 1	• Frontload Concept • Preteach Skills • Conventions/Writing
DAY 2	• Review Concept/Skills • Frontload and Read Main Selection • Conventions/Writing
DAY 3	• Review Concept/Skills • Reread Main Selection • Conventions/Writing
DAY 4	• Review Concept/Skills • Read ELL or ELD Reader • Conventions/Writing

3 Day Plan

DAY 1	• Frontload Concept • Preteach Skills • Conventions/Writing
DAY 2	• Review Concept/Skills • Frontload and Read Main Selection • Conventions/Writing
DAY 3	• Review Concept/Skills • Read ELL or ELD Reader • Conventions/Writing

This Week on Reading Street!

Question of the Week

How can unplanned situations have positive outcomes?

Daily Plan

Don't Wait Until Friday

Whole Group

- ◉ Draw Conclusions
- ◉ Unknown Words
- • Fluency/Accuracy
- • Research and Inquiry

MONITOR PROGRESS | Success Predictor

Day 1	Days 2–3	Day 4	Day 5
Check Oral Vocabulary	Check Retelling	Check Fluency	Check Oral Vocabulary

Small Group

Teacher-Led

- • Reading Support
- • Skill Support
- • Fluency Practice

Practice Stations

Independent Activities

Customize Literacy More support for a balanced literacy approach, see pp. CL•1–CL•47

Customize Writing More support for a customized writing approach, see pp. CW•1–CW•10

Whole Group

- • Writing: Journal Entry
- • Conventions: Modifiers
- • Spelling: Suffixes -ous, -sion, -ion, -ation

Assessment

- • Weekly Tests
- • Day 5 Assessment
- • Fresh Reads

You Are Here!
Unit 6
Week 1

This Week's Reading Selections

Main Selection
Genre: **Expository Text**

Paired Selection
Genre: **Autobiography**

Leveled Readers

ELL and ELD Readers

Resources on Reading Street!

	Build Concepts	Comprehension
Whole Group	 Let's Talk About pp. 318–319	 Envision It! Skills/ Strategies  Comprehension Skills Lesson pp. 320–321
Go Digital	• Concept Talk Video	• Envision It! Animations • eSelections
Small Group and Independent Practice	 The Truth About Austin's Amazing Bats pp. 324–325 ELL and ELD Readers Leveled Readers	 The Truth About Austin's Amazing Bats pp. 324–325 ELL and ELD Readers Leveled Readers Envision It! Skills/ Strategies Reader's and Writer's Notebook Practice Station Flip Chart
Go Digital	• eReaders • eSelections	• Envision It! Animations • eSelections • eReaders
Customize Literacy	• Leveled Readers	• Envision It! Skills and Strategies Handbook • Leveled Readers
Go Digital	• Concept Talk Video • Big Question Video • eReaders	• Envision It! Animations • eReaders

Question of the Week
How can unplanned situations have positive outcomes?

Vocabulary	Fluency	Conventions and Writing

Envision It! Vocabulary Cards — Vocabulary Skill Lesson pp. 322–323	Let's Learn It! pp. 342–343	Let's Write It! pp. 338–339
• Envision It! Vocabulary Cards • Vocabulary Activities	• eSelections • eReaders	• Grammar Jammer

Envision It! Vocabulary Cards — The Truth About Austin's Amazing Bats pp. 324–325 — Practice Station Flip Chart Words! — Reader's and Writer's Notebook	The Truth About Austin's Amazing Bats pp. 324–325 — Practice Station Flip Chart Leveled Readers — ELL and ELD Readers	Reader's and Writer's Notebook — The Truth About Austin's Amazing Bats pp. 324–325 Practice Station Flip Chart
• Envision It! Vocabulary Cards • Vocabulary Activities • eSelections	• eSelections • eReaders	• Grammar Jammer
• Envision It! Vocabulary Cards	• Leveled Readers	• Reader's and Writer's Notebook
• Vocabulary Activities	• eReaders	• Grammar Jammer

You Are Here! Unit 6 Week 1

My 5-Day Planner for Reading Street!

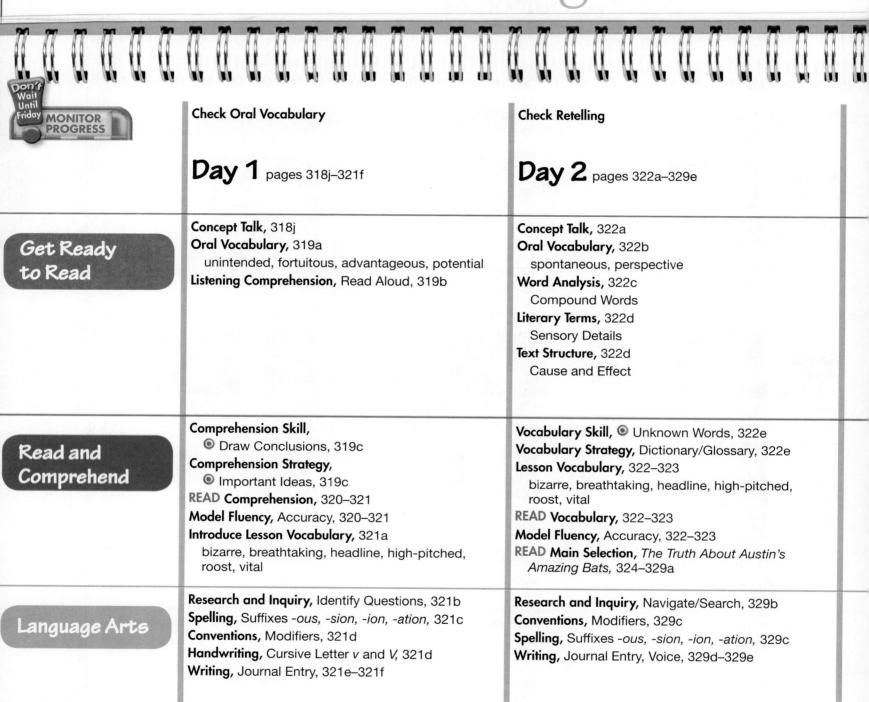

MONITOR PROGRESS
Don't Wait Until Friday

	Check Oral Vocabulary **Day 1** pages 318j–321f	**Check Retelling** **Day 2** pages 322a–329e

Get Ready to Read	**Concept Talk,** 318j
	Oral Vocabulary, 319a
	  unintended, fortuitous, advantageous, potential
	Listening Comprehension, Read Aloud, 319b
		Concept Talk, 322a
		Oral Vocabulary, 322b
		  spontaneous, perspective
		Word Analysis, 322c
		  Compound Words
		Literary Terms, 322d
		  Sensory Details
		Text Structure, 322d
		  Cause and Effect

Read and Comprehend	**Comprehension Skill,**
	  ◉ Draw Conclusions, 319c
	Comprehension Strategy,
	  ◉ Important Ideas, 319c
	READ Comprehension, 320–321
	Model Fluency, Accuracy, 320–321
	Introduce Lesson Vocabulary, 321a
	  bizarre, breathtaking, headline, high-pitched, roost, vital
		Vocabulary Skill, ◉ Unknown Words, 322e
		Vocabulary Strategy, Dictionary/Glossary, 322e
		Lesson Vocabulary, 322–323
		  bizarre, breathtaking, headline, high-pitched, roost, vital
		READ Vocabulary, 322–323
		Model Fluency, Accuracy, 322–323
		READ Main Selection, *The Truth About Austin's Amazing Bats,* 324–329a

Language Arts	**Research and Inquiry,** Identify Questions, 321b **Spelling,** Suffixes -ous, -sion, -ion, -ation, 321c **Conventions,** Modifiers, 321d **Handwriting,** Cursive Letter v and V, 321d **Writing,** Journal Entry, 321e–321f	**Research and Inquiry,** Navigate/Search, 329b **Conventions,** Modifiers, 329c **Spelling,** Suffixes -ous, -sion, -ion, -ation, 329c **Writing,** Journal Entry, Voice, 329d–329e

You Are Here!
Unit 6
Week 1

Question of the Week

How can unplanned situations have positive outcomes?

Check Retelling	Check Fluency	Check Oral Vocabulary
Day 3 pages 330a–339c	**Day 4** pages 340a–343e	**Day 5** pages 343f–343q

Concept Talk, 330a
Oral Vocabulary, 330b
   happenstance, occurrences
Comprehension Check, 330c
Check Retelling, 330d
	Concept Talk, 340a
	Oral Vocabulary, 340b
	   perceptive, unaware
	Genre, Autobiography:
	   Point of View, 340c
		Concept Wrap Up, 343f
		Check Oral Vocabulary, 343g
		   unintended, fortuitous, advanta-
		   geous, potential, spontaneous,
		   perspective, happenstance,
		   occurrences, perceptive, unaware
		Amazing Ideas, 343g
		Review ⊙ Draw Conclusions, 343h
		Review ⊙ Unknown Words, 343h
		Review Word Analysis, 343i
		Review Literary Terms, 343i

READ Main Selection, *The Truth About Austin's Amazing Bats,* 330–335a
Retelling, 336–337
Think Critically, 337a
Model Fluency, Accuracy, 337b
Reasearch and Study Skills,
   Follow/Clarify Directions, 337c
	READ Paired Selection,
	   "The Animals in My Life,"
	   340–341a
	Let's Learn It! 342–343a
	   Fluency: Accuracy
	   Vocabulary: Unknown Words
	   Listening and Speaking:
	   Debate
		Fluency Assessment,
		   wcpm, 343j–343k
		Comprehension Assessment,
		   ⊙ Draw Conclusions, 343l–343m

Research and Inquiry, Analyze, 337d
Conventions, Modifiers, 337e
Spelling, Suffixes *-ous, -sion, -ion, -ation,* 337e
Let's Write It! Journal Entry, 338–339a
Writing, Journal Entry, Voice, 339a–339c
	Research and Inquiry,
	   Synthesize, 343b
	Conventions, Modifiers, 343c
	Spelling, Suffixes *-ous, -sion, -ion, -ation,* 343c
	Writing, Journal Entry, Revising, 343d–343e
		Research and Inquiry,
		   Communicate, 343n
		Conventions, Modifiers, 343o
		Spelling Test, Suffixes *-ous, -sion, -ion, -ation,* 343o
		Writing, Journal Entry, Modifiers, 343p–343q
		Quick Write for Fluency, 343q

Grouping Options for Differentiated Instruction
Turn the page for the small group time lesson plan.

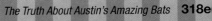

Planning Small Group Time on *Reading Street!*

SMALL GROUP TIME RESOURCES

Look for this Small Group Time box each day to help meet the individual needs of all your students. Differentiated Instruction lessons appear on the DI pages at the end of each week.

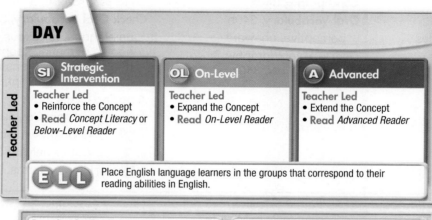

DAY 1

Teacher Led

SI Strategic Intervention	**OL** On-Level	**A** Advanced
Teacher Led	**Teacher Led**	**Teacher Led**
• Reinforce the Concept	• Expand the Concept	• Extend the Concept
• Read *Concept Literacy or Below-Level Reader*	• Read *On-Level Reader*	• Read *Advanced Reader*

ELL Place English language learners in the groups that correspond to their reading abilities in English.

Practice Stations
• Read for Meaning
• Get Fluent
• Word Work

Independent Activities
• Concept Talk Video
• Reader's and Writer's Notebook
• Research and Inquiry

ELL

ELL Reader
Advanced
Advanced High

ELD Reader
Beginning
Intermediate

ELL Poster

You Are Here!
Unit 6
Week 1

Day 1

SI Strategic Intervention	Reinforce the Concept, DI•1–DI•2 Read **Concept Literacy Reader** or **Below-Level Reader**
OL On-Level	Expand the Concept, DI•7 Read **On-Level Reader**
A Advanced	Extend the Concept, DI•12 Read **Advanced Reader**
ELL English Language Learners	DI•16–DI•25 Frontload Concept Preteach Skills Writing

Reading Street
Response to
Intervention Kit

Reading Street
Practice Stations Kit

SI Strategic Intervention

Concept Literacy Reader

OL On-Level

On-Level Reader

A Advanced

Advanced Reader

Below-Level
Reader

The Truth About Austin's Amazing Bats pp. 324–325

The Animals in My Life pp. 340–341

Small Group Weekly Plan

Day 2	Day 3	Day 4	Day 5
Reinforce Comprehension, DI•3 **Revisit Main Selection**	**Reinforce Vocabulary,** DI•4 **Read/Revisit Main Selection**	**Reinforce Comprehension,** Practice Retelling DI•5 Genre Focus **Read/Revisit Paired Selection**	**Practice Fluency,** DI•6 **Reread Concept Literacy Reader** or **Below-Level Reader**
Expand Comprehension, DI•8 **Revisit Main Selection**	**Expand Vocabulary,** DI•9 **Read/Revisit Main Selection**	**Expand Comprehension,** Practice Retelling DI•10 Genre Focus **Read/Revisit Paired Selection**	**Practice Fluency,** DI•11 **Reread On-Level Reader**
Extend Comprehension, DI•13 **Revisit Main Selection**	**Extend Vocabulary,** DI•14 **Read/Revisit Main Selection**	**Extend Comprehension,** Genre Focus DI•15 **Read/Revisit Paired Selection**	**Practice Fluency,** DI•15 **Reread Advanced Reader**
DI•16–DI•25 **Review Concept/Skills** **Frontload Main Selection** **Practice**	DI•16–DI•25 **Review Concept/Skills** **Reread Main Selection** **Practice**	DI•16–DI•25 **Review Concept** **Read ELL/ELD Readers** **Practice**	DI•16–DI•25 **Review Concept/Skills** **Reread ELL/ELD Reader** **Writing**

Practice Stations for Everyone on Reading Street!

Word Wise
Greek word parts

Objectives
• Spell words with Greek word parts.

Materials
• *Word Wise* Flip Chart Activity 26
• word cards
• paper • pencil

Differentiated Activities

🔵 Choose five words cards. Write the words in a list. Circle the Greek word part in each one. Write a sentence for each of your words. Add other words with these Greek word parts to your list.

🔺 Choose six word cards. List the words, and circle the Greek word part in each one. Write sentences using each of your words. Add other words with these Greek word parts to your list.

◼ Choose eight word cards, and write the words in a list. Circle the Greek word part in each word. Write sentences using each word. Add other words with these word parts to the list.

Technology
• Online Dictionary

Word Work
Greek word parts

Objectives
• Identify and write words with Greek word parts.

Materials
• *Word Work* Flip Chart Activity 26
• word cards
• paper • pencil

Differentiated Activities

🔵 Choose four word cards with different Greek word parts. Make a four-column chart. Use the word parts as headings. Quietly say each word aloud. Fill in your chart. Add other words you know.

🔺 Choose five word cards with different Greek word parts. Make a five-column chart using the word parts as headings. Quietly say each word. Fill in the chart, and add other words with these parts.

◼ Sort the word cards by Greek word part. Make a chart using the word parts as headings. Quietly say each word. Fill in the chart with the words on the cards. Add other words with these word parts.

Technology
• Modeled Pronunciation Audio CD

Words to Know
Prefixes *over-* and *in-*

Objectives
• Determine the meaning of words with prefixes *over-* and *in-*.

Materials
• *Words to Know* Flip Chart Activity 26
• word cards
• paper • pencil

Differentiated Activities

🔵 Choose three word cards with words that have each prefix. Write your words in a list. Circle the prefix in each word. Write a sentence for each of your words. Add other words you know with these prefixes to your list.

🔺 Choose four word cards with words that have each prefix. Write your words in a list. Circle the prefix in each word, and write a sentence for each word. Add other words you know with these prefixes to your list.

◼ Choose six word cards with words that have each prefix, and write your words in a list. Circle each word's base word, and write sentences using the words. Add other words you know with these prefixes to your list.

Technology
• Online Dictionary

You Are Here!
Unit 6
Week 1

Key

● Below-Level Activities

▲ On-Level Activities

■ Advanced Activities

Practice Station Flip Chart

Let's Write!
Summary

Objectives
· Write a summary.

Materials
· *Let's Write!* Flip Chart Activity 26
· paper · pencil

Differentiated Activities

● Think of book you read recently. Write a summary of the book. Explain what the book is about. Include the book's most important events and details in your summary.

▲ Write a summary of a book you read recently. Explain what the book is about, and include only the most important ideas and details in your summary.

■ Write a summary of a book you read recently. Provide an explanation of what the book is about, and summarize the book's most important facts and details.

Technology
· Online Graphic Organizers

Read for Meaning
Generalize

Objectives
· Make a generalization based on text evidence.

Materials
· *Read for Meaning* Flip Chart Activity 26
· Leveled Readers
· paper · pencil

Differentiated Activities

● Choose and read one of the books your teacher provides. Write a sentence stating a generalization. Base your generalization on information in the text. Include a sentence with a detail from the text to support your generalization.

▲ Choose and read one of the books your teacher provides, and write a sentence stating a generalization. Base your generalization on information in the text. Write sentences with details to support your generalization.

■ Choose and read one of the books your teacher provides. Write sentences stating two generalizations you made based on information in the text. For each generalization, write sentences that include evidence from the text to support your opinion.

Technology
· Leveled Reader Database

Get Fluent
Practice fluent reading.

Objectives
· Read aloud at an appropriate rate.

Materials
· *Get Fluent* Flip Chart Activity 26
· Leveled Readers

Differentiated Activities

● Work with a partner. Choose a Concept Literacy Reader or Below-Level Reader. Take turns reading a page from the book. Use the reader to practice appropriate rate. Provide feedback as needed.

▲ Work with a partner. Choose an On-Level Reader. Take turns reading a page from the book. Use the reader to practice appropriate rate. Provide feedback as needed.

■ Work with a partner. Choose an Advanced Reader. Take turns reading a page from the book. Use the reader to practice appropriate rate. Provide feedback as needed.

Technology
· Leveled Reader Database
· Reading Street Readers CD-ROM

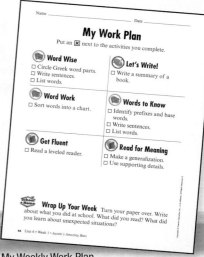

My Weekly Work Plan

Week 1

Objectives
- Introduce the weekly concept.
- Develop oral vocabulary.

Today at a Glance

Oral Vocabulary
unintended, fortuitous, advantageous, potential

Comprehension
- Draw conclusions
- Important ideas

Reading
"The Mystery of the Monarchs"

Fluency
Accuracy

Lesson Vocabulary
Tested vocabulary

Research and Inquiry
Identify questions

Spelling
Suffixes *-ous, -sion, -ion, -ation*

Conventions
Modifiers

Handwriting
Cursive letters *v* and *V*

Writing
Journal entry

Concept Talk

Question of the Week

How can unplanned situations have positive outcomes?

Introduce the concept

To further explore the unit concept of The Unexpected, this week students will read, write, and talk about how things that happen by accident can have surprising results. Write the Question of the Week on the board.

ROUTINE — Activate Prior Knowledge — Team Talk

1. **Think** Have students think about instances where something unplanned brought about a happy result.

2. **Pair** Have pairs of students discuss the Question of the Week, considering each other's suggestions.

3. **Share** Call on a few students to share their ideas with the group. Guide the discussion and encourage elaboration with prompts such as:

   - Can inventors stumble upon new inventions by accident? How?

   - What books, movies, or TV shows have you seen about a chance event that leads to something good?

Routines Flip Chart

Anchored Talk

Develop oral vocabulary

Have students turn to pp. 318–319 in their Student Editions. Look at each of the photos. Then, use the prompts to guide discussion and create the *How unplanned situations have positive outcomes* concept map.

- What is going on at the table? (**The girl is being surprised with a birthday cake.**) She might have expected a cake, but she probably didn't expect it to be so fancy with sparkling candles. Let's add *Surprises* to our map.

- What's unexpected about the hippo and a bird? (**Most people wouldn't expect to see them "hanging out" together.**) I wonder if there's something advantageous about this situation that helps both of them. Let's add *Unexpected situation* to our concept map.

Student Edition pp. 318–319

Oral Vocabulary

Let's Talk About

Unplanned Situations, Positive Outcomes

● Describe ways unplanned situations can have positive outcomes.

● Listen to and interpret messages other students have about unplanned situations.

● Ask questions to clarify classmates' messages.

READING STREET ONLINE
CONCEPT TALK VIDEO
www.ReadingStreet.com

● You've learned
2 5 0
★ Amazing Words ★
so far this year!

319

Amazing Words

You've learned **2 5 0** words so far.

You'll learn **0 1 0** words this week!

unintended	perspective
fortuitous	happen-
advantageous	stance
potential	occurrences
spontaneous	perceptive
	unaware

Writing on Demand

Ask students to respond to the photos on pp. 318–319 by writing as well as they can and as much as they can about how unplanned situations can have positive outcomes.

- Do you think there's a potential for a big smile from Mom? Why? (The kids are going to surprise her with flowers.)

- Ask: How can unplanned situations have positive outcomes?

```
        How
     unplanned
    situations can
    have positive
       outcomes
       |        |
  Unexpected   Surprises
  situation
```

Connect to reading

Tell students that this week they will be reading about unexpected situations with positive outcomes. Encourage students to add concept-related words to the week's concept map.

ELL Preteach Concepts Use the Day 1 instruction on ELL Poster 26 to assess and build background knowledge, develop concepts, and build oral vocabulary.

ELL

English Language Learners

ELL support Additional ELL support and modified instruction is provided in the *ELL Handbook* and in the ELL Support lessons on pp. DI•16–DI•25.

Listening comprehension English learners will benefit from additional visual support to understand the key terms in the concept map. Use the pictures on pp. 318–319 to scaffold understanding.

Frontload for Read Aloud Use the modified Read Aloud on page DI•19 of the ELL Support lessons to prepare students to listen to "A Lucky Accident" on p. 319b.

ELL Poster 26

Objectives
- Develop listening comprehension.
- Develop oral vocabulary.

Check Oral Vocabulary
SUCCESS PREDICTOR

Oral Vocabulary
Amazing Words

Introduce Amazing Words

"A Lucky Accident" on p. 319b is about some inventions that were discovered by accident. Tell students to listen for this week's Amazing Words—*unintended, fortuitous, advantageous,* and *potential*—as you read.

Model fluency

As you read "A Lucky Accident," model accuracy with smooth, fluent reading.

Teach Amazing Words

Amazing Words Oral Vocabulary Routine

unintended
fortuitous
advantageous
potential

1 Introduce Write the word *unintended* on the board. Have students say the word with you. In "A Lucky Accident," we learn that the microwave oven was invented when something *unintended* happened. Does the author include any context clues that tell me the meaning of this word? Supply a student-friendly definition.

2 Demonstrate Break into groups. Have students elicit suggestions from other group members to demonstrate understanding. Why do you think *unintended* happenings lead to new inventions? Is it possible to prepare yourself for *unintended* happenings?

3 Apply Ask students to tell about an *unintended* happening.

See p. OV•1 to teach *fortuitous, advantageous,* and *potential.*

Routines Flip Chart

Apply Amazing Words

To build oral language, discuss the meanings of Amazing Words.

 Don't Wait Until Friday

MONITOR PROGRESS **Check Oral Vocabulary**

During discussion, listen for students' use of Amazing Words.

If... students are unable to use the Amazing Words to discuss the concept,

then... use the Oral Vocabulary Routine in the Routines Flip Chart to demonstrate words in different contexts.

Day 1	Days 2–3	Day 4	Day 5	
Check Oral Vocabulary	Check Retelling	Check Fluency	Check Oral Vocabulary	Success Predictor

A Lucky Accident

I scream, you scream, we all scream for… but wait! Hold that thought a minute, folks, because I'm supposed to tell you a story first. Golly, it's hard to stay focused when you've got you-know-what on your mind. Don't worry, though—I keep my stories short and sweet. Did I just say *sweet?* Oh my, there's just no doubt that it's the sweetest, creamiest, most honest to goodness delicious…but wait! From now on, I'll stick to the story.

So want to hear something fun I just learned? Turns out that some of the greatest inventions were discovered by accident. That's right—all it took was for something unintended to happen, and bingo! Suddenly the world was a better place. Take microwave ovens. Somebody who wasn't even looking discovered the secret behind those little miracles, and now movie night is a whole lot better with microwave pop-corn. And what about penicillin? You know, the medicine we sometimes have to take when we're sick? It may not be the tastiest stuff, but it sure helps us get better quicker. That, too, was a fortuitous discovery. Kind of makes you wonder how things would be if a few lucky accidents didn't happen. By the way, there's a word for the discovery of something advantageous by accident. It's called serendipity. Kind of fun to say, isn't it? *Serendipity*.

Well anyway, I've got serendipity to thank for bringing about one of the best inventions of all time. Some folks might call it no big deal, but I beg to differ. It might not make life easier or healthier, but it sure makes it nicer. Here's what happened. Way back in 1904, St. Louis, Missouri had itself a World's Fair. Lots of people stopped by to see the sights and eat the treats. And I bet you know what treat sold out faster than you can blink an eye. That's right: ice cream! But in those days, ice cream was served only in dishes. Can you imagine that? Nobody had ever even heard of an ice cream cone! Well, the story goes that the gentleman selling the ice cream ran out of dishes. Luckily, the stall next door happened to be selling waffles. So he rolled up one of those waffles, plopped a scoop on top, and just like that, the world's first ice cream cone was born! Now, nobody knows if this was really the first time people ate ice cream cones, but it sure makes for a good story, doesn't it? Reminds us to keep our eyes and minds open, because events with unexpected potential happen all the time. Right now, though, the time has come for my favorite snack. I scream, you scream, we all scream for ice cream!

Oral Vocabulary

Success Predictor

Objectives

◎ Draw conclusions from information presented by an author.

◎ Use the important ideas strategy to aid comprehension.

• Read grade-level text with accuracy.

Skills Trace

◎ **Draw Conclusions**

Introduce U4W1D1; U4W5D1; U6W1D1

Practice U4W1D2; U4W1D3; U4W5D2; U4W5D3; U6W1D2; U6W1D3

Reteach/Review U4W1D5; U4W2D2; U4W2D3; U4W4D2; U4W4D3; U4W5D5; U6W1D5; U6W3D2; U6W3D3; U6W5D2; U6W5D3

Assess/Test Weekly Tests U4W1; U4W5; U6W1

Benchmark Tests U4; U6

KEY:

U=Unit   W=Week   D=Day

Skill ⟷ Strategy
🔄 Draw Conclusions
🔄 Important Ideas

Student Edition p. EI•6

Introduce draw conclusions

Envision It!

When readers draw conclusions, what two things should they base their conclusions on? (Information from the text and information they already know) The third bullet tells you to support your conclusions with facts from the text. Why? (Otherwise you might be drawing an incorrect conclusion.) Have students turn to p. EI•6 in the Student Edition to review drawing conclusions. Then read "The Mystery of the Monarchs" with students.

Model the skill

Think Aloud Today we're going to read about monarch butterflies. Have students follow along as you read the first two paragraphs of "The Mystery of the Monarchs." I read some facts about the monarchs' journey. They migrate to Mexico for the winter. It's warm there. In spring, they fly as far north as Canada. I know that it gets cold in Canada in the winter. I also know that many animals migrate when food becomes scarce. I'll draw a conclusion: monarchs migrate to Mexico because they are not very suited to cold weather, and they can find more food there during the winter.

Guide practice

Have students finish reading "The Mystery of the Monarchs" on their own. After they read, have them use a graphic organizer like the one on p. 320 and draw conclusions based on information presented by the author and what they already know.

Strategy check

Important Ideas Remind students that if they have difficulty understanding the information in "The Mystery of the Monarchs," they can use the important ideas strategy. Model the strategy.

Model the strategy

Think Aloud I will look at each paragraph and determine the essential information and how those ideas are related to the ideas in surrounding paragraphs. Determining the most important ideas in a text helps me summarize the text. Have students summarize the important ideas in "The Mystery of the Monarchs," while maintaining the meaning and logical order of the passage. Then have students review the strategy of important ideas on p. EI•17 of the Student Edition.

Envision It!

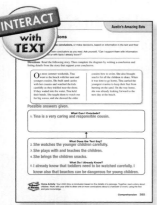
Reader's and Writer's Notebook, p. 385

Student Edition p. EI•17

On their own

Use p. 385 in the *Reader's and Writer's Notebook* for additional practice with drawing conclusions.

Objectives
• Draw conclusions about texts and evaluate how well the author achieves his or her purpose.

Envision It! Skill Strategy

Skill

Strategy

READING STREET ONLINE
ENVISION IT! ANIMATIONS
www.ReadingStreet.com

Comprehension Skill

Draw Conclusions

- Active readers make decisions based on evidence in the text or on their own background knowledge.
- When you form an idea or opinion about a text, you are drawing a conclusion.
- Examine your own conclusions as you read. Ask yourself if you can support them with facts from the text or facts you already know.
- Use a graphic organizer like the one below to draw conclusions about "The Mystery of the Monarchs."

Comprehension Strategy

Important Ideas

Good readers pay close attention to the important ideas in a piece of writing. Important ideas are the details and essential information that help you understand what an author is writing about.

The Mystery of the Monarchs

Have you ever seen the orange-and-black butterflies known as monarchs? If you have, it was probably autumn. The butterflies were migrating through your area on their way to Mexico.

All monarch butterflies spend the winter months in forests in Mexico, where it is warm. They fly there in large groups. In the spring these monarchs repeat the same flight in the other direction. They fly back to the North as far as Canada and lay eggs along the way. Then they die.

But when those eggs hatch, a new generation of butterflies is born. When another autumn comes, they take off for Mexico. They repeat the flight path of the original butterflies, and, amazingly, they fly to the same forests and sometimes the exact same trees where their parents came from previously. Think about it: they fly to the same forests and trees and they've never been there before!

Scientists think the butterflies begin their journey because of the position of the sun in the sky as the seasons change. But for now, though, no one can explain how the butterflies know where to go. That remains the "mystery of the monarchs."

Skill Draw a conclusion about why butterflies migrate to Mexico.

Strategy What information does this paragraph tell you? Is it important to understand these ideas to know what the author is writing about?

Skill What conclusion can you draw about ongoing study of the monarch butterflies?

Your Turn!

Need a Review? See the *Envision It! Handbook* for additional help with drawing conclusions and important ideas.

Let's Think About...

Ready to Try It? Talk about what you've learned about drawing conclusions and important ideas as you read *Austin's Amazing Bats.*

320

321

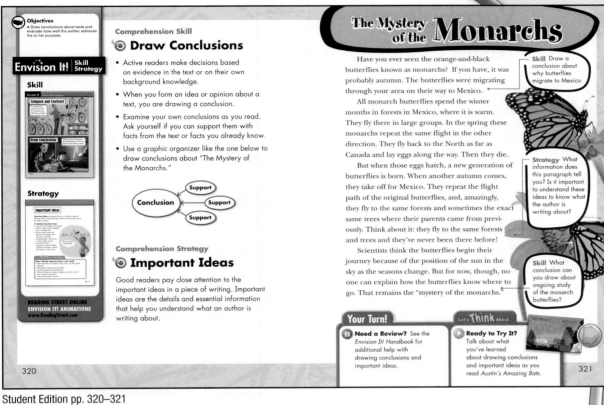

Student Edition pp. 320–321

Skill Monarch butterflies need warm weather to survive.

Strategy The offspring of Monarch butterflies return to the forests their parents came from without ever having seen them before. It is important because this is part of the mystery of the monarchs.

Skill Scientists will continue to try to figure out how the Monarchs know where to go.

Model Fluency

Accuracy

Model fluent reading

Have students listen as you read paragraph 3 of "The Mystery of the Monarchs" with accuracy. Explain that you will read steadily and clearly, being sure to read each word correctly.

ROUTINE Oral Rereading

1. **Read** Read paragraph 3 of "The Mystery of the Monarchs" aloud.
2. **Reread** To achieve optimal fluency, students should reread the text three to four times with accuracy.
3. **Corrective Feedback** Have students read aloud without you. Provide feedback about their accuracy and encourage them to look carefully at each word. Listen for accuracy.

Routines Flip Chart

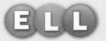

ELL

English Language Learners

Draw conclusions Provide oral practice by having students draw conclusions. Ask what conclusion they might draw from the following facts:

- Jan steps inside and leaves her wet umbrella on the porch.
- A sudden flash of light appears through the window.

Have students explain how they drew their conclusions.

Objectives
- Activate prior knowledge of unknown words.
- Identify questions for research.

Vocabulary
Tested Vocabulary

Lesson vocabulary

Have students complete sentences by filling in the blanks with lesson vocabulary words.

Display the lesson vocabulary and discuss what students already know about these words. Then write incomplete sentences on the board, such as those below. Have students identify the lesson word that completes each sentence and makes sense in context. Students may need to check the glossary or a print or electronic dictionary.

Activate prior knowledge

- The newspaper _____ said *Citizens speak out.* (headline)
- After climbing the tower, we had a _____ view. (breathtaking)
- Where will the hens _____ at night? (roost)
- We'd find it _____ if a snowstorm hit in the middle of summer. (bizarre)
- His trumpet made a _____ squeal. (high-pitched)
- Watering your plants often is _____ if you want them to stay healthy. (vital)

Related words

Ask what creature makes a *cock-a-doodle-doo* sound. Then ask how *roost* and *rooster* are related in meaning.

At the end of the week, students can review their fill-in-the-blank sentences or create their own with a partner.

Preteach Academic Vocabulary

 Academic Vocabulary Write the following words on the board:

modifiers	cause and effect
writer's personality	journal entry
directions	letter size

Have students share what they know about this week's Academic Vocabulary. Use the students' responses to assess their prior knowledge. Preteach then Academic Vocabulary by providing a student-friendly description, explanation, or example that clarifies the meaning of each term. Then ask students to restate the meaning of the Academic Vocabulary term in their own words.

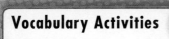
Research and Inquiry
Identify Questions

Teach

Discuss the Question of the Week: How can unplanned situations have positive outcomes? Tell them they will consult with others to choose and research an example of this topic, such as the discovery of X-rays or Rosa Park's role in the Civil Rights movement, and present their findings to the class on Day 5 in the form of a skit they will write and perform.

Model

Think Aloud I'll start with a list of open-ended questions about the situation and outcome I chose. Some possible questions could be Why did Rosa Parks refuse to give up her bus seat to a white passenger? What did she expect to happen when she refused to stand? and What happened to Rosa Parks after she was arrested?

Guide practice

Divide the class into small groups of students. After the groups have chosen a topic, have them write open-ended inquiry questions. Explain that tomorrow they will research online and print reference sources using their questions. Help students identify keywords that will guide their search.

On their own

Have students work in their small groups to write a research plan.

INTERNET GUY
Don Leu

21st Century Skills

Weekly Inquiry Project

Day 1 Identify Questions

Day 2 Navigate/Search

Day 3 Analyze

Day 4 Synthesize

Day 5 Communicate

Differentiated Instruction

A **Advanced**

Have students write a few sentences explaining why the situation's positive outcome is important and to whom.

Small Group Time

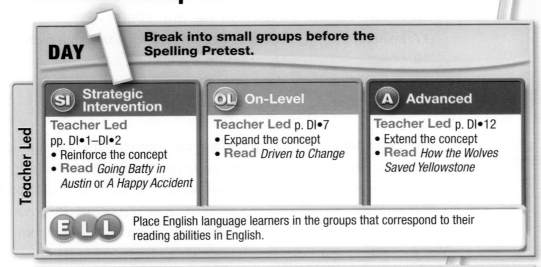

DAY 1

Break into small groups before the Spelling Pretest.

SI Strategic Intervention	**OL On-Level**	**A Advanced**
Teacher Led pp. DI•1–DI•2 • Reinforce the concept • **Read** *Going Batty in Austin* or *A Happy Accident*	Teacher Led p. DI•7 • Expand the concept • **Read** *Driven to Change*	Teacher Led p. DI•12 • Extend the concept • **Read** *How the Wolves Saved Yellowstone*

ELL Place English language learners in the groups that correspond to their reading abilities in English.

Practice Stations
• Read for Meaning
• Get Fluent
• Word Work

Independent Activities
• Concept Talk Video
• *Reader's and Writer's Notebook*
• Vocabulary Activities

English Language Learners

Multilingual word lists Students can apply knowledge of their home languages to acquire new English vocabulary by using the Multilingual Vocabulary Lists (*ELL Handbook*, pp. 431).

Objectives

• Spell words with *-ous*, *-sion*, *-ion*, and *-ation*.
• Use and understand modifiers.
• Write cursive capital letter *V* and lowercase *v* in words.

Spelling Pretest
Suffixes *-ous*, *-sion*, *-ion*, and *-ation*

Introduce
Ask students to think of words that end with the suffixes *-ous (jealous)*, *-sion (confusion)*, *-ion (rejection)*, and *-ation (quotation)*. This week we will use spelling patterns and rules to spell words with the suffixes *-ous*, *-sion*, *-ion*, and *-ation*.

Pretest
Use these sentences to administer the spelling pretest. Say each word, read the sentence, and repeat the word.

1. **famous**	He is **famous** for his cooking.	
2. **invention**	The telephone is a great **invention.**	
3. **election**	The **election** is still undecided.	
4. **furious**	She was **furious** when he lost the ticket.	
5. **imagination**	Writers use their **imagination.**	
6. **education**	I think **education** is a grand adventure.	
7. **nervous**	The **nervous** cat twitched its tail.	
8. **explanation**	His **explanation** made sense.	
9. **various**	There are **various** ways to walk to school.	
10. **decision**	Making a **decision** is not always easy.	
11. **relaxation**	A vacation is a time for **relaxation.**	
12. **conversation**	We had a long **conversation.**	
13. **tension**	Walking can get rid of **tension.**	
14. **humorous**	The **humorous** card made us laugh.	
15. **exhibition**	There's a new **exhibition** at the museum.	
16. **attraction**	Moths have an **attraction** to light.	
17. **invasion**	The ants staged an **invasion** at the picnic.	
18. **creation**	My **creation** is a clay sculpture.	
19. **occupation**	Her **occupation** is in the medical field.	
20. **destination**	We drove to our **destination.**	

Challenge words

21. **cancellation**   Snow caused the **cancellation** of tonight's concert.
22. **summarization**   His **summarization** of the story was thorough.
23. **glamorous**   The **glamorous** actress wore large diamonds.
24. **mysterious**   No one entered or left the **mysterious** house.
25. **administration**   The new **administration** will change some laws.

Self-correct
After the pretest, you can either display the correctly spelled words or spell them orally. Have students self-correct their pretests by writing misspelled words.

Let's Practice It!
TR DVD•306

On their own
For additional practice, use *Let's Practice It!* p. 306 on the *Teacher Resources DVD-ROM.*

Conventions
Modifiers

Teach

Display Grammar Transparency 26, and read aloud the explanation and examples in the box. Emphasize to students that writers should give careful consideration to the placement of modifiers in a sentence.

Model

Model how to identify the type of modifier underlined in sentences 1 and 2. Refer to the explanations in the box as you think aloud to answer the questions.

Guide practice

Guide students to complete items 3–6. Remind them that prepositional phrases begin with prepositions and end with nouns or pronouns. Record the correct responses on the transparency.

Daily Fix-It

Use Daily Fix-It numbers 1 and 2 in the right margin.

Connect to oral language

Have students read sentences 7–9 on the transparency and write the type of modifier to correctly complete each sentence.

Grammar Transparency 26

Handwriting
Cursive Letter *v* and *V*

Model letter formation

Display the cursive capital letter *V* and lowercase letter *v*. Follow the stroke instructions pictured to model letter formation.

Model letter size

Explain that letters need to be consistent in size. Some letters reach the top line, some touch the middle line, and others extend below the bottom line. The lowercase *v* touches the middle line while the capital *V* touches the top line. Model writing this sentence: *Vonda vaulted over the grape vines.* Make sure the letters aren't too light, dark, or jagged.

Guide practice

Have students write these sentences. *Vince will never vote for Veronica. Vivienne is available for various activities.* Circulate around the room, guiding students.

Academic Vocabulary

A **modifier** is a word or group of words that tell more about other words in a sentence.

Letter size is the appropriate size of letters in their formation so that they are neither too large nor too small.

Daily Fix-It

1. These bats are a famus cite to see. *(famous; sight)*
2. Lets see the bates in the cave. *(Let's; bats)*

 **E L L**

English Language Learners
Support Handwriting
Some students may not be accustomed to writing the letter *Vv*. Provide extra practice by saying aloud words with the letter *v* (*event, vicious, victory*) and Texas cities beginning with *V* (*Valley View, Vernon, Vidor, Van Horn*) and having students write them. Pair beginning English learners with more proficient English speakers. Have them take turns making up their own sentences that include words with the letter *v*. Have partners dictate the sentences while the other partner writes the words that contain the letter *v*.

The Truth About Austin's Amazing Bats **321d**

Writing—Journal Entry
Introduce

MINI-LESSON

MINI-LESSON

5 Day Planner
Guide to Mini-Lessons

DAY 1	Read Like a Writer
DAY 2	Organizing Story Parts
DAY 3	Writing with a Strong Voice
DAY 4	Revising Strategy: Adding
DAY 5	Proofread for Modifiers

Read Like a Writer

■ **Introduce** This week you will write a **journal entry.** A journal entry is usually a personal message that you write to yourself.

Prompt Think about a time you felt misunderstood. Write a journal entry about that experience.

Trait Voice

Mode Narrative

INTERACT with TEXT

Reader's and Writer's Notebook p. 386

■ **Examine Model Text** Let's read an example of a journal entry that describes a situation where the writer is misunderstood—and gets punished for it. Have students read the journal entry model on p. 386 of their *Reader's and Writer's Notebook.*

■ **Key Features** Journal entries usually record the date that the entry is written. This way writers can go back to recall when certain events happened in their lives. Have students circle the date in the sample journal entry.

Writers often use journal entries to express their personal ideas and experiences. What idea or experience does the writer of this journal entry express? Have students write a brief description of the main idea of the journal entry.

Journal entries are usually written by the writer for only the writer to read. The journal entry is a very personal and informal form of writing; writers can share thoughts and feelings that they wouldn't normally share with someone else. Discuss with students the ways in which this sample journal entry appears to be personal, or for the writer's "eyes only." Have them underline a few words and phrases that reveal the informality of the writing.

Review
Key features

Review the key features of a journal entry with students. You may want to post the key features in the classroom for students to refer to as they work on their compositions.

Key Features of a Journal Entry

- usually records the date
- expresses personal ideas and experiences

- often intended only for the writer to read
- may be experimental and informal

Write Guy
Jeff Anderson

Details, Details

Ask students to notice detail that is beyond the obvious. What evocative description reveals something new to readers?

Academic Vocabulary

A **journal entry** is a personal message that people write to themselves.

ROUTINE **Quick Write for Fluency** **Team Talk**

1. **Talk** Have pairs take a few minutes to discuss the features of a journal entry.

2. **Write** Each student writes a few sentences defining a journal entry in his or her own words.

3. **Share** Partners read their sentences to each other.

Routines Flip Chart

English Language Learners

Formal and Informal Language
Review the difference between formal and informal language. Read two sentences, and have students tell you which sentence is the one written in informal language.

Beginning *How are you? How's it going?*

Intermediate *Excuse me, please be quiet. Hey, keep it down!*

Advanced/Advanced High *I cannot visit you today. I can't come over today.*

Wrap Up Your Day

✔ **Build Concepts** Have students discuss how unplanned situations can have positive outcomes.

✔ **Oral Vocabulary** Have students use the Amazing Words they learned in context sentences.

✔ **Homework** Send home this week's Family Times newsletter on *Let's Practice It!* pp. 307–308 on the *Teacher Resources DVD-ROM.*

Preview DAY 2

Tell students that tomorrow they will read about the city of Austin, TX, and its population of bats.

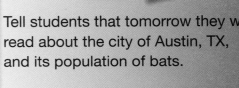

Let's Practice It!
TR DVD•307–308

Objectives
- Expand the weekly concept.
- Develop oral vocabulary.

Today at a Glance

Oral Vocabulary
spontaneous, perspective

Word Analysis
Compound words

Literary Terms
Sensory details

Text Structure
Cause and effect

Lesson Vocabulary
◉ Unknown words

Reading
"Ears for Eyes"

The Truth About Austin's Amazing Bats

Fluency
Accuracy

Research and Inquiry
Navigate/Search

Spelling
Suffixes *-ous, -sion, -ion, -ation*

Conventions
Modifiers

Writing
Journal entry

Concept Talk

Question of the Week
How can unplanned situations have positive outcomes?

Expand the concept

Remind students of the weekly concept question. Tell students that today they will begin reading *The Truth About Austin's Amazing Bats.* As they read, encourage students to think about how something that seems like a bad thing might turn out to be an amazing thing.

Anchored Talk

Develop oral vocabulary

Use the photos on pp. 318–319 and the Read Aloud, "A Lucky Accident," to talk about the Amazing Words: *unintended, fortuitous, advantageous,* and *potential.* Add these and other concept-related words to the concept map to develop students' knowledge of the topic. Have students break into groups to discuss the following questions. Encourage students to elicit suggestions from other group members.

- How do you react to *unintended* experiences? Why?
- How do people recognize that a discovery has *potential*? Can discoveries be *advantageous*?
- Tell about something *fortuitous* that has happened to you.

Oral Vocabulary
Amazing Words

Amazing Words

unintended	perspective
fortuitous	vigor
advantageous	devotion
potential	resist
spontaneous	discipline

Teach Amazing Words

Amazing Words Oral Vocabulary Routine

1 **Introduce** Write the Amazing Word *spontaneous* on the board. Have students say it aloud with you. Relate *spontaneous* to the photographs on pp. 318–319 and "A Lucky Accident." Have you ever given anybody a *spontaneous* gift, one you thought of on the spur of the moment like the kids are doing with the flowers? Have students use the context to determine and clarify the definition of the word. Something *spontaneous* is done without planning ahead.

2 **Demonstrate** Have students answer questions to demonstrate understanding. You've read about how ice cream cones were invented. Do you think other kinds of foods had a *spontaneous* beginning? Why or why not?

3 **Apply** Have students apply their understanding. What would be some synonyms for *spontaneous*?

See p. OV•1 to teach *perspective*.

Routines Flip Chart

Apply Amazing Words

Help students establish a purpose for reading as they read "Ears for Eyes" on p. 323. Have them consider how the Amazing Words *spontaneous* and *perspective* apply to the way bats hunt.

Connect to reading

Explain that today students will read about a large group of bats that roost under a bridge in Austin, Texas. As they read, they should think about how the Question of the Week and the Amazing Words *spontaneous* and *perspective* apply to the Austin bats.

E L L **Reinforce Vocabulary** Use the Day 2 instruction on ELL Poster 26 to teach lesson vocabulary and the lesson concept.

E L L Poster 26

The Truth About Austin's Amazing Bats **322b**

Objectives

• Understand how compound words are formed.

• Understand how sensory details enhance comprehension.

• Use text structure to understand the relationships among ideas.

Word Analysis
Compound Words

Teach compound words

Model the skill

Tell students that compound words are made up of two words. Have students choose one word from the first column and find its match in the second column to build a compound word.

Think Aloud I will choose the word *high* from the first column and look for a word in the second column that can form a compound word.

I can add the word *way* in the second column to *high* to make the word *highway*. A *highway* is a road that links cities or towns.

First Word		Second Word			
high	tight	way	step	loose	rope
head	breath	rest	wear	bridge	ache
foot	sky	line	dress	path	band
		taking	light	hold	note

Guide practice

Have students combine words from both columns to build new compound words.

On their own

Have students use a printed or electronic dictionary or glossary to verify that the words they combined are in fact compound words and then determine their meaning. Follow the Strategy for Meaningful Word Parts to teach the word *headline.*

ROUTINE **Strategy for Meaningful Word Parts**

1. **Introduce word parts** Circle each smaller word of *headline.* I will circle *head* and *line.*

2. **Connect to meaning** Define each smaller word. *Head* means "at the top or front of." *Line* means "a group of words."

3. **Read the word** Blend the meaningful word parts together to read *headline.* Then blend the meanings to find the meaning of *headline.* *Headline* means "the group of words, or title, that comes at the beginning of a newspaper article."

Continue the routine with the word *breathtaking.*

Routines Flip Chart

Literary Terms
Sensory Details

Academic Vocabulary
cause and effect cause is *why* something happened and effect is *what* happened as a result

Teach sensory details

Tell students that authors often use sensory details to help readers visualize while reading. Write the following sentence on the board: *The breeze rippling through leaves made the sunlit trees shimmer and dance.* All the descriptive words in the sentence help readers create sensory images in their minds.

Model sensory details

Think Aloud Look back at "The Mystery of the Monarchs" on page 321. The author describes the butterflies as orange-and-black. What sensory details could you add to help readers visualize the migration? **(Answers will vary.)**

Guide practice

Find an example of a sensory detail in *The Truth About Austin's Amazing Bats.* Authors use these details to help readers visualize the text and monitor and adjust their comprehension.

On their own

Have students look for examples of sensory details in *The Truth About Austin's Amazing Bats* and tell how these sensory details help them create sensory images in their minds.

Text Structure
Cause and Effect

Teach cause and effect

One organizational pattern used in expository text is cause and effect. When using this text structure, an author shows the relationship between what happened and why.

Model the strategy

Think Aloud In "The Mystery of the Monarchs," the author first tells us that monarchs migrate over the same route and to the same destinations as their parents. Then we learn about a possible cause—the change in the position of the sun. Authors can describe the effect first then tell about the cause, or they can tell about the cause first and then describe the effect.

Guide practice

Discuss with students the cause-and-effect text structure of *The Truth About Austin's Amazing Bats.*

On their own

Have students look for examples of cause-and-effect organization as they read. Have them analyze how this organizational structure influences their understanding of the relationships among ideas in the text.

Objectives

◎ Use a dictionary or glossary to find the meaning of unknown words.

• Read grade-level text with accuracy.

Vocabulary Strategy for
🎯 Unknown Words

Teach unknown words

Envision It!

Tell students that when they encounter an unknown word, they should use the strategy of looking up its meaning in a print or electronic dictionary or glossary. Explain how a dictionary and glossary can help students understand the meanings of unknown words. Point out that they can also find a word's pronunciation, syllabication, and part of speech in a dictionary or glossary. Refer students to *Words!* on p. W•14 in the Student Edition for additional practice.

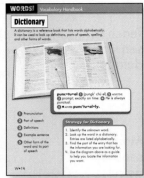

Student Edition p. W•14

Model the strategy

Think Aloud

Write on the board: *My friend told me the play had a bizarre ending.* I don't know what *bizarre* means, so I don't know what the ending of that play was like. I'll look up the word *bizarre* in a dictionary or glossary. When I do, I see that it means "strange, weird, or very unusual." Now I understand that the play had a strange ending—one my friend did not expect. But I see more information than that. I also see the word's pronunciation (bə zär), syllabication (bi zarre´), and part of speech (adjective). I also see that *strange, weird,* or *unusual* are alternate word choices for *bizarre.* If my friend wants to write about the *bizarre* ending to that play, she might want to use some of those other words too.

Guide practice

Write this sentence on the board: *Mr. Jackson worried when his car made a high-pitched sound.* Have students first use context clues to help them think about the meaning of *high-pitched.* Then have them look the word up in a dictionary or a glossary to confirm or clarify its meaning. Ask them to identify the word's meaning, pronunciation, syllabication, and part of speech. For additional support, use *Envision It! Pictured Vocabulary Cards* or *Tested Vocabulary Cards*.

On their own

Have students read "Ears for Eyes" on p. 323. Have students use a dictionary or glossary to list the definitions for the lesson vocabulary words. Have students also write down the syllabication, pronunciation, and part of speech for each word. For additional practice use *Reader's and Writer's Notebook* p. 387.

Reader's and Writer's Notebook p. 387

Objectives
• Use a dictionary, a glossary, or a thesaurus to locate information about words.

Envision It! | Words to Know

bizarre

headline

roost

breathtaking
high-pitched
vital

READING STREET ONLINE
VOCABULARY ACTIVITIES
www.ReadingStreet.com

322

Vocabulary Strategy for
◎ Unknown Words

Dictionary/Glossary Sometimes a writer doesn't include context clues in the sentences surrounding an unknown word. In this case, you have to look up the word in a dictionary or glossary to find its meaning, pronunciation, part of speech, and syllabication. Choose one of the *Words to Know*, and then follow these steps.

1. Check the back of the book for a glossary, or use a dictionary.

2. Find the word entry. If the pronunciation and syllabication are given, read the word aloud. You may recognize the word when you hear yourself say it.

3. Look at all the meanings and parts of speech listed in the entry. Try each meaning in the sentence that contains the unknown word.

4. Choose the meaning that makes sense in your sentence.

Read "Ears for Eyes" on page 323. Use a dictionary or a glossary to determine the meanings of words you cannot figure out from the text.

Words to Write Reread "Ears for Eyes." Think of other mammals that hunt at night and write an article about them. Use words from the *Words to Know* list in your article.

Ears for Eyes

What do bats and dolphins have in common? It's certainly not where they live! It's echolocation, the process of using sound to "see" in the dark. Instead of relying on eyesight, these mammals locate prey with high-pitched sounds, creating for each other a breathtaking symphony.

Echolocation is bizarre, and you won't read explanations of it in newspaper headlines. Here's how it works. Mammals that use echolocation listen to the differences in sound between their right and left ears to locate objects. As sounds emitted by the mammals bounce off an object and come back, the mammals keep track of the time it takes for the sound to reflect off the object. In this way, they are able to calculate where their prey is—all in a matter of seconds!

It might seem strange that mammals use their ears instead of their eyes to locate prey. Why do they? For one, echolocation provides them an ecological advantage. For example, if bats can roost during the day and hunt at night, they can take advantage of prey when it is vulnerable. Also, bats can hunt while their predators are sleeping. Indeed, echolocation is vital to these mammals' survival.

Your Turn!

⏸ **Need a Review?**
For additional help with using a dictionary or glossary, see *Words!*

▶ **Ready to Try It?**
Read *The Truth About Austin's Amazing Bats* on pp. 324–335.

323

Student Edition pp. 322–323

Reread for Fluency
Accuracy

Model fluent reading

Read paragraph 1 of "Ears for Eyes" aloud, concentrating on reading clearly and accurately. Point out that you are working to read each word correctly.

ROUTINE — Choral Reading

1. **Select a passage** For "Ears for Eyes," use paragraph 1.

2. **Model** Have students track the print as you read with accuracy.

3. **Guide practice** Have students read along with you.

4. **On their own** Have the class read aloud without you. For optimal fluency, students should reread three or four times with accuracy.

Routines Flip Chart

Lesson Vocabulary

bizarre strange; weird; very unusual

breathtaking so surprising, impressive, or beautiful that it could make people gasp

headline the title of an article in the newspaper

high-pitched describes a sound that is higher than most other sounds

roost a place to rest and sleep

vital necessary; crucial

Differentiated Instruction

SI Strategic Intervention

Unknown Words Have students work in pairs to list additional unknown words they find in "Ears for Eyes." If neither partner can tell the meaning of the word, they should use a dictionary or glossary to look it up and then write the definition.

ELL

English Language Learners

Cognates Point out the Spanish cognate in this week's lesson vocabulary: *vital/vital*.

Build Academic Vocabulary Use the lesson vocabulary pictured on p. 322 to teach the meanings of *bizarre, headline,* and *roost*. Call on pairs to write the words on sticky notes and use them to label images of the words on the ELL Poster.

Objectives

- Understand the elements of expository text.
- Use text features to preview and predict.
- Set a purpose for reading.

The Truth About **Austin's Amazing Bats**

- By Ron Fridell

Genre **Expository texts** tell about what certain things are and how they came to be. As you read, notice how the author explains how bats came to live in Austin, Texas.

Question of the Week
How can unplanned situations have positive outcomes?

324

Let's **Think** About **Reading!**

Student Edition pp. 324–325

Build Background

Discuss bats

Team Talk Have students turn to a partner and discuss the Question of the Week and these questions about bats by eliciting and considering suggestions from each group member.

- Why are so many people afraid of bats?
- Do you think bats are mostly helpful or mostly harmful?
- Would you like to see a bat up close in nature? Why or why not?

Connect to selection

Have students discuss their answers with the class. Encourage students to listen attentively and ask questions to clarify the speaking student's perspective. Possible responses: Some people are afraid of bats because they've seen movies or heard tales about bats that suck blood. Bats are harmful because they can spread disease, but they are also helpful because they eat bugs. I would like to see a bat up close because I am curious about the shape of their wings. For additional opportunities to build background, use the Background Building Audio.

Prereading Strategies

Genre

Explain that **expository text** communicates factual information about real people, things, or events. It has a text structure such as cause-and-effect, comparison-contrast, or problem-solution. It often includes photographs, maps, or other graphic features to help readers understand the information in the text.

Preview and predict

Have students preview the title and photographs in *The Truth About Austin's Amazing Bats.* Have them predict what kind of information they will find in the selection.

Set purpose

Prior to reading, have students set their own purposes for reading this selection. To help students set a purpose, ask them to think about what it would be like to see a large number of bats flying overhead.

Strategy Response Log

 INTERACT with TEXT

Have students use p. 32 in the *Reader's and Writer's Notebook* to review and use the strategy of important ideas.

Small Group Time

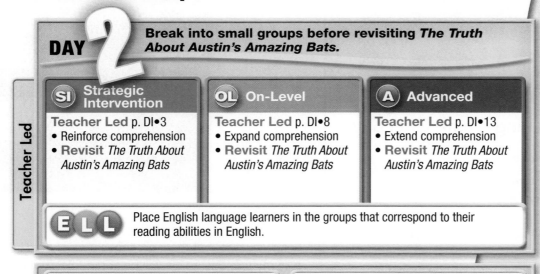

DAY 2 Break into small groups before revisiting *The Truth About Austin's Amazing Bats.*

Teacher Led

(SI) Strategic Intervention
Teacher Led p. DI•3
• Reinforce comprehension
• **Revisit** *The Truth About Austin's Amazing Bats*

(OL) On-Level
Teacher Led p. DI•8
• Expand comprehension
• **Revisit** *The Truth About Austin's Amazing Bats*

(A) Advanced
Teacher Led p. DI•13
• Extend comprehension
• **Revisit** *The Truth About Austin's Amazing Bats*

ELL Place English language learners in the groups that correspond to their reading abilities in English.

Practice Stations
• Words to Know
• Get Fluent
• Word Wise

Independent Activities
• Background Building Audio
• *Reader's and Writer's Notebook*
• Research and Inquiry

Differentiated Instruction

 **A Advanced**

Have students write a paragraph telling whether or not they think they would like to encounter a large number of bats in nature. Tell them to explain why they feel as they do.

Multidraft Reading

For **Whole Group** instruction, choose one of the reading options below. For each reading, have students set the purpose indicated.

Option 1
Day 2 Read the selection. Use Guide Comprehension to monitor and clarify understanding.
Day 3 Reread the selection. Use Extend Thinking to develop higher-order thinking skills.

Option 2
Day 2 Read the first half of the selection, using both Guide Comprehension and Extend Thinking instruction.
Day 3 Read the second half of the selection, using both Guide Comprehension and Extend Thinking instruction.

ELL

English Language Learners
Build background To build background, review the summary selection in English *(ELL Handbook* p. 181). Use the Retelling Cards to provide visual support for the summary.

Guide Comprehension Skills and Strategies

Teach Unknown Words

Unknown Words Have students read p. 326. The author talks about an imposing sculpture in the shape of a bat. What does the word *imposing* mean? **(very big, impressive)**

Corrective Feedback

If... students are unable to figure out the meaning of *imposing*,

then... model using a dictionary to determine the correct meaning.

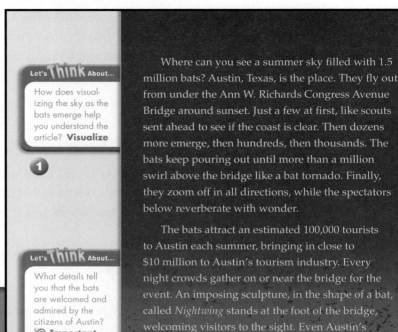

Reader's and Writer's Notebook p. 391

Model the Skill

Think Aloud I don't know this word, so I'll look it up in a dictionary. *Imposing* could be the present tense of the verb *impose.* I see that *impose* is "to force a rule or punishment on somebody, to expect too much from someone."

Let's Think About...

How does visualizing the sky as the bats emerge help you understand the article? **Visualize**

1

Let's Think About...

What details tell you that the bats are welcomed and admired by the citizens of Austin? **Important Ideas**

2

Where can you see a summer sky filled with 1.5 million bats? Austin, Texas, is the place. They fly out from under the Ann W. Richards Congress Avenue Bridge around sunset. Just a few at first, like scouts sent ahead to see if the coast is clear. Then dozens more emerge, then hundreds, then thousands. The bats keep pouring out until more than a million swirl above the bridge like a bat tornado. Finally, they zoom off in all directions, while the spectators below reverberate with wonder.

The bats attract an estimated 100,000 tourists to Austin each summer, bringing in close to $10 million to Austin's tourism industry. Every night crowds gather on or near the bridge for the event. An imposing sculpture, in the shape of a bat, called *Nightwing* stands at the foot of the bridge, welcoming visitors to the sight. Even Austin's former professional hockey team, the Ice Bats, embraced the creatures. The team's mascot was a fierce-looking cartoon bat gripping a hockey stick. Austin loves its bats so much that it holds a two-day summer Bat Festival to honor the flying mammals.

326

Student Edition pp. 326–327

Extend Thinking Think Critically

Higher-Order Thinking Skills

Unknown Words • Synthesis Look up the word *reverberate* in the dictionary. Use what you find to rewrite the following sentence about the bats: *Finally, they zoom off in all directions, while the spectators below reverberate with wonder.* Possible response: As the bats zoomed away, a sense of wonder echoed through the crowd.

Let's Think About...

1 I can visualize that there are thousands of bats in the sky. This tells me that this article will be about this exciting, but scary, scene.

2 They installed a statue of a bat to welcome the visitors and tourists.

3 The clues *once upon a time* and *after* tell me this text is written in sequential order.

Does that make sense here? (no) I also see the adjective *imposing* as a separate entry. It means "very large and impressive." Does that make sense? Why? (Yes, the statue was meant to welcome tourists.)

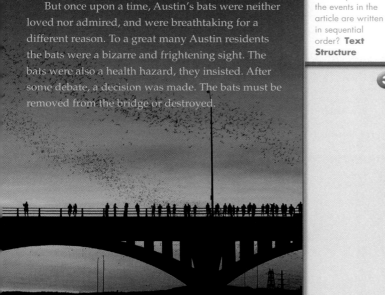

Spectators watch the nightly display from all sorts of places, high and low. Some watch from up on the Congress Avenue Bridge. Others watch from the lake below. The bridge spans Town Lake on the Colorado River, where people watch the bats from rowboats, canoes, and kayaks. There is even a riverboat that gives special bat cruises. Some people spread blankets on the lake's grassy shores to watch. Nearby downtown restaurants have tables set up on patios for viewing. When the bats come out, the guests put down their knives and forks to watch a breathtaking display of nature in the city.

But once upon a time, Austin's bats were neither loved nor admired, and were breathtaking for a different reason. To a great many Austin residents the bats were a bizarre and frightening sight. The bats were also a health hazard, they insisted. After some debate, a decision was made. The bats must be removed from the bridge or destroyed.

Let's Think About...

What clues in the text tell you that the events in the article are written in sequential order? **Text Structure**

3

327

On Their Own

Have students look up the words *impose* and *imposing* in the dictionary. Have them record the pronunciations, the syllabications, and the parts of speech, and use each word in a sentence. For additional practice, use *Reader's and Writer's Notebook* p. 391.

Fact and Opinion • Evaluation In the last paragraph on page 327, the author says *The bats were also a health hazard, they insisted.* Does he present the health hazard as a fact or an opinion? How can you tell? **Possible response:** an opinion because he adds "they insisted"; If he wanted to present it as fact, he would have said, "The bats were also a health hazard."

Genre • Synthesis When rereading expository text, it is important to synthesize all the new ideas that you read and make logical connections between ideas in the text. Synthesize the ideas you learned in paragraph 2 on page 326 by summarizing. What logical connections can you make between the idea of tourism and the idea of business? **Possible response:** The city of Austin has learned to value the bats; Businesses need tourists to come and spend money in their shops in order to be successful.

Differentiated Instruction

SI Strategic Intervention

Cause and Effect Help students understand the connection between businesses and their customers. According to the text, how many tourists come to Austin to see the bats each summer? (about 100,000) What are some ways restaurants and other businesses could get tourists to come in? (by providing them with opportunities to see the bats)

Connect to Science

Bats are the only mammals that can truly fly. Like all mammals, and unlike birds, bats have hair, and produce milk to feed their young. Like most mammals, bats give birth to live young—they do not lay eggs.

ELL

English Language Learners

Activate prior knowledge Ask volunteers to tell about any experiences they may have had with bats in particular. Then ask them to tell about times they were amazed by something they saw in nature. Encourage them to use descriptive words.

Objectives

◎ Draw conclusions to enhance comprehension.

OPTION 1

Skills and Strategies, continued

Teach Draw Conclusions

Draw Conclusions Have students read p. 328. Think about the engineers who designed the bridge. What opinion do you think they had of the bats? How did you reach that conclusion? (Possible response: They thought the bats were undesirable; they would have changed the design to one that was not bat-friendly.)

Corrective Feedback

If... students have difficulty drawing a conclusion,

then... model how to draw a conclusion.

Let's Practice It!
TR DVD•309

Model the Skill

Think Aloud The engineers didn't know they were creating a great habitat for the bats. What would they have done if they had known? (They would have changed the design.)

Student Edition pp. 328–329

OPTION 2

Think Critically, continued

Higher-Order Thinking Skills

Draw Conclusions • Evaluation Does the author think people's fears about the bats are valid? How can you tell? Possible response: The author does not think the fears are valid; he says their reasons are based on fear and misinformation.

Let's **Think** About...

What can you do to better understand why Austin's bat population doubles in size during August? **Monitor and Clarify**

4

How were Austin's bats saved? The story begins in 1980. That's when workers began reconstructing the Congress Avenue Bridge. The bridge is a landmark in the heart of downtown, just ten blocks from the Texas state capitol. The engineers in charge of the project didn't know that their work would create an ideal habitat for bats. Otherwise they would not have left so many openings on the bridge's concrete underside.

The long, narrow, dark crevices became instantly popular with migrating bats, because bats prefer to make cozy spots to roost and raise their young. Most of the bats are pregnant females. In March they fly north from Mexico to give birth and raise their young, called pups. That's why in August the bridge's bat population of 1.5 million is double what it was in March. Austin's human population is about 740,000. That means that in summer, Austin has twice as many bats as people!

328

Let's **Think** About...

4 I can look back in the text. It says that in March, the bats fly to Mexico and give birth and take care of their young.

5 The author asks and then answers questions to help the reader better understand the content. The question might be something the reader would have wondered.

They would have tried to keep the bats out. I know they would not have done that if they thought the bats were a good thing, so they must have thought the bats were a bad thing.

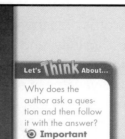

Why were so many people so scared of the bats beneath the bridge? The reasons are based on fear and misinformation. Fear of the dark is one reason. Many children—and even some adults—are afraid of the dark, and bats are creatures of the night. During the day they inhabit dark spaces such as caves and tunnels. At night they come out to hunt. Bats' anatomy and appearance scares some people too, with their pointed ears and noses and sharply curved wings. And when people think of bats, they often think of vampires, mythical creatures that drink blood. Or they picture a great big bat flying blindly at them and getting all tangled in their hair, or biting them and giving them rabies.

Let's **Think** About...

Why does the author ask a question and then follow it with the answer?

Important Ideas

⑤

329

On Their Own

Have students draw a conclusion about how the bats get into and out of the bridge, based on the information in paragraph 1 on p. 328. For additional practice, use *Let's Practice It!* p. 309 in the *Teacher Resources DVD-ROM*.

Sensory Details • Analysis What words do you think of when you hear the word *cozy*? What do you think the author means by *cozy*? Possible response: I think of the words *warm, fuzzy,* and *snug.* The author probably means *dark, enclosed,* and *safe.*

Background Knowledge • Evaluation • Text to World Compare and contrast what you read about bats with what you know about dogs or other popular pets.

Possible response: Both are animals, but bats come out at night; dogs are awake during the day. Bats are associated with vampire myths; dogs are called "man's best friend."

Check Predictions Have students look back at the predictions they made earlier and discuss whether they were accurate. Then have students preview the rest of the selection and either adjust their predictions accordingly or make new predictions.

Differentiated Instruction

 Strategic Intervention

Prior knowledge Have students work in pairs to construct a Venn diagram to compare and contrast bats and another kind of animal. Suggest they start by listing bat traits. They can then think of whether the other animal is alike or different than bats for each trait.

Ⓐ Advanced

Have students read p. 329 and choose the best argument for why bats should be feared. Have them explain their reasoning.

ⒺⓁⓁ

English Language Learners

Vocabulary: Idioms Focus students' attention on the expression "the heart of downtown" in the first paragraph on p. 328. Explain *the heart of* is an idiom that means the central or busiest part of a place or the most important part of something, such as in "getting to the heart of the matter." Ask students to tell about a situation where they might use either expression.

Draw Conclusions Encourage students to use a graphic organizer to help them draw conclusions as they read. The organizer should have three columns, labeled *Clues from the text, What I already know,* and *Conclusion.*

If you want to teach this selection in two sessions, stop here.

The Truth About Austin's Amazing Bats **329a**

Research and Inquiry
Navigate/Search

Teach

Have students search the Internet and print references using their inquiry questions and keywords. Tell them to carefully evaluate each potential source for relevance, validity, and reliability. Point out that, since they will be writing and performing a skit based on the material they gather, they may wish to look for eyewitness accounts or newspaper and magazine articles from the time (if available for the time and place of the situation they chose) that may help them bring out the drama of the situation. Remind students to take careful notes as they gather information from both online and print resources.

Model

Think Aloud When searching for information about Rosa Parks, I came up with millions of hits. Some will not be relevant. Others will relate to Rosa Parks, her arrest, and the civil rights movement but will not give accurate, factual information. I do see a publisher's Web site that features an interview with Rosa Parks. I'll try using *Rosa Parks interview* as a search term.

Guide practice

Have students review Web sites they've identified. Point out that they must evaluate each site to determine if it is relevant, valid, and reliable. Explain that not everyone who claims to be a part of something is credible, so students should look for ways to verify information they find. For example, if they are looking for interviews, they should look for trustworthy sources, such as major news outlets, museums, educational institutions, and so on.

On their own

As they take notes, have students write down print publication information (author, date, title) and Web addresses, authors, and the dates the Web sites were last updated to create a Works Cited page. Remind them to always identify the source of their notes.

Conventions
Modifiers

Teach

Remind students that modifiers are words or groups of words that tell more about other words in a sentence. Adjectives, adverbs, and prepositional phrases are modifiers.

Guide practice

Remind students that it is very important to place modifiers as close as possible to the words they modify. Write these sentences, and help students correctly reposition the prepositional phrases.

> **The dog sat on the porch with blue eyes.**
>
> **In the sky Quan tried to take a picture of the eagle soaring.**
>
> **Mrs. Huff discussed how to fill in the blanks with students.**

Daily Fix-It

Use Daily Fix-It numbers 3 and 4 in the right margin.

Connect to oral language

Have students identify a variety of modifiers in *The Truth About Austin's Amazing Bats*.

On their own

For additional practice, use *Reader's and Writer's Notebook* p. 388.

Spelling
Suffixes *-ous, -sion, -ion,* and *-ation*

Teach

Remind students that adding a suffix to a word can change the word's meaning. Adding *-ation, -ion,* or *-sion* changes a verb to a noun. Adding *-ous* changes the word from a noun to an adjective. When adding a suffix, the spelling of some base words may change. A final *e* or *y* may be dropped or changed (*fame/famous; fury/furious*).

Guide practice

Write *invent/invention* and *humor/humorous*. Use the words in sentences to illustrate how the verb *invent* changes to the noun *invention* and the noun *humor* changes to the adjective *humorous*. Have students work in pairs to circle the spelling list words that have no change to their base when the suffix is added.

On their own

For additional practice, use *Reader's and Writer's Notebook* p. 389.

Daily Fix-It

3. The bats was darting between Sam and I. *(were; and me)*

4. Dad saw too bats over the bridge flying low. *(Over the bridge, Dad saw two bats flying low.)*

Reader's and Writer's Notebook p. 388

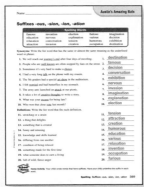

Reader's and Writer's Notebook p. 389

English Language Learners

Practice conventions
Students may have difficulty understanding how adverbs modify verbs. Model acting out modifiers in sentences: *He walked slowly. She made a sandwich quickly. He tip-toed quietly.* Have students come up with their own sentences that include actions to model modifiers.

Objectives
- Organize ideas to prepare for writing.

Writing—Journal Entry
Writing Trait: Voice

Introduce the prompt

Review the key features of a journal entry. Remind students that they should think about these features as they plan to write their own journal entry. Then explain that they will begin the writing process today. Read aloud the writing prompt.

Writing Prompt

Think about a time you felt misunderstood. Write a journal entry about that experience.

Select a topic

 To choose a topic for this writing prompt, you will have to search through your memories. It might help if you work with a few of your classmates and brainstorm ideas together. Have students get into small groups for brainstorming.

Gather information

Remind students that they can use a graphic organizer to help them organize ideas as they brainstorm. Write a three-column chart on the board with headings like the ones below. Model for students how to use the chart to record ideas. You might use the examples provided, or you might model using your own experiences.

Event/Experience	How I felt	Why I was misunderstood
I got in trouble for talking in class.	Embarrassed; upset	I was telling others to stop talking when I got in trouble for talking
I forgot about the big science test.	Nervous; frustrated; embarrassed	No misunderstanding

Point out to students that, in the second example, organizing ideas in a chart helped the writer realize that there was actually no misunderstanding in that event. The writer had only made a mistake in forgetting the test; he or she was not misunderstood.

Corrective feedback

Circulate around the room as students use the chart to organize their brainstorming ideas. Conference briefly with any students who are having difficulty choosing a topic for their journal entry. Ask each struggling student to try to remember a time when something happened to them that they thought was unfair. Lead them to understand how they felt they were misunderstood even if they only thought of the situation as unfair.

Organizing Story Parts

■ Even though journal writing is informal, it is a good idea to pause and organize your ideas before you begin. A story sequence chart will help us and keep track of the details in the story we are relating and allow us to identify the problem and the solution in our story.

■ Let's fill in this graphic organizer with details from the model in your *Reader's and Writer's Notebook.* Display a story sequence chart. Guide students in using the details from the model to fill in the organizer.

Have students use the graphic organizer on p. 390 of their *Reader's and Writer's Notebook* to plan their own journal entries. Explain that they will fill in the organizer with details about the experience they chose to write about.

ROUTINE   Quick Write for Fluency   Team Talk

1 **Talk** Have pairs discuss the topic they have chosen for their journal entry.

2 **Write** Each student summarizes their topic in one sentence.

3 **Share** Partners read each other's sentence and ask questions about the topic.

Routines Flip Chart

Wrap Up Your Day

✔ **Build Concepts** Have students discuss the different ways people reacted to the bats.

✔ **Draw Conclusions** What conclusion did you draw about why many people feared the bats?

✔ **Important Ideas** What are some of the important ideas in the article so far?

Differentiated Instruction

 Advanced

Graphic organizers Have students work in a small group to identify other graphic organizers that would help them write a journal entry. Ask them to skim their *Reader's and Writer's Notebooks* to review the other graphic organizers they have used throughout the year. Have each group choose one graphic organizer and explain why that one would be helpful to use to plan their writing.

Reader's and Writer's Notebook p. 390

Teacher Tip

Do a periodic check of students' Quick Writes to make sure they are on task and communicating effectively with their partners.

Preview DAY 3

Tell students that tomorrow they will read about how BCI educated the public about the benefits of bats.

Objectives
- Expand the weekly concept.
- Build oral vocabulary.

Today at a Glance

Oral Vocabulary
happenstance, occurrences

Comprehension Check/Retelling
Discuss questions

Reading
The Truth About Austin's Amazing Bats

Think Critically
Retelling

Fluency
Accuracy

Research and Study Skills
Follow and clarify directions

Research and Inquiry
Analyze

Spelling
Suffixes *-ous, -sion, -ion, -ation*

Conventions
Modifiers

Writing
Journal entry

Concept Talk

Question of the Week

How can unplanned situations have positive outcomes?

Expand the concept

Remind students of the weekly concept question. Discuss how the question relates to the Austin bats. Tell students that today they will read about how Austin residents' attitudes toward the bat changed. Encourage students to think about the bats from the residents' *perspective*.

Anchored Talk

Develop oral vocabulary

Use text features—illustrations and captions—to review pp. 324–329 of *The Truth About Austin's Amazing Bats.* Discuss the Amazing Words *spontaneous* and *perspective.* Add these words to the concept map. Use the following questions to develop students' understanding of the concept. Break into groups and have students identify points of agreement and disagreement.

- Think about the bats from the *perspective* of a tourist. How would you describe them?

- People in Austin might make a *spontaneous* outing to see the bats. What might you see or do on a *spontaneous* outing?

Oral Vocabulary
Amazing Words

Amazing Words

unintended	perspective
fortuitous	happenstance
advantageous	occurrences
potential	perceptive
spontaneous	unaware

Teach Amazing Words

Amazing Words Oral Vocabulary Routine

1 Introduce Write the word *occurrences* on the board. Have students say it with you. Yesterday we learned that many people watch some interesting *occurrences* in Austin. Have students use context clues to determine a definition of *occurrence*. (An *occurrence* is a happening.)

2 Demonstrate Have students answer questions to demonstrate understanding. Before the bridge attracted the bats, did Austin planners expect such an *occurrence*? (No) Do you think a bat festival is a common *occurrence*? Why or why not? (Possible response: A bat festival is probably not a common occurrence because bats are not very popular in most places.)

3 Apply Have students apply their understanding. Describe the most unusual *occurrence* you've ever seen.

See p. OV•1 to teach *happenstance*.

Routines Flip Chart

Apply Amazing Words

Help students establish a purpose for reading as they read pp. 330–335 of *The Truth About Austin's Amazing Bats.* Have them consider how the Amazing Words *happenstance* and *occurrences* apply to the bats and the residents of Austin.

Connect to reading

Explain that today students will read about how the people of Austin changed their minds about the bats. As they read, students should think about how the Question of the Week and the Amazing Words *happenstance* and *occurrences* apply to this journey.

ELL Expand Vocabulary Use the Day 3 instruction on ELL Poster 26 to help students expand vocabulary.

ELL Poster 26

Objectives
◉ Identify important ideas in text.
◉ Practice drawing conclusions.
◉ Use a dictionary or glossary to define unknown words.

Comprehension Check

Have students discuss each question with a partner. Ask several pairs to share their responses.

✓ Genre • Evaluation

In *The Truth About Austin's Amazing Bats,* the author begins an expository text with a scene that includes many descriptive details. Why do you think he did that? Did he achieve his goal? **Possible response: He wants readers to envision the scene and realize how special the bats are. Then they will care about the issues surrounding the bats.**

✓ Draw Conclusions • Analysis

Do you think the city of Austin encourages or discourages crowds of out-of-towners to come see the bats? How can you tell? **Possible response: They encourage people to come see the bats. They host a Bat Festival, which probably brings a lot of money into the city.**

✓ Important Ideas • Synthesis

Summarize the most important idea you've read so far about Austin's bats. **Possible response: People love the bats now, but they used to be afraid of them and worry that they were a health problem.**

✓ Unknown Words • Synthesis

On page 328, the text talks about *crevices.* What does the word *crevice* mean? Use a dictionary to find the meaning and pronunciation of *crevice.* **Possible response: The definition of *crevice* (krev´ is) is "a narrow crack."**

✓ Connect text to world

Do you think it's important to protect bats and other kinds of animals in urban areas? Why or why not? What happens when protected animals interfere with human activities? **Possible response: It's important to protect animals in all areas, because they are part of the food web and are needed to keep a balance. If they interfere with human activities, residents should look for a compromise, such as moving their activities or finding a new place for the animals.**

Strategy Response Log

Have students list 2–3 important ideas presented in *The Truth About Austin's Amazing Bats* on p. 32 in the *Reader's and Writer's Notebook.*

Check Retelling

Have students retell *The Truth About Austin's Amazing Bats,* summarizing information in the text in a logical order. Encourage students to use the text features in their retellings.

Corrective feedback

If... students leave out important details,

then... have students look back through the illustrations in the selection.

Small Group Time

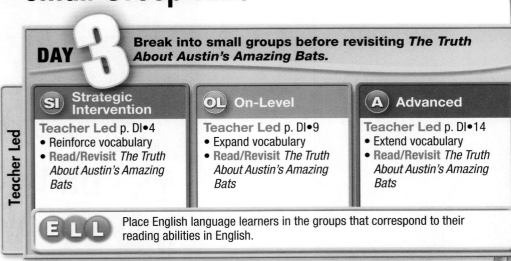

DAY 3 Break into small groups before revisiting *The Truth About Austin's Amazing Bats.*

Teacher Led

SI Strategic Intervention
Teacher Led p. DI•4
• Reinforce vocabulary
• **Read/Revisit** *The Truth About Austin's Amazing Bats*

OL On-Level
Teacher Led p. DI•9
• Expand vocabulary
• **Read/Revisit** *The Truth About Austin's Amazing Bats*

A Advanced
Teacher Led p. DI•14
• Extend vocabulary
• **Read/Revisit** *The Truth About Austin's Amazing Bats*

ELL Place English language learners in the groups that correspond to their reading abilities in English.

Practice Stations
• Let's Write
• Get Fluent
• Word Work

Independent Activities
• AudioText of *Austin's Amazing Bats*
• *Reader's and Writer's Notebook*
• Research and Inquiry

English Language Learners

Check retelling To support retelling, review the multilingual summary for *The Truth About Austin's Amazing Bats* with the appropriate Retelling Cards to scaffold understanding.

Objectives

◎ Use the important ideas strategy to improve comprehension.

OPTION **1** Skills and Strategies, continued

Teach Important Ideas

◉ **Important Ideas** What important ideas do you see in the first paragraph on page 330? (In the past, Austin residents feared the bats and wanted them gone. Newspapers portrayed the bats as something to be feared.)

Corrective Feedback

If... students have difficulty identifying important ideas,
then... model how to determine the importance of ideas.

 **Multidraft Reading**

If you chose...

Option 1 Return to Extend Thinking instruction starting on p. 326–327.
Option 2 Read pp. 330–335. Use the Guide Comprehension and Extend Thinking instruction.

Student Edition pp. 330–331

OPTION **2** Think Critically, continued

Higher-Order Thinking Skills

◉ **Important Ideas • Evaluation** Look at the first paragraph on page 331. Would the following sentence be a good way of summarizing the important ideas in the paragraph? *The more you know about bats, the less they will bother you.* Why or why not? **Possible responses:** Yes, because it tells in just a few words that people are only bothered by bats because they don't know enough about them, and it maintains the meaning and logical order of the text.

Model the Strategy

Think Aloud I read that the Austin residents used to be fearful. I think that's what this paragraph is going to be about, so it must be an important idea. Then I read about the newspapers.

Austin resident Mari Murphy remembers how fearful Austin residents used to be. "For years, local newspapers had carried headlines like 'Bat colonies sink teeth into city' and 'Mass fear in the air as bats invade Austin,'" she writes. "Misinformation abounded, and the bats that made Austin, Texas, their summer home were regarded as something to be eliminated, not as something wonderful to see."

Ms. Murphy belongs to Bat Conservation International (BCI). BCI's mission is to teach people the truth about bats and to protect and conserve bats' habitats. BCI moved their headquarters to Austin in 1986. One of their goals was to protect the bats that spent summers under the Congress Avenue Bridge.

Let's Think About...
What essential information does the author give to help you understand the BCI's mission?
◉ **Important Ideas**

6

The Daily Journal

MASS FEAR IN TH[
AS BATS INVADE A[

Facts on the Fly!
THINGS **YOU** CAN DO TO PROMOTE BAT CONSERVATION

330

Let's Think About...

6 The BCI's mission is to teach people the truth about bats and to protect and conserve bats' habitats.

7 Vampire bats drink the blood of birds, goats, and cattle.

How did the newspapers portray the bats? (as something to be feared) I know that because I see words like *sink teeth into* and *invade.* I think that's important because it tells me one of the reasons why people were afraid—they got misinformation from the newspaper.

On Their Own

As students read the selection, have them summarize the important ideas they notice, maintaining the meaning and logical order of the text.

There's a saying that goes "The more you know about bugs, the less they will bug you." The same can be said of bats. That's why BCI members told Austin residents all about the bats under the bridge. Their plan: Bring all the fears and misinformation about bats out into the open, and then show Austin's residents what bats are really like. Then they will learn to like, and even love, the bats. With this plan in mind, BCI members set to work spreading the truth about bats.

Yes, they told Austin residents, there are such things as vampire bats. They drink the blood of birds, goats, and cattle. First they lick the animal's skin in a spot where the blood vessels are close to the surface. Then they bite the skin and drink. A vampire bat will drink about four teaspoons of blood per day. But no, they do not prey on humans, and there are no vampire bats in Austin.

Let's **Think** About…

No vampire bats prey on humans. On what animals do they prey?
Questioning

⑦

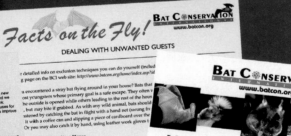

331

Draw Conclusions • Synthesis Based on what you know about news headlines, draw a conclusion or make an inference about why a newspaper would use terms like *invade* rather than *visit* when talking about the bats? Possible response: The more dramatic headline will probably sell more papers.

Review **Generalize • Synthesis** Based on the evidence in the text, what generalization can you infer about the relationship between vampire bats and humans? Possible response: All vampire bats prey on animals, but never humans.

E L L

English Language Learners

Prefixes Explain to students that the prefix *mis-* on p. 331 means "bad; wrong." Ask students to determine the meaning of the word *misinformation.* Ask: Can you think of a time when you got or gave *misinformation*?

Objectives

◎ Draw conclusions based on the text to aid comprehension.

OPTION 1 Skills and Strategies, continued

Teach Draw Conclusions

🔵 **Draw Conclusions** Have students read pp. 332–333. What conclusion can you draw regarding Paul Garret's feelings toward bats? What evidence did you use? (Possible response: He is impressed rather than frightened by them. I know this because he says their ability is amazing.)

Corrective Feedback

If... students are unable to draw a conclusion,
then... model how to draw a conclusion from textual evidence.

Student Edition pp. 332–333

OPTION 2 Think Critically, continued

Higher-Order Thinking Skills

🔵 **Draw Conclusions • Analysis** Do you think bats have more to fear from people or do people have more to fear from bats? What evidence supplied by the author supports your conclusion? Possible response: Bats have more to fear from people because people spread poisonous pesticides and destroy roosting spots.

Model the Skill

Think Aloud The author doesn't tell me how Paul Garret feels about bats, but I can look at the way he describes them. What word does he use to describe their ability to fly in a small space? (amazing)

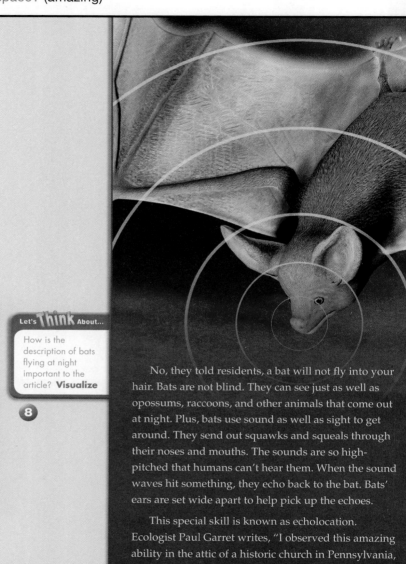

Let's Think About...

How is the description of bats flying at night important to the article? **Visualize**

8

No, they told residents, a bat will not fly into your hair. Bats are not blind. They can see just as well as opossums, raccoons, and other animals that come out at night. Plus, bats use sound as well as sight to get around. They send out squawks and squeals through their noses and mouths. The sounds are so high-pitched that humans can't hear them. When the sound waves hit something, they echo back to the bat. Bats' ears are set wide apart to help pick up the echoes.

This special skill is known as echolocation. Ecologist Paul Garret writes, "I observed this amazing ability in the attic of a historic church in Pennsylvania,

332

Let's Think About...

8 It shows how bats use sounds and their echoes when flying in the dark, and that they aren't blind and won't fly into your hair.

9 I can look back at the text and read the information again. If I still don't understand, I can look it up in an encyclopedia.

125 933

(They pollinate flowers, scatter seeds, and help control crop bugs.) I also see information about echolocation, but that tells me how bats hunt, not why they benefit humans, so I will not count that as evidence for my generalization.

On Their Own

Have students find another generalization about the benefits of bats and identify textual evidence that supports the generalization. For additional practice, use *Let's Practice It!* p. 310 on the *Teacher Resources DVD-ROM*.

The people who live in the city have their own special reasons for loving the Free-tails. For one thing, Austin's bats eat loads of mosquitoes. If not for the bats, Austin's residents would have tons more mosquitoes biting their skin and sucking their blood on summer evenings.

August is the best month for bat-watching. That's when most of the young pups are ready to leave the roost and join their mothers to hunt. The bats usually start coming out from under the bridge between 8:00 and 8:30 p.m. People can call the special Bat Hotline for updates on the most likely time that night, and BCI members are at the bridge each night to hand out information and answer questions. They want to make sure that everyone knows the truth about Austin's amazing bats.

What is it about the bats—besides the benefits to farming and tourism—that captivates visitors and residents of Austin? City dwellers often forget about the natural world beyond their streets and skyscrapers, but when they watch the bats soar, they rediscover the joy and mystery of nature. Some believe that observing the bats links spectators to nature, and that the resulting thrill is unforgettable. Photographer Tim Flach writes, "I've been fortunate enough to see a number of natural wonders, but the bats will stay in mind for the rest of my life."

 Let's **Think** About...

What clues make you think the author wants people to care for the natural world?
Inferring

335

Differentiated Instruction

 Strategic Intervention

Generalize Point out that when students read a generalization, they should look for evidence to support the generalization. Point out that some nearby information may provide details that, while interesting, do not support the generalization. Have pairs of students read the second paragraph on p. 335 and decide whether or not each sentence supports the generalization *August is the best month for bat-watching*.

A **Advanced**

Ask students to create a flyer encouraging tourists to come see Austin's bats. Remind them to pay special attention to word choice and other persuasive techniques to make their point.

ELL

English Language Learners

Word choice Point out the phrase *tons more mosquitoes*. Tell students that the term *ton* is a unit of measure equal to 2,000 pounds, but that the author does not mean for *tons* to be taken literally. Do you think the author means there are a lot of mosquitoes or a few mosquitoes? Point out that the author may have used *tons* rather than *a lot* because it sounds more dramatic.

Comprehension Check

Spiral Review

Author's Purpose • Evaluation What is the author's purpose in writing *The Truth About Austin's Amazing Bats?* How well does he achieve that goal? Explain. **Possible response:** His purpose is to inform people about bats and to help readers see how amazing the Austin bats are. He succeeds because I learned a lot I didn't know, and now I would like to see the Austin bats myself.

Check Predictions Have students return to the predictions they made earlier and confirm whether they were accurate.

Objectives

◎ Draw conclusions to enhance comprehension.

◎ Use important ideas strategy to enhance comprehension.

Check Retelling
SUCCESS PREDICTOR

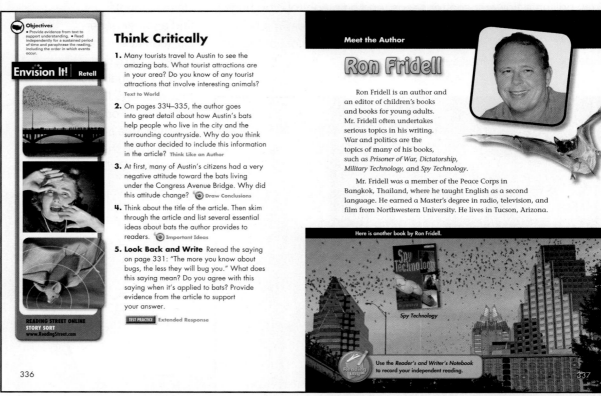

Objectives
• Provide evidence from text to support understanding. • Read independently for a sustained period of time and paraphrase the reading, including the order in which events occur.

Envision It! Retell

READING STREET ONLINE
STORY SORT
www.ReadingStreet.com

336

Think Critically

1. Many tourists travel to Austin to see the amazing bats. What tourist attractions are in your area? Do you know of any tourist attractions that involve interesting animals? **Text to World**

2. On pages 334–335, the author goes into great detail about how Austin's bats help people who live in the city and the surrounding countryside. Why do you think the author decided to include this information in the article? **Think Like an Author**

3. At first, many of Austin's citizens had a very negative attitude toward the bats living under the Congress Avenue Bridge. Why did this attitude change? **Draw Conclusions**

4. Think about the title of the article. Then skim through the article and list several essential ideas about bats the author provides to readers. **Important Ideas**

5. **Look Back and Write** Reread the saying on page 331: "The more you know about bugs, the less they will bug you." What does this saying mean? Do you agree with this saying when it's applied to bats? Provide evidence from the article to support your answer.

TEST PRACTICE Extended Response

Meet the Author

Ron Fridell

Ron Fridell is an author and an editor of children's books and books for young adults. Mr. Fridell often undertakes serious topics in his writing. War and politics are the topics of many of his books, such as *Prisoner of War, Dictatorship, Military Technology,* and *Spy Technology.*

Mr. Fridell was a member of the Peace Corps in Bangkok, Thailand, where he taught English as a second language. He earned a Master's degree in radio, television, and film from Northwestern University. He lives in Tucson, Arizona.

Here is another book by Ron Fridell.

Spy Technology

Use the *Reader's and Writer's Notebook* to record your independent reading.

337

Student Edition pp. 336–337

Retelling

Envision It! Have students work in pairs to retell the selection, using the Envision It! Retelling Cards as prompts. Remind students that they should maintain meaning and logical order in their summaries. Monitor students' retellings.

Scoring rubric

> **Top-Score Response** A top-score response makes connections beyond the text, describes the main topic and important ideas using accurate information, evaluates facts and opinions, and draws conclusions from the text.

Plan to Assess Retelling

☑ **This week assess Strategic Intervention students.**

☐ **Week 2** Assess Advanced students.

☐ **Week 3** Assess Strategic Intervention students.

☐ **Week 4** Assess On-Level students.

☐ **Week 5** Assess any students you have not yet checked during this unit.

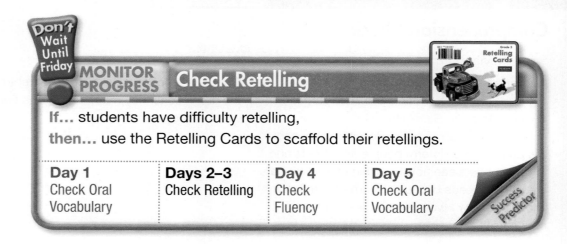

Don't Wait Until Friday

MONITOR PROGRESS Check Retelling

Retelling Cards

If... students have difficulty retelling,

then... use the Retelling Cards to scaffold their retellings.

Day 1	Days 2–3	Day 4	Day 5
Check Oral Vocabulary	Check Retelling	Check Fluency	Check Oral Vocabulary

Success Predictor

Think Critically

Text to world

1. Possible response: In our city, we have museums with gardens and a zoo. We also have an aquarium where you can see sharks, rays, and other animals up close.

Think like an author

2. Possible response: He wanted to show that bats are not harmful to people but instead are helpful in many ways—so people should not be afraid of them.

** Draw conclusions**

3. Possible response: They found out that much of what they thought they knew about bats was actually wrong and that bats would not hurt them. You can infer from the text that citizens probably liked the tourist business the bats brought to Austin.

Important ideas

4. Possible response: Bats like to roost in dark caves or tunnels. Many people are afraid of bats, but bats are helpful because they eat lots of bugs and pollinate plants. Bats use echolocation to avoid hitting things and to help them hunt. Bats are in danger because of human activities, such as spraying pesticides and destroying places where bats roost.

Writing on Demand

5. **Look Back and Write** To build writing fluency, assign a 10–15 minute time limit.

Suggest that students use a prewriting strategy, such as brainstorming or using a graphic organizer, to organize their ideas. Remind them to establish a topic sentence and support it with organized facts, details, or explanations from the text. As students finish their multi-paragraph essays, encourage them to reread their responses, revise for organization and support, and proofread for errors in grammar and conventions.

Scoring rubric

> **Top-Score Response** A top-score response uses details to tell about misinformation regarding bats.
>
> **A top-score response should include:**
>
> - People wrongly think bats will hurt them.
> - Few bats carry rabies and vampire bats do not feed on humans.
> - Bats help people by pollinating plants and eating insects.

Differentiated Instruction

SI Strategic Intervention

Have students work in pairs to brainstorm details about information that could help people see bats differently.

Meet the Author

Have students read about author Ron Fridell on p. 337. Ask them if they think Fridell considers nature a serious topic.

Independent Reading

After students enter their independent reading information into their Reading Logs, have them paraphrase a portion of the text they have just read. Remind students that when we paraphrase, we express the meaning of a passage using other words and maintaining logical order.

ELL

English Language Learners

Retelling Use the retelling cards to discuss the selection with students. Point to each card and have students tell how it shows information they learned in the selection.

Objectives

• Read grade-level text with accuracy.
• Reread for fluency.
• Follow and clarify directions.

Model Fluency
Accuracy

Model fluent reading

Have students turn to p. 332 of *The Truth About Austin's Amazing Bats.* Have students follow along as you read this page. Tell them to notice spelling and punctuation as they listen to the way you say each word and sentence. Be sure to enunciate clearly for accuracy.

Guide practice

Have the students follow along as you read the page again. Then have them reread the page as a group without you until they read with no mistakes. Ask questions to be sure students comprehend the text. Continue in the same way on p. 333.

Reread for Fluency

Corrective feedback

If... students are having difficulty reading with accuracy, **then...** prompt:

• What word is a problem?
• Read the sentence again to be sure you understand it.
• Tell me the sentence. Now read it with accuracy.

ROUTINE Paired Reading

 Select a passage For *The Truth About Austin's Amazing Bats,* use pp. 332–333.

 Reader 1 Students read the pages, switching readers at the end of each paragraph.

Reader 2 Partners reread the pages. This time the other student begins.

Reread For optimal fluency, have partners continue to read three or four times.

 Corrective Feedback Listen as students read. Provide feedback about their accuracy. If needed, make suggestions to help them increase their accuracy, such as slowing down or analyzing words that give them particular trouble.

Routines Flip Chart

Research and Study Skills
Follow/Clarify Directions

Academic Vocabulary

directions a list of steps in a process that tells how to make or do something

Teach

Ask students where they might find a list of directions. Students may mention cookbooks, textbooks with science experiments, or packages of products such as cameras. Display a recipe or directions for an experiment and use it to discuss these ideas:

- **Directions** are instructions that explain how to make or do something. They are often presented as a numbered list.

- Read directions through completely before you begin. Use text features, such as numbered items and graphics, to gain an overview and locate information.

- When you follow directions, you go through the explanation and perform each step in the process, one step at a time.

- Directions often include labeled diagrams or pictures of what happens at each stage to help you understand what to do.

- If any part of the directions is not clear, clarify the directions by rereading the steps, going back to the last step you did correctly, checking pictures, diagrams, and charts, or asking questions.

Provide groups with different types of directions. Have each group present its directions to the class, explaining how details from the text could be used to help someone complete a task, solve a problem, or perform a procedure.

Guide practice

Discuss these questions:

How are all these directions alike? How are they different? (They all show how to do something, but they have different kinds of steps and graphics.)

Which directions would be easiest to follow? Why? (The easiest directions may offer fewer steps, include a materials list to help get ready for the project, and include clear graphics and text features.)

On their own

Have students complete pp. 392–393 of the *Reader's and Writer's Notebook*.

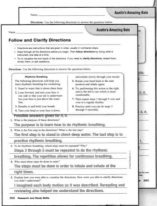

Reader's and Writer's Notebook pp. 392–393

ELL

English Language Learners

Expand Vocabulary To help students prepare for the paired reading, point out content-area vocabulary found in the selected text: *echolocation, ecologist, colony, disease, poisonous,* and *pesticides.* Ask volunteers to tell what each word means. Then have the class repeat each word several times so they will be better able to read them in context.

Objectives
- Analyze data for usefulness.
- Identify and correctly use modifiers.
- Spell frequently misspelled words.

Research and Inquiry
Analyze

Teach

Tell students that today they will analyze their findings. They may need to change or adjust the focus of their original inquiry question as dictated by the answers to secondary questions they have asked.

Model

Think Aloud

Originally I was looking for information about the arrest of Rosa Parks and what happened immediately afterward because of it. However, my research kept turning up the Montgomery Bus Boycott. Now I realize that the boycott was important to the beginning of the Civil Rights movement—and it would also be a really dramatic event to show in a skit. Now, my inquiry question is *How did Rosa Parks and the Montgomery Bus Boycott help launch the Civil Rights movement?* The new question still talks about an unplanned incident—Rosa Park's actions and her arrest—but it tells more about the chain of events that finally led to social changes.

Guide practice

Have students analyze their findings. They may need to refocus their inquiry question to better fit the information they have found or look for different ways to find information they seek. Remind students that if they have difficulty improving their focus they can ask a reference librarian or a local expert for guidance.

On their own

Have student groups discuss their findings. Point out that they should look for holes in the knowledge that they need to tell a story in a skit. Have them arrange their ideas on a time line to help them decide which areas they need to further explore. Stress the importance of historical accuracy in their skits. As they begin to outline their skits using information they have found, have them review the sources of their notes to be sure the information is relevant, valid, and reliable.

Conventions
Modifiers

Review

Remind students that this week they learned about modifiers:

- Adjectives, adverbs, and prepositional phrases are modifiers.
- Adjectives modify nouns and pronouns. Adverbs modify verbs, adjectives, or other adverbs.
- Prepositional phrases can act as adjectives or adverbs.
- Place modifiers next to the words they modify to avoid confusion.

Daily Fix-It

Use Daily Fix-It numbers 5 and 6 in the right margin.

Connect to oral language

Write this sentence one the board: *Riley took the pen.* Then, write these modifiers on the board: *red, from her pocket, quickly.* Have students use the modifiers to extend the sentence. After each addition, have them say the new sentence aloud.

On their own

For additional practice, use *Let's Practice It!* p. 311 on the *Teacher Resources DVD-ROM.*

Let's Practice It!
TR DVD•311

Spelling
Suffixes *-ous, -sion, -ion,* and *-ation*

Frequently misspelled words

The words *didn't, said,* and *don't* are often misspelled by students, along with the words *decision* and *humorous* from your spelling list. I'm going to read a sentence. Choose the correct word to complete the sentence and then write it correctly. Use a dictionary to check your spellings.

1. We saw a very _____ movie this week. (humorous)

2. Mateo _____, "Let's try looking over here!" (said)

3. Anthony _____ understand the assignment. (didn't)

4. Li made a _____ about basketball camp. (decision)

5. "_____ pull on the dog's tail!" Mom yelled. (Don't)

On their own

For additional practice, use *Reader's and Writer's Notebook* p. 394.

Differentiated Instruction

 Strategic Intervention

Modifiers Tell students that mistakes with the placement of the word *only* are common. These mistakes usually happen when its placement in a sentence makes the meaning unclear. Encourage them to think about what *only* modifies in a sentence and then decide whether it is placed correctly. Guide students in identifying the differences in meaning based on the placement of *only* in these sentences:

Only take advice from Pat. (Take nothing else from Pat but advice.)

Take advice from Pat only. (Don't take advice from anyone but Pat.)

Daily Fix-It

5. The girl taked pictures of them bats. (*took; those* or *these*)

6. Soon uncle Bob will make a desicion. (*Uncle; decision*)

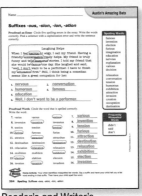

Reader's and Writer's Notebook p. 394

Objective
• Understand the criteria for writing an effective journal entry.

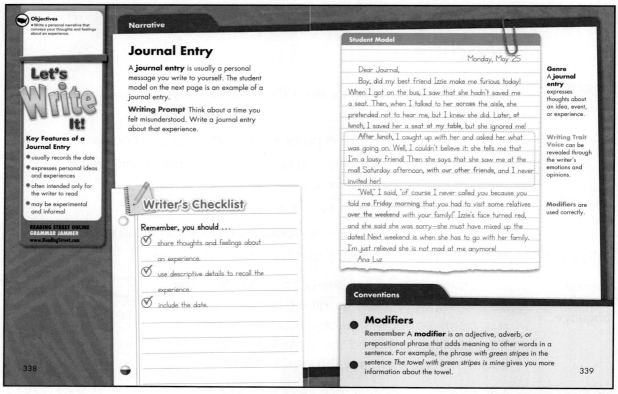
Student Edition pp. 338–339

Let's Write It!
Journal Entry

Teach

Use pp. 338–339 in the Student Edition. Direct students to read the key features of a journal entry which appear on p. 338. Then have students read the remainder of p. 338. Remind students that they can refer to the information in the Writer's Checklist as they write their own journal entries.

Read the student model on p. 339. Point out the key features, such as the date at the top of the page, the ideas and experience shared by the writer, and the informality of the writing.

Connect to conventions

Remind students that adjectives, adverbs, and prepositional phrases are called modifiers. Point out the correct use of modifiers in the model.

Writing—Journal Entry
Writing Trait: Voice

Display rubric

Display Scoring Rubric 26 from the *Teacher Resources DVD* and go over the criteria for each trait under each score. Then, using the model in the Student Edition, choose students to explain why the model should score a 4 for one of the traits. If a student offers that the model should score below 4 for a trait, the student should offer support for that response. Explain that this rubric will be used to evaluate the journal entry they write.

Scoring Rubric: Journal Entry

	4	3	2	1
Focus/Ideas	Journal entry is focused and clearly tells the story of writer's experience feeling misunderstood	Mostly focused journal entry; adequately relates writer's experience feeling misunderstood	Mostly unfocused entry; writer's experience feeling misunderstood undeveloped	Unfocused narrative; fails to relate experience feeling misunderstood
Organization	Clear beginning, middle, and end; effectively relates the story of event or experience	Identifiable beginning, middle, and end; adequately relates story of event or experience	Somewhat unclear beginning, middle, and end; story of event or experience disrupted	No clear beginning, middle, or end, obscuring retelling of event or experience
Voice	Engaging; shows writer's thoughts and feelings about the event or experience being shared	Voice apparent; reveals some thoughts and feelings about the event or experience	Weak voice; little explanation of thoughts and feelings about the event or experience	Flat writing with no identifiable voice
Word Choice	Vivid, precise word choice; abundant personal details to establish voice	Accurate word choice; adequate personal details to establish voice	Limited or repetitive word choice; few personal details	Incorrect or limited word choice; lack of personal details
Sentences	Varied sentences in logical progression	Not as much variety; order mostly logical	Too many similar sentences	Many fragments and run-ons
Conventions	Excellent control and accuracy; modifiers used correctly	Good control, few errors; modifiers generally used correctly	Weak control; modifiers used incorrectly	Serious errors that obscure meaning

Story sequence

Have students get out the story sequence graphic organizers that they worked on yesterday. If their organizers are not complete, offer students some time to complete them. Encourage all students to consider the rubric and add any details to their writing plans as appropriate.

Write

You will be using your graphic organizer as you write the draft of your journal entry. Concentrate only on capturing the story in some detail when you draft. You can add additional details when you revise and correct errors when you proofread.

Objectives
- Write a first draft of a journal entry.
- Include details and vivid words to establish a strong voice.

Writing, continued
Writing Trait: Voice

MINI-LESSON

Writing with a Strong Voice

■ **Introduce** Explain to students that a writer's voice is like a person's personality—it is the thing that makes each of us unique. We show our personalities through the things we say and do, as well as through our ideas and feelings. Sharing strong ideas and feelings is one way to create an engaging voice in writing. Display the Drafting Tips for students. Then display Writing Transparency 26A.

Writing Transparency 26A, TR DVD

Drafting Tips

✔ Begin by following the plan you created when you completed your story sequence graphic organizer.

✔ Make sure you clearly retell an experience that you have had where you felt misunderstood.

✔ Include strong words to show how you feel about the event or experience you are describing.

Think Aloud This is another sample of a journal entry written to the same prompt that you will write to this week. It tells the story of a misunderstanding between two friends. Notice that the writer was concerned only with capturing her story. She can fix the spelling and grammar errors later. **Point students to the second sentence of the third paragraph.** When the writer says, "I'd rather be friends with her than wear any bracelet in the world," she is showing her feelings and creating a strong voice in her writing. Tomorrow we will see how the writer revised this entry to make her voice even stronger. **Direct students to use the Drafting Tips to guide them in writing their drafts. Remind them to share their feelings and ideas as they tell their story.**

ROUTINE Quick Write for Fluency Team Talk

1. **Talk** Have students discuss ways that they could create a strong voice when they revise their journal entries.

2. **Write** Each student writes a paragraph explaining his or her plans for revising to create a strong voice.

3. **Share** Partner's check each other's paragraphs for the correct use and placement of modifiers.

Routines Flip Chart

Wrap Up Your Day

✔ **Build Concepts** Have students discuss how the bat situation in Austin had a positive outcome.

✔ **Draw Conclusions** Why did people come to love the bats?

✔ **Important Ideas** How did identifying important ideas help you to understand why people changed their minds about the bats?

Differentiated Instruction

SI Strategic Intervention

Writer's voice Work in a small group with students to point out the characteristics of a strong writing voice in other pieces of writing. You might use the journal entry models, models for another writing product, or the program literature.

Academic Vocabulary

A **writer's personality** is shown through the word choice and the tone of the writing.

Preview DAY 4

Tell students that tomorrow they will read about the author of *The Truth About Austin's Amazing Bats.*

Today at a Glance

Oral Vocabulary
perceptive, unaware

Genre
Autobiography

Reading
"The Animals in My Life"

Let's Learn It!
Fluency: Accuracy
Vocabulary: Unknown words
Listening/Speaking: Debate

Research and Inquiry
Synthesize

Spelling
Suffixes *-ous, -sion, -ion, -ation*

Conventions
Modifiers

Writing
Journal entry

Concept Talk

? Question of the Week
How can unplanned situations have positive outcomes?

Expand the concept

Remind students that this week they have read about how bats found a home in Austin through *happenstance*. Tell students that today they will read about the unexpected *occurrence* that gave Ron Fridell the idea to write *The Truth About Austin's Amazing Bats.*

Anchored Talk

Develop oral vocabulary

Use text features—illustrations and captions—to review pp. 330–335 of *The Truth About Austin's Amazing Bats.* Discuss the Amazing Words *happenstance* and *occurrences.* Add these words to the concept map. Use the following questions to develop students' understanding of the concept. Break into groups and have students identify points of agreement and disagreement.

• Do you think tourists are more likely to visit a place for its everyday *occurrences* or for its special festivals? Why do you think so?

• What role does *happenstance* play in the big decisions people make?

Strategy Response Log

Have students complete p. 32 in *Reader's and Writer's Notebook*. Then have students summarize the important ideas that they found in the selection.

Oral Vocabulary
Amazing Words

unintended	perspective
fortuitous	happenstance
advantageous	occurrences
potential	perceptive
spontaneous	unaware

 Amazing Words Oral Vocabulary Routine

Teach Amazing Words

1 Introduce Write the concept word *unaware* on the board. Have students say it aloud with you. Use context clues in this sentence to help you come up with a definition for the word *unaware: Austin residents used to be* unaware *of the good things bats do, but now they know how helpful bats are.* (The words *used to, good things, but now they know,* and *helpful* help me understand that the word means "not noticing, not knowing, not realizing.")

2 Demonstrate Have students answer questions to demonstrate understanding. Why does BCI care if people are *unaware* of how bats really live? (If people have the wrong ideas about bats, they may want to harm or get rid of them.)

3 Apply Have students apply their understanding. What would some antonyms be for *unaware*?

See p. OV•1 to teach *perceptive*.

Routines Flip Chart

Apply Amazing Words

Help students establish a purpose for reading as they read "The Animals in My Life" on pp. 340–341. Have them think about how people who are *perceptive* can notice things about animals that people who are *unaware* may not.

Connect to reading

As students read today's selection about a writer who writes about nature, have them think about how this week's Question of the Week and the Amazing Words *perceptive* and *unaware* apply to wildlife viewing.

ELL Produce Oral Language Use the Day 4 instruction on ELL Poster 26 to extend and enrich language.

ELL Poster 26

Let's Think About Genre
Autobiography: Point of View

Introduce the genre

Explain to students that what we read is structured differently depending on the author's reasons for writing and what kind of information he or she wishes to convey. Different types of texts are called genres. Tell them that autobiography is one type of genre.

Discuss the genre

Discuss autobiography with students. Ask: What is an autobiography? (the story of a real person's life told by that person) How is it different from a biography? (Possible response: Biographies are told by someone else.) Explain: Biographies and autobiographies both tell about a real person's life—the difference is point of view. Biographies are usually told in the third-person objective, using words such as *he, him, she,* and *her,* and can only tell what the author has learned about the person. Autobiographies are told in the first-person point of view, using words such as *I* and *me,* and often give insight into what the person was thinking or feeling. Point out some of the literary language and devices authors of autobiography use to present major life events. For example, they may embellish or leave out details or make up dialogue to tell a better story.

On the board, draw a Venn diagram like the one below, labeled *Biography* and *Autobiography.* Ask the following questions:

• In which point of view would you write a biography? (third-person) An autobiography? (first-person)

• In which genre would you expect to hear a person's exact thoughts? (autobiography) In which genre would you expect to hear what many other people said about the person? (biography)

Biography   **Autobiography**

third-person objective
he, she, they

The life story of a real person

first-person subjective
I, we, me

Guide practice

Have students work in pairs to identify words or phrases they could add to the Venn diagram.

Connect to reading

Tell students that they will now read an autobiography by the author of *The Truth About Austin's Amazing Bats.* Have the class think about the author's point of view, as well as the language and devices he uses to tell about his life.

Small Group Time

DAY 4 — Break into small groups before reading or revisiting "The Animals in My Life."

Teacher Led

(SI) Strategic Intervention

Teacher Led p. DI•5
- Practice retelling
- Genre focus
- **Read/Revisit** "The Animals in My Life"

(OL) On-Level

Teacher Led p. DI•10
- Practice retelling
- Genre focus
- **Read/Revisit** "The Animals in My Life"

(A) Advanced

Teacher Led p. DI•15
- Genre focus
- **Read/Revisit** "The Animals in My Life"

 Place English language learners in the groups that correspond to their reading abilities in English.

Practice Stations
- Read for Meaning
- Get Fluent
- Words to Know

Independent Activities
- AudioText: "The Animals in My Life"
- *Reader's and Writer's Notebook*
- Research and Inquiry

Objectives
- Make connections between and among texts. • Identify the language and devices used in biographies and autobiographies, including how authors present major events in a person's life.

Science in Reading

Genre
Autobiography

- An autobiography is the story of a person's life written by the person who lived it.
- Autobiographies are written in the first person, using *I, me,* and *my.*
- The events in an autobiography are actual events and experiences in a person's life.
- Read "The Animals in My Life." Look for elements that make this story an autobiography. What language does the author use when he discusses major events in his life?

THE ANIMALS IN MY LIFE
By Ron Fridell

I have been writing nonfiction for my entire adult life. I've written on many science topics, from the life cycle of the pumpkin to fingerprinting, from water pollution to space travel. But my favorite topic is animals.

The very first animal I wrote about was my collie dog, Ranger. I wrote action-packed tales of our fictional adventures together. We would battle everything from dinosaurs to pirates. Whenever I was in trouble, my brave and clever Ranger was always there to rescue me. I was in the third grade at the time.

Since then I've written about many animals, small and big. Ants, spiders, frogs, turtles, vultures, camels, elephants—and now bats.

Why the Austin bats? I saw them fly out from under the Congress Avenue Bridge once, in the 1980s. I'd forgotten all about them until the summer of 2008. That's when I learned that Mexican Long-tongued bats were visiting my hummingbird feeder.

I live in southern Arizona, out on the desert. The feeder is right outside the kitchen window. I wait until dark. Then I shine a flashlight through the window. And there they are with their big eyes and long, long tongues.

The Long-tongued bats reminded me of the Austin bats, so I did some Internet research. To my surprise, I read that the Austin bats are now a huge tourist attraction, thanks to the good people at Bat Conservation International. I also talked with a scientist at BCI by e-mail. I loved what I discovered in my research. I don't like to see anyone misunderstood, whether it's a person or an animal. And I love happy endings. That's why I had to write about the Austin bats. I hope their story makes my readers feel happy too.

Let's Think About...
How does the point of view tell you this is an autobiography? **Autobiography**

1

Let's Think About...
Reading Across Texts After reading about Austin's bats and about the author, what conclusions can you draw about the author?

Writing Across Texts Imagine that you are a member of BCI. Write a journal entry about your life helping Austin's bats.

340

341

Student Edition pp. 340–341

Guide Comprehension
Skills and Strategies

Teach the genre

Genre: Autobiography Have students read pp. 340–341. Then ask: The author could tell about many other events in his life. Why does he choose to tell about seeing bats in Austin and then at his bird feeder?

Corrective feedback

If... students have difficulty understanding how literary devices are used in an autobiography,
then... use the model to guide students in understanding a literary device, such as sequence of events.

Model

Think Aloud I know that autobiography usually has a story structure based on sequence of events. I read that first Ron Fridell saw the Austin bats. Then he saw the bats at his feeder. Finally, he researched and wrote *The Truth About Austin's Amazing Bats*. I think he is telling me about his encounters with bats to explain why he wrote *The Truth About Austin's Amazing Bats*.

On their own

Have students list some of the events they would include if they were writing an autobiography and explain why each is important.

Extend Thinking
Think Critically

Higher-order thinking skills

 Draw Conclusions • Analysis Reread the second paragraph on page 341. Describe how the author's use of language helps you envision the scene. Possible response: He uses rhythm as well as details. He uses two short, direct sentences, *I wait until dark. Then I shine a flashlight through the window.* He then describes the bats' shiny eyes and their long, long tongues, which helps me see them in my mind.

Author's Purpose • Evaluation What is the author's goal in wanting you to picture the scene at the bird feeder? How well does he achieve that goal? Explain. Possible response: He wants me to feel as if I'm there and see the incident through his eyes. Yes, he fully achieves that goal because I can picture the scene and imagine the bats.

Let's Think About...

 I can tell this selection is an autobiography because it is told from the point of view of the person who lived through these things. The author uses the words *I* and *me.*

Reading Across Texts

Have students construct a Venn diagram to help them organize what they know about Ron Fridell from reading *The Truth About Austin's Amazing Bats* and "The Animals in My Life." Point out that, while only the autobiography provides direct information about the author and his life, *The Truth About Austin's Amazing Bats* does offer clues about what the author thinks and feels.

Writing Across Texts

Suggest that students think about what a member of BCI would consider challenging and rewarding about helping Austin's bats.

Objectives

- Read with fluency.
- ◎ Use a dictionary or glossary to determine the meanings of unknown words.
- Participate in a debate.

Fluency: WCPM
SUCCESS PREDICTOR

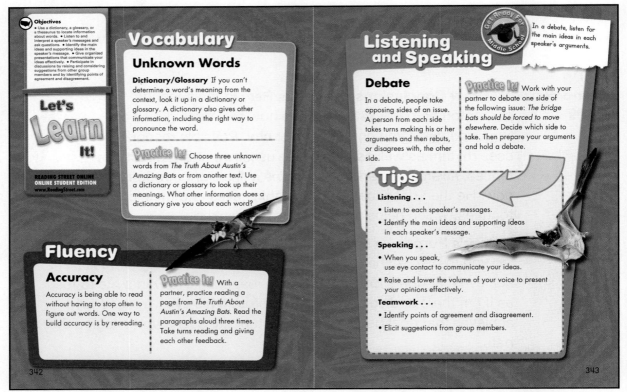

Student Edition pp. 342–343

Fluency
Accuracy

Guide practice

Use the Student Edition activity as an assessment tool. Make sure the reading passage is at least 200 words in length. As students read aloud with partners, make sure they are reading accurately.

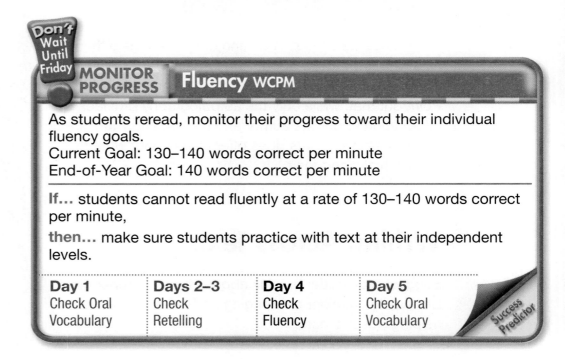

Don't Wait Until Friday

MONITOR PROGRESS **Fluency WCPM**

As students reread, monitor their progress toward their individual fluency goals.
Current Goal: 130–140 words correct per minute
End-of-Year Goal: 140 words correct per minute

If... students cannot read fluently at a rate of 130–140 words correct per minute,

then... make sure students practice with text at their independent levels.

Day 1	Days 2–3	Day 4	Day 5
Check Oral Vocabulary	Check Retelling	Check Fluency	Check Oral Vocabulary

Success Predictor

Vocabulary
Unknown Words

Teach unknown words

Dictionary/Glossary Write this sentence on the board: *Bats are nocturnal animals.* Underline the word *nocturnal* but do not say it aloud. Point out that the context does not make the meaning or pronunciation of this word clear.

Guide practice

Have students use a print or electronic dictionary or glossary to find the meaning and pronunciation of *nocturnal.* Also have students find the syllabication and part of speech of the word.

On their own

Have students tell a partner which words they chose, what each word means, how to pronounce it correctly, and its syllabication and part of speech.

Listening and Speaking
Debate

Teach

Tell students that to prepare for a debate, each team must be very organized and thoroughly discuss the arguments they will use to present their side of the issue. Explain that team members should elicit and consider suggestions from other members of their group. Students should also identify points of agreement and disagreement between members of their own group to help them prepare for the debate. This preparation will help when they face a team on the opposing side of the issue as they can use points of agreement or disagreement to argue for their side.

Guide practice

As they practice, remind students that good speakers maintain eye contact with listeners, speak at an appropriate rate and volume with clear enunciation, make natural gestures with their hands and body, and use proper conventions of language while speaking. Also remind the students to listen attentively to the speaker and to take notes and ask questions to help them accurately interpret the speaker's verbal and nonverbal messages and clarify the speaker's perspective.

On their own

Have students engage in an organized debate. You might want to have students from another class judge the debates, telling which side they feel won the debate and explaining why.

Debate

Explain to students that a debate is an attempt at persuasion. Point out that when they debate, they should state a clear position and provide relevant support. They should bring in strong, provable facts to persuade audience members to agree with them.

ELL

English Language Learners

Practice pronunciation Assist students as they prepare for their debate. Model correct pronunciation of words they have difficulty with. Have them repeat the words after you.

Fluency

Succes
Predict

Objectives

- Synthesize research findings into a skit.
- Review modifiers.
- Spell words with suffixes *-ous*, *-sion*, *-ion*, and *-ation*.

Research and Inquiry
Synthesize

Teach

Have students synthesize research findings from multiple sources into a skit that portrays the event they researched. Remind them that the skit should be about an unplanned situation with a positive outcome.

Guide practice

Have students meet with their group and assign roles. One student may be the narrator. Show examples of scripts. Each line should begin with a character's name, followed by a semicolon. Students may also wish to note stage directions in italics.

Although props are unnecessary, students should discuss how the "stage" should be set up and where characters should stand and sit. For example, a Rosa Parks skit would take place on a bus, so students would need to set up chairs in rows, including a place for the driver.

On their own

Have students use a word-processing program to create their script. Check to make sure that students are listening to each other and following the time line they created on Day 3.

After they finish the script, groups should rehearse together to prepare for their performance. Walk around and give students advice on how to portray their characters accurately.

Conventions
Modifiers

Test practice

Remind students that grammar skills, such as modifiers, are often assessed on important tests. Review with students that modifiers—adjectives, adverbs, and prepositional phrases—tell more about other words in a sentence. Tell students to make sure modifiers are correctly placed in sentences to avoid confusion and, on tests, incorrect answers.

Daily Fix-It

Use Daily Fix-It numbers 7 and 8 in the right margin.

On their own

For additional practice, use *Reader's and Writer's Notebook* p. 395.

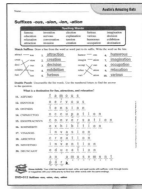

Reader's and Writer's
Notebook p. 395

Spelling
Suffixes *-ous, -sion, -ion,* and *-ation*

Practice spelling strategy

Have students write sentences using as many list words as possible. Challenge them to use at least two list words per sentence. Students may also illustrate their sentences to show their understanding of the words and how they have used them in the sentences. When finished, have student share their work with a partner and discuss the rules and patterns they used to spell each word correctly. Have students use dictionaries to check for correct spellings.

On their own

For additional practice, use *Let's Practice It!* p. 312 on the *Teacher Resources DVD-ROM.*

Let's Practice It!
TR DVD•312

Daily Fix-It

7. I chose a cart when I went to the store <u>with a squeaky wheel.</u> (*I chose a cart <u>with a squeaky wheel</u> when I went to the store.*)

8. The beach is the better place of all to go for relaxasion. *(best; relaxation)*

Differentiated Instruction

 Advanced

Modifiers Have students work in pairs to experiment with the placement of the underlined modifiers in each sentence. Pairs should move the modifier to various positions in the sentence (noted by asterisks) and then describe how each sentence's meaning changes.

1. Mia put the puppy * in the bed <u>with the curly tail</u>.
2. Ellie <u>barely</u> tried to * win the game.
3. James had more points than any <u>other</u> player on any * team in the * league.
4. <u>Only</u> the * cat in the * cage * plays with the * red toy *.

Objectives
- Revise draft of a journal entry.
- Apply the revising strategy Adding.

Writing—Journal Entry
Revising Strategy

MINI-LESSON

Revising Strategy: Adding

Writing Transparency 26B

- Yesterday we wrote journal entries about a time we felt misunderstood. Today we will revise our drafts.

- Display Writing Transparency 26B. Remind students that revising does not include corrections of grammar and mechanics. Then introduce the revising strategy of adding.

- When you revise, you ask yourself *Does my voice come through in my writing? Have I captured and expressed my feelings about the experience I am describing?* The revising strategy of adding is the strategy in which more details are added to make the writer's voice stronger and the writing more engaging for readers. Let's look at the first paragraph on the model. This paragraph does a good job of beginning the story, but I feel like I learned more about Tara than I did about the writer. The writer can add a sentence or two to help readers get to know him or her better. **Have students reread their own journal entries to find places where more personal details will enhance their writing voice.**

Revising Tips

✔ Review writing to make sure that it is well-organized and engaging.

✔ Add sentences and words as necessary to enhance voice and clarify meaning.

✔ Don't look for grammar and spelling errors; you will have time to make those corrections during the editing stage.

Peer conferencing

Peer Revision Have pairs of students exchange papers for peer revision. Have each student write three suggestions for strengthening their partner's voice to make the story more engaging. Refer to *First Stop* for more information about peer conferencing.

Have students revise their journal entries using the suggestions their partner wrote during Peer Revision as well as the key features of a journal entry to guide them. Be sure that students are using the revising strategy of adding.

Corrective feedback

Circulate around the room to monitor students as they revise. Remind any students correcting errors that they will have time to edit tomorrow. They should be working on content and organization today.

Write Guy
Jeff Anderson

Life in a Fishbowl

When a teacher can't confer with every student, a "fishbowl conference" with one willing student can allow other students to observe, listen, and explore how to appropriately respond to others' writing. It's important to reflect what the student is doing well and how a draft might be revised and improved.

ROUTINE Quick Write for Fluency **Team Talk**

1. **Talk** Have pairs discuss how Austin's bats were once misunderstood and unwanted and how the bats' presence became a positive thing for the city and its residents.

2. **Write** Students write a paragraph summarizing their ideas about the changing perceptions of Austin's bats.

3. **Share** Partners check each other's paragraphs for correct use of modifiers.

Routines Flip Chart

English Language Learners
Peer conferencing Students might benefit from working with the same partner to complete the Day 4 and the Day 5 steps of the writing lesson. Encourage students to monitor their own understanding of the journal entry writing process and to seek help from you or more English-proficient students as necessary.

Wrap Up Your Day

✔ **Build Concepts** What did you learn about why Ron Fridell writes about animals?

✔ **Oral Vocabulary** Monitor students' use of oral vocabulary as they respond: What words could a writer use to describe the effects of unplanned situations?

✔ **Text Structure** Discuss how seeing Mexican long-tongued bats at his hummingbird feeder caused Fridell to write about the Austin bats.

Preview DAY 5

Remind students to think about how unplanned situations can have positive outcomes.

Objectives
- Review the weekly concept.
- Review oral vocabulary.

Today at a Glance

Oral Vocabulary

Comprehension
◉ Draw conclusions

Lesson Vocabulary
◉ Unknown words

Word Analysis
Compound words

Literary Terms
Sensory details

Assessment
Fluency
Comprehension

Research and Inquiry
Communicate

Spelling
Suffixes *-ous, -sion, -ion, -ation*

Conventions
Modifiers

Writing
Journal entry

Check Oral Vocabulary
SUCCESS PREDICTOR

Concept Wrap Up

? Question of the Week
How can unplanned situations have positive outcomes?

Review the concept
Have students look back at the reading selections to find examples that best demonstrate how unexpected events can lead to good surprises.

Review Amazing Words
Display and review this week's concept map. Remind students that this week they have learned ten Amazing Words related to unplanned situations with positive outcomes. Break into groups. Have students use the Amazing Words and the concept map to answer the question *How can unplanned situations have positive outcomes?* Encourage students to consider suggestions from all group members.

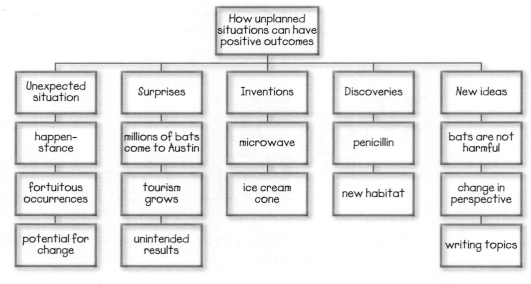

How unplanned situations can have positive outcomes

Unexpected situation	Surprises	Inventions	Discoveries	New ideas
happen-stance	millions of bats come to Austin	microwave	penicillin	bats are not harmful
fortuitous occurrences	tourism grows	ice cream cone	new habitat	change in perspective
potential for change	unintended results			writing topics

ELL **Check Concepts and Language** Use the Day 5 instruction on ELL Poster 26 to monitor students' understanding of the lesson concept.

ELL Poster 26

Amazing Ideas

Connect to the Big Question

Have pairs of students discuss how the Question of the Week connects to the Big Question: *What can we learn from encounters with the unexpected?* Tell students to use the concept map and what they have learned from this week's Anchored Talks and reading selections to form an Amazing Idea—a realization or "big idea" about The Unexpected. Then ask pairs to share their Amazing Ideas with the class.

Amazing Ideas might include these key concepts:

- Sometimes the most amazing things are the unexpected ones.
- Great inventions and discoveries sometimes come about when we're open to the unexpected.
- Fear of the unknown can keep us from appreciating the unexpected.

Write about it

Have students write a few sentences about their Amazing Idea, beginning with "This week I learned…"

 It's Friday

MONITOR PROGRESS | **Check Oral Vocabulary**

Have individuals use this week's Amazing Words to describe meeting challenges. Monitor students' abilities to use the Amazing Words and note which words you need to reteach.

If… students have difficulty using the Amazing Words,

then… reteach using the Oral Vocabulary Routine, pp. 319a, 322b, 330b, 340b, OV•1.

Day 1	**Days 2–3**	**Day 4**	**Day 5**
Check Oral Vocabulary	Check Retelling	Check Fluency	Check Oral Vocabulary

Success Predictor

Amazing Words

unintended	perspective
fortuitous	happenstance
advantageous	occurrences
potential	perceptive
spontaneous	unaware

E L L

English Language Learners
Concept map Work with students to add new words to the concept map.

Oral Vocabulary

Succe Predicto

Objectives
- Review drawing conclusions.
- Review unknown words.
- ◎ Review compound words.
- ◎ Review sensory details.

Comprehension Review
↻ Draw Conclusions

Envision It! Visual Skills Handbook

Student Edition p. EI•6

Teach draw conclusions

Envision It!

Review the definition of drawing conclusions on p. 320. Remind students that readers should draw conclusions based on information presented by the author of a text and on their own knowledge. For additional support, have students review p. EI•6 on drawing conclusions.

Guide practice

Have student pairs draw a conclusion from the information presented by the author of *The Truth About Austin's Amazing Bats.* Then have the pairs tell what information from the text and from their own knowledge they used to draw their conclusion.

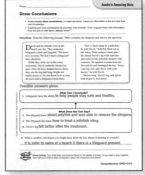

Let's Practice It!
TR DVD•313

On their own

For additional practice with drawing conclusions, use *Let's Practice It!* p. 313 on the *Teacher Resources DVD-ROM.*

Vocabulary Review
↻ Unknown Words

Teach unknown words

Remind students to use a dictionary or glossary to help them understand the meanings of unknown words and to determine pronunciations, syllabications, and parts of speech.

Guide practice

Review with students how to find the meaning, pronunciation, syllabication and part of speech of the word *vital* by using a printed or electronic dictionary or glossary.

On their own

Have students look up the lesson vocabulary words in a printed or electronic dictionary or glossary to determine each word's meaning, pronunciation, syllabication and part of speech. Have them write a fill-in-the-blank sentence for each word. Then have students trade sentences with a partner and try to fill in the blanks with the correct vocabulary word.

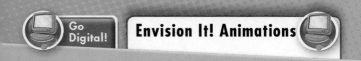

Word Analysis Review
Compound Words

Teach compound words
Review the definition of compound words with students. Discuss the meanings of these compound words: *riverboat* and *newspapers*.

Guide practice
Display the following words: *landmark, downtown, echolocation,* and *skyscrapers.* Use the Strategy for Meaningful Word Parts to teach the word *landmark.*

ROUTINE Strategy for Meaningful Word Parts

1. **Introduce the word parts** Have students circle each smaller word in *landmark.*

2. **Connect to meaning** Define each smaller word. *Land* means "a piece of Earth's surface; ground." *Mark* means "a symbol or sign."

3. **Read the word** Blend the meaningful word parts together to read *landmark.* Then use the meanings of the smaller words to determine the meaning of the new word. A *landmark* is "a sign, such as a building, that helps you know where you are."

Routines Flip Chart

On their own
Have students work in pairs to identify word parts and define *downtown, echolocation,* and *skyscrapers.*

Literary Terms Review
Sensory Details

Teach sensory details
Have students reread pp. 331–335 of *The Truth About Austin's Amazing Bats.* Remind students that sensory details are those that help readers draw on their five senses to better understand the text.

Guide practice
Find an example of a sensory detail, such as "First they lick the animal's skin in a spot where the blood vessels are close to the surface," on p. 331. Discuss how these details help readers picture what is happening.

On their own
Have students make a T-chart with the headings *sensory detail* and *sense.* Ask them to list examples of sensory details from the selection and tell which of the five senses it draws on.

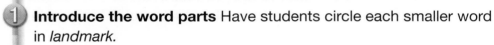
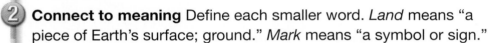

English Language Learners
Draw Conclusions If students have trouble drawing conclusions, supply them with a conclusion, such as *People do not need to worry about vampire bats drinking all their blood.* Ask: According to the author, whose blood do vampire bats drink? (animals) In your own life, do you think it makes sense to worry about something that can't happen to you? (no) Then supply students with another conclusion and ask them to use ideas from the text and from their own knowledge to support the conclusion.

Compound words Supply students with a list of compound words. Have students draw a line between the two words of each compound word.

Objective
- Read grade-level text with fluency.

Plan to Assess Fluency

☑ **This week assess Advanced students.**

☐ **Week 2** Assess Strategic Intervention students.

☐ **Week 3** Assess On-Level students.

☐ **Week 4** Assess Strategic Intervention students.

☐ **Week 5** Assess any students you have not yet checked during this unit.

Set individual goals for students to enable then to reach the year-end goal.
- Current Goal: 130–140 WCPM
- Year-End Goal: 140 WCPM

Assessment

Check words correct per minute

Fluency Make two copies of the fluency passage on page 343k. As the student reads the text aloud, mark mistakes on your copy. Also mark where the student is at the end of one minute. To check the student's comprehention of the passage, have him or her retell what was read. To figure words correct per minute (WCPM), subtract the number of mistakes from the total number of words read in one minute.

Corrective feedback

If... students cannot read fluently at a rate of 130–140 WCPM,
then... make sure they practice with text at their independent reading level. Provide additional fluency practice by pairing nonfluent readers with fluent readers.

If... students already read at 140 WCPM,
then... have them read a book of their choice independently.

Small Group Time

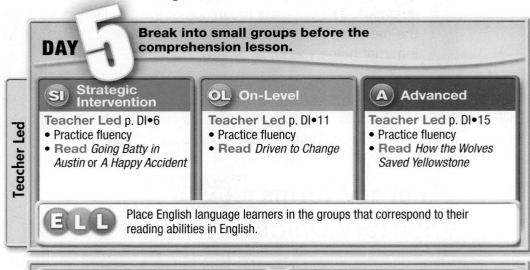

DAY 5 Break into small groups before the comprehension lesson.

Teacher Led

SI Strategic Intervention
Teacher Led p. DI•6
- Practice fluency
- Read *Going Batty in Austin* or *A Happy Accident*

OL On-Level
Teacher Led p. DI•11
- Practice fluency
- Read *Driven to Change*

A Advanced
Teacher Led p. DI•15
- Practice fluency
- Read *How the Wolves Saved Yellowstone*

ELL Place English language learners in the groups that correspond to their reading abilities in English.

Practice Stations
- Words to Know
- Get Fluent
- Read for Meaning

Independent Activities
- Grammar Jammer
- Concept Talk Video
- Vocabulary Activities

Spelling Test
Suffixes *-ous, -sion, -ion,* and *-ation*

Spelling test To administer the spelling test, refer to the directions, words, and sentences on p. 321c.

Conventions
Extra Practice

Teach This week we learned about modifiers. A modifier is an adjective, adverb, or prepositional phrase. Modifiers tell more about other words in a sentence. To avoid confusion, always place modifiers as closely as possible to the words they modify.

Guide practice Write the following sentence frames on the board, and have students work in pairs to fill in the blanks with the appropriate modifiers. Answers will vary.

- The [adjective] kite with the [adjective] tail got stuck [prepositional phrase].
- Ryan [adverb] searched for his [adjective] book [prepositional phrase].

Daily Fix-It Use Daily Fix-It numbers 9 and 10 in the right margin.

On their own Write these sentences. Have students look back in *The Truth About Austin's Amazing Bats* to find the correct modifiers to fill in the blanks. Remind students that a modifier might be an adjective, and adverb, or a prepositional phrase. Students should complete *Let's Practice It!* p. 314 on the *Teacher Resources DVD-ROM.*

1. **Some people spread blankets _____ to watch.** (on the lake's grassy shores)
2. **To a great many Austin residents the bats were a _____ sight.** (bizarre and frightening)
3. **The long, narrow, dark crevices became _____ popular with migrating bats.** (instantly)
4. **_____, BCI members set to work spreading the truth about bats.** (With this plan in mind)
5. **Bats, on the other hand, _____ ever carry the disease.** (hardly)

Daily Fix-It

9. Austins' bats are amazeing. (*Austin's; amazing*)
10. People comes from miles around to see the attracion. (*come; attraction*)

Let's Practice It!
TR DVD•314

Objectives
- Proofread drafts of a journal entry, including correct use of modifiers.
- Create and present final draft.

Writing—Journal Entry
Modifiers

Review Revising

Remind students that yesterday they revised their journal entries, paying particular attention to adding details to strengthen the writer's voice. Today they will proofread their journal entries.

MINI-LESSON

Proofread for Modifiers

■ **Teach** When we proofread, we look closely at our work, searching for errors in mechanics such as spelling, capitalization, punctuation, and grammar. Today we will focus on making sure that modifiers are used correctly.

Writing Transparency 26C

■ **Model** Display Writing Transparency 26C. Let's look at this paragraph from the model we've been using. Explain that you will be looking for errors in the use of modifiers. I see an error in the first sentence. Look at the modifier *for me* at the end of the sentence. Its placement makes the meaning unclear. Does Tara have the bracelet for the writer? By moving the modifier closer to the word it modifies—*bought*—the meaning is clear. Point out the other misplaced modifiers in the second and the final sentences. Then, discuss with students the other errors that are corrected on the transparency. Remind students that they should read their composition several times, each time looking for a different type of error.

Proofreading Tips

✔ Be sure that all modifiers are used correctly.

✔ Check for correct spelling, punctuation, capitalization, and grammar.

✔ Reread writing several times focusing on finding one type of error each time.

Proofread

Display the Proofreading Tips. Ask students to proofread their compositions, using the Proofreading Tips and paying particular attention to modifiers. Circulate around the room answering students' questions. When students have finished editing their own work, have pairs proofread one another's journal entries.

Present

Have students incorporate revisions and proofreading edits into their journal entries to create a final draft.

Give students two options for presenting: A bound class booklet or an informal reading-circle oral presentation. Have the class vote on which option the entire class will use. If students choose an oral presentation, encourage audience members to consider how well the presenter let his or her personality show in the writing. Suggest that audience members write one compliment and one helpful suggestion for each presenter. If students create a class journal, have them include a hand-printed or typed copy of their journal entry along with appropriate illustrations or photographs for their page. When students have finished, have each complete a Writing Self-Evaluation Guide.

ROUTINE · Quick Write for Fluency · Team Talk

 Talk Pairs discuss what they learned about writing journal entries this week.

 Write Each student writes a paragraph exploring how journal writing might benefit them.

 Share Partners read each other's paragraphs and discuss their ideas.

Routines Flip Chart

Teacher Note

Writing Self-Evaluation Guide Make copies of the Writing Self-Evaluation Guide on p. 39 of the *Reader's and Writer's Notebook* and hand out to students.

English Language Learners

Poster preview Prepare students for next week by using Unit 6, Week 2, ELL Poster 27. Read the Poster Talk-Through to introduce the concept and vocabulary. Ask students to identify and describe objects and actions in the art.

Selection summary Send home the summary of *The Mystery of Saint Matthew Island* in English and in the students' home languages, if available. They can read the summary with family members.

Preview NEXT WEEK

What unexpected effects can humans have on nature? Tell students that next week they will read about nature and the unexpected.

Weekly Assessment

Use pp. 187–192 of *Weekly Tests* to check:

✔ **Word Analysis** Compound Words

✔ 💿 **Comprehension Skill** Draw Conclusions

✔ Review **Comprehension Skill**
Generalize

✔ **Lesson Vocabulary**

bizarre	roost
breathtaking	vital
headline	
high-pitched	

Weekly Tests

Advanced

On-Level

Differentiated Assessment

Use pp. 151–156 of *Fresh Reads for Fluency and Comprehension*
to check:

✔ 💿 **Comprehension Skill** Draw Conclusions

✔ Review **Comprehension Skill** Generalize

✔ **Fluency** Words Correct Per Minute

**Strategic
Intervention**

Fresh Reads for Fluency and Comprehension

Managing Assessment

Use *Assessment Handbook* for:

✔ **Weekly Assessment Blackline Masters for Monitoring Progress**

✔ **Observation Checklists**

✔ **Record-Keeping Forms**

✔ **Portfolio Assessment**

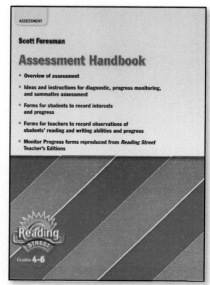

Assessment Handbook

Teacher Notes

Small Group Time

Pacing Small Group Instruction

🕐 15–20 mins.

5-Day Plan

DAY 1	• Reinforce the concept • Read Leveled Readers Concept Literacy Below Level
DAY 2	• 👁 Draw Conclusions • 👁 Important Ideas • Revisit Student Edition pp. 324–329
DAY 3	• 👁 Unknown Words • Revisit Student Edition pp. 330–335
DAY 4	• Practice Retelling • Read/Revisit Student Edition pp. 340–341
DAY 5	• Reread for fluency • Reread Leveled Readers

3- or 4-Day Plan

DAY 1	• Reinforce the concept • Read Leveled Readers
DAY 2	• 👁 Draw Conclusions • 👁 Important Ideas • Revisit Student Edition pp. 324–329
DAY 3	• 👁 Unknown Words • Revisit Student Edition pp. 330–335
DAY 4	• Practice Retelling • Read/Revisit Student Edition pp. 340–341 • Reread for fluency • Reread Leveled Readers

-Day Plan: Eliminate the shaded box.

SI Strategic Intervention

DAY 1

Build Background

■ **Reinforce the Concept** Connect the weekly question *How can unplanned situations have positive outcomes?* Discuss with students situations in which something they first thought was a problem turned out to be a benefit. For example, you and a friend might plan to play soccer at the park, but a sudden storm means you have to stay home. While you're home, your parents decide to take everyone out for pizza. Making plans can be very helpful, but sometimes unplanned events work out even better. Discuss the words on the concept map on p. 318–319 in the Teacher Edition.

■ **Connect to Reading** Ask students if they have ever had an experience with something they feared that turned out not to be scary after all. Maybe they were afraid of a neighbor's dog, which turned out to be friendly once they got to know it. Point out that these kinds of experiences are not uncommon. This week you will read about different kinds of unplanned situations and their outcomes. In the Read Aloud "A Lucky Accident" the outcome was clear right away—the invention of the ice cream cone. In other cases, a positive outcome might not be easy to see. It might take research and education to show people what the benefits are.

Objectives
• Interpret a speaker's messages (both verbal and nonverbal).

 **SI** *Strategic Intervention*

For a complete literacy instructional plan and additional practice with this week's target skills and strategies, see the **Leveled Reader Teaching Guide.**

Concept Literacy Reader

- **Read** *Going Batty in Austin*

- **Before Reading** Preview the selection with students, focusing on key concepts and vocabulary. Then have them set a purpose for reading.

- **During Reading** Read the first two pages of the selection aloud while students track the print. Then have students finish reading the selection with a partner.

- **After Reading** After students finish reading the selection, connect it to the weekly question *How can unplanned situations have positive outcomes?*

Below-Level Reader

- **Read** *A Happy Accident*

- **Before Reading** Have students preview the selection, using the illustrations. Then have students set a purpose for reading.

- **During Reading** Do a choral reading of pp. 5–8, and have students read and discuss the remainder of the book with a partner. Have partners discuss the following questions:

- What is the "accident" that happens in the selection? *(The main character's brother takes his brother's essay to college by mistake.)*

- Why does this seem like a problem? *(The essay can't be entered into the contest.)*

- **After Reading** Have students look at and discuss the concept map. Connect the Below-Level Reader to the weekly question *How can unplanned situations have positive outcomes?* In *A Happy Accident,* how did the main character experience a positive outcome? *(He won the contest.)*

MONITOR PROGRESS

If... students have difficulty reading the selection with a partner,

then... have them follow along as they listen to the Leveled Readers DVD-ROM.

If... students have trouble understanding the meaning of the title *A Happy Accident.*

then... review the resolution of the story.

Objectives
- Interpret a speaker's messages (both verbal and nonverbal).

Small Group Time

Student Edition p. EI•6

More Reading

Use additional Leveled Readers or other texts at students' instructional levels to reinforce this week's skills and strategies. For text suggestions, see the Leveled Reader Database or the Leveled Readers Skills Chart on pp. CL24–CL29.

Reinforce Comprehension

Skill Draw Conclusions Review with students *Envision It!* p. EI•6 on Draw Conclusions. Then use p. 320 to review the definition. Drawing conclusions means making decisions based on information in the text combined with your own knowledge.

Strategy Important Ideas Review the definition of important ideas. Remind students to identify the main points that the author wants readers to know as they read the selection. Encourage them to think about which details support the main ideas. For additional support, refer students to *Envision It!* p. EI•17.

Revisit *The Truth About Austin's Amazing Bats* on pp. 324–329. As students read, have them apply the comprehension skill and strategy to the selection.

- The author says the bats are active only at night. What conclusion can you draw about the kinds of insects they do NOT hunt? *(insects that are only active during the day)*

- What does the author mean on p. 327 when he writes that once the bats were "breathtaking for a different reason"? *(People were afraid of them.)*

- What clue words in the nearby text helped you figure out the previous question? *(bizarre, frightening)*

- What conclusion can you draw about why bats prefer dark and narrow places to raise their young? *(They feel that they can protect their young better because it's difficult or seems threatening for other animals to enter.)*

Use the During Reading Differentiated Instruction for additional support for struggling readers.

MONITOR PROGRESS

If... students have difficulty reading along with the group,
then... have them follow along as they listen to the AudioText.

Objectives
- Draw conclusions from the information presented by an author.
- Summarize main ideas in a text in ways that maintain meaning.

Strategic Intervention

DAY **3**

Reinforce Vocabulary

Unknown Words/Dictionary/Glossary Say the word *reverberate* as you write it on the board. Then read the sentence from the text, "Finally they zoom off in all directions, while the spectators below reverberate with wonder." With an unknown word such as *reverberate* I might first try other strategies to figure out what it means. But even knowing what words such as *spectators* mean doesn't help much, nor does recognizing the prefix *re-*. At this point, I would look up *reverberate* in a dictionary. There I would find that *reverberate* means "echo."

Revisit *The Truth About Austin's Amazing Bats* on pp. 330–335. Review *Words!* on p. W•14. As students finish reading the selection, encourage them to identify unknown words and use a dictionary or the glossary to learn their meanings.

- Point out the word *bizarre* on p. 327. Look up *bizarre* in a dictionary. Besides the word's meaning, what other information does the dictionary provide? *(pronunciation, syllabification, and part of speech)*

- Guide students to understand that many words in the article can be used as different parts of speech, and that realizing this can help when using a dictionary. Look at words such as *hazard* and *project*. They can be verbs as well as nouns. How are they used here? *(as nouns)* When I look up unknown words like these in the dictionary, I need to pay attention to their part of speech so that I find the meaning that matches the text.

Use the During Reading Differentiated Instruction for additional support for struggling readers.

MONITOR PROGRESS

If... students need more practice with the lesson vocabulary, **then...** use *Envision It! Pictured Vocabulary Cards*.

Student Edition p. W•14

More Reading

Use additional Leveled Readers or other texts at students' instructional levels to reinforce this week's skills and strategies. For text suggestions, see the Leveled Reader Database or the Leveled Readers Skills Chart on pp. CL24–CL29.

Objectives
- Use a dictionary or glossary (printed or electronic) to determine meanings of words.

Small Group Time

DAY **4**

Practice Retelling

- **Retell** Have students work in pairs and use the Retelling Cards to retell *Austin's Amazing Bats*. Monitor retelling and prompt students as needed:

- Tell me what this selection is about in a few sentences.

- How have Austin's residents changed their attitudes toward the bats?

If students struggle, model a fluent retelling.

Genre Focus

- **Before Reading or Revisiting** "The Animals in My Life" on pp. 340–341, read aloud the genre information about autobiographies on p. 340.

Then have students preview "The Animals in My Life."

- Based on the kind of animals shown and the title, what do you think is the author's connection to these animals? Could they be pets, for example? *(These are probably not pets but wild animals the author has written about.)*

Have students set a purpose for reading based on their preview.

- **During Reading or Revisiting** Have students read along with you while tracking the print or do a choral reading of the autobiography. Stop to discuss any unfamiliar words or phrases, such as *collie* or *life cycle*.

- **After Reading or Revisiting** Have students share their reactions to the autobiography. Then guide them through the Reading Across Texts and Writing Across Texts activities.

MONITOR PROGRESS

If... students have difficulty retelling the selection,

then... have them review the selection using the photos and text features.

Objectives
- Identify literary devices used in biographies, including how authors present major events in a person's life.

For a complete literacy instructional plan and additional practice with this week's target skills and strategies, see the **Leveled Reader Teaching Guide.**

Concept Literacy Reader

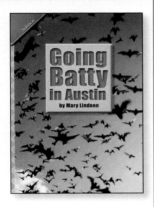

■ **Model** Model the fluency skill of accuracy for students. Ask students to listen carefully as you read aloud the first two pages of *Going Batty in Austin*. Have students note how you slow down and pronounce words and phrases correctly so that the author's meaning is conveyed accurately.

■ **Fluency Routine**

1. Have students reread passages from *Going Batty in Austin* with a partner.

2. For optimal fluency, students should reread three to four times.

3. As students read, monitor accuracy and provide corrective feedback. Encourage to read for accuracy, self-correcting as needed, and not continuing until they have read words and phrases correctly.

See *Routines Flip Chart* for more help with fluency.

■ **Retell** Have students retell *Going Batty in Austin*. Prompt as necessary.

Below-Level Reader

■ **Model** Ask students to listen carefully as you read aloud pp. 3–4 of *A Happy Accident,* emphasizing accuracy.

■ **Fluency Routine**

1. Have students reread passages from *A Happy Accident* with a partner or individually.

2. For optimal fluency, students should reread three to four times.

3. As students read, monitor accuracy and provide corrective feedback. Point out that reading with accuracy does not simply convey information correctly, but also helps express feelings better, as in dialogue. Emphasize that students should improve accuracy first before increasing their rate.

See *Routines Flip Chart* for more help with fluency.

■ **Retell** For additional practice, have students retell *A Happy Accident* page-by-page, using the illustrations. Prompt as necessary.

• What happens in this part?

• What is the selection about?

MONITOR PROGRESS

If... students have difficulty reading fluently,

then... provide additional fluency practice by pairing nonfluent readers with fluent ones.

Objectives
• Read aloud grade-level stories with fluency.

Small Group Time

Pacing Small Group Instruction

5-Day Plan

DAY 1	• Expand the concept • Read On-Level Reader
DAY 2	• ◉ Draw Conclusions • ◉ Important Ideas • Revisit Student Edition pp. 324–329
DAY 3	• ◉ Unknown Words • Revisit Student Edition pp. 330–335
DAY 4	• Practice Retelling • Read/Revisit Student Edition pp. 340–341
DAY 5	• Reread for fluency • Reread On-Level Reader

3- or 4-Day Plan

DAY 1	• Expand the concept • On-Level Reader
DAY 2	• ◉ Draw Conclusions • ◉ Important Ideas • Revisit Student Edition pp. 324–329
DAY 3	• ◉ Unknown Words • Revisit Student Edition pp. 330–335
DAY 4	• Practice Retelling • Read/Revisit Student Edition pp. 340–341 • Reread for fluency • Reread On-Level Reader

3-Day Plan: Eliminate the shaded box.

Build Background

■ **Expand the Concept** Connect the weekly question *How can unplanned situations have positive outcomes?* and expand the concept. Sometimes it takes a crisis to get people to change. That is what is beginning to happen as both governments and ordinary people take the threat of global warming more seriously. Discuss the meaning of the words on the Concept Map on p. 318–319 in the Teacher Edition.

On-Level Reader

For a complete literacy instructional plan and additional practice with this week's target skills and strategies, see the **Leveled Reader Teaching Guide.**

■ **Before Reading** *Driven to Change,* have students preview the reader by looking at the title, cover, and pictures in the book.

• What is the topic of this book? *(global warming and ways to fight it)*

• What is causing people and governments to change the ways they think and act about energy? *(Fossil fuel use and other processes are causing global temperatures to rise.)*

Have students create webs with the title *Responses to Global Warming* in the center oval. Some of the strategies in this book involve reducing energy consumption while others focus on finding alternative energy sources to fossil fuels. As you read, identify these strategies and their details. On your web, record each strategy and some of its details, including scientific and technological terms and concepts.

■ **During Reading** Read aloud the first three pages of the book as students follow along. Then have them finish reading the book on their own. Remind students to add strategies and terms to their webs as they read.

■ **After Reading** Have partners compare their webs.

• Which strategies to combat global warming do you think are the most important?

• How does the topic relate to the weekly question *How can unplanned situations have positive outcomes?*

Objectives
• Interpret a speaker's messages (both verbal and nonverbal).

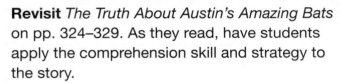
On-Level   DAY 2

Expand Comprehension

◉ **Skill** **Draw Conclusions** Use p. 320 to review the definition of draw conclusions. For additional review, see p. EI•6 in *Envision It!* Good readers question their own conclusions as they keep reading to see if there is supporting evidence.

◉ **Strategy** **Important Ideas** Review the definition of important ideas, and encourage students to identify the main points as they read. For additional support, use the Extend Thinking questions and refer students to *Envision It!* p. EI•17.

Revisit *The Truth About Austin's Amazing Bats* on pp. 324–329. As they read, have students apply the comprehension skill and strategy to the story.

- What important idea does the author want to convey by describing the spectators watching the bats? *(The positive response of the spectators makes the bats seem appealing.)*

- Think about the details presented in the first two pages of the article. What conclusion can you draw about the bats' economic impact? *(Their presence seems to help a variety of businesses.)*

- What evidence in the text supports the conclusion that the fear of bats was unreasonable? *(The text mentions fear of the dark, fear of the bats' anatomy and appearance, associations of the bats with vampires, and fear of being attacked or given rabies by bats.)*

Student Edition p. EI•6

More Reading

Use additional Leveled Readers or other texts at students' instructional levels to reinforce this week's skills and strategies. For text suggestions, see the Leveled Reader Database or the Leveled Readers Skills Chart on pp. CL24–CL29.

Objectives
- Draw conclusions from the information presented by an author.
- Summarize main ideas in a text in ways that maintain meaning.

On-Level

Expand Vocabulary

Unknown Words/Dictionary/Glossary Read the following sentence from the text: "An imposing sculpture, in the shape of a bat, called *Nightwing* stands at the foot of the bridge, welcoming visitors to the sight." The context does not provide sufficient clues to determine the meaning of *imposing*. When I can't determine the meaning of a word from its context or structure, I need to look it up in a dictionary or glossary. The dictionary tells me that *imposing* means "impressive." I can check to see if the meaning is correct by substituting this definition to see if it makes sense in the sentence.

Write the sentences below on the board. Have students look up the meanings of the italicized words in a dictionary and then rewrite the sentences, substituting the dictionary meanings for the unfamiliar words.

- Bats *emerge* nightly from under the bridge. *(Bats come out nightly from under the bridge.)*

- The *anatomy* of bats scares some people. *(The physical structure of bats scares some people.)*

- Bats help plants grow by *pollinating* flowers. *(Bats help plants grow by fertilizing flowers.)*

Revisit *The Truth About Austin's Amazing Bats* on pp. 330–335. Review *Words!* on p. W•14. As students finish reading *The Truth About Austin's Amazing Bats*, ask them to use dictionaries and glossaries to figure out the meaning of any unknown words.

Have students recall what happened in the selection. Encourage them to think critically.

- What beliefs about bats did you have that turned out to be wrong?

- What did you think was the most interesting part of *The Truth About Austin's Amazing Bats?*

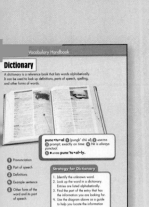

Student Edition p. W•14

More Reading

Use additional Leveled Readers or other texts at students' instructional levels to reinforce this week's skills and strategies. For text suggestions, see the Leveled Reader Database or the Leveled Readers Skills Chart on pp. CL24–CL29.

Objectives
- Use a dictionary or glossary (printed or electronic) to determine meanings of words.

On-Level

DAY **4**

Practice Retelling

■ **Retell** To assess students' comprehension, use the Retelling Cards. Monitor retelling and prompt students as needed.

Genre Focus

■ **Before Reading or Revisiting** "The Animals in My Life" on pp. 340–341, read aloud the information about autobiographies on p. 340. Have students preview "The Animals in My Life" and set a purpose for reading.

● What visuals and words in the selection stand out? *(wild animal photos, first-person pronouns)*

● Look at the kinds of animals pictured. What do you think most people's attitudes towards these animals are, and what does this suggest about the author's purpose? *(Many people would probably be uncomfortable with tarantulas, buzzards, and even frogs, so the author could be pointing out that he's drawn to unusual animals.)*

■ **During Reading or Revisiting** Have students read along with you while tracking the print.

● What details about the author's life does the text provide? *(his career, childhood pet, and his interest in bats)*

● What does the first-person point of view allow the author to do? *(to tell readers directly about his thoughts and feelings about the animals in the book and to explain why or how he did something)*

■ **After Reading or Revisiting** Have students share their reaction to the autobiography. Then have them write an autobiographical paragraph about an encounter—pleasant or unpleasant—that they had with a pet, insect, or other animal.

Objectives
• Identify literary devices used in biographies, including how authors present major events in a person's life.

 **On-Level**  **DAY 5**

On-Level Reader

■ **Model** Model the fluency skill of accuracy for students. Read aloud the first two pages of *Driven to Change*, emphasizing accuracy. Stress the importance of reading expository text accurately.

■ **Fluency Routine**

1. Have students reread passages from *Driven to Change* with a partner.

2. For optimal fluency, students should reread passages three to four times.

3. As students read, monitor fluency and provide corrective feedback. Point out to students that they can preview the page to see if there are words they don't know how to pronounce or difficult passages that might give them trouble. Have students practice pronouncing the words or rereading difficult passages. Discuss how reading with accuracy can help listeners better understand the text.

See *Routines Flip Chart* for more help with fluency.

■ **Retell** For additional practice, have students use headings and photographs as a guide to retell *Driven to Change*. Prompt as necessary.

• What is this selection mostly about? *(how people and governments are responding to global warming)*

• What did you learn from reading this selection *(Global warming is having some positive effects because it is causing people and governments to think about energy in new ways.)*

Objectives
• Read aloud grade-level stories with fluency.

 **A** Advanced

DAY 1

Build Background

- **Extend the Concept** Expand the weekly question *How can unplanned situations have positive outcomes?* Why do you think it might be difficult for governments and businesses to do things differently if there were no clear threats to people? *(Governments and businesses tend not to want to change unless they have to.)*

Advanced Reader

For a complete literacy instructional plan and additional practice with this week's target skills and strategies, see the **Leveled Reader Teaching Guide.**

- **Before Reading** *How the Wolves Saved Yellowstone,* tell students to recall the Read Aloud "A Lucky Accident."

How the Wolves Saved Yellowstone
by Meish Goldish

- What does *serendipity* mean? *(discovery of something advantageous by accident)*

- What serendipity is described in "A Lucky Accident"? *(the accidental discovery of the ice cream cone)*

Serendipity is about an unexpected—and fortunate—result. Today you'll read about how wolves, often depicted negatively, can actually help the environment in unexpected ways.

Have students look at the book's illustrations and use them to predict what will happen. Then have students set a purpose for reading.

- **During Reading** Have students read the Advanced Reader independently. Encourage them to think critically. For example, ask:

- What do you think people's fear of wolves is based upon?

- What other animals do you know that play a role in their environment similar to that of the wolves in Yellowstone?

- **After Reading** Have students review the concept map and explain how *How the Wolves Saved Yellowstone* helps students answer the weekly question *How can unplanned situations have positive outcomes?* Prompt as necessary.

- What were some of the unexpected benefits at Yellowstone?

- Why is it hard to plan for everything when it comes to wilderness environments?

- **Now Try This** Assign "Now Try This" at the end of the Advanced Reader.

Objectives
- Interpret a speaker's messages (both verbal and nonverbal).

Pacing Small Group Instruction
15–20 mins.

5-Day Plan

DAY 1	• Extend the concept • Read Advanced Reader
DAY 2	• Draw Conclusions • Important Ideas • Revisit Student Edition pp. 324–329
DAY 3	• Unknown Words • Revisit Student Edition pp. 330–335
DAY 4	• Autobiography • Read/Revisit Student Edition pp. 340–341
DAY 5	• Reread for fluency • Reread Advanced Reader

3- or 4-Day Plan

DAY 1	• Extend the concept • Advanced Reader
DAY 2	• Draw Conclusions • Important Ideas • Revisit Student Edition pp. 324–329
DAY 3	• Unknown Words • Revisit Student Edition pp. 330–335
DAY 4	• Autobiography • Read/Revisit Student Edition pp. 340–341 • Reread for fluency • Reread Advanced Reader

3-Day Plan: Eliminate the shaded box.

More Reading

Use additional Leveled Readers or other texts at students' instructional levels to reinforce this week's skills and strategies. For text suggestions, see the Leveled Reader Database or the Leveled Readers Skills Chart on pp. CL24–CL29.

A Advanced

DAY 2

Extend Comprehension

⊙ Skill Draw Conclusions Review the definition of draw conclusions. Emphasize that a conclusion is a decision that is supported by a text's facts or details. Encourage students to distinguish between conclusions that can be drawn logically and those that cannot. Recall the book *How the Wolves Saved Yellowstone*. Imagine a reader concluded that introducing a nonnative species of predators into Yellowstone would produce the same results. Would this be a logical conclusion or not?

⊙ Strategy Important Ideas Review the definition of the strategy. Remind students to identify important ideas as they read. During reading, use the Extend Thinking questions and the During Reading Differentiated Instruction for additional support.

■ **Revisit** *The Truth About Austin's Amazing Bats* on pp. 324–329. As students begin reading the selection, prompt them to use the comprehension skill and strategy.

● What do you think is the basic response of most people who observe the flight of the Austin bats? *(wonder at the huge number of the animals)*

● Would it be logical to conclude that people would respond the same way to large numbers of any species of animals? *(No; their response would be very different if the animals were really dangerous or destructive.)*

■ **Critical Thinking** Encourage students to think critically as they read *The Truth About Austin's Amazing Bats*.

● Would the current attitude toward Austin's bats exist without the efforts of Bat Conservation International? *(probably not, because BCI has played a key role in educating the public about bats)*

● How might people's experience of the bats change their response to environmental issues? *(They might begin to better appreciate the interactions of different elements in the environment.)*

Objectives
• Draw conclusions from the information presented by an author.
• Summarize main ideas in a text in ways that maintain meaning.

Advanced

DAY **3**

Extend Vocabulary

◉ Unknown Words/Dictionary/Glossary
Remind students that when they cannot determine the meaning of an unfamiliar word from context, they should look it up in a dictionary or glossary. Have students decide if there are sufficient context clues in the text to determine the meaning of the following words. If there are, have them write the definition. If not, have them look the words up in a dictionary and write down the meaning.

- emerge *(sufficient context; "come out")*

- imposing *(insufficient context; "impressive")*

- mammal *(insufficient context; "warm-blooded animal")*

- kayak *(sufficient context; "a type of boat")*

- bizarre *(insufficient context; "very strange")*

- crevice *(sufficient context; "narrow opening")*

- anatomy *(insufficient context; "physical structure")*

- rabies *(insufficient context; "an infectious disease")*

- pollinating *(insufficient context; "fertilizing")*

■ **Revisit** *The Truth About Austin's Amazing Bats* on pp. 330–335. Remind students to use a dictionary or glossary when context clues are insufficient to determine the meaning of unknown words.

■ **Critical Thinking** Have students recall what the selection was about. Encourage them to think critically.

- Bats have some unusual habits and skills. How do you think these habits and skills made people more afraid of them?

- Do you think people would still support the bats if their nightly flight was not so spectacular? Why or why not?

More Reading

Use additional Leveled Readers or other texts at students' instructional levels to reinforce this week's skills and strategies. For text suggestions, see the Leveled Reader Database or the Leveled Readers Skills Chart on pp. CL24–CL29.

Objectives
- Use a dictionary or glossary (printed or electronic) to determine meanings of words.

A — Advanced · DAY 4

Genre Focus

- **Before Reading or Revisiting** "The Animals in My Life" on pp. 340–341, read the sidebar information on autobiographies on p. 340. Ask students to use the text features to preview the selection and then set a purpose for reading on their own.

- **During Reading or Revisiting** Ask students to share information about the author contained in "The Animals in My Life" that might not appear in other genres of expository text on the same topic. Write a list on the board. Note how the author explains his thoughts and feelings. Which details remind you of events or feelings in your own life? Explain that autobiographies are often written in an informal style and voice because the author wants to connect directly with readers.

- **After Reading or Revisiting** Have students discuss Reading Across Texts. Then have them do Writing Across Texts independently.

Objectives
- Identify literary devices used in biographies, including how authors present major events in a person's life.

A — Advanced · DAY 5

- **Reread For Fluency** Have students silently reread passages from *How the Wolves Saved Yellowstone*. Then have them reread aloud with a partner or individually. As students read, monitor accuracy and provide corrective feedback. If students read accurately on the first reading, they do not need to reread three to four times. Assess the fluency of students in this group using p. 343j.

- **Retell** Have students summarize the main idea and key details from the Advanced Reader *How the Wolves Saved Yellowstone*.

- **Now Try This** Have students complete their projects. You may wish to review their work before they share it with classmates.

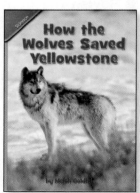

Objectives
- Read aloud grade-level stories with fluency.

Support for English Language Learners

The ELL lessons are organized by strands. Use them to scaffold the weekly curriculum of lessons or during small group time instruction.

Academic Language

Students will hear or read the following academic language in this week's core instruction. As students encounter the vocabulary, provide a simple definition or concrete example. Then ask students to suggest an example or synonym of the word and identify available cognates.

Skill Words	important (importante) prefix (prefijo) cause (causar) effect	modifier (modificador) journal conclusion (conclusión) details
Concept Words	unplanned positive (positivo)	situation (situación) outcome

*Spanish cognates in parentheses

Concept Development

How can unplanned situations have positive outcomes?

■ **Preteach Concept**

- **Prior Knowledge** Have students turn to pp. 318–319 in the Student Edition. Call attention to the picture of the girl with the birthday cake and tap into students' knowledge of surprise parties. Focus on the basic vocabulary: *Surprise* and *happy.* Do you think she is happy about her surprise? What surprises have you gotten?

- **Discuss Concept** Elicit students' knowledge and experience of surprises that turned out well. Be sure students understand the important details in discussion about the student Edition pages, which may include a topic and situation unfamiliar to Students. Have students talk about surprises in their own lives.

- **Poster Talk-Through** Read aloud the Poster Talk-Through on ELL Poster 26 and work through the Day 1 activities.

■ **Daily Concept and Vocabulary Development** Use the daily activities on ELL Poster 26 to build concept and vocabulary knowledge.

Objectives
- Use prior knowledge and experiences to understand meanings in English.
- Listen to and derive meaning from a variety of media such as audio tape, video, DVD, and CD ROM to build and reinforce concept and language attainment.

Content Objectives
- Learn basic and concept vocabulary related to unexpected situations with positive outcomes.

Language Objectives
- Express ideas in response to art and discussion.
- Understand details of spoken language.
- Use media to build concept attainment.

Daily Planner	
DAY 1	• **Frontload Concept** • **Preteach** Comprehension Skill, Vocabulary, Phonics/Spelling, Conventions • **Writing**
DAY 2	• **Review Concept,** Vocabulary, Comprehension Skill • **Frontload Main Selection** • **Practice** Phonics/Spelling, Conventions/Writing
DAY 3	• **Review Concept,** Comprehension Skill, Vocabulary, Conventions/Writing • **Reread** Main Selection • **Practice** Phonics/Spelling
DAY 4	• **Review Concept** • **Read ELL/ELD Readers** • **Practice** Phonics/Spelling, Conventions/Writing
DAY 5	• **Review Concept,** Vocabulary, Comprehension Skill, Phonics/Spelling, Conventions • **Reread ELL/ELD Readers** • **Writing**

*See the ELL Handbook for ELL Workshops with targeted instruction.

Concept Talk Video

Use the Concept Talk Video Routine (*ELL Handbook,* p. 477) to build background knowledge about unplanned situations. After viewing, ask students what they learned about the concept.

The Truth About Austin's Amazing Bats **DI•16**

Support for English Language Learners

Language Objectives

- Understand and use basic vocabulary.
- Learn meanings of grade-level vocabulary.
- Use strategies to acquire basic vocabulary.
- Respond to questions.

Language Opportunity: Listening

Use an oral reading to provide an opportunity for students to answer questions about vocabulary words. Turn to p. 323 in the Student Edition to review lesson words. Read the passage aloud. Ask questions that have lesson words either in the questions or the answer, such as What kinds of sounds do bats make? *(high-pitched)* What is vital to the survival of bats? (echolocation)

Basic Vocabulary

- **High-Frequency Words** Use the vocabulary routines and the high-frequency word list on p. 455 of the *ELL Handbook* to systematically teach newcomers the first 300 sight words in English. Students who began learning ten words per week at the beginning of the year are now learning words 251–260. Have students use a strategy such as drawing to learn the words. For example, Accidents could draw to represent *company,* a *week,* a *room,* a *figure,* and *nature.*

Lesson Vocabulary

- **Preteach** Introduce the Lesson Vocabulary using this routine:

    1. Distribute copies of this week's Word Cards *(ELL Handbook, page 179).*

    2. Display ELL Poster 26 and reread the Poster Talk-Through.

    3. Using the poster illustrations, model how a word's meaning can be expressed with other similar words: The *caterpillar,* or long bug with many legs, crawled across the grass.

    4. Use these sentences to reveal the meaning of the other words.

        - The *migrant* bird flew away. (animal or insect that flies to warmer places)
        - The butterfly came out of the *cocoon*. (protective case a bug grows in)
        - She *sketched* a picture. (drew)
        - The students showed *disrespect* by talking in class. (not respecting rules)
        - He *unscrewed* the top of the bottle. (took off by turning)
        - The mouse *emerged* from the hole in the wall. (came out of)

Objectives

- Use strategic learning techniques such as concept mapping, drawing, memorizing, comparing, contrasting, and reviewing to acquire basic and grade-level vocabulary.
- Internalize new basic and academic language by using and reusing it in meaningful ways in speaking and writing activities that build concept and language attainment.

 English Language Learners

■ **Reteach** Distribute a copy of the Word Cards (*ELL Handbook*, p. 179) to each pair of students.

- Have partners write a clue or simple picture on each card to help them understand each word. Provide an example clue such as: *drew* (sketched).

- Ask questions about the Lesson Vocabulary to check students' understanding.

  - Which bug is longer, an ant or a *caterpillar*? (caterpillar)

  - What is an example of a *migrant* animal? (duck)

  - What insect comes out of a *cocoon*? (a butterfly)

  - If you have *sketched* something, have you written a paragraph about it? (no)

  - What is an example of *disrespect*? (talking in class)

  - What is something that can be *unscrewed*? (a screw)

  - Where would a snake *emerge* from? (a hole in the ground)

Have students speak using the words. Have them use synonyms for words, such as *sketch* (draw), *disrespect* (rudeness), *unscrewed* (removed), *emerged* (left).

■ **Writing** Place students in mixed proficiency groups. Put the Word Cards facedown and have each group pick two cards. Have students create a newspaper headline using the two words. Groups can use a two-column chart to record their words and headline examples. Circulate to provide assistance. Also provide examples of newspaper headlines for students to use for reference.

Beginning Have students draw pictures to illustrate a headline. Then have them write the Lesson Vocabulary word.

Intermediate Have students describe their ideas for a headline using the selected vocabulary words.

Advanced/Advanced High Challenge these students to write the first one or two sentences of the news story under the headline. Explain that they should tell what happened and where.

Language Objectives

- Produce drawings, phrases, or short sentences to show understanding of Lesson Vocabulary.

- Speak using learning strategies.

ELL Teacher Tip

For beginning writers, it can help to include both words and pictures in early writing. Experts in English language learning advise teachers to have students write words and attempt sentences to accompany their pictures. Graphic organizers help students record and organize their ideas.

 Transfer Skills

Directionality Some languages, such as Arabic and Hebrew, read from right-to-left instead of left-to-right. Students who speak languages with a reverse directionality may need time to adjust to reading left to right. They may spell some English words backward.

Objectives
- Use strategic learning techniques such as concept mapping, drawing, memorizing, comparing, contrasting, and reviewing to acquire basic and grade-level vocabulary.
- Internalize new basic and academic language by using and reusing it in meaningful ways in speaking and writing activities that build concept and language attainment.

Support for English Language Learners

Content Objectives

- Monitor and adjust oral comprehension.

Language Objectives

- Discuss oral passages.
- Use a graphic organizer to take notes.

ELL Teacher Tip

Ask students questions to help them focus on facts and identify the problem and solution. For example: What job did the man have? How did he serve ice cream? What happened? Why was this a problem? What did he do? What became the new way to serve ice cream?

ELL English Language Learners

Listening Comprehension

Read Aloud

A Sweet Treat

I just learned that some great inventions were discovered by accident. Something unplanned happened. Microwave ovens are one of those accidents. Penicillin, the medicine, was discovered by accident too. When something good is discovered by accident, it is called "serendipity."

One of the best inventions happened unexpectedly in 1904 in St. Louis, Missouri. There was a World's Fair in St. Louis then. Lots of people came to see the sights and eat good food. One treat sold faster than any other treat. It was ice cream! In those days, ice cream was served only in dishes. The man who sold the ice cream ran out of clean dishes. He saw that the food stall next to him sold waffles. The ice cream man rolled up a waffle and put a scoop of ice cream inside. Success! He kept serving his ice cream in rolled waffles. His customers loved it. Some people say that was the invention of the world's first ice cream cone. It makes a sweet story. The story reminds us to look for events that may have unexpected results. But now it's time for my favorite snack. Can you guess what that is?

Prepare for the Read Aloud The modified Read Aloud above prepares students for listening to the oral reading A Lucky Accident on p. 319b.

■ **First Listening: Listen to Understand** Write the title of the Read Aloud on the board. This is about an accidental invention. Listen to learn about a man who served ice cream at a fair. What did he do when he ran out of dishes? Afterward, ask the question again and have students share their answers.

■ **Second Listening: Listen to Check Understanding** Use a Problem and Solution chart (*ELL Handbook,* p. 490) to help students identify the problem that led to the invention of the ice cream cone. Record their ideas in the Problem and Solution boxes. Now listen again to check that you identified the problem and what the man did to solve it.

Objectives

- Understand the general meaning, main points, and important details of spoken language ranging from situations in which topics, language, and contexts are familiar to unfamiliar.
- Monitor understanding of spoken language during classroom instruction and interactions and seek clarification as needed.

ELL *English Language Learners*

Phonics and Spelling

■ **Suffixes** *-sion, -tion, -ation*

- **Preteach** Write these words: *invention, relaxation, exhibition, invasion.* Tell students that each of these words is made up of a root word and a suffix. Have students look at the beginning of each word to find its root word (*invent, relax, exhibit, invade*). Circle the suffix *-tion* in the first word. Ask volunteers to find the suffixes in the other three words. Point out the English spelling rule for changing the base word to add the suffix. In the word *invasion*, the final *-de* is dropped before adding *-sion*.

- **Teach Spellings** Explain that *-sion, -tion,* and *-ation* have the same meaning, "an action or a state of being." The suffixes change verbs or adjectives into nouns. Write these examples on the board: *perfection, imagination, decision.* Ask students to provide additional examples.

- **Practice** Have students write these suffixes and root words on index cards: *-tion, -sion, -ation, confuse, react, converse.* Tell students to use the cards to make words with suffixes. Have students use spelling rules to change the base words.

Word Analysis: Prefix *dis-*

■**Preteach and Model** Write *agree* on the board. When we talk about our ideas and opinions, what does it mean when we agree with each other? Discuss what the word *agree* means. Can you think of a prefix we could add to make a word that means the opposite of agree? Write *dis-* on the board. The prefix *dis-* means "not." When you add it to the beginning of the word, it changes the meaning. Write *disagree.* This word means "not agree."

■**Practice** Write on the board: *appear, continue, approve, believe.* Have a volunteer read a word in the frame: I _____. Another student uses the word in this sentence frame: I do not _____. A third student adds the prefix *dis-* to the beginning word and completes this sentence frame using it: I _____.

Content Objectives
- Identify prefixes in words.
- Identify suffixes in words.
- Identify how suffixes change a verb to a noun.

Language Objectives
- Apply phonics and decoding skills to vocabulary.
- Discuss meaning of words with the prefix *dis-*.
- Use English spelling rules and patterns with accuracy.

Objectives
- Spell familiar English words with increasing accuracy, and employ English spelling patterns and rules with increasing accuracy as more English is acquired.

Content Objectives

- Use the analytical skill of drawing conclusions.
- Form opinions and make decisions about text.

Language Objectives

- Demonstrate and expand comprehension with inferential skills.
- Identify text and visual support for conclusions.
- Use details from text to write a conclusion.
- Use nature language for classroom communication.
- Demonstrate listening comprehension by taking notes.

Language Opportunity: Take Notes

Have students employ their inferential skills by taking notes on a graphic organizer. On a concept web, write a conclusion that can be drawn by reading p. 326 of the Student Edition: *People in Austin admire the bats.* Then have them read for details that support this conclusion and add to the concept web. *(sculpture, ice hockey team, Bat Festival)* Students can expand their inferential skills by creating a similar graphic organizer for another page in the student edition.

ELL English Language Learners

Comprehension
Draw Conclusions

■ **Preteach** When you make a decision or form an opinion about what you read, you draw a conclusion. To draw a conclusion, use ideas and details from the text. Put them together with what you already know. Have students turn to Envision It! on p. El•6 in the Student Edition. Read aloud the text together. Discuss the visual clues on the page. Have them use their analytical skills to consider the clues and what they already know about storms to analyze and draw conclusions.

■ **Reteach** Distribute copies of the Picture It! (*ELL Handbook,* p. 180). Have students look at the images. Have the students listen for details about why the townspeople praised the "clothes" during the parade. Ask students what they know about emperors and townspeople. Finally, ask the students to draw a conclusion about why the people did not tell the truth. (Details: The cloth can't be seen by anyone who is stupid. Emperors have lots of power over townspeople. Conclusion: The townspeople were fearful the king would think they were stupid and fire them from their jobs.)

Beginning/Intermediate Choral read the passage with the students. List details and ask students which are supported by the story.

Advanced/Advanced High Have students read the passage with a partner. Ask students to underline sentences that give information about the emperor.

MINI-LESSON

Academic Language

Draw conclusions is routine classroom language. Provide practice for using this routine language. Take out a math textbook and write a math problem on the board. Have students draw a conclusion. Provide this sentence frame. I conclude that ____. (you are about to start a math lesson.) The details that support my conclusion are ____. (the textbook, writing on the board)

Objectives

- Internalize new basic and academic language by using and reusing it in meaningful ways in speaking and writing activities that build concept and language attainment.

Reading Comprehension
The Truth About Austin's Amazing Bats

Student Edition pp. 324–325

■ **Frontloading** Ask students to share if they have heard about or seen the bats in Austin or have observed bats flying at dusk. I wonder what is amazing about the bats in Austin. Guide students on a picture walk through *The Truth About Austin's Amazing Bats.* Ask students to predict how bats can be amazing. Provide students with a K-W-L chart to fill out as they read the selection.

Sheltered Reading Ask questions such as the following to guide students' comprehension and develop their vocabulary:

- p. 326: What Texas city is home to millions of bats? (Austin)

- p. 327: How did people in Austin feel about the bats several years ago? (They thought the bats were bizarre, frightening, and a health hazard.)

- p. 330: Which organization helped change people's ideas and feelings about the bats? (Bat Conservation International)

- pp. 331–333: What did BCI do to change people's feelings about bats? (They told the truth about bats.)

- p. 334: How are Austin's bats vital to farmers? (They pollinate flowers and scatter seeds.)

■ **Fluency: Read with Accuracy** Remind students that reading with accuracy means to read each word in the text with correct pronunciation. Read the last paragraph on p. 334. Model accurate reading. Have pairs choose a paragraph on p. 327. Have students read accurately as their partners listen and offer feedback.

After Reading Have students use the Retelling Cards on p 336 of the Student Edition for a listening activity with peers. Pair students. Have one use the retelling cards to retell the story. The other student should listen, summarize, and add any missing information. Then students can switch roles.

Content Objectives

- Monitor and adjust comprehension.

- Make and adjust predictions.

Language Objectives

- Read grade-level text with accuracy.

- Summarize text using visual support.

- Collaborate with peers.

- Use media to build language attainment.

Audio Support

Students can prepare for reading *The Truth About Austin's Amazing Bats* by using the eSelection or the AudioText CD. After listening, have students note any language that was difficult to understand. Have them listen again to challenging language and read along with the audio and selection.

ELL Teaching Routine

For more practice summarizing, use the Retelling/Summarizing Nonfiction Routine (*ELL Handbook,* p. 476).

Objectives
- Understand the general meaning, main points, and important details of spoken language ranging from situations in which topics, language, and contexts are familiar to unfamiliar.
- Demonstrate listening comprehension of increasingly complex spoken English by following directions, retelling or summarizing spoken messages, responding to questions and requests, collaborating with peers, and taking notes commensurate with content and grade-level needs.

Support for English Language Learners

For additional leveled instruction, see the **ELL/ELD Reader Teaching Guide.**

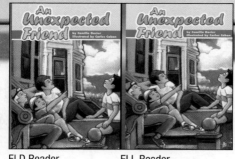

ELD Reader   ELL Reader

Comprehension
An Unexpected Friend

■ **Before Reading** Distribute copies of the ELL and ELD Readers, *An Unexpected Friend,* to students at their reading level.

• **Preview** Read the title aloud with students: This is a fiction text about a boy who finds a friend in a new school in an unexpected way. Invite students to look through the pictures and name what they see. Have them predict how David finds his new friend Ased on the picture clues.

• **Set a Purpose for Reading** Let's read to find out how meeting a friend can be unexpected.

■ **During Reading** Follow the Reading Routine for both reading groups.

1. Read the entire Reader aloud slowly.

2. Reread pp. 2–4, pausing to build background or model comprehension. Have Beginning students finger-point as you read. Use the questions in the chart to check students' comprehension.

3. Have students reread pp. 2–4 independently.

4. Repeat steps 2–3 for pp. 5–8.

■ **After Reading** Use the exercises on the inside back cover of each Reader and invite students to share their writing. In a whole-group discussion, ask students, How can a friend be unexpected? Record their answers on the board and invite them to point to pictures in the book to support their answers.

ELD Reader   Beginning/Intermediate

■ **p. 2** What does the main character like to do? (talk with his friends)

■ **p. 7** Could the main character and the stranger become friends? (yes) How do you know? (The stranger smiled and introduced himself.)

Writing What sentence helps you conclude that David is unhappy on his first day in a new school? Find and copy the sentence. Read it aloud to your partner.

ELL Reader   Advanced/Advanced High

■ **pp. 2–4** What will David have to do again when he moves? (start over at a new school)

■ **p. 8** Does David feel better the second day at lunch than he did on the first day? (yes)

Study Guide Distribute copies of the ELL Reader Study Guide (*ELL Handbook,* p. 184). Help students draw conclusions about David's feelings and fill in the chart. Review their responses together. (**Answers** See *ELL Handbook,* pp. 209–212.)

Objectives
• Demonstrate English comprehension and expand reading skills by employing inferential skills such as predicting, making connections between ideas, drawing inferences and conclusions from text and graphic sources, and finding supporting text evidence commensurate with content area needs.

 English Language Learners

Conventions
Modifiers

- **Preteach** Point to an item in the classroom. *That is a chair. The word* chair *is a noun. If I say* big chair, soft chair, *or* brown chair, *those describing words are adjectives. They tell more about the noun. If I say* The chair squeaks loudly, *the word* loudly *is an adverb. It tells more about the verb* squeaks *by answering how.* Have students suggest other words to describe nouns or verbs.

- **Teach/Model** Display the following sentences: *Jose is a smart student. He talks softly as he quickly answers questions. He also tells funny jokes.* Have students identify the modifiers (*smart, softly, quickly, funny*). Remind students that modifiers can be adjectives or adverbs.

- **Practice** List these modifiers on the board: *loudly, clearly, easy, strong.*

 Leveled LS Support

Beginning/Intermediate Have Beginning students point to the adverbs (*loudly, clearly*) and then the adjectives (*easy, strong*) as Intermediate students say the words.

Advanced/Advanced High Have advanced students think of nouns and verbs that can be described with these modifiers. Advanced High students can then write sentences using each modifier and a noun or a verb.

- **Reteach**

  - Display the following chart on the board. Review adjectives and adverbs and what they modify.

Sentence	Modifier	Word that is Modified
The cat walks softly.		
The sweater is blue.		

 Leveled LS Support

Beginning Have students go to the board and underline the modifier in each sentence. (*softly, blue*)

Intermediate Ask students to write the modifier in each sentence in the second column. Then have them name the type of modifier. (*adverb, adjective*)

Advanced Call on students to write the word that is modified and identify it as a noun or verb. (*walks,* verb; *sweater,* noun)

Advanced High Have students speak to the class using the modifiers in new sentences. Ask other students to write the new sentences.

Objectives
- Speak using a variety of grammatical structures, sentence lengths, sentence types, and connecting words with increasing accuracy and ease as more English is acquired.

Content Objectives
- Identify modifiers as adjectives and adverbs.
- Identify adjectives and adverbs that modify nouns and verbs.

Language Objectives
- Speak using modifiers.
- Write phrases and sentences with adjectives and adverbs.

 **Transfer Skills**

Adjectives Spanish adjectives have endings that match the gender and number of nouns they modify. Assure students that English adjectives do not have these endings. In Spanish and Vietnamese, adjectives often follow nouns.

Adverbs English learners may use adjectives as adverbs. Point out to Spanish speakers that the adverb suffix *-ly* is like the ending *-mente* in Spanish. Give examples with cognates such as *rapidly/rápidamente.*

Support for English Language Learners

Content Objectives
- Express the writer's personality through relating feelings about a personal experience.

Language Objectives
- Write a journal entry about a personal experience.
- Share feedback for editing and revising.
- Distinguish between formal and informal English.
- Narrate with increasing specificity and detail.

Tell students that writing a journal entry is narrating, or telling a story. Turn to the prompt on p. 338 of the Student Edition. Read the prompt and the Writer's Checklist. Then have students tell others in groups about their experiences. Prompt them to narrate with details and specificity by asking clarifying questions.

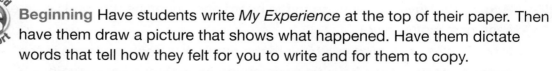

ELL English Language Learners

Writing a Journal Entry

■ **Introduce** Display the journal entry model and read it aloud. Review that a journal entry relates a personal experience, including the writer's feelings. Point out the date as correct format for a journal entry. What experience does the entry tell about? (dropping books in school) How did the writer feel? (embarrassed) Why did the writer feel he or she was misunderstood? (The girl looked at him in a way that showed she thought he was not nice.)

Writing Model
Tuesday, September 6

I had hoped that I would make new friends in school today, but the day did not go as I had planned. I was rushing to a class when I stumbled and dropped my books. A girl stopped to help me pick them up. I was so embarrassed that I did not even say thanks. By the way she looked at me, I know she thought I was not very nice. I have to think of some way to explain to her how I felt.

Point out that, in a journal, the writer's personality usually comes through.

■ **Practice** Provide a frame for students to use to help them plan their journal entry about a time they felt misunderstood. Remind them to date the entry. The date is ____. I remember a time when I felt ____. This is what happened: ____. I felt ____. Everyone thought I was ____. I was misunderstood because ____.

Discuss whether journal entries include formal or informal English. Journal entries are often written only for the writer to read, so informal English is appropriate. Have students point out informal English in the model.

■ **Write** Have students use their frame to write a journal entry about a personal experience in which they felt misunderstood. For ideas, have students think about what David in *An Unexpected Friend* would write in his journal.

Leveled Support

Beginning Have students write *My Experience* at the top of their paper. Then have them draw a picture that shows what happened. Have them dictate words that tell how they felt for you to write and for them to copy.

Intermediate Have students use their frame as their journal entry. Ask them to complete each sentence orally as you write. Then have them copy the entry.

Advanced/Advanced High Have students write journal entries independently. Then have pairs exchange papers and provide feedback for revising.

Objectives
- Narrate, describe, and explain with increasing specificity and detail to fulfill content area writing needs as more English is acquired.
- Share information in cooperative learning interactions.

This Week on Reading Street!

Question of the Week

What unexpected effects can humans have on nature?

Daily Plan

Don't Wait Until Friday

Whole Group

- ◉ Main Idea and Details
- ◉ Endings -s, -es
- • Fluency/Appropriate Phrasing/Punctuation Cues
- • Research and Inquiry

MONITOR PROGRESS	Success Predictor		
Day 1 Check Oral Vocabulary	Days 2–3 Check Retelling	Day 4 Check Fluency	Day 5 Check Oral Vocabulary

Small Group

Teacher-Led

- • Reading Support
- • Skill Support
- • Fluency Practice

Practice Stations

Independent Activities

Customize Literacy More support for a balanced literacy approach, see pp. CL•1–CL•47

Customize Writing More support for a customized writing approach, see pp. CW•1–CW•10

Whole Group

- • Writing: Mystery
- • Conventions: Conjunctions
- • Spelling: Final Syllable -ant, -ent, -ance, -ence

Assessment

- • Weekly Tests
- • Day 5 Assessment
- • Fresh Reads

You Are Here!
Unit 6
Week 2

This Week's Reading Selections

Main Selection
Genre: **Expository Text**

Paired Selection
Genre: **Expository Text**

Leveled Readers

ELL and ELD Readers

Resources on Reading Street!

	Build Concepts	**Comprehension**
Whole Group	 Let's Talk About pp. 344–345	  Envision It! Skills/ Strategies Comprehension Skills Lesson pp. 346–347
 *Go Digital*	• Concept Talk Video	• Envision It! Animations • eSelections
Small Group and Independent Practice	 The Mystery of St. Matthew Island pp. 350–351 ELL and ELD Readers Leveled Readers	 The Mystery of St. Matthew Island pp. 350–351 ELL and ELD Readers Leveled Readers  Envision It! Skills/ Strategies Reader's Practice and Writer's Station Notebook Flip Chart
Go Digital	• eReaders • eSelections	• Envision It! Animations • eSelections • eReaders
Customize Literacy	• Leveled Readers	• Envision It! Skills and Strategies Handbook • Leveled Readers
 *Go Digital*	• Concept Talk Video • Big Question Video • eReaders	• Envision It! Animations • eReaders

Question of the Week
What unexpected effects can humans have on nature?

Vocabulary

Envision It!
Vocabulary
Cards

Vocabulary Skill Lesson
pp. 348–349

- Envision It! Vocabulary Cards
- Vocabulary Activities

Fluency

Let's Learn It!
pp. 368–369

- eSelections
- eReaders

Conventions and Writing

Let's Write It! pp. 362–363

- Grammar Jammer

Envision It!
Vocabulary
Cards

The Mystery of
St. Matthew Island
pp. 350–351

Practice
Station
Flip Chart

Words!

Reader's
and Writer's
Notebook

The Mystery of
St. Matthew Island
pp. 350–351

Practice
Station
Flip Chart

ELL and ELD
Readers

Leveled
Readers

Reader's
and Writer's
Notebook

The Mystery of
St. Matthew Island
pp. 350–351

Practice
Station
Flip Chart

- Envision It! Vocabulary Cards
- Vocabulary Activities
- eSelections

- eSelections
- eReaders

- Grammar Jammer

- Envision It! Vocabulary Cards

- Leveled Readers

- Reader's and Writer's Notebook

- Vocabulary Activities

- eReaders

- Grammar Jammer

You Are Here!
Unit 6
Week 2

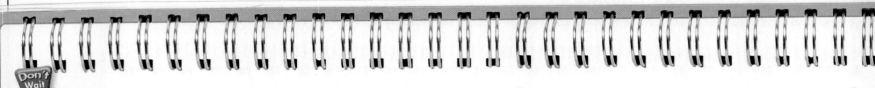

My 5-Day Planner for Reading Street!

	Check Oral Vocabulary **Day 1** pages 344j–347f	**Check Retelling** **Day 2** pages 348a–355e

Get Ready to Read	**Concept Talk,** 344j
	Oral Vocabulary, 345a
	  accommodates, refuge, domesticated, contaminated
	Listening Comprehension, Read Aloud, 345b
		Concept Talk, 348a
		Oral Vocabulary, 348b
		  grandiose, prune
		Word Analysis, 348c
		  Russian Word Origin
		Literary Terms, 348d
		  Word Choice
		Text Features, 348d
		  Maps

Read and Comprehend	**Comprehension Skill,**
	  ◉ Main Idea and Details, 345c
	Comprehension Strategy,
	  ◉ Text Structure, 345c
	READ Comprehension, 346–347
	Model Fluency, Appropriate Phrasing/Punctuation Cues, 346–347
	Introduce Lesson Vocabulary, 347a
	  bleached, carcasses, decay, parasites, scrawny, starvation, suspicions, tundra
		Vocabulary Skill, ◉ Endings -s, -es, 348e
		Vocabulary Strategy, Word Structure, 348e
		Lesson Vocabulary, 348–349
		  bleached, carcasses, decay, parasites, scrawny, starvation, suspicions, tundra
		READ Vocabulary, 348–349
		Model Fluency, Appropriate Phrasing/Punctuation Cues, 348–349
		READ Main Selection, *The Mystery of Saint Matthew Island*, 350–355a

Language Arts	**Research and Inquiry,** Identify Questions, 347b **Spelling,** Final Syllable -ant, -ent, -ance, -ence, 347c **Conventions,** Conjunctions, 347d **Handwriting,** Cursive Letter z and Z, 347d **Writing,** Mystery, 347e–347f	**Research and Inquiry,** Navigate/Search, 355b **Conventions,** Conjunctions, 355c **Spelling,** Final Syllable -ant, -ent, -ance, -ence, 355c **Writing,** Mystery, Focus/Ideas, 355d–355e

You Are Here! Unit 6 Week 2

Question of the Week
What unexpected effects can humans have on nature?

Check Retelling	Check Fluency	Check Oral Vocabulary
Day 3 pages 356a–363c	**Day 4** pages 364a–369e	**Day 5** pages 369f–369q

Concept Talk, 356a
Oral Vocabulary, 356b
  composition, depletion
Comprehension Check, 356c
Check Retelling, 356d
	Concept Talk, 364a
	Oral Vocabulary, 364b
	  natural resources, aggravate
	Genre, Expository Text:
	  Graphic Sources, 364c
		Concept Wrap Up, 369f
		Check Oral Vocabulary, 369g
		  accommodates, refuge, domesticated, contaminated, grandiose, prune, composition, depletion, natural resources, aggravate
		Amazing Ideas, 369g
		`Review` ◉ Main Idea and Details, 369h
		`Review` ◉ Endings *-s, -es,* 369h
		`Review` Word Analysis, 369i
		`Review` Literary Terms, 369i

READ **Main Selection,** *The Mystery of Saint Matthew Island,* 356–359a
Retelling, 360–361
Think Critically, 361a
Model Fluency, Appropriate Phrasing/Punctuation Cues, 361b
Research and Study Skills, Time Line, 361c
	READ **Paired Selection,** "City Hawks," 364–367a
	Let's Learn It! 368–369a
	  Fluency: Appropriate Phrasing/Punctuation Cues
	  Vocabulary: Endings *-s, -es*
	  Listening and Speaking: Interview
		Fluency Assessment, wcpm, 369j–369k
		Comprehension Assessment, ◉ Main Idea and Details, 369l–369m

Research and Inquiry, Analyze, 361d **Conventions,** Conjunctions, 361e **Spelling,** Final Syllable *-ant, -ent, -ance, -ence,* 361e **Let's Write It!** Mystery, 362–363a **Writing,** Mystery, Details, 363a–363c	**Research and Inquiry,** Synthesize, 369b **Conventions,** Conjunctions, 369c **Spelling,** Final Syllable *-ant, -ent, -ance, -ence,* 369c **Writing,** Mystery, Revising, 369d–369e	**Research and Inquiry,** Communicate, 369n **Conventions,** Conjunctions, 369o **Spelling Test,** Final Syllable *-ant, -ent, -ance, -ence,* 369o **Writing,** Mystery, Conjunctions, 369p–369q **Quick Write for Fluency,** 369q

Grouping Options for Differentiated Instruction
Turn the page for the small group time lesson plan.

Planning Small Group Time on Reading Street!

SMALL GROUP TIME RESOURCES

Look for this Small Group Time box each day to help meet the individual needs of all your students. Differentiated Instruction lessons appear on the DI pages at the end of each week.

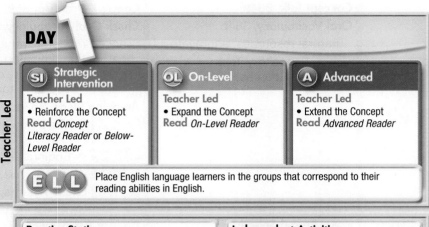

DAY 1

Teacher Led

SI Strategic Intervention	OL On-Level	A Advanced
Teacher Led	**Teacher Led**	**Teacher Led**
• Reinforce the Concept	• Expand the Concept	• Extend the Concept
Read *Concept Literacy Reader* or *Below-Level Reader*	Read *On-Level Reader*	Read *Advanced Reader*

ELL Place English language learners in the groups that correspond to their reading abilities in English.

Practice Stations
• Read for Meaning
• Get Fluent
• Word Work

Independent Activities
• Concept Talk Video
• *Reader's and Writer's Notebook*
• Research and Inquiry

ELL Reader
Advanced
Advanced High

ELD Reader
Beginning
Intermediate

ELL Poster

You Are Here!
Unit 6
Week 2

Day 1

SI Strategic Intervention	**Reinforce the Concept,** DI•26–DI•27 **Read Concept Literacy Reader** or **Below-Level Reader**
OL On-Level	**Expand the Concept,** DI•32 **Read On-Level Reader**
A Advanced	**Extend the Concept,** DI•37 **Read Advanced Reader**
ELL English Language Learners	DI•41–DI•50 **Frontload Concept** **Preteach Skills** **Writing**

Reading Street Response
to Intervention Kit

Reading Street
Practice Stations Kit

What unexpected effects can humans have on nature?

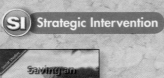

SI Strategic Intervention

Below-Level
Reader

Nature's Balance

Concept Literacy Reader

OL On-Level

On-Level Reader

A Advanced

Advanced
Reader

The Mystery of Saint Matthew Island pp. 350–351

City Hawks pp. 364–365

Small Group Weekly Plan

Day 2	Day 3	Day 4	Day 5
Reinforce Comprehension, DI•28 **Revisit Main Selection**	**Reinforce Vocabulary,** DI•29 **Read/Revisit Main Selection**	**Reinforce Comprehension,** Practice Retelling DI•30 Genre Focus **Read/Revisit Paired Selection**	**Practice Fluency,** DI•31 **Reread Concept Literacy Reader** or **Below-Level Reader**
Expand Comprehension, DI•33 **Revisit Main Selection**	**Expand Vocabulary,** DI•34 **Read/Revisit Main Selection**	**Expand Comprehension,** Practice Retelling DI•35 Genre Focus **Read/Revisit Paired Selection**	**Practice Fluency,** DI•36 **Reread On-Level Reader**
Extend Comprehension, DI•38 **Revisit Main Selection**	**Extend Vocabulary,** DI•39 **Read/Revisit Main Selection**	**Extend Comprehension,** Genre Focus DI•40 **Read/Revisit Paired Selection**	**Practice Fluency,** DI•40 **Reread Advanced Reader**
DI•41–DI•50 **Review Concept/Skills** **Frontload Main Selection** **Practice**	DI•41–DI•50 **Review Concept/Skills** **Reread Main Selection** **Practice**	DI•41–DI•50 **Review Concept** **Read ELL/ELD Readers** **Practice**	DI•41–DI•50 **Review Concept/Skills** **Reread ELL/ELD Readers** **Writing**

Practice Stations for
Everyone on Reading Street!

Word Wise
Suffixes *-ous, -sion, -ion,* and *-ation*

Objectives
• Spell words with suffixes *-ous, -sion, -ion,* and *-ation.*

Materials
• *Word Wise* Flip Chart Activity 27
• Teacher-made word cards
• paper • pencil

Differentiated Activities

⬤ Choose five word cards. Write the words in a list. Circle the suffix in each word. Write a sentence using some of the words. Add other words with these suffixes to your list.

▲ Choose seven word cards, and write your words in a list. Circle the suffix in each word. Write a sentence using each of your words. Add other words you know with these suffixes to your list.

■ Choose nine word cards, and write your words in a list. Circle the suffix in each word. Write sentences using each word. Add other words to your list that share these suffixes.

Technology
• Online Dictionary

Word Work
Suffixes *-ous, -sion, -ion,* and *-ation*

Objectives
• Identify and write words with suffixes *-ous, -sion, -ion,* and *-ation.*

Materials
• *Word Work* Flip Chart Activity 27
• Teacher-made word cards
• paper • pencil

Differentiated Activities

⬤ Choose ten word cards. Make a four-column chart using the suffixes as headings. Write the words in the correct column. Quietly say each word aloud. Write each word's base word.

▲ Choose fifteen word cards. Make a four column chart, and use the suffixes as headings. Write the words in the correct column. Quietly say each word aloud. Write each word's base word.

■ Group the word cards by suffix. Quietly say each word aloud. Make a four-column chart, and use the suffixes as headings. Write the words in the correct column. Write each word's base word.

Technology
• Modeled Pronunciation Audio CD

Words to Know
Unknown words.

Objectives
• Use a dictionary to find the meaning of unknown words.

Materials
• *Words to Know* Flip Chart Activity 27
• magazines • dictionary
• paper • pencil

Differentiated Activities

⬤ Use the magazines to find three unknown words. Write the words in a list. Use the dictionary to look up each word's definition. Write sentences using each of your words.

▲ Use the magazines to find four unknown words. Write the words in a list, and use the dictionary to look up each word's definition. Write sentences using each of your words.

■ Use the magazines to find six unknown words. Write the words in a list, and use the dictionary to determine each word's meaning. Write sentences using each of your words.

Technology
• Online Dictionary check definitions.

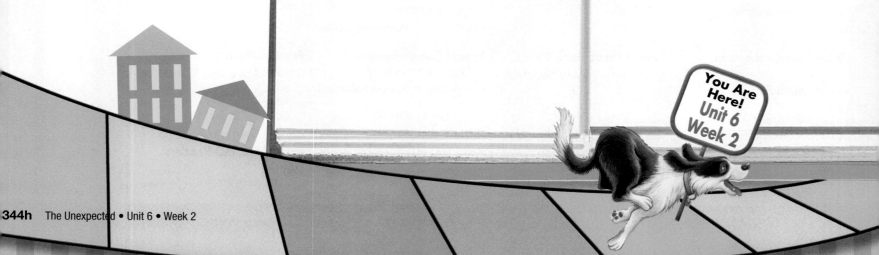

You Are Here!
Unit 6
Week 2

Key

● Below-Level Activities

▲ On-Level Activities

■ Advanced Activities

Practice Station Flip Chart

Let's Write!
Journal entry

Objectives
• Write a journal entry.

Materials
• *Let's Write!* Flip Chart Activity 27
• paper • pencil

Differentiated Activities

● Think about a day that was exciting for you. Write a journal entry that tells about the day's events. Include one detail to explain why the day was so exciting. Write in a voice that shows your excitement.

▲ Write a journal entry describing a day that was especially memorable to you. Include at least three details that tell about the day's events. Write your entry in a voice that reflects your personality.

■ Write a journal entry describing a weekend that was especially memorable to you. Include several details telling about the weekend's events. Write your entry using a voice that reflects your personality and excitement.

Technology
• Online Graphic Organizers

Read for Meaning
Draw conclusions

Objectives
• Draw conclusions based on text evidence.

Materials
• *Read for Meaning* Flip Chart Activity 27
• Leveled Readers
• paper • pencil

Differentiated Activities

● Read one of the books your teacher provides. Draw conclusions based on the information in the text. Write one sentence stating a conclusion. Write one sentence with a detail from the text to support your reasoning.

▲ Read one of the books your teacher provides. Draw conclusions based on information in the text. Write one sentence stating your conclusion. Write two sentences that give details from the selection to support your conclusion.

■ Read one of the books your teacher provides. As you read, draw conclusions based on information in the text. Write a short paragraph that states your conclusion. Include details from the text to support your conclusion.

Technology
• Leveled Reader Database

Get Fluent
Practice fluent reading.

Objectives
• Read aloud with accuracy.

Materials
• *Get Fluent* Flip Chart Activity 27
• Leveled Readers

Differentiated Activities

● Work with a partner. Choose a Concept Literacy Reader or Below-Level Reader. Take turns reading a page from the book. Use the reader to practice accuracy. Provide feedback as needed.

▲ Work with a partner. Choose an On-Level Reader. Take turns reading a page from the book. Use the reader to practice accuracy. Provide feedback as needed.

■ Work with a partner. Choose an Advanced Reader. Take turns reading a page from the book. Use the reader to practice accuracy. Provide feedback as needed.

Technology
• Leveled Reader Database
• Reading Street Readers CD-ROM

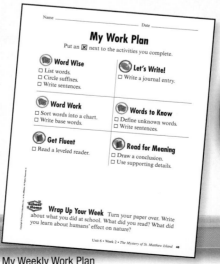

Name _____ Date _____

My Work Plan
Put an ☒ next to the activities you complete.

Word Wise
□ List words.
□ Circle suffixes.
□ Write sentences.

Let's Write!
□ Write a journal entry.

Word Work
□ Sort words into a chart.
□ Write base words.

Words to Know
□ Define unknown words.
□ Write sentences.

Get Fluent
□ Read a leveled reader.

Read for Meaning
□ Draw a conclusion.
□ Use supporting details.

Wrap Up Your Week Turn your paper over. Write about what you did at school. What did you read? What did you learn about humans' effect on nature?

Unit 6 • Week 2 • *The Mystery of St. Matthew Island*

My Weekly Work Plan

Objectives
- Introduce the weekly concept.
- Develop oral vocabulary.

Today at a Glance

Oral Vocabulary
accommodates, refuge, domesticated, contaminated

Comprehension
◉ Main idea and details
◉ Text structure

Reading
"Works of Art or Works of Aliens?"

Fluency
Appropriate phrasing/punctuation cues

Lesson Vocabulary
Tested vocabulary

Research and Inquiry
Identify questions

Spelling
Final syllable *-ant, -ent, -ance, -ence*

Conventions
Conjunctions

Handwriting
Cursive Letters *z* and *Z*

Writing
Mystery

Concept Talk

? Question of the Week
What unexpected effects can humans have on nature?

Introduce the concept

To further explore the unit concept of The Unexpected, this week students will read, write, and talk about how people can unknowingly upset the balance of nature. Write the Question of the Week on the board.

ROUTINE | **Activate Prior Knowledge** | **Team Talk**

1. **Think** Have students think about how human beings might affect nature.

2. **Pair** Have pairs of students discuss the Question of the Week. Have students identify points of agreement and disagreement.

3. **Share** Call on a few students to share their ideas with the group. Guide the discussion and encourage elaboration with prompts such as:

- Which human actions can affect nature?

- What movies, TV shows, or books have you seen about the ways people can influence the course of nature?

Routines Flip Chart

Anchored Talk

Develop oral vocabulary

Have students turn to pp. 344–345 in their Student Editions. Look at each of the photos. Then, use the prompts to guide discussion and create the *Unexpected human effects on nature* concept map.

- How does the sign pictured here show humans helping wildlife? (The sign keeps the public out of the area to protect the wildlife.) Let's add *helping* to the concept map.

- How does this photograph of the factories show the negative effects of human actions? (The photograph shows industry using natural resources and damaging the air.) Let's add *natural resources* and *damage* to the concept map.

Objectives
• Listen to and interpret a speaker's messages and ask questions.

Oral Vocabulary

Let's Talk About

Humans' Effect on Nature

● Share what you know about humans' effects on nature.

● Listen to a classmate's messages about humans and nature.

● Ask questions to clarify classmates' messages.

READING STREET ONLINE
CONCEPT TALK VIDEO
www.ReadingStreet.com

You've learned **260** Amazing Words ⭐ so far this year!

Student Edition pp. 344–345

Amazing Words

You've learned **260** words so far

You'll learn **010** words this week!

accommo-dates	prune
refuge	composition
domesticated	depletion
contaminated	natural resources
grandiose	aggravate

Writing on Demand ⏱

Writing Fluency

Ask students to respond to the photos on pp. 344–345 by writing as well as they can and as much as they can about the unexpected effects humans can have on nature.

• What does this huge stone sculpture indicate about how humans can directly shape nature? (It indicates that humans can use nature to make something beautiful.) Let's add *show beauty* to the concept map.

• After discussing the photos, ask: What unexpected effects can humans have on nature?

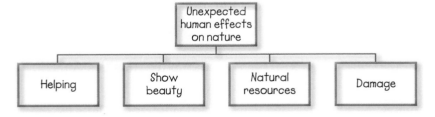

Connect to reading

Tell students that this week they will be reading about different ways humans can have an effect on natural processes. Encourage students to add concept-related words to this week's concept map.

ELL **Preteach Concepts** Use the Day 1 instructions on ELL Poster 27 to assess and build background knowledge, develop concepts, and build oral vocabulary.

ELL

English Language Learners

ELL support Additional ELL support and modified instruction is provided in the *ELL Handbook* and in the ELL Support lessons on pp. DI•41–DI•50.

Listening comprehension
English learners will benefit from additional visual support to understand the key terms in the concept map. Use the pictures on pp. 344–345 to scaffold understanding.

Frontload for Read Aloud Use the modified Read Aloud on page DI•44 of the ELL Support Lessons to prepare students to listen to "All the King's Animals" p. 345b.

ELL Poster 27

The Mystery of Saint Matthew Island **344–345**

Objectives
- Develop listening comprehension.
- Develop oral vocabulary.

Check Oral Vocabulary
SUCCESS PREDICTOR

Oral Vocabulary
Amazing Words

Introduce Amazing Words

"All the King's Animals" on p. 345b is about the unexpected effects humans can have on nature. Tell students to listen for this week's Amazing Words—*accommodates*, *refuge*, *domesticated*, *contaminated*— as you read.

Model fluency

As you read "All the King's Animals," model appropriate phrasing by grouping words in a meaningful way and playing attention to punctuation cues.

Teach Amazing Words

Amazing Words — Oral Vocabulary Routine

| accommo-dates |
| refuge |
| domesticated |
| contaminated |

1 Introduce Write the word *accommodates* on the board. Have students say the word aloud with you. In "All the King's Animals, " we learn that Swaziland *accommodates* many kinds of wildlife. Does the author include any context clues that tell me the meaning of *accommodates*? Supply a student-friendly definition.

2 Demonstrate Break students into groups. Have students elicit suggestions for uses of the word from other group members to demonstrate understanding. What country accommodates many wild animals?

3 Apply Ask students to tell how a region *accommodates* wildlife.

See p. OV•2 to teach *refuge, domesticated,* and *contaminated.*

Routines Flip Chart

Apply Amazing Words

To build oral language, have students discuss the Amazing Words.

MONITOR PROGRESS — Check Oral Vocabulary

During discussion, listen for students' use of the Amazing Words.

If... students are unable to use the Amazing Words to discuss the concept,

then... use the Oral Vocabulary Routine in the Routines Flip Chart to demonstrate words in different contexts.

Day 1	Days 2–3	Day 4	Day 5
Check Oral Vocabulary	Check Retelling	Check Fluency	Check Oral Vocabulary

Success Predictor

All the King's Animals

by Cristina Kessler

Swaziland is a small country located at the southern tip of Africa. Its diverse land accommodates a variety of wildlife and plant life, especially in the lush "Valley of Heaven." Swaziland is an ideal location for the wildlife refuge that the Swazi people have recently created; however, people haven't always been so kind to their land.

"Swaziland's earliest residents were the San. These short, sturdy people lived in total harmony with their surroundings. For thousands of years they wandered across southern Africa. Living in small groups, the San collected wild plants and fruits, pods and berries. They hunted to feed themselves or to appease their ancestors with ceremonial offerings. The land remained unchanged as both people and wild animals thrived.

In the fifteenth century the Nguni (N-GU-NEE) people from the north moved into the region. The ancestors of the modern Swazi people brought with them domesticated cattle and a system of farming. They changed the land, but a balance with nature still existed. Nguni cattle grazed on the plains side by side with wild herds of wildebeest, zebras, impala, warthogs, and rhinoceroses.

The first European settlers arrived in Swaziland in the 1850s. Their records describe vast herds covering the land. Giraffe, impala, kudu, and rhinoceros roamed as far as the eye could see. The Europeans' arrival signaled dramatic changes for Swaziland's wildlife.

The settlers hunted game in large numbers for sport. But a far greater problem was a disease that spread from the north in 1886. Contaminated cattle carried rinderpest disease from Europe to North Africa. This deadly virus passed from domestic cattle to wild animals that shared their grazing land.

The Cattle Plague swept south across Africa killing domestic and wild herd animals in its path. By 1896 it had reached Swaziland and killed almost the entire populations of impala, roan antelope, hartebeest and wildebeest.

The disappearing herds left Swaziland's fertile highlands and lowveld empty. European settlers quickly moved on to the land. They raised sheep and cattle where wildebeest had wandered and antelope once grazed. They cleared land and planted cotton and corn. Their lives were going well until 1930, when something incredible occurred.

One day countless thousands of wildebeest arrived from the north. The herds were so large they filled the horizon from one sunrise

(Continued on p. 369s)

Oral Vocabulary

Succes
Predicto

Objectives

◎ Identify main idea and details.

◎ Analyze the organizational pattern of a text.

- Read grade-level text with appropriate phrasing.

Skills Trace

◉ **Main idea and details**

Introduce U3W2D1; U3W4D1; U6W2D1

Practice U3W2D2; U3W2D3; U3W4D2; U3W4D3; U6W2D2; U6W2D3

Reteach/Review U3W2D5; U3W3D2; U3W3D3; U3W4D5; U5W2D3; U6W2D5; U6W4D2; U6W4D3

Assess/Test Weekly Tests U3W2; U3W4; U6W2 Benchmark Tests U3

KEY:

U=Unit   W=Week   D=Day

Skill ↔ Strategy
Main Idea and Details
Text Structure

Student Edition p. EI•12

Introduce main idea and details

Envision It!

The main idea is the most important idea about a topic. How can I tell the main idea from the details that support it? (Look for a direct statement or find the small pieces of information that tell more about the main idea.) The main idea is not always directly stated. How can I identify a main idea that is not stated? (See what the supporting details add up to.) Have students turn to p. EI•12 in the Student Edition to review main idea and details. Then read "Works of Art or Works of Aliens?" with students.

Model the skill

Think Aloud Today we're going to read about the mystery of crop circles. Have students follow along as you read the first paragraph of "Works of Art or Works of Aliens?." The first paragraph of "Works of Art or Works of Aliens?" has a number of details about crop circles of southern England. The author tells about the size of the crop circles and the materials used to make them. The last sentence asks how the crop circles came to be. The author does not state the main idea, so I will have to figure it out. I think main idea is that when crop circles first appeared, they were very mysterious.

Guide practice

Have students finish reading "Works of Art or Works of Aliens?" on their own. After they read, have them use a graphic organizer like the one on p. 346 and summarize main ideas and supporting details from the passage maintaining meaning and logical order.

Strategy check

Text Structure Remind students that if they have difficulty understanding they can use the strategy of text structure. Model the strategy of determining text structure to help comprehension.

Model the strategy

Envision It!

Think Aloud I see that after the author asks how the crop circles came to be, he or she explains the cause in the next few paragraphs. The author is using a cause-and-effect text structure. Recognizing this helps me understand how the author has organized his or her ideas. Have students review the strategy of text structure on p. EI•24 of the Student Edition.

On their own

Use p. 396 in the *Reader's and Writer's Notebook* for additional practice with main idea and supporting details.

Student Edition p. EI•24

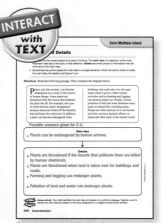

Reader's and Writer's Notebook p. 396

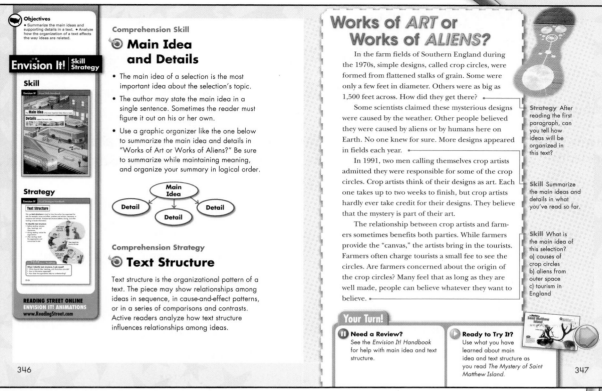

Student Edition pp. 346–347

Model Fluency
Appropriate Phrasing

Model fluent reading

Have students listen as you read paragraph 2 of "Works of Art or Work of Aliens?" with appropriate phrasing. Explain that you will follow punctuation cues to emphasize meaning and read text smoothly.

ROUTINE Oral Rereading

1. **Read** Have students read paragraph 2 of "Works of Art or Works of Aliens?" orally.

2. **Reread** To achieve optimal fluency, students should reread the text three to four times with appropriate phrasing.

3. **Corrective Feedback** Have students read aloud without you. Provide feedback about their phrasing and encourage them to note punctuation that shows when to pause or come to a stop. Listen for use of appropriate phrasing.

Routines Flip Chart

ELL

English Language Learners

Main idea and details Have students reread the last paragraph of "Works of Art or Works of Aliens?" Write these sentences on the board and read them aloud. Have students identify whether each sentence is a main idea or a supporting detail.

- Crop artists and farmers help each other.
- Farmers charge tourists a small fee.
- Artists bring in tourists.

The Mystery of Saint Matthew Island **346–347**

Vocabulary
Tested Vocabulary

Lesson vocabulary

Use the following question and answer activity to help students acquire word knowledge.

Activate prior knowledge

Display the lesson words. Invite students to tell what they already know about these words. Then ask questions like those below. Students should give reasons for their answers.

- If something is *bleached,* how does it look?
- When we find animal *carcasses,* are the animals alive?
- If a building is in a state of *decay,* would it be pleasant to live there?
- Are *parasites* easier to see under a microscope?
- If an animal is *scrawny,* is it getting enough to eat?
- What might cause the *starvation* of a herd of animals?
- When you have *suspicions,* how can you prove them true or false?
- In what part of the world would you find the *tundra?*

By the end of the week, students should know the vocabulary words. Have them use each word in a sentence.

Use the word decay in a sentence: *If you leave fruit or vegetables in the refrigerator for too long, they will begin to soften, decay, and turn colors.* Have students use the context of the sentence to determine the meaning of the word *decay.* Then ask students to use a thesaurus to find synonyms for the word *decay,* such as *rot, spoil,* and *go bad.*

Preteach Academic Vocabulary

 Academic Vocabulary Write the following words on the board:

word choice	**paraphrase**
coordinating conjunctions	**syllable**
subordinating conjunctions	**time line**

Have students share what they know about this week's Academic Vocabulary. Use the students' responses to assess prior knowledge. Preteach the Academic Vocabulary by providing a student-friendly description, explanation, or example. Then ask students to define the term in their own words.

Research and Inquiry
Identify Questions

Teach   Discuss the question of the week: *What unexpected effects can humans have on nature?* Tell students they will investigate how the actions of people can sometimes have a negative impact on nature. They will brainstorm ideas and consult with multiple sources of information, including experts, in order to create a time line that provides important facts and dates related to the topic. They will present their time lines to the class on Day 5.

Model   I'll get started by brainstorming ideas about the unexpected effects humans can have on nature. I already know that some chemicals are bad for wildlife. I'd like to find out what happens when we use pesticides. Some open-ended questions I could investigate are: *How do pesticides affect the environment in general? What are some of the unexpected effects that common pesticides have on the air, land, or water?*

Guide practice   After students have brainstormed topics and inquiry questions, explain that tomorrow they will follow a research plan to answer their questions, looking online, reading print references, and consulting experts. Help students identify keywords that will guide their search.

On their own   Have students work individually, in pairs, or in small groups to write an inquiry question.

INTERNET GUY
Don Leu

21st Century Skills

Weekly Inquiry Project

Day 1 Identify Questions

Day 2 Navigate/Search

Day 3 Analyze

Day 4 Synthesize

Day 5 Communicate

Small Group Time

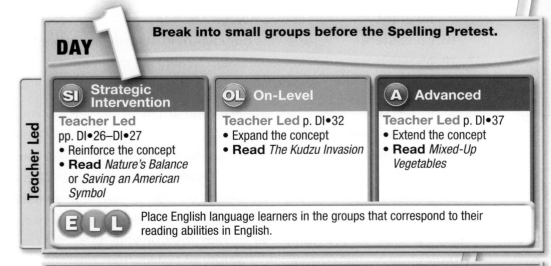

Break into small groups before the Spelling Pretest.

DAY 1

Teacher Led

SI Strategic Intervention

Teacher Led pp. DI•26–DI•27
- Reinforce the concept
- **Read** *Nature's Balance* or *Saving an American Symbol*

OL On-Level

Teacher Led p. DI•32
- Expand the concept
- **Read** *The Kudzu Invasion*

A Advanced

Teacher Led p. DI•37
- Extend the concept
- **Read** *Mixed-Up Vegetables*

ELL Place English language learners in the groups that correspond to their reading abilities in English.

Practice Stations
- Read for Meaning
- Get Fluent
- Word Work

Independent Activities
- Concept Talk Video
- *Reader's and Writer's Notebook*
- Vocabulary Activities

ELL

English Language Learners

Multilingual word lists students can apply knowledge of their home languages to acquire new English vocabulary by using the Multilingual Vocabulary Lists *(ELL Handbook,* pp. 431–444).

Word webs Students can make word webs of vocabulary that relates to their general topic. These word webs can become the basis of keywords and phrases when they do their online research.

Objectives

- Spell words with Latin-derived suffixes, *-ant, -ent, -ance,* and *-ence.*
- Define and identify conjunctions.
- Understand and use subordinating conjunctions.
- Write cursive lowercase *z* and capital letter *Z* in words.

Spelling Pretest
Final Syllable *-ant, -ent, -ance, -ence*

Introduce   Words ending in *-ant, -ance,* and *-ence* are sometimes difficult to spell because it is hard to hear whether an *a* or an *e* is used in the syllable. This week we will spell words with the final syllable *-ant, -ance,* and *-ence.* Remind students to listen for syllables, which can help them spell words correctly.

Pretest   Use these sentences to administer the spelling pretest. Say each word, read the sentence, and repeat the word.

1. **important**	Though small, ants are **important** in nature.
2. **experience**	Common sense is based on **experience.**
3. **ignorant**	Being **ignorant** of botany, he didn't know the plant.
4. **entrance**	They met in front at the main **entrance.**
5. **difference**	There's a big **difference** between cats and dogs.
6. **instance**	In this **instance,** he was right to feel proud.
7. **absence**	The **absence** of a fence allowed the cows to stray.
8. **appearance**	The home's **appearance** improved with new paint.
9. **intelligent**	An **intelligent** person invented airplanes.
10. **evidence**	The **evidence** shows that smoking is bad.
11. **pollutant**	Smog is a **pollutant** that harms children and adults.
12. **clearance**	The store had a **clearance** sale before the holiday.
13. **confidence**	He has **confidence** when he knows the facts.
14. **conference**	The principal will speak at the school **conference.**
15. **insurance**	He wants health **insurance** in case he becomes ill.
16. **ambulance**	She called an **ambulance** when her friend fell.
17. **hesitant**	He was **hesitant** to ride the elephant at the fair.
18. **consistent**	She was **consistent** in studying for every test.
19. **excellence**	He worked hard to achieve **excellence.**
20. **persistent**	Being **persistent,** she finally got the tent erected.

Challenge words

21. **iridescent**	The water is **iridescent** in the sunlight.
22. **coincidence**	By **coincidence,** I have the same birthday as you.
23. **convenient**	It's more **convenient** to walk than to ride the bus.
24. **significant**	The most **significant** meal for me is breakfast.
25. **alliance**	To become class president, you need an **alliance.**

Self-correct   After the pretest, you can either display the correctly spelled words or spell them orally. Have students self-correct their pretests by writing misspelled words.

On their own   For additional practice, use *Let's Practice It!* p. 315 on the *Teacher Resources DVD-ROM.*

Let's Practice It!
TR DVD•315

Conventions
Conjunctions

Teach

Display Grammar Transparency 27. Read aloud the definition. Point out the first sentence. In this sentence, *or* is the conjunction. A conjunction is a word that joins words, phrases, or sentences. The words *and, but* and *or* are known as coordinating conjunctions. Coordinating conjunctions are used to join two sentence parts that are equal, such as subjects, predicates, and sentences. Review the definition of subordinating conjunctions and point out the two joined clauses in each example sentence.

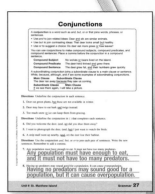
Grammar Transparency 27
TR DVD

Model

Model identifying the conjunctions in sentences 1, 2, and 3. Explain whether they join related or contrasting ideas or offered a choice; then show how you determined the correct answer.

Guide practice

Guide students through items 4–6. Remind them that a coordinating conjunction joins equal elements. Have students identify those elements. Record the correct responses on the transparency.

Daily Fix-It

Use Daily Fix-It numbers 1 and 2 in the right margin.

Connect to oral language

Have students read sentences 7 and 8 on the transparency and write the conjunction to correctly complete each sentence.

Handwriting
Cursive Letters z and Z

Model letter formation

Display the capital cursive letter *Z* and the lowercase letter *z*. Follow the stroke instructions pictured to model letter formation.

Model letter shape

Explain that writing legibly means letters have the correct shape. Students should make sure that their *Z*s are looped below the bottom line and that they are also rounded but not closed above the bottom line. Model writing this sentence: *Zeke saw zebras at the zoo.* Make sure to join *z* to the letters that follow them.

Guide practice

Have students write this sentence: *Zanya thinks the zucchini pizza is zesty.* Circulate around the room, guiding students.

Academic Vocabulary

A **coordinating conjunction** is a word such as *and, but,* or *or* that, with a comma, can combine two sentences or phrases.

A **subordinating conjunction,** such as *while, because,* or *if,* can connect a subordinate clause to a main clause or sentence.

A **syllable** is a word part that is pronounced as a unit.

Daily Fix-It

1. Living at the north pole would be a frigid experiance. *(North Pole; experience)*

2. Some plants can live in the arctic cold and most cannot survive. *(Arctic cold, but)*

ELL

English Language Learners

Cognates Point out the Spanish cognates for this week's lesson on conventions and spelling:

conjunctions/conjunciones, important/importante experience/experiencia ignorant/ignorante difference/diferencia

intelligent/inteligente evidence/evidencia conference/conferencia ambulance/ambulancia excellence/excelencia persistent/persistente

The Mystery of Saint Matthew Island **347d**

Objectives
• Identify the elements of a mystery.

Writing—Mystery
Introduce

MINI-LESSON

5-Day Planner
Guide to Mini-Lessons

DAY 1	Read Like a Writer
DAY 2	Creating a Recipe for a Mystery
DAY 3	Developing Clues in a Mystery
DAY 4	Revising Strategy: Clarifying
DAY 5	Proofread for Conjunctions

MINI-LESSON

Read Like a Writer

■ **Introduce** This week you will write a mystery story. A mystery is an imaginative story in which clues are presented in such a way that readers have a chance to solve the problem.

Prompt	In *The Mystery of Saint Matthew Island*, a scientist discovers what was happening to the reindeer on Saint Matthew Island. Now write your own mystery. Explain what the mystery is, then use clues to reveal what happened, how it happened, and why.
Trait	Focus/Ideas
Mode	Narrative

INTERACT with TEXT

Reader's and Writer's Notebook p. 397

■ **Examine Model Text** Let's read an example of a mystery about a missing recipe card and three suspects. Have students read "It's in the Cards" on p. 397 of their *Reader's and Writer's Notebook*.

■ **Key Features** A mystery or problem is **presented early** in the story. The writer's focus is clearly defined. Have students locate the problem in the story. *(The card with the recipe has vanished.)*

Mysteries can be set in any time. **Settings should be specific, believable, and described with sensory details.** Where does the narrator see the suspects? Have students underline each suspect's setting.

Plot is clearly defined, usually involves suspense, and uses facts, details, and examples to solve the mystery. What actions does our narrator take? How does he or she use details? Have students circle key plot events: narrator interviews suspects, asks the same question, listens to their words, and observes behavior.

The mystery is **resolved by end of the story.** What did the nurse reveal that led to the solution of the mystery? Have students underline the resolution that the nurse knew more about the missing card than the narrator had told her.

Review key features

Review the key features of a mystery with students. You may want to post the key features in the classroom for students to refer to while they work on their own mysteries.

Key Features of a Mystery

- presents a problem or mystery early in the story with a clearly defined focus

- has a specific, believable setting described with sensory detail

- has a clearly defined plot with facts, details, and examples to help explain and solve the mystery

- explains or resolves the mystery by the end of the story

Write Guy
Jeff Anderson

Two Words: Subject, Verb!

Challenge students to find favorite sentences in books and then whittle them down to the simple subject and the verb. This paves the way for supporting grammar in student's writing.

ROUTINE — Quick Write for Fluency — Team Talk

1. **Talk** Have pairs of students discuss the features of a mystery.
2. **Write** Each student writes a short paragraph explaining the role of plot in a mystery.
3. **Share** Partners read their paragraphs to one another.

Routines Flip Chart

Wrap Up Your Day

- ✔ **Build Concepts** What did you learn about the unexpected effects that humans can have on nature?

- ✔ **Oral Vocabulary** Have students use the Amazing Words they learned in context sentences.

- ✔ **Homework** Send home this week's Family Times newsletter on *Let's Practice It!* pp. 316–317 on the *Teacher Resources DVD-ROM.*

Let's Practice It!
TR DVD•316–317

E L L

English Language Learners

Preteach writing Read the writing model aloud. Help students understand that this mystery is about something missing that a character values. Tell students that *value* can mean price, quality, or importance. Ask students if there was a time when they couldn't find something that had value. Was the value price or importance? Was it lost or misplaced? What steps did they take to find the missing object?

Preview DAY 2

Tell students that tomorrow they will read about a scientist who investigates the deaths of thousands of reindeer on a remote island.

Objectives
• Expand the weekly concept.
• Develop oral vocabulary.

Today at a Glance

Oral Vocabulary
grandiose, prune

Word Analysis
Russian word origins

Literary Terms
Word choice

Text Features
Maps

Lesson Vocabulary
◉ Endings -s, -es

Reading
"Cleanup by Mother Nature"
The Mystery of Saint Matthew Island

Fluency
Appropriate phrasing/Punctuation cues

Research and Inquiry
Navigate/Search

Spelling
Final syllable -ant, -ent, -ance, -ence

Conventions
Conjunctions

Writing
Mystery

Concept Talk

Question of the Week

? **What unexpected effects can humans have on nature?**

Expand the concept

Remind students of the weekly concept question. Tell students that today they will begin reading *The Mystery of Saint Matthew Island.* As they read, encourage students to think about how people can change the course of nature by their actions.

Anchored Talk

Develop oral vocabulary

Use the photos on pp. 344–345 and the Read Aloud, "All the King's Animals," to talk about the Amazing Words—*accommodates, refuge, domesticated,* and *contaminated*. Add these words to the concept map to develop students' knowledge of the topic. Have students break into groups. Then have them use the following questions to elicit suggestions from each group member and develop their understanding of the concept in a discussion.

• What kind of land *accommodates* and provides a *refuge* for many kinds of wild animals?

• How are *domesticated* animals different from wild animals?

• Why is it important to protect wildlife from *contaminated* food?

Prereading Strategies

Genre

Expository Texts tell about real people, things, or events. They may have more than one organizational pattern, such as sequence and cause and effect. A case study focuses on solutions to a mystery or problem.

Preview and predict

Have students preview the title, illustrations, and maps in *The Mystery of Saint Matthew Island* to gain an overview of the contents. Have them predict what they will find out as they read.

Set purpose

Prior to reading, have students set their own purposes for reading this selection. Ask them to think about how people's actions can affect nature.

Strategy Response Log

Have students use p. 33 in the *Reader's and Writer's Notebook* to review three types of text structures.

INTERACT with TEXT

Small Group Time

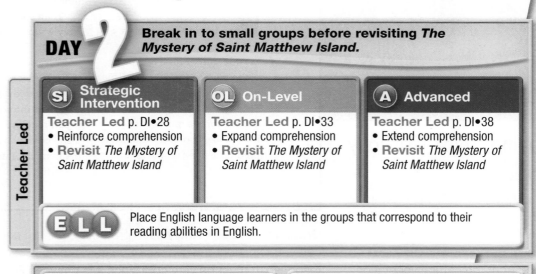

DAY 2 Break in to small groups before revisiting *The Mystery of Saint Matthew Island.*

Teacher Led

SI Strategic Intervention
Teacher Led p. DI•28
• Reinforce comprehension
• Revisit *The Mystery of Saint Matthew Island*

OL On-Level
Teacher Led p. DI•33
• Expand comprehension
• Revisit *The Mystery of Saint Matthew Island*

A Advanced
Teacher Led p. DI•38
• Extend comprehension
• Revisit *The Mystery of Saint Matthew Island*

ELL Place English language learners in the groups that correspond to their reading abilities in English.

Practice Stations
• Words to Know
• Get Fluent
• Word Wise

Independent Activities
• Background Building Audio
• *Reader's and Writer's Notebook*
• Research and Inquiry

Objectives

◎ Identify main ideas and details in a text.

OPTION 1 Guide Comprehension Skills and Strategies

Teach Main Idea and Details

👁 **Main Idea and Details** Write the following sentences on the board and have students determine which states a main idea and which states a detail: *Saint Matthew Island is in the midst of the Bering Sea.* (detail) *Scientists wanted to increase the reindeer herd on Saint Matthew Island, but failed.* (main idea)

Corrective Feedback

If... students are unable to distinguish between main ideas and details, **then...** model guiding students in identifying main ideas and details.

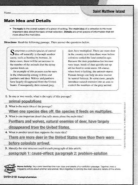

Let's Practice It!
TR DVD●318

Model the Skill

 Think Aloud How could I determine whether the first sentence is the main idea? (ask myself, *Is this the most important point here?*)

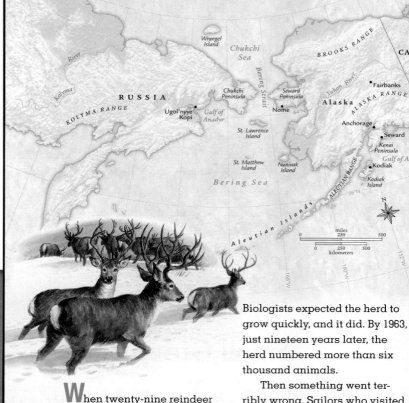

Biologists expected the herd to grow quickly, and it did. By 1963, just nineteen years later, the herd numbered more than six thousand animals.

Then something went terribly wrong. Sailors who visited Saint Matthew to hunt reindeer in 1965 found the island littered with reindeer skeletons. They saw only a few live reindeer.

When the sailors' disturbing report reached Dr. David Klein, a scientist who had studied the herd, he immediately made

When twenty-nine reindeer were released on Saint Matthew Island in 1944, the future of the herd seemed bright. This island in the midst of the Bering Sea offered plenty of plants and lichens for the reindeer to eat. No wolves, bears, or other large predators lived on the island.

352

Student Edition pp. 352–353

OPTION 2 Extend Thinking Think Critically

Higher-Order Thinking Skills

👁 **Main Idea and Details • Analysis** Find the main idea of the first two paragraphs on page 352. Summarize the idea in a way that maintains the meaning and logical order of the text. **Possible response:** Reindeer were released on the island with plenty of food from the natural vegetation. Years later, almost the entire herd had died off.

Graphic Sources • Analysis Interpret the map on page 352. What can you tell about the climate of Saint Matthew Island? **Possible response:** It must be very cold since it is between Russia and Alaska.

No, this sentence does not state the most important point. The fact that the island is in the midst of the Bering Sea is a detail, not a main idea. The second sentence tells the main idea.

plans to investigate. Arranging transportation to the remote island was difficult. Located halfway between Alaska and Siberia, this American island is so far from anywhere that it is nearly impossible to reach. No one lives there, so the island has no airports, and it is too far offshore for small planes to venture. For most of the year, it is surrounded by polar sea ice and thus unreachable even by boat. So it was over a year before Klein and two co-workers were able to reach the island by Coast Guard ship. With camping gear, food, and a promise that they would be

picked up within two weeks, the investigators were left on the lonely shore.

The first step of their investigation was to determine if the disaster report was true. On his two previous visits to Saint Matthew years before, Klein had seen small groups of reindeer everywhere. But now the island was strangely still. The bleached skeletons of reindeer lay scattered across the tundra. Klein had a few suspicions about the disaster based on his earlier trips to the island. But to solve the mystery, he needed to conduct a thorough investigation.

As a first step, the researchers explored the mountainous island. After several days of difficult hiking, they found that only forty-two live animals remained on the entire island. All of these were adult females, except one scrawny adult male. There were no calves. The absence of calves meant that the lone male was unable to sire young. So the herd was doomed to disappear

353

Cause and Effect • Analysis According to the information on p. 353, what caused the absence of young reindeer on the island? Possible response: There was only one surviving male deer left on the island. The male deer was not able to sire young, which meant the island would not repopulate naturally.

On Their Own

Have students reread pp. 352–353 to find the main ideas of different sections. Ask students to summarize the main idea and details in ways that maintain meaning and logical order. For additional practice, use *Let's Practice It!* p. 318 on the *Teacher Resources DVD-ROM.*

Differentiated Instruction

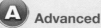 **Strategic Intervention**
Graphic sources Have students work in small groups to look at the map on p. 352. Students can share their knowledge of geography to support understanding.

A Advanced
Have students discuss the relationship of habitat to the way species adapt. Have them answer the question: What does a species need to do to survive in a particular region?

Six Pillars of Character

Responsibility We show responsibility when we think before we act and are accountable for our actions. Have students discuss how the scientists on Saint Matthew Island showed responsibility.

ELL

English Language Learners
Activate prior knowledge Create a two-column chart to record students' prior knowledge of arctic climate and terrain. Have students explain what animals might need to survive in an arctic region. Record students' observations on the chart.

Text features Have students locate the island on the map of the Bering Sea. Have them discuss the effect of its location on climate.

Objectives
- Identify sequence to aid comprehension.

Teach Sequence

Review Sequence On p. 354, the author discusses Klein's attempt to figure out when the reindeer died. Ask students: At what point did most of the herd die off?

Corrective Feedback

If... students are unable to understand the sequence of the text,

then... use the Model to help them identify sequential text structure.

Let's Practice It!
TR DVD•319

Model the Skill

Think Aloud When had the animals died? (The decline happened between 1963 and 1964.) I can use the text structure, which presents events in sequence, to help me understand what happened.

completely someday. When and how had the other six thousand animals perished? And why had such a disaster happened to this once healthy herd?

Perhaps there was a clue in the reindeer skeletons. Klein noticed that nearly all of the

skeletons were in the same state of decay. That meant the entire herd had died at about the same time. Based on the moss growing on the bones and their bleached condition, Klein estimated that the carcasses had lain around for at least three years. Klein had counted six thousand animals when he visited the island in summer 1963, so he concluded that the reindeer had died sometime between that summer and the summer of 1964.

ABOVE: In addition to the large colonies of seabirds that use Saint Matthew Island, it's the only place in the world that the rare McKay's Bunting breeds.

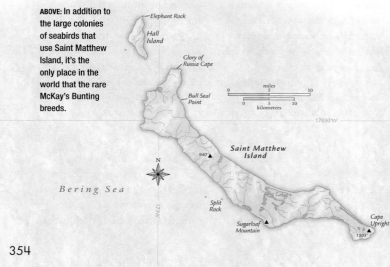

354

Student Edition pp. 354–355

Higher-Order Thinking Skills

Review Sequence • Analysis Identify an event that occurred before the female reindeer were able to give birth to their young. Possible response: Before the female reindeer could bear their young, the reindeer population died off dramatically.

Monitor and Clarify • Analysis Read the last paragraph on page 355. Why could Klein tell that human predators had not killed the reindeer? Possible response: Klein knew that few people visited the island.

In the last sentence on page 354 the author tells me that Klein counted 6,000 animals in 1963. Next, we learn that Klein concluded that the animals died before the summer of 1964. So I can say that the animals died sometime between 1963 and 1964.

RIGHT: Part of the Saint Matthew herd when it was six thousand strong, silhouetted against a stormy sky in 1963.

Klein examined the skeletons more carefully, hoping to find more clues about the date of the die-off. He soon found the tiny, newly formed bones of baby reindeer that had died while still inside their mothers. These tiny bones told Klein that the female reindeer had died in late winter when their calves were still developing.

With the time of death narrowed down to late winter 1963–1964, Klein searched for clues about the cause of death. No predators lived on the island, and people rarely visit it. So neither of these potential killers were suspects in the case.

LEFT: The vole that lives on Saint Matthew Island has developed into its own species, having arrived more than 10,000 years ago, when the oceans were lower and the island was connected to the mainland.

355

On Their Own

Have students reread pp. 354–355. Ask them to analyze how the time-order organizational pattern of this section of the article helps them understand what happened to the reindeer on the island. For additional practice, use *Let's Practice It!* p. 319 on the *Teacher Resources DVD-ROM.*

Draw Conclusions • Evaluation In this part of the selection, the author describes one man's attempt to understand a natural catastrophe, the sudden decline of the reindeer population. Does this remind you of any other situation in which a group of animals is threatened by natural causes? Explain. Possible response: I know that bald eagles were threatened with extinction. That had happened when people interfered with their nesting habits due to building and use of chemicals.

Check Predictions Have students look at the predictions they made earlier and discuss whether they were accurate. Then have students preview the rest of the selection and either adjust their predictions accordingly or make new predictions.

Differentiated Instruction

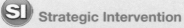 Strategic Intervention

Sequence Have students work in pairs to determine the exact sequence of events up to this point in the selection. They should record their responses on a timeline.

 Advanced

Have volunteers identify other selections they've read in which the text structure can be used to help identify main ideas.

Connect to Science

Reindeer live in herds on the Arctic tundra, as well as in the mountain and forest regions. The deer is important to native peoples such as the Lapps because it provides food as well as transportation.

ELL

English Language Learners
Vocabulary: Idioms Direct students to the phrase "lain around" in the second paragraph of p. 354. To "lie around" is to remain in a particular condition, like the deer bones that had been on the ground for some time.

Text structure If students have difficulty analyzing the text structure, help them create a time line to organize the events in the text.

 If you want to teach this selection in two sessions, stop here.

Objectives
- Find pertinent information from print, electronic, and expert sources.
- Identify and understand the function of conjunctions.
- Spell words with the final syllable *-ant*, *-ent*, *-ance*, or *-ence*.

Research and Inquiry
Navigate/Search

Teach

Have students follow their research plans to search the Internet and interview experts about their chosen topic. Remind students to take notes as they gather information from a variety of sources, paying particular attention to facts and dates they can add to their timeline.

Model

Think Aloud I found this information online: *Bald eagles were victims of a pesticide called DDT.* I can use keywords such as *bald eagles DDT* to find appropriate Web sites. I will also call a bird expert at the zoo or at a wildlife center to find out how DDT has harmed bald eagles and what has been done about the problem.

Guide practice

Have students evaluate the relevance, validity, and reliability of each source. Remind them that Web addresses ending in *.gov, .org,* or *.edu* tend to be more reliable than sites that end in *.com.* Students should use several sources, including print references and experts, to get an accurate and balanced overview of the topic.

On their own

Have students make a list of potential experts to contact in person, on the phone, or online. Ask them to make a list of questions for their interview, focusing on facts, events and dates. Allow students to work with a partner to practice interview techniques. They may want to interview some experts in groups. Ask partners about their topics to make sure students are contacting appropriate experts.

Conventions
Conjunctions

Teach

Write these sentences on the board:

Ty likes cats. Mary likes dogs. Ty likes cats, and Mary likes dogs. He has a cold. John will not go swimming. Because he has a cold, John will not go swimming.

For the first group of sentences, point out: A coordinating conjunction is used to form a compound sentence. Both parts are equal. For the second group of sentences, point out: A subordinating conjunction shows a relationship in which one part depends on the other.

Guide practice

Write the following sentence on the board, and have students identify the conjunction and its type. *Although she could walk to the mall on most days, Maria would rather ride.* (subordinating conjunction, *although*)

Daily Fix-It

Use Daily Fix-It numbers 3 and 4 in the right margin.

Connect to oral language

Have students look for and read aloud conjunctions in *The Mystery of Saint Matthew Island.* (*Thus Klein suspected that the Saint Mathew Island reindeer had been unhealthy or had run out of food during the winter of 1963–64,* p. 356.)

On their own

For more practice, use the *Reader's and Writer's Notebook* p. 399.

Spelling
Final Syllable *-ant, -ent, -ance, -ence*

Teach

Remind students that words with *-ant, -ent, -ance,* and *-ence* are difficult to spell because it is hard to hear whether an *a* or an *e* is used in the last syllable. Listen for syllables, which can help you spell the words correctly.

Guide practice

Write *confidence* on the board, replacing the first *e* with a blank line. Have students say the word aloud. Write an *e* on the line. Remind students that they have to memorize the spelling of some words. Model finding words in a dictionary. Have students use a dictionary to find other words with these endings.

On their own

For more practice, use *Reader's and Writer's Notebook,* p. 400.

Daily Fix-It

3. One different between desert or tundra is temperature. *(difference; desert and)*

4. Both places is very dry. And their life forms must adapt to this condition. *(are very dry, and)*

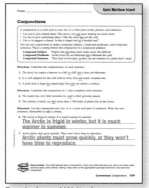

Reader's and Writer's Notebook p. 399

Reader's and Writer's Notebook p. 400

ELL

English Language Learners
Conventions To provide students with practice on conjunctions use the modified grammar lessons in the *ELL Handbook* and the Grammar Jammer! online at: www.ReadingStreet.com

Conjunctions Model writing conjunctions by acting out those you can physically demonstrate. *We like to laugh and clap. We like to run or walk.* Then ask students to write their own sentences with which they can act out the use of conjunctions. Circulate among students as they work to make sure they are correctly using conjunctions in their sentences.

Objectives
- Organize ideas to prepare for writing.

Writing—Mystery
Writing Trait: Focus/Ideas

Introduce the prompt

Yesterday we learned that a mystery is a type of narrative fiction that focuses on a problem or mystery to be solved. A mystery may describe past, future, or present events, but the setting is specific and believable. The plot is clearly defined and includes facts and details to solve the mystery by the end of the story.

Today we will begin the writing process for a mystery. Let's look at the writing prompt. **Display and read aloud the writing prompt.**

> **Writing Prompt**
>
> In *The Mystery of Saint Matthew Island,* a scientist discovers what was happening to the reindeer on Saint Matthew Island. Now write your own mystery. Explain what the mystery is, then use clues to reveal what happened, how it happened, and why.

Select a topic

To write a mystery, you begin with a topic. To find an idea, ask friends and family if they know of a mystery. Think about their story and see if you can turn it into a problem you can use in a mystery. What if your mom discovered your family car was out of gas one morning, yet when she drove it last, it had plenty of gas? Let's list that on a T-chart and decide how we can turn it into a mystery story. **Write this as Item 1 on your T-chart.** Think about news stories. What ideas could we find in the news? Write class suggestions in appropriate columns.

Gather information

Remind students that they can interview people or conduct research to find more information or details for their mysteries. Remember to keep this chart as the students will refer back to it tomorrow as they draft.

Source/Idea	Mystery
1. Mom: discovers car is out of gas, but when she drove it last, it had gas	1. Something missing. What? How? Why?
2. News: lost pet	2. Is the pet a runaway or pet-napped?

Corrective feedback

Have students individually continue the chart with ideas of their own. Circulate around the room, assisting students with *what if?* questions.

MINI-LESSON

Creating a Recipe for a Mystery

■ I remember my grandmother talking about a strange noise that awakened her at night when she was little girl. In the mornings, she would find scraps of tinfoil on her bed. Tiny bows from her quilt would be missing. It was a pack rat. I think I can turn that into a mystery. My recipe for a mystery will have five ingredients **Make a single-column list of the five items below.** Let's start with the idea and problem.

1. <u>Idea/Problem:</u> Strange noise at night. Who or what and why?

2. <u>Setting and Mood</u>: Farm, bedroom. Night. Sinister. Baffling.

3. <u>Characters</u>: Main: little girl. Minor: mother, father, and brother. They think she's dreaming or removing bows in her sleep.

4. <u>Clues</u>: Noises occur only at night in the dark. Missing bows. Tinfoil.

5. <u>Ending</u>: A little pack rat is swapping tinfoil for the bows.

■ Have students begin their own recipes using the form on p. 401 of their *Reader's and Writer's Notebook.*

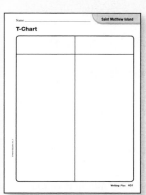

Reader's and Writer's Notebook p. 401

ROUTINE

Quick Write for Fluency

Team Talk

① **Talk** Pairs discuss their focus and ideas for their mystery stories.

② **Write** Each student writes a short description of their mystery.

③ **Share** Partners read each other's descriptions.

Routines Flip Chart

ELL

English Language Learners

Support prewriting Help students understand the writing prompt. Explain that fictional mysteries can be based on actual events. Pair beginning English learners with more proficient English speakers and have them discuss the difference between fiction and nonfiction.

Wrap Up Your Day

✔ **Build Concepts** Have students discuss the investigation of the deaths of reindeer.

✔ **Main Idea and Details** What is the main idea of *The Mystery of Saint Matthew Island*?

✔ **Text Structure** Does the author reveal the main idea or do you have to figure it out?

Preview DAY 3

Tell students that tomorrow they will continue to read about how Dr. Klein discovered the cause of the deaths of thousands of reindeer.

Objectives
- Expand the weekly concept.
- Develop oral vocabulary.

Today at a Glance

Oral Vocabulary
composition, depletion

Comprehension Check/Retelling
Discuss questions

Reading
The Mystery of Saint Matthew Island

Think Critically
Retelling

Fluency
Appropriate phrasing

Research and Study Skills
Time line

Research and Inquiry
Analyze

Spelling
Final syllable *-ant, -ent, -ance, -ence*

Conventions
Conjunctions

Writing
Mystery

Concept Talk

Question of the Week

❓ What unexpected effects can humans have on nature?

Expand the concept

Remind students of the weekly concept question. Discuss how the question relates to Saint Matthew Island. Tell students that today they will read about a scientist's search for clues to a natural mystery. Encourage students to think about how human planning shaped nature.

Anchored Talk

Develop oral vocabulary

Use text features—illustrations, captions, diagrams and maps—to review pp. 350–355 of *The Mystery of Saint Matthew Island*. Discuss the Amazing Words *grandiose* and *prune*. Add these and other concept-related words to the concept map. Have students break into groups. Ask students to elicit suggestions from one another to answer the following questions and develop their understanding of the concept.

- Stocking the island with reindeer could be considered a *grandiose* plan. Think about what it means to be *grandiose*. What are some ways that people can be *grandiose*?

- Think about why it might be helpful to *prune* a bush. Why would a gardener *prune* bushes or other plants?

Oral Vocabulary
Amazing Words

Amazing Words

accommodates	depletion
refuge	composition
domesticated	natural
contaminated	resources
grandiose	aggravate
prune	

Amazing Words — Oral Vocabulary Routine

Teach Amazing Words

1 Introduce Write the word *depletion* on the board. Have students say it with you. Yesterday, we learned that the *depletion* of the reindeer population puzzled Dr. Klein. Have students use the context to determine a definition of *depletion*. (*Depletion* is the reduction or using up of something.)

2 Demonstrate Have students answer questions to demonstrate understanding. How did researchers find out about the *depletion* of the herd? (They tracked down the remaining reindeer on the island to see how many were left.)

3 Apply Have students apply their understanding. In what ways does the *depletion* of one animal species affect our world?

See p. OV•2 to teach *composition*.

Routines Flip Chart

Apply Amazing Words

As students read pp. 356–359 of *The Mystery of Saint Matthew Island,* have them consider how the Amazing Words *depletion* and *composition* apply to the deaths of the reindeer on Saint Matthew Island.

Connect to reading

Help students establish a purpose for reading. Explain that today students will read about how Dr. Klein solved the mystery of the decreasing reindeer population. As they read, students should think about how the Question of the Week and the Amazing Words *depletion* and *composition* apply to Klein's discovery.

ELL **Expand Vocabulary** Use the Day 3 instruction on ELL Poster 27 to help students expand vocabulary.

ELL Poster 27

Objectives

◎ Summarize main ideas and details to aid comprehension.

◎ Analyze text structure to understand cause-and-effect relationships.

◎ Understand -s and -es endings.

Comprehension Check

Have students discuss each question with a partner. Ask several pairs to share their responses.

☑ **Genre • Synthesis**

Why do you think the author uses illustrations, maps, and graphs? Possible response: Graphics make the information more clear. For example, maps show the island's location and geography. The illustrations make the text more exciting.

☑ **Main idea and details • Analysis**

The author indicates that the decline of the herd was mysterious to Dr. Klein. Which details suggest that the reindeer should have been thriving when Dr. Klein returned to the island? Possible response: At one point there were over six thousand reindeer; there were no predators or humans and plenty of food on the island.

☑ **Text structure • Evaluation**

What was the cause-and-effect relationship between the absence of other large mammals on the island and the researchers' predictions about the reindeer population? Possible response: The absence of predators on the island caused researchers to assume that the reindeer population would grow.

☑ **Endings -s, -es • Analysis**

Find the phrase *lonely shore* on page 353. To make *shore* plural, would we add -s or -es? Explain. Add -s because *shore* ends with e, and *shorees* isn't a word.

☑ **Connect text to self**

Dr. Klein's scientific investigation into what happened on Saint Matthew Island could be described as a case study. How would you apply Dr. Klein's procedure to a scientific investigation of your own? Possible response: First, I would clearly identify the problem. Then, I would make a list of possible causes. I would go down the list one-by-one, investigating each possible cause.

Strategy Response Log

Have students identify the text structures the author used for *The Mystery of Saint Matthew Island* on p. 33 in the *Reader's and Writer's Notebook*.

INTERACT with TEXT

Check Retelling

Have students retell what they have read so far of *The Mystery of Saint Matthew Island,* summarizing main ideas in the text in a logical order. Encourage students to use the graphics in their retellings.

Corrective feedback

If... students leave out important details,
then... have students look back at the graphics and illustrations in the selection.

Small Group Time

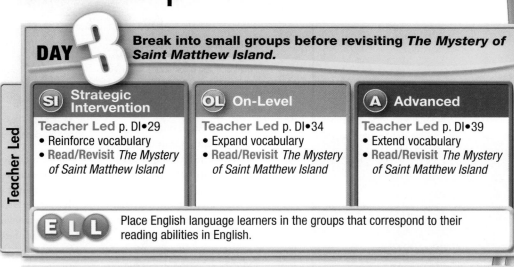

Teacher Led

DAY 3 Break into small groups before revisiting *The Mystery of Saint Matthew Island.*

SI Strategic Intervention
Teacher Led p. DI•29
• Reinforce vocabulary
• **Read/Revisit** *The Mystery of Saint Matthew Island*

OL On-Level
Teacher Led p. DI•34
• Expand vocabulary
• **Read/Revisit** *The Mystery of Saint Matthew Island*

A Advanced
Teacher Led p. DI•39
• Extend vocabulary
• **Read/Revisit** *The Mystery of Saint Matthew Island*

ELL Place English language learners in the groups that correspond to their reading abilities in English.

Practice Stations
• Let's Write
• Get Fluent
• Word Work

Independent Activities
• AudioText: *Saint Matthew Island*
• *Reader's and Writer's Notebook*
• Research and Inquiry

English Language Learners
Check retelling To support retelling, review the multilingual summary for *The Mystery of Saint Matthew Island* with the appropriate Retelling Cards to scaffold understanding.

Objectives

◎ Analyze cause and effect as a text structure.

 OPTION 1 Skills and Strategies, continued

Teach Text Structure

🔁 **Text Structure** Write the following sentences on the board: *The bone marrow of the reindeer had little fat in it when the deer died. The deer did not have enough vegetation to eat.* Ask students which is the cause and which is the effect.

Corrective Feedback

If... students are unable to identify a cause-and-effect text structure, **then...** model identifying cause and effect.

 **Multidraft Reading**

If you chose...

Option 1 Return to Extend Thinking instruction starting on p. 352–353.
Option 2 Read pp. 356–359. Use the Guide Comprehension and Extend Thinking instruction.

Student Edition pp. 356–357

OPTION 2 Think Critically, continued

Higher-Order Thinking Skills

🔁 **Text Structure • Analysis** What is the main idea of the last paragraph on page 357? Possible response: Dr. Klein found that the food crop that was critical to the deer's survival had been severely damaged. What is the cause and what is the effect? How can the text structure of cause and effect help you understand the main idea?

Model the Strategy

Think Aloud What is the relationship between these two events? (When an animal doesn't have enough to eat, it loses fat.)

During the winter, the reindeer fed off vegetation such as lichen (TOP LEFT), sedge (TOP RIGHT), and willow (RIGHT), which grew on the windswept areas of the island where the snow is often blown free.

Klein ruled out diseases and parasites because he had found almost no signs of disease or parasites on his earlier visits to Saint Matthew. And it was not possible that an infected animal from somewhere else had brought in any disease or parasite. Saint Matthew Island is too remote.

Klein found skeletons from animals of all ages. Therefore old age was not the cause of the die-off either. That left weather and starvation as possible causes.

Weather seemed likely to be involved. The 1963–64

winter included some of the deepest snows and the coldest temperatures ever recorded in the Bering Sea area. But Klein thought a severe winter alone should not have caused such a massive die-off. Reindeer are arctic animals. As long as they have enough food, most healthy reindeer should be able to survive, even in a severe winter.

Thus Klein suspected that the Saint Matthew Island reindeer had been unhealthy or had run out of food during the winter of 1963–64. With this

356

Possible response: The damage to the food supply was the cause, and the threat to the deer's survival is the effect. Thinking about cause-and-effect relationships helps me analyze the relationships among ideas presented in the text.

So the cause is the lack of vegetation, and the effect is that the bone marrow had little fat in it. **The text is structured in a way that helps readers see this relationship between ideas.**

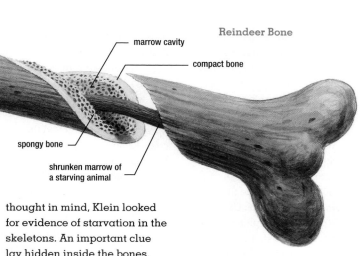

Reindeer Bone

marrow cavity

compact bone

spongy bone

shrunken marrow of a starving animal

thought in mind, Klein looked for evidence of starvation in the skeletons. An important clue lay hidden inside the bones. A well-fed animal has fat in its bone marrow. This fatty marrow remains in the bones for five years or more after an animal dies. Knowing this, Klein cracked open the leg bones of the skeletons to examine the marrow. Bone after bone, skeleton after skeleton, the marrow was completely gone. None of the animals had fat in their bone marrow when they died. This was clear evidence that the herd had starved to death.

When Klein visited the island three years earlier, he had noticed that some impor-

tant winter food plants of the reindeer looked overgrazed. When he looked around this time, he noticed more severe damage. Many of the small plants looked as if they had been clipped back. And lichens, mosslike organisms that once carpeted the island, were now absent from many areas. Klein observed that the most serious damage was on hilltops and ridges, where winds keep the ground snow-free in winter. Such places would have been used heavily by reindeer during winter.

357

On Their Own

Have students reread pp. 356–357 to find more cause-and-effect relationships. Then have students analyze how this organizational pattern influences their understanding of the text and the relationships among ideas.

Connect to Science

A *lichen (LY kun)* consists of a fungus and algae or bacteria that live together in a mutually-beneficial relationship. The fungus benefits from the food produced by the algae or bacteria. In turn, the algae or bacteria obtain shelter and water from the fungus.

 ELL

English Language Learners
Monitor understanding Have groups of students create a time line showing the events in the selection so far, focusing on events between 1963 and 1966. Ask: When did the reindeer get to the island? When did Klein return? When did it seem that the population died off?

With students, read aloud paragraph 4 on p. 356. What did Klein think happened to the reindeer in the winter of 1963 to 1964? Why did he guess this?

Graphic Sources • Analysis How does interpreting the factual information in the diagram on page 357 help you gain an overview of the text and locate information? Possible response: It shows the outside and inside of a reindeer bone so I know that this page has something to do with what happens to an animal's bones when it is starving.

Context Clues • Synthesis Which context clues on page 356 help you determine the meaning of the word *severe*? Possible response: *deepest snows and coldest temperatures ever recorded in the Bering Sea area*

Objectives

◎ Determine the meaning of grade-level academic English words with endings -s and -es.

Teach Endings -s, -es

◉ **Endings -s, -es** Write these words on the board: *diseases, animals.* Have students identify the ending in each word and its part of speech.

Corrective Feedback

If... students are unable to identify the word ending or part of speech, **then...** model guiding students in breaking down word structure.

Reader's and Writer's Notebook, p. 402

Model the Skill

 Think Aloud What is the singular form of *diseases*? **(disease)** What is the singular form of *animals*? **(animal)**

The damaged plant life led Klein to suspect that the reindeer had run out of nutritious food. Knowing that a lack of healthy food would show up in the weights of the reindeer, Klein reviewed the records from his earlier visits to Saint Matthew. The animals he had examined in 1957 weighed 199 to 404 pounds—more than most reindeer elsewhere. Clearly, the animals had plenty of food then. In contrast, the reindeer Klein had weighed in 1963 averaged 50 to 120 pounds less in weight. These lower weights showed that when the herd had numbered six thousand animals, many of the reindeer were not getting enough to eat. Klein next weighed a few of the live reindeer that remained on the island. These animals still weighed less than normal. They were not getting enough good food. That clinched the case. Klein was now certain what had happened.

Without predators or disease to limit its numbers, the small reindeer herd had grown quickly. Many young were born, and all the animals had plenty to eat. But after a few years, there were too many animals. The reindeer ate and trampled the tundra plants and lichens faster than these could grow. Crowded onto the windswept

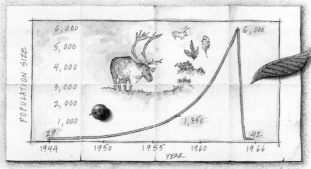

Assumed population of the Saint Matthew Island reindeer herd. Actual counts are indicated on the population curve.

358

Student Edition pp. 358–359

Higher-Order Thinking Skills

◉ **Endings -s, -es • Analysis** What are the plural forms of *lichen,* and *weight*? *(lichens, weights)* What are the parts of speech of each word? **(nouns)** How do the word endings help you determine the meaning of each word? **Possible response:** Since I know the ending -s is used to make singular things plural, I know that words with this ending are nouns, which helps me determine their meanings.

Word Choice • Synthesis How do words and phrases like *destroyed, disaster was inevitable,* and *eaten themselves out of house and home* help you monitor and adjust your comprehension of the text? **Possible response:** These descriptive words and phrases create negative and somber sensory images that help me understand the seriousness of the situation for the reindeer on the island.

I can use the words in a sentence to help determine their part of speech: *There are many diseases that can make animals sick.* Both of these words are nouns in this sentence.

RIGHT: View of Bull Seal Point, Saint Matthew Island.

BELOW: The very last reindeer. She was last seen in 1982.

ridges in winter, the large herd destroyed the lush lichen carpet. When the most nutritious plants and lichens became scarce, the reindeer began to lose weight. In poor condition, and with little food to sustain them, disaster was inevitable. The harsh winter of 1963–64 spelled the end for the once healthy herd. The Saint Matthew Island reindeer had literally eaten themselves out of house and home. By their numbers alone, they had destroyed their island home and their future.

On Their Own

Have students reread pp. 358–359 to find other plural nouns to use in sentences. Then have students use a print or electronic dictionary to determine or verify the meaning and part of speech of each word they find. For additional practice, use *Reader's and Writer's Notebook,* p. 402.

When Klein and his co-workers left Saint Matthew Island, they brought with them an important understanding of the connections between animals and their environment. Populations of all living things can skyrocket in numbers, like the reindeer herd. Usually, however, animal numbers are kept in check by predators, parasites and diseases, or other factors. The mystery of the Saint Matthew Island reindeer showed that in the absence of these natural checks, a growing population eventually destroys its own environment. And disaster strikes.

359

Comprehension Check

Spiral Review

Graphic Sources • Analysis Use the graph on page 358 to locate information about the approximate number of reindeer on Saint Matthew Island in 1955. Possible response: There were slightly below one thousand reindeer on the island at that time. What happened between 1955 and 1963? The reindeer population steadily increased.

Author's Purpose • Evaluation Why do you think the author includes a photo of the very last reindeer on Saint Matthew Island? Possible response: The photo is eerie and sad. The author wants the reader to think about what happened to the reindeer on Saint Matthew Island. By showing the very last one, the author hopes the reader will think about how humans can affect nature.

Check Predictions Have students return to the predictions they made earlier and confirm whether they were accurate.

Differentiated Instruction

 Strategic Intervention

Graphic sources Have students work in pairs to obtain information from the graph on p. 358. They can estimate population numbers from each year and then compare notes with other student pairs.

A **Advanced**

Word choice Have students locate other words and phrases in the text that help contribute to a somber, serious tone about what happened on the island.

ELL

English Language Learners

Monitor and clarify Have students ask questions about any words in the reading selection that confuse them or are unfamiliar. Then have other students answer the questions with the help of a dictionary.

The Mystery of Saint Matthew Island **359a**

Objectives
• Provide evidence from text to support understanding. • Read independently for a sustained period of time and paraphrase the reading, including the order in which events occur.

Envision It! Retell

READING STREET ONLINE
STORY SORT
www.ReadingStreet.com

360

Think Critically

1. Think of other mysteries you have read. How would you compare "The Mystery of Saint Matthew Island" to another mystery you have read? How are the mysteries similar? How are they different? Text to Text

2. Dr. David Klein did not guess at answers. He searched for them and found them. How does the author portray Dr. Klein as a scientist rather than a guesser? Think Like an Author

3. Think of the main idea of the selection as a piece of advice for both animals and humans. What would the advice be? Use details from the selection to support your answer. ◎ Main Idea and Details

4. The selection can be seen as a series of clues that add up to a solution. Identify and list the major clues, from start to finish. Then discuss how they add up to the solution. ◎ Text Structure

5. **Look Back and Write** Reread the end of the selection on page 359. The author's last line in the selection talks about disaster striking. Why did disaster strike for the reindeer? Write an explanation to this question. Provide evidence to support your answer.

TEST PRACTICE Extended Response

Meet the Author
Susan E. Quinlan

Susan E. Quinlan loves wildlife. She says, "It's hard to draw a line between what I do for a living and what I do for hobbies." As a biologist and naturalist guide, she has explored environments in many parts of the world. "The Mystery of Saint Matthew Island" is one of fourteen accounts in *The Case of the Mummified Pigs and Other Mysteries in Nature*. To write the book, she followed up on "wisps of knowledge" she had collected from her experiences in the field and from interviewing scientists.

Ms. Quinlan says, "My primary career interest is to share my fascination with nature and science with other people. Through my years of education and work as a wildlife biologist, I gradually realized that people who are trained as biologists look at nature differently from other people. This different way of looking at things results from acquired nature observation skills and from learning about the research of other scientists. One of my goals as a writer is to help others learn to look at nature in the ways that a biologist might. I also want to interpret the research work of scientists in ways that children and non-scientists can understand and enjoy."

Here are other books by Susan E. Quinlan.

The Case of the Monkeys That Fell from the Trees and Other Mysteries in Tropical Nature

THE CASE OF THE MONKEYS THAT FELL FROM THE TREES

THE CASE OF THE MUMMIFIED PIGS and Other Mysteries in Nature

The Case of the Mummified Pigs and Other Mysteries in Nature

Use the Reader's and Writer's Notebook to record your independent reading.

361

Student Edition pp. 360–361

Retelling

Envision It!

Have students work in pairs to retell the selection, using the Envision It! Retelling Cards as prompts. Remind students that they should maintain meaning and logical order in their retelling. Monitor students' retellings.

Scoring rubric

Top-Score Response A top-score response makes connections beyond the text, describes the main topic and important details using accurate information, and draws conclusions from the text.

Plan to Assess Retelling

☑ **Week 1** Assess Strategic Intervention students.

☑ **This week assess Advanced students.**

☐ **Week 3** Assess Strategic Intervention students.

☐ **Week 4** Assess On-Level students.

☐ **Week 5** Assess any students you have not yet checked during this unit.

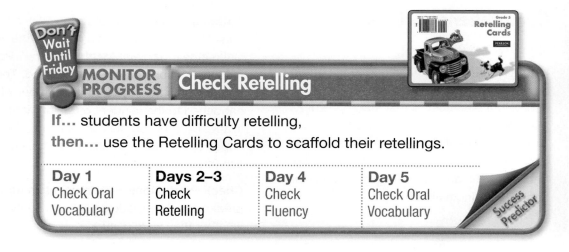

Don't Wait Until Friday

MONITOR PROGRESS Check Retelling

Grade 5 Retelling Cards

If... students have difficulty retelling,

then... use the Retelling Cards to scaffold their retellings.

Day 1	Days 2–3	Day 4	Day 5
Check Oral Vocabulary	Check Retelling	Check Fluency	Check Oral Vocabulary

Success Predictor

Think Critically

Text to text

1. I would compare this mystery to *The Dinosaur Bones of Waterhouse Hawkins.* Klein and Waterhouse both use science to solve their mysteries, but Waterhouse uses art to interpret the evidence, and Klein does not.

Think like an author

2. Dr. Klein is shown to be a good scientist because he forms a theory from reason and physical evidence. He carefully rules out several possible causes until there is only one good explanation. A guesser would not have been as thorough and careful.

Main idea and details

3. The advice is to respect natural checks or else the whole population could be at risk of extinction. Without natural checks, such as predators, parasites, and diseases, the reindeer herd had become too large for the island to support.

Text structure

4. Skeletons in the same state of decay showed that the deaths happened at the same time; bones of unborn reindeer showed the deaths were in late winter; skeletons of all ages ruled out old age; skeletons showed no signs of disease or parasites; bones showed an absence of marrow. The last clue guaranteed that starvation was the answer. It agreed with everything Klein had observed the last time he visited the island.

 Writing on Demand

5. **Look Back and Write** To build writing fluency, assign a 10–15 minute time limit.

Suggest that students use a prewriting strategy, such as a graphic organizer, to organize ideas. Remind them to establish a topic sentence and support it with facts and explanations. As students finish, encourage them to reread their responses, revise for organization and support, and proofread for errors in grammar and conventions.

Scoring rubric

Top-Score Response A top-score response uses details to synthesize and connect ideas about the decline of the reindeer population.

A top-score response should include:

• The reindeer had no natural predators or diseases.

• The reindeer population had grown too large.

• When food became scarce, the reindeer starved to death.

Differentiated Instruction

 Strategic Intervention
Have students work in small groups to identify the main idea of paragraph 1 on p. 358.

Meet the Author

Have students read about author Susan E. Quinlan on p. 361. Ask students to explain why *The Mystery of Saint Matthew Island* shows Quinlan's concern for wildlife and the environment.

Independent Reading

After students enter their independent reading information into their Reading Logs or a journal, have them summarize what they have read. Remind students that a summary should be no more than a few sentences about the main idea of a text.

ELL

English Language Learners
Retelling Use the Retelling Cards to discuss the selection with students. Then have students make their own cards showing other passages or events from the selection. When they are finished, have partners take turns describing their cards.

Retelling

Success
Predicto

Model Fluency
Appropriate Phrasing

Model fluent reading

Have students turn to p. 357 of *The Mystery of Saint Matthew Island*. Have students follow along as you read this page. Tell them to listen to your phrasing as you group words meaningfully, pausing at commas and coming to a full stop at periods.

Guide practice

Have students follow along as you read the page again. Then have them reread the page as a group without you until they read with appropriate phrasing and with no mistakes. Ask questions to be sure students comprehend the text. Continue in the same way on p. 358.

Reread for Fluency

Corrective feedback

If... students are having difficulty reading with the right phrasing, **then...** prompt:

• Where can we break up this sentence? Which words are related?
• Read the sentence again. Pause after each group of words.
• Tell me the sentence. Now read it with pauses after each group of words.

> **ROUTINE Choral Reading**
>
> 1. **Select a passage** For *The Mystery of Saint Matthew Island*, use p. 355.
> 2. **Model** Read aloud p. 355. Have students listen as you read with appropriate phrasing and attention to punctuation cues.
> 3. **Guide practice** Have students read along with you.
> 4. **On their own** Have the class read aloud without you. For optimal fluency, students should reread aloud three or four times with appropriate phrasing. To check the student's comprehension of the passage, have him or her retell what was read.
>
> Routines Flip Chart

Research and Study Skills
Time Line

Teach

Ask students what type of visual aid shows things in chronological order. Students may need prompting before they mention time lines. Show a time line to students, perhaps one from their social studies text. Then explain these features:

- A **time line** presents information in chronological order. The points on the main line show dates and events.

- Time lines can be very specific (a time line of your day) or very general (a time line of world history).

- Electronic time lines on CD-ROMS and the Internet often contain underlined words, colored type, hypertext, or links that will take you to another site for more information.

- A time line gives a visual summary of information.

Provide groups with examples of time lines from different content areas. Have each group show its time line to the class, telling what the main focus of the time line is and what it shows.

Guide practice

Discuss these questions:

How do you know what information the time line shows? (Each point on the line shows a date and an event.)

How are these example time lines alike and different? (Possible response: They all show events in chronological order, but some are vertical, and some are horizontal; some are about science, and some are about history.)

After groups describe their time lines, ask specific questions about the information on their time lines. Have students take written notes on the information presented in the time line. Then have students use these graphics to locate and interpret specific factual and/or quantitative information. For example, ask questions starting with *Who, Where, When,* and *How many.*

On their own

Have students complete pp. 403–404 of the *Reader's and Writer's Notebook.*

Academic Vocabulary

time line a vertical or horizontal line that visually displays the order in which events occur; a time line may present narrative (fiction) or chronological (nonfiction) information

Differentiated Instruction

 Strategic Intervention

Graphic organizer Students can work in groups to make a main idea and supporting details chart that includes events and dates from *The Mystery of Saint Matthew Island.* Then have them take these key points and arrange them on a time line.

 Advanced

Graphic organizer Have students select a relevant topic from history or science. Then ask them to create a time line organized around a main idea that includes supporting details such as dates, events, and discoveries of that topic or event.

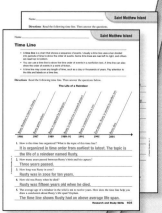

Reader's and Writer's Notebook pp. 403–404

Objectives
- Analyze data for usefulness.
- Review conjunctions.
- Spell frequently misspelled words.

Research and Inquiry
Analyze

Teach

Tell students that today they will analyze their findings to focus on specific facts and dates appropriate for their time lines. Have them ask themselves questions to refine and focus their inquiry topics.

Model

Think Aloud In my research, I found that bald eagle populations have declined steadily since the 1700s. There are several reasons for this, including habitat destruction, hunting, and food and water contamination as well as pesticides such as DDT. I ask myself, *Which of this information should I include in my time line?* I'd like to focus on DDT, which causes bald eagle eggs to thin. I will include the incidents and statistics I found on my time line. Now my inquiry question is, *How has DDT affected the bald eagle population?*

Guide practice

Have students analyze their findings. Help students who are having difficulty by pairing them with other students. They should also narrow down their research by highlighting or putting sticky notes on events they plan to include in their time line.

On their own

Remind students that they will use a time line to provide a visual representation of their findings and to help them organize information. Have them look for a few images, such as photographs or illustrations, to serve as visual aids in their time line.

Conventions
Conjunctions

Review

Remind students that this week they learned about conjunctions--words that join words, phrases, or sentences.

- A coordinating conjunction, such as *and, but,* and *or,* joins two parts of a sentence of equal importance.

- A subordinating conjunction, such as *because, if, when, before, after, then,* and *although,* introduces a clause that depends on the other part of the sentence.

Daily Fix-It

Use Daily Fix-It numbers 5 and 6 in the right margin.

Connect to oral language

Display the following sentences and have students read from the board, guiding them to supply an appropriate conjunction.

> **We had crackers for a snack, _____ Mom had suggested veggies.** (but)
>
> **_____ I got to up this morning, I had breakfast.** (When)

On their own

For additional practice, use *Let's Practice It!* p. 320 on the *Teacher Resources DVD-ROM.*

Let's Practice It!
TR DVD•320

Spelling
Final Syllable *-ant, -ent, -ance, -ence*

Frequently misspelled words

The words *off, one,* and *tired* are words that we often misspell. I'm going to read a sentence. Choose the right word to complete the sentence, and then write it correctly.

> **1. The only _____ to forget his homework was Kyle.** (one)
>
> **2. Turn _____ the lights when you leave the room.** (off)
>
> **3. She was _____ after the marathon.** (tired)

On their own

For additional practice, use the *Reader's and Writer's Notebook,* page 405.

Differentiated Instruction

SI Strategic Intervention

Compound sentences Remind students that a compound sentence has two independent clauses that are separated by a comma. Example: *Zoo animals adjust to zoo life, but they may fail to mate.* Have small groups of students find one or two examples of compound sentences in the selection.

Daily Fix-It

5. The Bering Sea lies between Alaska and siberia, ships can travel there only a few months. *(Siberia. Ships)*

6. Can you locate St. Matthew island on a map. *(Island; map?)*

Reader's and Writer's Notebook p. 405

Objectives
• Understand the criteria for an effective mystery.

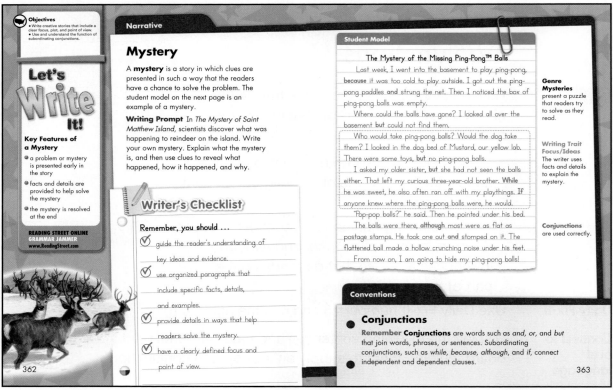

Student Edition pp. 362–363

Let's Write It!
Mystery

Teach

Use pages 362–363 in the Student Edition. Direct students to read the key features of a mystery which appear on page 362. Remind students that they can refer to the information in the Writer's Checklist as they write their own case study.

Read the student model on page 363. Point out the clear focus, point of view, and plot events in the model.

Connect to conventions

Remind students that conjunctions are words that join words, phrases, or sentences. Point out the correct use of conjunctions in the model.

Writing—Mystery
Writer's Craft: Details

Display rubric

Display Scoring Rubric 27 from the *Teacher Resources DVD* and go over the criteria for each trait under each score. Then, using the model in the Student Edition, choose students to explain why the model should score a 4 for one of the traits. If a student offers that the model should score below 4 for a particular trait, the student should offer support for that response. Remind students that this is the rubric that will be used to evaluate the mystery they write.

Scoring Rubric: Mystery

	④	③	②	①
Focus/Ideas	Problem stated early in the story; facts and details strong, help solve the mystery; no unnecessary details	Problem occurs early on, and facts and details provide some help in solving the mystery; no unnecessary details	Problem vague or takes time to understand; facts and details barely helpful in solving mystery; some unrelated details	Problem not clear or occurs too late; facts and details not sufficient to solve mystery; many unrelated details
Organization	Orderly, well-crafted plot with solid clues and logical end	Well-crafted plot with clues and understandable end	Plot is difficult to follow, clues and end lack focus	Lacks plot and organization; clues and end are a mystery
Voice	Involved throughout; engages readers	Involved most of the time	Not fully engaged	Writer not engaged
Word Choice	Strong sensory details to build mood and create setting	Good use of sensory details to build mood and describe setting	Some vague or repetitive words; no sense of mood or description of setting	Poor word choice; words do not build mood or create setting
Sentences	Well-crafted sentences varied in length and type	Smooth sentences with some variety	Too many short, choppy sentences; no variety of type	Many fragments and run-ons
Conventions	Excellent control and accuracy; confident and correct use of conjunctions	Good control; conjunctions used correctly, but not consistently	Errors that may prevent understanding; show lack of understanding of how to use conjunctions	Frequent errors that interfere with meaning; conveys no understanding of how to use conjunctions

List

Have students get out the recipe for a mystery lists that they worked on yesterday. If their lists are not complete, have students work with a partner to brainstorm ideas to complete them.

Write

You will be using your list as you write the paragraphs for the first draft of your mystery. When you are drafting, don't worry if your mystery does not sound exactly as you want it to. You will have a chance to revise it tomorrow.

Differentiated Instruction

SI **Strategic Intervention**

Provide students with a short sample of a mystery story. Read it aloud together. Then have each group evaluate it according to the six traits included in the rubric.

English Language Learners

Support drafting Help students focus on factual evidence about their topics. Remind students of the difference between facts and opinion *(The recipe is missing.) (The recipe is valuable.)* To help beginning English language learners, ask them to think of other adjectives that are opinions (good, bad, nice, terrible).

Objectives
- Write a first draft of a mystery.
- Include facts and details in the form of clues.

Writing, continued
Writer's Craft: Details

MINI-LESSON

Developing Clues in a Mystery

■ **Introduce** Explain that the facts and details in a mystery can help create the clues that readers will use to make predictions about the problem's solution. These clues should provide some but not all of the information the reader needs to find the solution. Remind students that if their mysteries are based on true stories, they will need to paraphrase the clues and details, or put the information into their own words. Display the Drafting Tips for students. Remind them that the focus of drafting is to get their ideas down in a logical and organized way. Then display Writing Transparency 27A.

Sounds by Night

Heather wasn't sure if she was awake or dreaming, but she heard a noise. There was something moving in the dark in her bedroom. She sucked in her breath and listened. There was nothing. Maybe it was just a dream, she thought, and went back to sleep.

When she slipped from bed the next morning, something crinkled beneath her foot. It was a piece of tinfoil. Bobby, her brother, must have put it there to play a joke. But then she noticed one of the little bows on her bed quilt was missing. Why would Bobby take that?

By the time she went to bed that night, she had forgotten all about the incident. But the next morning, the same thing had happened. This time, she figured the cat must have done it.

"Don't blame the cat," mother said, "because she was in our room until sunup."

Bobby came to dinner that night with a picture he had taken with his homemade box camera. Bobby was an amateur photographer, taking and even his own pictures. "Maybe I should take a picture of the evidence," he volunteered.

Heather looked at her brother. "Can you set up your camera so that something moving at night can trigger a picture?" she asked.

"Sure," Bobby said.

That night, Bobby had braced the camera and the flash, and rigged up a trip wire that ran from the dresser, past the foot of the bed and to the window. Heather turned off the light and climbed into bed. A brilliant flash of light exploded in her head and popped open her eyes. She turned on her light and ran to her brother's room. It worked, she cried.

They retrieved the camera and raced to the basement darkroom. It seemed like it took forever. They couldn't make out the negative so Bobby printed a picture and put in the chemical tray. And image began to appear. The pair gasped at what they saw. It was a pack rat and it had the funniest look on its little face, the way a pack rat would look if it knew it had been caught red-handed.

Unit 6 The Mystery of Saint Matthew Island   Writing: Model **27A**

Writing Transparency 27A, TR DVD

Drafting Tips

✔ Remember that your mystery is presented early in the story. Plan the ending of your mystery before you begin so that you know where you will end your story.

✔ Make a list of the facts and details you will provide as clues.

✔ If your mystery is based on a true story, paraphrase any facts or details you include.

Think Aloud I'm going to write a draft of a mystery based on my grandmother's hearing strange noises at night when she was a little girl. I will reveal the problem in the first sentence. Now, I will look at my list of clues. The mysterious noise at night was the first clue. Stepping on tinfoil was another. The missing bows and frayed thread were also clues. I will refer to my list to make sure I've included all the right details.

Direct students to use the drafting tips to guide them in developing their drafts. Remind them to provide clues in the story that will enable the reader to solve the problem.

ROUTINE **Quick Write for Fluency** Team Talk

1 **Talk** Pairs talk about strange and mysterious things they have heard their family talk about.

2 **Write** Each student writes a brief paragraph about a conflict, mystery, or problem they heard from their family. The paragraph will use a subordinating conjunction to compare or contrast the conflict.

3 **Share** Partners check each other's paragraphs for correct use of the subordinating conjunction.

Routines Flip Chart

SI Strategic Intervention
Have groups of two or three students work together to create introductory sentences for their mystery stories.

Academic Vocabulary

Paraphrase means to rephrase and simplify text or ideas in your own words.

Wrap Up Your Day

✔ **Build Concepts** What did you learn about the role humans played in the death of the reindeer herd on Saint Matthew Island?

✔ **Main Idea and Details** What important details of the article helped you determine the main idea?

✔ **Text Structure** How did the organization of "The Mystery of Saint Matthew Island" help you determine the main idea?

Preview DAY 4

Tell students that tomorrow they will read a new selection about red-tailed hawks living in the urban environment of New York City.

Objectives
- Expand the weekly concept.
- Develop oral vocabulary.

Today at a Glance

Oral Vocabulary
natural resources, aggravate

Genre
Expository text

Reading
"City Hawks"

Let's Learn It!
Fluency: Appropriate phrasing
Vocabulary: Endings *-s, -es*
Listening/Speaking: Interview

Research and Inquiry
Synthesize

Spelling
Final syllable *-ant, -ent, -ance, -ence*

Conventions
Conjunctions

Writing
Mystery

Concept Talk

Question of the Week

What unexpected effects can humans have on nature?

Expand the concept

Remind students that this week they have read about the way people can alter the composition of the natural world, creating new problems in the process. Tell students that today they will read about a student who uses e-mail and the Internet to find information about the relationship of people to wildlife and the environment.

Anchored Talk

Develop oral vocabulary

Use the text features—illustrations and maps—to review pp. 356–359 of *The Mystery of Saint Matthew Island.* Discuss the Amazing Words *composition* and *depletion.* Add these and other concept-related words to the concept map. Then have students get into groups. Have them use the following questions to elicit and consider suggestions from each other, identify points of agreement and disagreement among group members, use context to find the meaning of the unfamiliar Amazing Words, and develop their understanding of the concept.

- Think about how people can change the *composition* of the natural world. What are some of the ways people change the *composition* of a beach, for instance?

- Why should we avoid the *depletion* of natural resources, such as fresh water and forests?

Strategy Response Log

INTERACT with TEXT

Have students complete p. 33 in the *Reader's and Writer's Notebook.* Then have students summarize the selection.

Oral Vocabulary
Amazing Words

Amazing Words

accommodates depletion
refuge   composition
domesticated natural
contaminated   resources
grandiose   aggravate
prune

Amazing Words Oral Vocabulary Routine

Teach Amazing Words

1 Introduce Write the phrase *natural resources* on the board. Have students say it aloud with you. We read about how *natural resources* like lichen and mosses on an island were depleted by the increased reindeer population. Have students use context clues to help them determine the definition of *natural resources.* (Natural resources are things that occur in nature that can be useful to people or animals.)

2 Demonstrate Have students answer questions to demonstrate understanding. What are two *natural resources*? (coal, water) How can we use *natural resources* wisely to protect the future of Earth? (conserve, replace, recycle)

3 Apply Have students apply their understanding. What is an example of a wise use of a *natural resource*?

See p. OV•2 to teach *aggravate.*

Routines Flip Chart

Apply Amazing Words

As students read "City Hawks" on pp. 364–367, have them think about the kinds of natural resources on which wildlife depend.

Connect to reading

As students read today's section about hawks in urban areas, have them think about how the Question of the Week and the Amazing Words *natural resources* and *aggravate* apply to hawks.

E L L Produce Oral Language Use the Day 4 instruction on ELL Poster 27 to extend and enrich language.

E L L Poster 27

Let's Think About Genre

Expository Text: Graphic Sources

Introduce the genre

Explain to students that what we read is structured differently depending on the author's reasons for writing and what kind of information he/she wishes to convey. Different types of texts are called genres. Tell them that expository text is one type of genre.

Discuss the genre

Tell students that many expository texts have graphic sources that give additional information, summarize information, or clarify information by helping you to visualize it. Examples of graphic sources include time lines and photographs with explanatory captions.

On the board, draw a time line like the one below. Label it *Reindeer of Saint Matthew Island.* Ask the following questions:

- How do photographs support information in an expository text? **Possible response: Photographs give visual information about a topic to help readers visualize aspects of the writer's subject.**

- What kinds of information might you find on a time line? **Possible responses: dates of important events in history, dates of discoveries or inventions; 21 years**

- How do time lines support information in an expository text? How might a time line clarify the information in a text? **Possible response: Time lines summarize when things happened by placing them in sequential order. One way this could clarify text is by showing that one event caused some other event.**

| 1944 | 1947 | 1950 | 1953 | 1956 | 1959 | 1962 | 1965 |

Reindeer of Saint Matthew Island

Guide practice

Have students look back at *The Mystery of Saint Matthew Island* and fill in significant dates related to what happened to the reindeer between 1944 and 1965.

Connect to reading

Tell students that they will now read an expository text that is an article about hawks nesting in a city environment. Have the class think about times when reading an article about wildlife might be interesting or informative.

Small Group Time

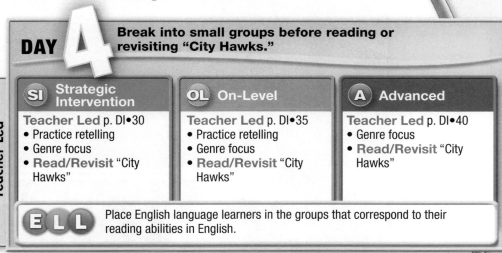

DAY 4 Break into small groups before reading or revisiting "City Hawks."

Teacher Led

SI Strategic Intervention
Teacher Led p. DI•30
• Practice retelling
• Genre focus
• **Read/Revisit** "City Hawks"

OL On-Level
Teacher Led p. DI•35
• Practice retelling
• Genre focus
• **Read/Revisit** "City Hawks"

A Advanced
Teacher Led p. DI•40
• Genre focus
• **Read/Revisit** "City Hawks"

ELL Place English language learners in the groups that correspond to their reading abilities in English.

Practice Stations
• Read for Meaning
• Get Fluent
• Words to Know

Independent Activities
• AudioText: "City Hawks"
• *Reader's and Writer's Notebook*
• Research and Inquiry

Objectives

- Understand the use of graphic sources in expository text.
- Use multiple text features to locate information and aid comprehension.
- Synthesize and make logical connections between texts.

Student Edition pp. 364–365

Guide Comprehension

Teach the genre

Genre: Expository Text Have students preview "City Hawks" on pp. 364–367. Ask them to examine the photographs and caption on the first two pages. Ask: What do these photographs and the caption tell you about the birds?

Corrective feedback

If… students are unable to get meaningful information from the photographs and caption,

then… use the model to guide students in using the photographs.

Model the genre

Think Aloud As I look at the photograph I see that these birds are large hawks. I see that they have a nest on a building, which is unusual. This narrow photo in the middle shows me that the nest is in a very big city. The bottom photo shows baby hawks, and the caption tells me which bird is Lola, and which is Pale Male.

On their own

Have students work in pairs to write a brief summary of what they can learn from the photographs in "City Hawks."

Extend Thinking
Think Critically

Higher-order thinking skills

Graphic Sources • Evaluation How well do the captions in "City Hawks" support the photographs? **Possible response:** Very well because the captions tell me the names of the birds in the pictures and connect the pictures to the text.

Draw Conclusions • Synthesis Why do you think the presence of Pale Male's nest on a New York City building was unusual? Possible response: Most hawks live outside cities and migrate every year, rather than nest permanently in one spot.

Let's Think About...

1 The photographs help me see exactly where the hawks are and the captions help me understand what is happening in the photos.

Differentiated Instruction

SI **Strategic Intervention**

Graphic sources Work with students to identify how captions provide information about photos. Have students work in groups to paraphrase the information in the captions.

A **Advanced**

Critical thinking Have students identify the photograph which they think best illustrates why the male hawk was named Pale Male and write a brief explanation defending their choice.

English Language Learners
Clarify content Have students discuss where birds usually build their nests (trees, cliffs). Ask: How would birds live and nest if they were in a big city with many tall buildings? Where might a bird build its nest in a city? What would be safe or unsafe about nesting on a building?

Objectives

- Understand the use of graphic sources in expository text.
- Use multiple text features to locate information and aid comprehension.
- Synthesize and make logical connections between texts.

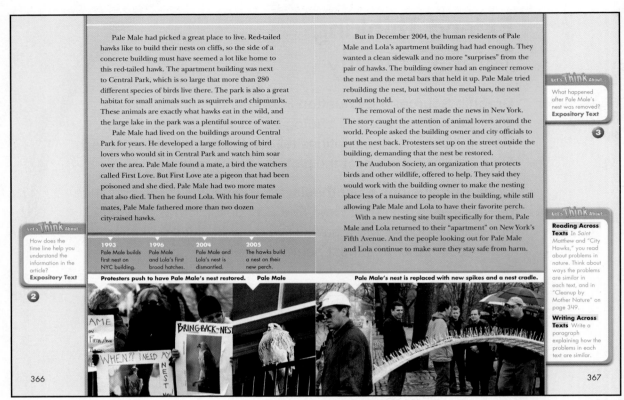

Pale Male had picked a great place to live. Red-tailed hawks like to build their nests on cliffs, so the side of a concrete building must have seemed a lot like home to this red-tailed hawk. The apartment building was next to Central Park, which is so large that more than 280 different species of birds live there. The park is also a great habitat for small animals such as squirrels and chipmunks. These animals are exactly what hawks eat in the wild, and the large lake in the park was a plentiful source of water.

Pale Male had lived on the buildings around Central Park for years. He developed a large following of bird lovers who would sit in Central Park and watch him soar over the area. Pale Male found a mate, a bird the watchers called First Love. But First Love ate a pigeon that had been poisoned and she died. Pale Male had two more mates that also died. Then he found Lola. With his four female mates, Pale Male fathered more than two dozen city-raised hawks.

But in December 2004, the human residents of Pale Male and Lola's apartment building had had enough. They wanted a clean sidewalk and no more "surprises" from the pair of hawks. The building owner had an engineer remove the nest and the metal bars that held it up. Pale Male tried rebuilding the nest, but without the metal bars, the nest would not hold.

The removal of the nest made the news in New York. The story caught the attention of animal lovers around the world. People asked the building owner and city officials to put the nest back. Protesters set up on the street outside the building, demanding that the nest be restored.

The Audubon Society, an organization that protects birds and other wildlife, offered to help. They said they would work with the building owner to make the nesting place less of a nuisance to people in the building, while still allowing Pale Male and Lola to have their favorite perch.

With a new nesting site built specifically for them, Pale Male and Lola returned to their "apartment" on New York's Fifth Avenue. And the people looking out for Pale Male and Lola continue to make sure they stay safe from harm.

Let's Think About...
How does the time line help you understand the information in the article?
Expository Text

Let's Think About...
What happened after Pale Male's nest was removed?
Expository Text

1993	1996	2004	2005
Pale Male builds first nest on NYC building.	Pale Male and Lola's first brood hatches.	Pale Male and Lola's nest is dismantled.	The hawks build a nest on their new perch.

Protesters push to have Pale Male's nest restored. Pale Male   Pale Male's nest is replaced with new spikes and a nest cradle.

366   367

Let's Think About...
Reading Across Texts In *Saint Matthew* and "City Hawks," you read about problems in nature. Think about ways the problems are similar in each text, and in "Cleanup by Mother Nature" on page 349.

Writing Across Texts Write a paragraph explaining how the problems in each text are similar.

Student Edition pp. 366–367

Guide Comprehension

Teach the genre

Genre: Expository Text Have students examine the time line on p. 366. Ask: How does the time line on p. 366 help you understand the key events in "City Hawks"?

Corrective feedback

If... students are unable to explain the purpose and content of the time line,

then... use the model to guide students in understanding time lines.

Model the genre

Think Aloud At a glance what I see in this time line is a summary of the main events described in the text. However, the time line not only summarizes key events, it also gives me additional details that are not in the main text. For example, I didn't know that Pale Male's first nest was built in 1993. I can see that by the time his new nest was built in 2005, Pale Male had been living in the city for 13 years.

On their own

Have students work in pairs to think of additional details they could add to the time line.

Extend Thinking
Think Critically

Higher-order thinking skills

Summarize • Synthesis Using the text and time line on page 366, how would you explain what happened to Pale Male during his first three years in New York City? Possible response: Pale Male's first nest was built in 1993. Then he lost two mates before he and Lola hatched their first brood in 1996.

Text Structure • Analysis What text structure did the author use to organize the information on page 367? Possible response: The author used sequence.

Let's Think About...

2 I know that the events in the article happened over a period of time. The time line helps me understand what and when events happened.

3 People were upset and protested outside the building. Then the building owner and the Audubon Society worked together to build a new nest that made everyone happy.

Reading Across Texts

Have students create a three-column chart to show the differences and similarities in the problems and solutions in each text.

Writing Across Texts

Students can use their charts to help them write their paragraphs. Encourage them to consider what the people in each selection learned about the balance of nature or the effects of human actions.

Differentiated Instruction

 Strategic Intervention

Graphic sources Work with students to identify how time lines can provide quick visual information. Have students work in groups to practice creating time lines based on what they did in class this past week.

 Advanced

Critical thinking Have students use the Internet to find out what has happened to the hawks in the years since the article was first published.

Connect to Social Studies

Between 2004 and 2008, Pale Male and Lola have tried to hatch out a brood, but the eggs haven't hatched so far. There is some speculation that the spikes on the nesting structure may be stopping Lola from rolling the eggs over, an important part of the nesting experience. There may also be other factors, which naturalists are investigating.

ELL

English Language Learners
Graphic organizer Provide support to students when creating their three-column charts. Help them choose labels for each column, and then work together to add details.

Objectives

- Read with fluency and comprehension.
- Identify word endings and how they affect parts of speech.
- Conduct an interview.

Check Fluency WCPM
◆ SUCCESS PREDICTOR

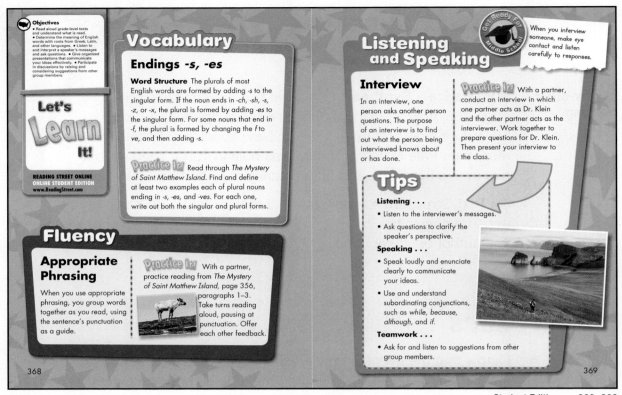

Objectives
- Read aloud grade-level texts and understand what is read.
- Determine the meaning of English words with roots from Greek, Latin, and other languages. • Listen to and interpret a speaker's messages and ask questions. • Give organized presentations that communicate your ideas effectively. • Participate in discussions by raising and considering suggestions from other group members.

Vocabulary

Endings -s, -es

Word Structure The plurals of most English words are formed by adding -s to the singular form. If the noun ends in -ch, -sh, -s, -z, or -x, the plural is formed by adding -es to the singular form. For some nouns that end in -f, the plural is formed by changing the f to ve, and then adding -s.

Let's Learn It!

READING STREET ONLINE
ONLINE STUDENT EDITION
www.ReadingStreet.com

Practice It! Read through *The Mystery of Saint Matthew Island*. Find and define at least two examples each of plural nouns ending in -s, -es, and -ves. For each one, write out both the singular and plural forms.

Fluency

Appropriate Phrasing

When you use appropriate phrasing, you group words together as you read, using the sentence's punctuation as a guide.

Practice It! With a partner, practice reading from *The Mystery of Saint Matthew Island*, page 356, paragraphs 1–3. Take turns reading aloud, pausing at punctuation. Offer each other feedback.

368

Listening and Speaking

Get Ready For Middle School
When you interview someone, make eye contact and listen carefully to responses.

Interview

In an interview, one person asks another person questions. The purpose of an interview is to find out what the person being interviewed knows about or has done.

Practice It! With a partner, conduct an interview in which one partner acts as Dr. Klein and the other partner acts as the interviewer. Work together to prepare questions for Dr. Klein. Then present your interview to the class.

Tips

Listening . . .
- Listen to the interviewer's messages.
- Ask questions to clarify the speaker's perspective.

Speaking . . .
- Speak loudly and enunciate clearly to communicate your ideas.
- Use and understand subordinating conjunctions, such as *while, because, although,* and *if.*

Teamwork . . .
- Ask for and listen to suggestions from other group members.

369

Student Edition pp. 368–369

Fluency
Appropriate Phrasing/Punctuation Cues

Guide practice

Use the Student Edition activity as an assessment tool. Make sure the reading passage is at least 200 words in length. As students read aloud with partners, walk around to make sure their phrasing is appropriate and that it follows punctuation cues to enhance the meaning of the text.

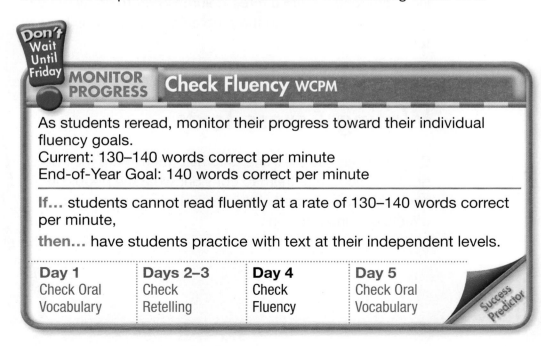

Don't Wait Until Friday

MONITOR PROGRESS **Check Fluency WCPM**

As students reread, monitor their progress toward their individual fluency goals.
Current: 130–140 words correct per minute
End-of-Year Goal: 140 words correct per minute

If... students cannot read fluently at a rate of 130–140 words correct per minute,

then... have students practice with text at their independent levels.

Day 1	Days 2–3	Day 4	Day 5
Check Oral Vocabulary	Check Retelling	Check Fluency	Check Oral Vocabulary

Success Predictor

Vocabulary
 Endings -s, -es

Teach word endings

Word Structure Write these selection–related words on the board:

| females | skeletons | carcasses | calves | wolves | foxes |

Point out the endings -s and -es on these words and explain any spelling changes that were made.

Guide practice

Have students circle the ending of each word and write the correct spelling for the singular word, before the addition of the ending.

On their own

Walk around the room as students work with partners to identify and define the words from *The Mystery of Saint Matthew Island.* Make sure students understand when to use -s and -es to form plurals.

Listening and Speaking
Interview

Teach

Tell students that in order for an interview to be successful, the interviewer needs to be organized, and the interviewee needs to be open and honest. Remind the students pretending to be Dr. Klein to think about the kinds of opinions and experiences the real Dr. Klein would have. When the interviewer asks them questions, they should respond how he would respond. Remind the interviewing students to ask relevant questions to clarify the interviewee's purpose or perspective. Tell students that the interviewer's point of view can influence the entire interview based on the kinds of questions that he or she asks.

Guide practice

Be sure students are asking relevant questions and answering using accurate information. Remind students that good speakers maintain eye contact with listeners, speak at an appropriate rate and volume with clear enunciation, make natural gestures with their hands and body, and use proper conventions of language while speaking. Also remind the students to listen attentively to the speaker and to take notes to help them accurately interpret the speaker's verbal and nonverbal message.

On their own

Have students conduct the interview with their partners.

Interview

Remind students that they should interpret and respond to questions and evaluate responses as both an interviewer and an interviewee. Tell students that anticipating a person's responses in an interview can help them have pertinent questions prepared.

ELL

English Language Learners
Practice syllabification of endings -s, -es Assist pairs of students by modeling the correct syllabification of the -s, -es words related to the selection, then have students repeat after you.

Fluency

Succes
Predicto

Objectives

- Analyze data for usefulness.
- Review conjunctions.
- Spell words with Latin-derived suffixes *-ant, -ent, -ance,* and *-ence.*

Research and Inquiry
Synthesize

Teach

Draw a sample time line on the board. In the bald eagle example, time line markers might include statistics about how many eagles were left in a given year, or events such as when the eagles were put on the endangered species list.

Show the arrow at either end of the time line clearly, and show where photos or illustrations could go. Years should be clearly marked in even intervals. Students should include at least five events on their time line. Ask questions to make sure students can interpret factual or quantitative information from the time line on the board.

Guide practice

Have students draw or use a word processor to synthesize their findings into a time line. Remind them to use data or information from multiple sources. They should paste the time line, as well as any illustrations or visual aids, on a poster board for their Day 5 presentation. Check to see that students are labeling their time lines with dates, events, and data relevant to the topic.

On their own

Have students work together to practice presenting their time line. Encourage students to give each other feedback on their time lines as well as ideas for the presentation.

Grammar Jammer

Conventions
Conjunctions

Test practice

Remind students that grammar skills, such as recognizing and using conjunctions correctly, are often assessed on important tests. Remind students that conjunctions are words that join other words, phrases, or sentences.

- Use the coordinating conjunctions *and, but,* and *or* and a comma to make compound subjects, compound predicates, and compound sentences.

- Use subordinating conjunctions such as *because, if, when, before, after, then* and *although* to make complex sentences.

Daily Fix-It

Use Daily Fix-It numbers 7 and 8 in the right margin.

On their own

For additional practice, use the *Reader's and Writer's Notebook* p. 406.

Reader's and Writer's Notebook p. 406

Daily Fix-It

7. The polar bear be my favorite animal at the zoo? *(is; zoo.)*

8. The bear fascinates that there man with huge paws. *(The bear with huge paws fascinates that man.)*

Spelling
Suffixes *-ant, -ent, -ance, -ence*

Practice spelling strategy

Have partners take turns quizzing each other on spelling the list words. Have one student dictate as the other writes each word. Have them review each other's work and continue quizzing and checking until each partner spells all the words correctly.

On their own

For additional practice, use *Let's Practice It!* p. 321 on the *Teacher Resources DVD-ROM.*

Let's Practice It!
TR DVD•321

Objectives

- Apply revising strategy of clarifying
- Include supporting sentences with facts, details, and explanations.

Writing — Mystery
Revising Strategy

MINI-LESSON

Revising Strategy: Clarifying

Writing Transparency 27B, TR DVD

■ Yesterday we wrote a draft of a mystery. Today we will revise our drafts. The goal is to make your writing clearer, more interesting, and more informative.

■ Display Writing Transparency 27B. Remind students that revising does not include corrections of grammar and mechanics. Tell them that this will be done as they proofread their work. Then introduce the revising strategy of clarifying.

■ When we revise, we ask ourselves, *Are my ideas and focus clear? Will readers understand the clues and examples I present in my mystery?* The revising strategy of clarifying is the process by which ideas are made clearer in order to construct a logical solution to our mystery. I am going to revise my draft by clarifying certain details and adding additional information. **Add in details to clarify the clues presented to the reader. For instance, add in the detail concerning the father's story of a ghost. Also, clarify the fact that Heather closed the door to keep the cat out.**

Tell students that as they revise, not only should they clarify the clues they present, but they should also make sure they use sensory words to create a specific mood and build suspense in their stories.

Revising Tips

✔ Is your problem stated early and is it clear and focused?

✔ Are your characters distinct and individual? Does each character contribute to or further the plot?

✔ Make sure you add information or clues to clarify the mystery.

✔ Make sure your ending is a logical and reasonable solution to the problem you presented in your opening.

Peer conferencing

Peer Revision Students should write three questions about the partner's writing. Questions should focus on where their partner could add information to make the writing more informative. Refer to *First Stop* for more information about peer conferencing. Have students revise their mysteries using the questions their partner wrote during Peer Revision as well as the key features of a mystery to guide them.

Corrective feedback

Circulate around the room to monitor students as they revise. Remind students that they should be working on clues and plot today.

Write Guy
Jeff Anderson

The Sunny Side

I like to look for what's *right* in students' writing rather than focusing on things I can edit or fix. Most students don't write flawlessly—who does? However, they will learn what they are doing well if we point it out.

ROUTINE **Quick Write for Fluency** **Team Talk**

1. **Talk** Pairs discuss what they read about human effects on nature in *The Mystery of Saint Matthew Island*.

2. **Write** Each student writes a brief introductory paragraph about one of those effects.

3. **Share** Partners check each other's paragraph for paragraph structure and correct use of conjunctions.

Routines Flip Chart

English Language Learners
Preteach revising For students who need help with clarifying information, have them brainstorm ideas about unexpected events that may lead to a mystery *(I got a coat when we moved, but it disappeared; I got a towel for the beach, but it disappeared.)* Tell them that this will help bring more focus to their ideas. Have students list ideas aloud while you write them on the board in an Event-Mystery table.

Wrap Up Your Day

✔ **Build Concepts** What did you learn about how humans affected Pale Male's home?

✔ **Oral Vocabulary** Monitor students' use of oral vocabulary as they respond: What are some unexpected effects humans can have on nature?

✔ **Text Features** How did the time line in "City Hawks" help you to understand the selection?

Preview DAY 5

Remind students to think about what we can learn from encounters with the unexpected.

Objectives
- Review the weekly concept.
- Review oral vocabulary.

Today at a Glance

Oral Vocabulary

Comprehension
◉ Main idea and details

Lesson Vocabulary
◉ Endings -s, -es

Word Analysis
Russian word origins

Literary Terms
Word choice

Assessment
Fluency
Comprehension

Research and Inquiry
Communicate

Spelling
Final syllable -ant, -ent, -ance, -ence

Conventions
Conjunctions

Writing
Mystery

Check Oral Vocabulary
SUCCESS PREDICTOR

Concept Wrap Up

Question of the Week
What unexpected effects can humans have on nature?

Review the concept

Have students look back at the reading selections to find examples that best demonstrate how humans sometimes affect Earth's natural balance.

Review Amazing Words

Display and review this week's concept map. Remind students that this week they have learned ten Amazing Words related to the natural world. Have students use the Amazing Words and the concept map to answer the question *What unexpected effects can humans have on nature?*

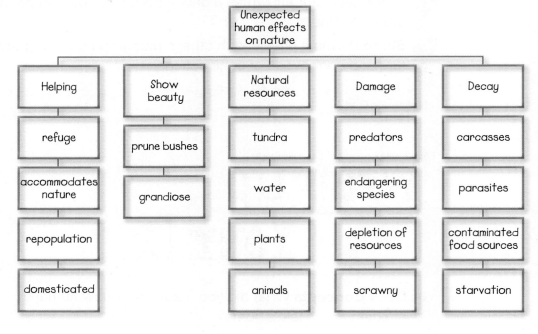

Concept map:
- **Unexpected human effects on nature**
  - **Helping**: refuge, accommodates nature, repopulation, domesticated
  - **Show beauty**: prune bushes, grandiose
  - **Natural resources**: tundra, water, plants, animals
  - **Damage**: predators, endangering species, depletion of resources, scrawny
  - **Decay**: carcasses, parasites, contaminated food sources, starvation

ELL Check Concepts and Language Use the Day 5 instruction on ELL Poster 27 to monitor students' understanding of the lesson concept.

ELL Poster 27

Amazing Ideas

accommodates
refuge
domesticated
contaminated
grandiose
prune

depletion
composition
natural
  resources
aggravate

Connect to the Big Question

Have pairs of students discuss how the Question of the Week connects to the Big Question: *What can we learn from encounters with the unexpected?* Encourage students to identify points of agreement and disagreement. Tell students to use the concept map and what they have learned from this week's Anchored Talks and reading selections to form an Amazing Idea—a realization or "big idea" about The Unexpected. Then ask pairs to share their Amazing Ideas with the class.

Amazing Ideas might include these key concepts:

- You can't predict what will happen when you try to influence nature.

- People need to be careful not to deplete natural resources.

- Unexpected events teach us new ideas.

Write about it

Have students write a few sentences about their Amazing Idea, beginning with "This week I learned…."

 It's Friday

MONITOR PROGRESS | **Check Oral Vocabulary**

Have individuals use this week's Amazing Words to describe the unexpected effects humans can have on nature. Monitor students' abilities to use the Amazing Words and note which words you need to reteach.

If… students have difficulty using the Amazing Words,

then… reteach using the Oral Vocabulary Routine on pp. 345a, 348b, 356b, 364b, OV•2.

Day 1	Days 2–3	Day 4	Day 5
Check Oral Vocabulary	Check Retelling	Check Fluency	Check Oral Vocabulary

Success Predictor

 **E L L**

English Language Learners

Concept map Work with students to add new words to the concept map.

Oral Vocabulary Success Predictor

Objectives
◎ Review main idea and details.
◎ Review endings *-s* and *-es*.
• Review Russian word origins.
• Review word choice.

Comprehension Review
🔄 Main Idea and Details

Teach main idea and details

Review the definition of main idea and details on p. 346. Remind students that the main idea of a selection is the most important point or idea. The author includes details that support or develop the main idea. For additional support have students review p. EI•12 on main idea and details.

Envision It!

Student Edition p. EI•12

Guide practice

Have partners identify the main ideas on pages 356–357 of *The Mystery of Saint Matthew Island* and evaluate whether the details supports those ideas. Have student pairs find an example of an important point that is supported by details on a different page of *The Mystery of Saint Matthew Island.* Then have students write a brief summary of both the main ideas and details of their chosen page, making sure to maintain meaning and logical order in their summaries.

On their own

For additional practice with main ideas and details, use *Let's Practice It!* p. 322 on the *Teacher Resources DVD-ROM.*

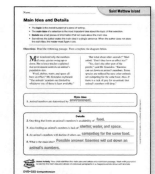
Let's Practice It!
TR DVD•322

Vocabulary Review
🔄 Endings -s, -es

Teach endings -s, -es

Remind students that the endings *-s* and *-es* are often used to form plurals. Nouns that end in *s, x, ch, zz,* or *ss* take *-es.* Nouns that end in *f* are made plural by changing the *f* to *ve* and adding *-s.*

Guide practice

Review with students how to form plurals by adding these endings. Point out that the spelling of some nouns changes when they become plural (*story-stories; berry-berries*).

On their own

Have students work with partners to write sentences using this week's lesson vocabulary words that end in *-s* and *-es.* Partners can trade sentences and identify whether the words are used correctly.

Word Analysis Review
Russian Word Origins

Teach Russian word origins

Review the definition of Russian word origins with students. Have students come up with words they know that have Russian origins.

Guide practice

Display the following words: *tundra* and *czar.* Use the strategy for Multisyllabic Words to teach the word *tundra.*

 ROUTINE **Strategy for Multisyllabic Words**

1. **Look for recognizable word parts** Have students either look for meaningful word parts, or try chunking the word.

2. **Connect to sound-spelling** Break the word into two syllables: *tundra.* Students will check a dictionary to determine the origin and meaning of the word *tundra.*

3. **Blend** Have the students blend the syllables together to read *tundra.*

Routines Flip Chart

On their own

Have students work in pairs to determine the meaning of each word and circle the syllables.

Literary Terms Review
Word Choice

Teach word choice

Have students reread "Cleanup by Mother Nature" on p 349 and monitor and adjust their comprehension. Remind students authors choose specific and vivid words to effectively help readers create sensory images to monitor and adjust their comprehension.

Guide practice

Find an example of effective word choice from "Cleanup by Mother Nature." Discuss the striking words and phrases the author uses in paragraph 2. Have students point out words and phrases they feel are especially vivid and create strong sensory images.

On their own

Have students make a list of effective words and phrases. Make sure that students explain how these descriptive words and strong verbs create sensory images that helped them monitor and adjust their comprehension of the text.

Lesson Vocabulary

bleached whitened by exposing to sunlight or chemicals

carcasses the bodies of dead animals

decay the process of rotting

parasites living things that live on or in other living things and feed off of them

scrawny having little flesh; skinny

starvation suffering from extreme hunger

suspicions beliefs; feelings; or thoughts

tundra a vast, treeless plain in arctic regions

 ELL

English Language Learners

Russian word origins If students have trouble pronouncing the words with Russian origins, have them work in pairs to break down the words into syllables. Check on students to make sure they are correctly pronouncing the vowel patterns *-oi* and *-ai.* Ask: Can you think of other words with these vowel patterns? What is the correct way to pronounce these words?

Word choice Give students examples of sentences that are not especially effective due to vague or general language: *There were not many deer. The deer had died.* Ask them: What could I add to these sentences to make them stronger and more precise?

Objectives
- Read grade-level text with fluency.

Assessment

Check words correct per minute

Fluency Make two copies of the fluency passage on p. 369k. As the student reads the text aloud, mark mistakes on your copy. Also mark where the student is at the end of one minute. To check the student's comprehension of the passage, have him or her retell you what was read. To figure words correct per minute (WCPM), subtract the number of mistakes from the total number of words read in one minute.

Corrective feedback

If... students cannot read fluently at a rate of 130–140 WCPM,
then... make sure they practice with text at their independent reading level. Provide additional fluency practice by pairing nonfluent readers with fluent readers.

If... students already read at 140 WCPM,
then... have them read a book of their choice independently.

Plan to Assess Fluency

☑ **Week 1** Assess Advanced students.

☑ **This week assess Strategic Intervention students.**

☐ **Week 3** Assess On-Level students.

☐ **Week 4** Assess Strategic Intervention students.

☐ **Week 5** Assess any students you have not yet checked during this unit.

Set individual goals for students to enable them to reach the year-end goal.

- Current Goal: 130–140 WCPM
- Year-End Goal: 140 WCPM

Small Group Time

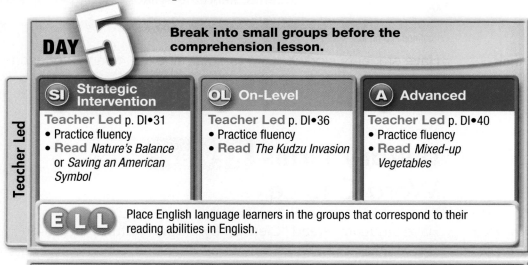

DAY 5 Break into small groups before the comprehension lesson.

Teacher Led

SI Strategic Intervention
Teacher Led p. DI•31
- Practice fluency
- **Read** *Nature's Balance* or *Saving an American Symbol*

OL On-Level
Teacher Led p. DI•36
- Practice fluency
- **Read** *The Kudzu Invasion*

A Advanced
Teacher Led p. DI•40
- Practice fluency
- **Read** *Mixed-up Vegetables*

ELL Place English language learners in the groups that correspond to their reading abilities in English.

Practice Stations
- Words to Know
- Get Fluent
- Read for Meaning

Independent Activities
- Grammar Jammer
- Concept Talk Video
- Vocabulary Acitivities

America's Eagle

Look at any American coin or dollar bill. Chances are you will see a   14

picture of the bald eagle. It has been on the Great Seal of the United States   30

since 1782. The bald eagle makes many people think of freedom.   41

But since the time it became an American symbol, the bald eagle started   54

to slowly disappear from the United States. By the late 1800s, towns and   67

cities had been built all the way across the country. This caused many of these   82

birds to lose their homes. In the 1900s, dangerous chemicals were used to kill   96

insects on farms. But animals as well as insects were affected. The chemicals   109

got into rivers and streams. Many eagles died from eating the fish from   122

these rivers and streams. Hunting was another reason the eagle was slowing   134

disappearing. By the 1970s, the bald eagle was almost gone forever.   145

Something had to be done to save our national bird. Laws were passed   158

that banned the use of certain chemicals. This kept many animals and their   171

homes much safer. Hunting the bald eagle is now against the law. People   184

set up special programs. They moved the few eagles that were left closer   197

together. This made it easier for the eagles to lay their eggs, keep their young   212

safe, and grow in number.   217

Efforts to save the bald eagle have paid off. The bird is no longer   231

endangered. But more work still needs to be done. Hopefully, one day there   244

will be as many bald eagles in America as there were when the country was   259

founded.   260

MONITOR PROGRESS   • Check Fluency

Assessment

Check main ideas and details

◉ **Main Idea and Details** Use "Thanks to Trees" on p. 369m to check students' understanding of main ideas and details.

1. If we cut down too many trees, what might happen to the animals that depend on trees for homes? **Possible response: The animals will have to find somewhere else to live.**

2. Summarize the main idea of the passage, maintaining meaning and logical order. **Possible response: We rely on trees for many things and can help plant more trees so that they are not in danger of disappearing.**

3. What things do we get from trees? **Possible response: food, shade, wooden objects, paper products**

4. What should we do to be sure that there will always be enough trees to meet our needs? **Possible response: We should replant more trees than we cut down.**

Corrective feedback

If... students are unable to answer the comprehension questions, **then...** use the Reteach lesson in the *First Stop* book.

Thanks to Trees

Think for a minute about all the things in your everyday life that come from trees. They provide shade on a hot, sunny day and supply us with fruits, nuts, and berries to eat. But trees give us even more than that.

We can thank trees for all of the wooden chairs, tables, homes, baseball bats, and other wooden items we see around us. We can thank trees for all of the paper we use for reading and writing. We even have handy products such as napkins and paper towels because of trees. Trees are one of the most useful natural resources in our modern world.

Cutting down trees for products is a big business. In fact, Americans alone use more paper each year than a forest can provide. It takes ten to twenty years for a tree to grow big enough to be harvested and used to make paper. During that time, the tree provides food and a home to many animals. When it is cut down, the ecosystem changes and the animals must find someplace else to live.

Fortunately, trees are a renewable resource, but it does take time for them to grow and be usable. There's a simple solution that keeps us from running out of forests. Plant more trees! Most companies in the United States that clear areas of the forests plant more trees than they cut down each year. While some areas are growing, others are being harvested for use. The forest can work in cycles for generations to come.

So, plant more trees! Not only do they help us meet our needs, they're also beautiful to look at. And the animals will thank you for it, too.

MONITOR PROGRESS

• **Main Idea and Details**

Objectives
- Communicate inquiry results.
- Take a spelling test.
- Review conjunctions.

Research and Inquiry
Communicate

Present ideas Have students display and explain the time lines they created on Day 4. Then have the class use their time lines and research findings to debate how much humans should be allowed to interfere with nature.

Listening and speaking Remind students how to be good speakers and how to communicate effectively with their audience.

- Explain the factual and quantitative information on the time line for the class.
- Speak loudly and with an appropriate rate.
- Keep eye contact with audience members.
- Enunciate clearly and use natural hand gestures as appropriate.
- Think before you speak in a debate. Make sure you have thought your point through before raising your hand to say it.

Remind students about these tips for how to be a good listener.

- Listen carefully and interpret the speaker's verbal and nonverbal messages.
- Use questions to clarify the speaker's purpose or perspective, not just to challenge arguments.
- Elicit suggestions from other students and consider those suggestions.
- Look for areas of agreement as well as disagreement when engaged in debate.
- Be polite, even if you disagree.

Spelling Test

Suffixes -ant, -ent, -ance, -ence

Spelling test To administer the spelling test, refer to the directions, words, and sentences on p. 347c.

Conventions

Extra Practice

Teach Remind students that conjunctions are words that join other words, phrases, or sentences.

- Coordinating conjunctions such as *and, but,* and *or* make compound subjects, compound predicates, and compound sentences.

- Subordinating conjunctions, such as *because, if, when, before, after, then* and *although,* are used to make complex sentences.

Guide practice Have students work with a partner to list their favorite color, food, story, or sport. Pairs then contrast their favorites with complete sentences using both their names and their favorites.

Daily Fix-It Use Daily Fix-It numbers 9 and 10 in the right margin.

---

1. _____ twenty-nine reindeer were released on St. Matthew Island in 1944, the future of the herd seemed bright. (When)

2. No wolves, bears, _____ other large predators lived on the island. (or)

3. No predators lived on the island, _____ people rarely visited it. (and)

On their own Write these sentences. Have students fill in the blanks with an appropriate conjunction. Students should complete *Let's Practice It!* p. 323 on the *Teacher Resources DVD-ROM.*

Daily Fix-It

9. These here birds fluff out they feathers to trap warm air. *(These birds; their)*

10. A bird must fead constantly to keep up its bodie heat. *(feed; body)*

Let's Practice It!
TR DVD•323

Objectives
- Edit for correct use of conjunctions.
- Create and present a final draft.

Writing—Mystery
Writer's Craft: Conjunctions

Review revising

Remind students that yesterday they revised their writing, paying particular attention to clarifying to make ideas and the relationships between ideas clear. Today students will proofread their mysteries.

MINI-LESSON

Proofread for Conjunctions

■ **Teach** When we proofread, we look closely at our work to find errors in mechanics such as spelling, capitalization, punctuation, and grammar.

■ **Model** Display Writing Transparency 27C. In the second paragraph, the conjunction "or" is used to end a list. That doesn't make sense. It should be "and." **Make the appropriate change on the transparency.** The sentence beginning with "She was tired" is clear but it sounds choppy. Let's insert the subordinating conjunction, *Although,* delete "and," and insert a comma. The sentence now reads "Although she was tired, she felt uneasy."

Now, let's check spelling. I see the word "Chemical" is misspelled. I will reread the passage looking for errors in punctuation, capitalization, and grammar.

Writing Transparency 27C, TR DVD

Proofread

Display the Proofreading Tips. Ask students to proofread their compositions, using the Proofreading Tips and paying particular attention to the correct use of conjunctions. Circulate around the room answering students' questions. When students have finished editing their own work, have pairs proofread one another's mysteries.

Proofreading Tips

✔ Be sure you have used conjunctions correctly.

✔ Look for one type of error at a time, such as spelling, then punctuation, then grammar.

✔ Make sure dialogue includes correct use of quotation marks and spacing.

Present

Have students incorporate revisions and proofreading edits into their compositions to create a final draft.

Give students two options for presenting: an oral-reading to the class or a picture book. Have students vote on which option they prefer. For the oral presentation, create a mysterious mood in the room. Allow students to bring in music or props that will enhance the mysterious tone of the presentations. For the picture book, have students hand- or computer-illustrate several scenes selected from the story. Students should bind their books and place them on display. When students have finished, have each complete a Writing Self-Evaluation Guide.

ROUTINE — Quick Write for Fluency — Team Talk

1. **Talk** Pairs discuss what they learned about writing mysteries.
2. **Write** Each student writes a paragraph about some aspect of their discussion.
3. **Share** Partners read one another's paragraphs.

Routines Flip Chart

Teacher Note
Writing Self-Evaluation Guide
Make copies of the Writing Self-Evaluation Guide on p. 39 of the *Reader's and Writer's Notebook* and hand out to students.

ELL

English Language Learners
Poster preview Prepare students for next week by using Week 3, ELL Poster 27. Read the Poster Talk-Through to introduce the concept and vocabulary. Ask students to identify and describe objects and actions in the art.

Selection summary Send home the summary of *King Midas and the Golden Touch* in English and the students' home languages, if available. Students can read the summary with family members.

Preview NEXT WEEK

How can we learn from the unexpected results of our actions? Tell students that next week they will read about a king who makes a wish that has unexpected results.

Weekly Assessment

Use pp. 193–200 of *Weekly Tests* to check:

✔ **Word Analysis** Russian Word Origin

✔ 🔘 **Comprehension Skill** Main Idea and Details

✔ Review **Comprehension Skill**
Sequence

✔ **Lesson Vocabulary**

bleached	scrawny
carcasses	starvation
decay	suspicions
parasites	tundra

Weekly Tests

Advanced

On-Level

Strategic Intervention

Differentiated Assessment

Use pp. 157–162 of *Fresh Reads for Fluency and Comprehension* to check:

✔ 🔘 **Comprehension Skill** Main Idea and Details

✔ Review **Comprehension Skill** Sequence

✔ **Fluency** Words Correct Per Minute

Fresh Reads for Fluency and Comprehension

Managing Assessment

Use *Assessment Handbook* for:

✔ **Weekly Assessment Blackline Masters for Monitoring Progress**

✔ **Observation Checklists**

✔ **Record-Keeping Forms**

✔ **Portfolio Assessment**

Assessment Handbook

All the King's Animals

Continued from p. 345b

to the next. It had taken thirty years, but the wilde-beest herds had finally recovered from the Cattle Plague.

5-Day Plan

DAY 1
- Reinforce the concept
- Read Leveled Readers Concept Literacy Below Level

DAY 2
- Main Idea and Details
- Text Structure
- Revisit Student Edition pp. 350–355

DAY 3
- Endings -s, -es
- Revisit Student Edition pp. 356–359

DAY 4
- Practice Retelling
- Read/Revisit Student Edition pp. 364–367

DAY 5
- Reread for fluency
- Reread Leveled Readers

3- or 4-Day Plan

DAY 1
- Reinforce the concept
- Read Leveled Readers

DAY 2
- Main Idea and Details
- Text Structure
- Revisit Student Edition pp. 350–355

DAY 3
- Endings -s, -es
- Revisit Student Edition pp. 356–359

DAY 4
- Practice Retelling
- Read/Revisit Student Edition pp. 364–367
- Reread for fluency
- Reread Leveled Readers

Day Plan: Eliminate the shaded box.

SI *Strategic Intervention* **DAY 1**

Build Background

- **Reinforce the Concept** Connect the weekly question *What unexpected effects can humans have on nature?* Ask students what they know about how human activity has affected animals in their area. For example, as cities expand, they destroy more wild habitats, forcing wild animals, such as raccoons, skunks, hawks, and crows, to live in cities. Humans are always changing the world around them. We can have positive or negative effects on nature, depending on what we do. Discuss the words on the concept map on p. 344–345 in the Teacher Edition.

- **Connect to Reading** This week you will read about the unexpected ways that humans affect nature. For instance, people can learn how to conserve and protect wildlife and the environment. On the other hand, when people bring their native animals with them into another country, the results can be disastrous. In "All the King's Animals," what happened to the animals in Swaziland when Europeans arrived? *(The European animals carried a disease that nearly killed all the impala, antelope, hartebeest, and wildebeest herds.)*

Objectives
- Interpret a speaker's messages (both verbal and nonverbal).

 SI Strategic Intervention

DAY 1

For a complete literacy instructional plan and additional practice with this week's target skills and strategies, see the **Leveled Reader Teaching Guide.**

Concept Literacy Reader

- **Read** *Nature's Balance*

- **Before Reading** Preview the selection with students, focusing on key concepts and vocabulary. Then have them set a purpose for reading.

- **During Reading** Read the first two pages of the selection aloud while students track the print. Then have students finish reading the selection with a partner.

Nature's Balance

- **After Reading** After students finish reading the selection, connect it to the weekly question *What unexpected effects can humans have on nature?*

Below-Level Reader

- **Read** *Saving an American Symbol*

- **Before Reading** Have students preview the selection, using the illustrations. Then have students set a purpose for reading.

- **During Reading** Do a choral reading of pp. 5–9, pausing along the way to discuss graphic sources. If students are able, have them read and discuss the remainder of the book with a partner. Have partners discuss the following questions:

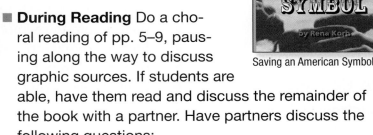
Saving an American Symbol

- What was one of the main causes of the decline in the buffalo population? *(People hunted and killed them by the millions.)*

- What changes helped bring the buffalo population back? *(Conservationists set aside protected land and helped get new laws passed.)*

- **After Reading** Have students look at and discuss the concept map. Connect the Below-Level Reader to the weekly question *What unexpected effects can humans have on nature?*

MONITOR PROGRESS

If... students have difficulty reading the selection with a partner,
then... have them follow along as they listen to the Leveled Readers DVD-ROM.

If... students have trouble understanding humans' effect on the buffalo population,
then... reread pp. 6–7 and discuss the graphics together.

Objectives
- Interpret a speaker's messages (both verbal and nonverbal).

Student Edition, p. El•12

More Reading

Use additional Leveled Readers or other texts at students' instructional levels to reinforce this week's skills and strategies. For text suggestions, see the Leveled Reader Database or the Leveled Readers Skills Chart on pp. CL 24–CL 29.

SI Strategic Intervention

DAY 2

Reinforce Comprehension

Skill Main Idea and Details Review with students *Envision It!* p. El•12 on Main Idea and Details. Then use p. 346 to review the definitions. The main ideas in a selection are the most important facts or conclusions about a topic. The author uses details to tell more about each main idea.

Strategy Text Structure Review the definition of text structure. Explain that authors need to organize information in a way that it makes it clear and easy for readers to follow. For example, descriptions of places are often in spatial order while those of events are put in chronological, or time, order. For additional support, refer students to *Envision It!* p. El•24.

Revisit *The Mystery of Saint Matthew Island* on pp. 350–355. As students read, have them apply the comprehension skill and strategy to the selection.

- How are the main events in the text organized? *(in chronological, or time, order)*

- When Dr. Klein arrived on the island to investigate, what important facts did he find? *(The reports were true: few reindeer survived, and the ones that did could not have calves.)*

- What details support the main idea that animal predators and human hunters did not cause the reindeer die-off? *(No predators lived on the island, and people rarely visited it.)*

- What main idea do the reindeer bones and body weights support? *(The reindeer starved to death.)*

Use the During Reading Differentiated Instruction for additional support for struggling readers.

MONITOR PROGRESS

If... students have difficulty reading along with the group,
then... have them follow along as they listen to the AudioText.

Objectives
- Summarize main ideas in a text in ways that maintain meaning.
- Analyze how the organizational pattern of a text influences the relationships among the ideas.

 SI Strategic Intervention

DAY 3

Reinforce Vocabulary

Endings -s, -es/Word Structure Write the following sentence on the board: "Klein packed a few boxes and took two jackets on his trip." Circle the words *boxes* and *jackets*. *I know the base words are* box *and* jacket. *The words "a few" and "took two" tell me that there is more than one box and more than one jacket. How do the endings* -es *and* -s *change the meaning of* box *and* jacket? *(They change the meaning from singular to plural:* box *to* boxes *and* jacket *to* jackets.)

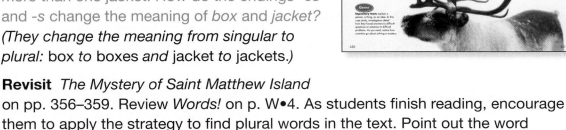

Revisit *The Mystery of Saint Matthew Island* on pp. 356–359. Review *Words!* on p. W•4. As students finish reading, encourage them to apply the strategy to find plural words in the text. Point out the word *carcasses* on p. 354 and read it aloud slowly, emphasizing the final syllable.

- The base word *carcass* means "a dead animal body." What ending tells you the word is plural? *(-es)*

- How does the ending change the meaning of the word? *(It changes it from meaning one dead animal body to meaning several dead animal bodies.)*

- Explain that some words look as if they have an *-es* ending when they really have only an *-s* ending.

Then write the following words on the board: *uses, skeletons, diseases, foxes.* Ask students to identify the base word and the ending for each word. *(uses = use + -s; skeletons = skeleton + -s; diseases = disease + -s; foxes = fox + -es)*

Use the During Reading Differentiated Instruction for additional support for struggling readers.

MONITOR PROGRESS

If... students need more practice with the lesson vocabulary,
then... use *Envision It! Pictured Vocabulary Cards.*

Student Edition, p. W•4

More Reading

Use additional Leveled Readers or other texts at students' instructional levels to reinforce this week's skills and strategies. For text suggestions, see the Leveled Reader Database or the Leveled Readers Skills Chart on pp. CL 24–CL 29.

 **Objectives**
- Recognize an ending on a base word.

Small Group Time

SI *Strategic Intervention*

DAY 4

Practice Retelling

- **Retell** Have students work in pairs and use the Retelling Cards to retell *The Mystery of Saint Matthew Island*. Monitor retelling and prompt students as needed.

  - Tell me what this selection is about in a few sentences.

  - Why do you think the author wrote this selection?

  If students struggle, model a fluent retelling.

Genre Focus

- **Before Reading or Revisiting** "City Hawks" on pp. 364–367, read aloud the genre information about expository text on p. 364. Explain to students that expository text contains facts and information about different subjects. Then have students preview "City Hawks."

  - What pictures and text features do you see? *(photos of hawks and people, captions, and a time line)*

  Have students set a purpose for reading based on their preview.

- **During Reading or Revisiting** Have students read along with you while tracking the print or do a choral reading of the expository text. Stop to discuss any unfamiliar words or phrases, such as *migrating* and *habitat*.

- **After Reading or Revisiting** Have students share their reactions to the expository text. Then guide them through the Reading Across Texts and Writing Across Texts activities.

MONITOR PROGRESS

If... students have difficulty retelling the selection,

then... have them review the selection using the photos, illustrations, and text features.

Objectives
- Synthesize ideas across two or three texts representing similar or different genres.

For a complete literacy instructional plan and additional practice with this week's target skills and strategies, see the **Leveled Reader Teaching Guide.**

Concept Literacy Reader

■ **Model** Model the fluency skill of appropriate phrasing and punctuation cues for students. Ask students to listen carefully as you read aloud the first two pages of *Nature's Balance.* Point out how your inflection matches the question mark on the first page, how you pause at the comma on the second page, and how you group words throughout.

Nature's Balance

■ **Fluency Routine**

1. Have students reread passages from *Nature's Balance* with a partner.

2. For optimal fluency, students should reread three to four times.

3. As students read, monitor fluency and provide corrective feedback. Encourage students to use punctuation cues to help achieve appropriate phrasing.

See *Routines Flip Chart* for more help with fluency.

■ **Retell** Have students retell *Nature's Balance.* Prompt as necessary.

Below-Level Reader

■ **Model** Ask students to listen carefully as you read aloud pp. 3–4 of *Saving an American Symbol,* emphasizing appropriate phrasing.

Saving an American Symbol

■ **Fluency Routine**

1. Have students reread passages from *Saving an American Symbol* with a partner or individually.

2. For optimal fluency, students should reread three to four times.

3. As students read, monitor fluency and provide corrective feedback. Point out that reading using punctuation cues can help them better group their words, emphasize the main ideas, and avoid skipping important details.

See *Routines Flip Chart* for more help with fluency.

■ **Retell** For additional practice, have students retell *Saving an American Symbol* page-by-page, using the illustrations. Prompt as necessary.

• What happens in this part?
• What are the problems in the book?

MONITOR PROGRESS

If... students have difficulty reading fluently,

then... provide additional fluency practice by pairing nonfluent readers with fluent ones.

Objectives
• Read aloud grade-level stories with fluency.

Small Group Time

5-Day Plan

DAY 1	• Expand the concept • Read On-Level Reader
DAY 2	• ◎ Main Idea and Details • ◎ Text Structure • Revisit Student Edition pp. 350–355
DAY 3	• ◎ Endings *-s, -es* • Revisit Student Edition pp. 356–359
DAY 4	• Practice Retelling • Read/Revisit Student Edition pp. 364–367
DAY 5	• Reread for fluency • Reread On-Level Reader

3- or 4-Day Plan

DAY 1	• Expand the concept • On-Level Reader
DAY 2	• ◎ Main Idea and Details • ◎ Text Structure • Revisit Student Edition pp. 350–355
DAY 3	• ◎ Endings *-s, -es* • Revisit Student Edition pp. 356–359
DAY 4	• Practice Retelling • Read/Revisit Student Edition pp. 364–367 • Reread for fluency • Reread On-Level Reader

3-Day Plan: Eliminate the shaded box.

OL On-Level

DAY 1

Build Background

■ **Expand the Concept** Connect the weekly question *What unexpected effects can humans have on nature?* and expand the concept. Often, the effects that humans have on nature do not appear to be harmful at first. In fact, some actions may appear to be helpful. That is what makes some negative effects all the more unexpected. Discuss the meaning of the words on the concept map on p. 344–345 in the Teacher Edition.

On-Level Reader

For a complete literacy instructional plan and additional practice with this week's target skills and strategies, see the **Leveled Reader Teaching Guide.**

■ **Before Reading** *The Kudzu Invasion,* have students preview the reader by looking at the title, cover, and pictures in the book.

The Kudzu Invasion

• What is the topic of this book? *(a plant that took over the countryside)*

• Which photos show situations that look potentially harmful or even dangerous? *(the plant growing on electric wires; people spraying the plant)*

Have students create T-charts with the labels *Kudzu: Pros* and *Kudzu: Cons.* This book tells the history of kudzu in this country and the advantages and disadvantages of planting it. As you read, look for facts about the pros and cons of kudzu, and record the facts in your T-chart.

■ **During Reading** Read aloud pp. 3–6 as students follow along. Then have them finish reading the book on their own. Remind students to add information to their T-charts as they read.

■ **After Reading** Have partners compare the facts on their T-charts.

• Which pros and cons of kudzu surprised you the most, based on your preview of the book?

• How does the topic relate to the weekly question *What unexpected effects can humans have on nature?*

Objectives
• Interpret a speaker's messages (both verbal and nonverbal).

 On-Level

DAY **2**

Expand Comprehension

Student Edition p. EI•12

Skill Main Idea and Details Use p. 346 to review the definitions of main idea and details. For additional review, see p. EI•12 in *Envision It!* Sometimes you will have to figure out the main idea based on the details that the author gives you.

Strategy Text Structure Review the definition of text structure, and encourage students to note the text structure, or the order in which information is presented when reading. For additional support, use the Extend Thinking questions and refer students to *Envision It!* p. EI•24.

Revisit *The Mystery of Saint Matthew Island* on pp. 350–355. Then have students begin reading the selection aloud. As they read, have them apply the comprehension skill and strategy to the story.

- What main idea about the effects of humans on nature is implied by the first paragraph? *(possible answer: Human actions had a beneficial effect on the reindeer.)*

- What details support this main idea? *(People had chosen an island with plenty of food and no predators; the herd grew from 29 to 6,000 in only 19 years.)*

- What is the main idea of the second paragraph? *(Something went terribly wrong.)*

- What details support this main idea? *(Sailors who visited St. Matthew found the island littered with reindeer skeletons. They saw only a few live reindeer.)*

More Reading

Use additional Leveled Readers or other texts at students' instructional levels to reinforce this week's skills and strategies. For text suggestions, see the Leveled Reader Database or the Leveled Readers Skills Chart on pp. CL 24–CL 29.

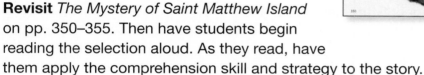

Objectives
- Summarize main ideas in a text in ways that maintain meaning.
- Analyze how the organizational pattern of a text influences the relationships among the ideas.

Student Edition, p. W•4

More Reading

Use additional Leveled Readers or other texts at students' instructional levels to reinforce this week's skills and strategies. For text suggestions, see the Leveled Reader Database or the Leveled Readers Skills Chart on pp. CL 24–CL 29.

DAY 3

Expand Vocabulary

Endings -s, -es/Word Structure Write these selection vocabulary words on the board as you say them aloud: *carcasses, parasites, suspicions.* Ask:

• Are these words singular or plural? *(plural)*

• What is the base word and ending of *suspicions? (suspicion + -s)*

• Which word has an *-es* ending, *carcasses, parasites,* or both? *(carcasses)* How do you know? *(Parasite ends in e and needs only -s to make it plural.)*

Then have students identify the base word and ending of each of the following plurals:

predators *(predator + -s)*
mosses *(moss + -es)*
skeletons *(skeleton + -s)*
females *(female + -s)*
investigators *(investigator + -s)*
boxes *(box + -es)*
bones *(bone + -s)*
suspects *(suspect + -s)*

• Based on this list of words, when do you use the *-es* ending to make a word plural? *(It is used only with words that end in x or double s.)*

Revisit *The Mystery of Saint Matthew Island* on pp. 356–359. As they finish reading the selection, remind students to use the strategy to help them identify plurals.

Then have students recall in the selection is about. Encourage them to think critically.

• How might reindeer be successfully reintroduced on Saint Matthew Island? *(Their numbers would have to be controlled through predators or hunting.)*

• How might the lesson of the Saint Matthew reindeer herd be applied to other environmental situations? *(Populations and resources have to be kept in balance.)*

Objectives
• Recognize an ending on a base word.

DAY 4

Practice Retelling

■ **Retell** To assess students' comprehension, use the Retelling Cards. Monitor retelling and prompt students as needed.

Grade 5
Retelling Cards
PEARSON

Genre Focus

■ **Before Reading or Revisiting** "City Hawks" on pp. 364–367, read aloud the information about expository text on p. 364. Have students preview the selection and set a purpose for reading.

• What text features does the expository text include? *(photos, captions, and a time line)*

• Look at the photos and read the captions. What do you think this article is about? *(Based upon the information about the nests and the signs of the protestors, it seems that a hawk named Pale Male has somehow been left without a home.)*

■ **During Reading or Revisiting** Have students read along with you while tracking the print.

• What background information does the text provide? *(It tells about the migration of red-tailed hawks and why the Central Park area would make a good home for them.)*

• What facts about the removal of the nest, the protest against it, and the eventual resolution does the author present? *(facts about how and why the engineer removed the nest, whom the protestors contacted, and how the Audubon Society stepped in to offer a solution)*

■ **After Reading or Revisiting** Have students share their reaction to the expository text. Then have them write a paragraph that tells about their community's wild animals or speculates about animals that could possibly make homes there.

Small Group Time

On-Level Reader

The Kudzu Invasion

■ **Model** Model the fluency skill of appropriate phrasing and punctuation cues for students. Read aloud p. 3 of the On-Level Reader *The Kudzu Invasion,* emphasizing how you group words for clarity and sense.

■ **Fluency Routine**

1. Have students reread passages from *The Kudzu Invasion* with a partner.

2. For optimal fluency, students should reread passages three to four times.

3. As students read, monitor fluency and provide corrective feedback. Encourage students to group words by using punctuation cues, such as commas, periods, question marks, and other punctuation. Discuss how using punctuation clues while reading leads to appropriate phrasing. Grouping your words makes the reading sound more like natural speech and can help you and your listeners better understand the ideas in the text.

See *Routines Flip Chart* for more help with fluency.

■ **Retell** For additional practice, have students use headings and photographs as a guide to retell *The Kudzu Invasion.* Prompt as necessary.

• What is this selection mostly about?

• What did you learn from reading it?

Objectives
• Read aloud grade-level stories with fluency.

Build Background

- **Expand the Concept** Discuss the weekly question *What unexpected effects can humans have on nature?* What effects can you think of that modern science has had on plants and animals? *(possible answers: genetic engineering of plants; cloning animals)*

Advanced Reader

For a complete literacy instructional plan and additional practice with this week's target skills and strategies, see the **Leveled Reader Teaching Guide.**

- **Before Reading** *Mixed-Up Vegetables,* tell students to recall the Read Aloud "All the King's Animals." What effects did Europeans have on the animal population of Swaziland? *(They hunted for sport and brought diseases that nearly wiped out some species.)* Today you will read about the positive and negative effects of genetically altering vegetables. Have students look at the book's illustrations and use them to predict what will happen. Then have students set a purpose for reading.

Mixed-Up Vegetables

- **During Reading** Have students read the Advanced Reader independently. Encourage them to think critically and solve problems as they read. Ask:

- What might be some additional unexpected effects on other species as a result of the techniques mentioned in the book?

- What is your opinion of the arguments under *Pro or Con?* at the end of the book? Explain your answer.

- **After Reading** Have students review the concept map and explain how *Mixed-Up Vegetables* helps students answer the weekly question *What unexpected effects can humans have on nature?* Prompt as necessary.

- What do you think might be some other unexpected positive or negative effects of transgenic crops in the future?

- What do the unexpected effects that humans have on nature reveal about the relationship between humans and nature?

- **Now Try This** Assign "Now Try This" at the end of the Advanced Reader.

Objectives
- Interpret a speaker's messages (both verbal and nonverbal).

15–20 mins.

Pacing Small Group Instruction

5-Day Plan

DAY 1	• Extend the concept • Read Advanced Reader
DAY 2	• ◉ Main Idea and Details • ◉ Text Structure • Revisit Student Edition pp. 350–355
DAY 3	• ◉ Endings *-s, -es* • Revisit Student Edition pp. 356–359
DAY 4	• Expository Text • Read/Revisit Student Edition pp. 364–367
DAY 5	• Reread for fluency • Reread Advanced Reader

3- or 4-Day Plan

DAY 1	• Extend the concept • Advanced Reader
DAY 2	• ◉ Main Idea and Details • ◉ Text Structure • Revisit Student Edition pp. 350–355
DAY 3	• ◉ Endings *-s, -es* • Revisit Student Edition pp. 356–359
DAY 4	• Expository Text • Read/Revisit Student Edition pp. 364–367 • Reread for fluency • Reread Advanced Reader

3-Day Plan: Eliminate the shaded box.

A Advanced

DAY 2

More Reading

Use additional Leveled Readers or other texts at students' instructional levels to reinforce this week's skills and strategies. For text suggestions, see the Leveled Reader Database or the Leveled Readers Skills Chart on pp. CL 24–CL 29.

Extend Comprehension

Skill Main Idea and Details Review the definitions of main idea and details. Explain that details can help readers determine the main idea when it is implied. Recall the book *Mixed-Up Vegetables.* The author provides details in support of two main ideas. What are those ideas? *(Transgenic vegetables offer advantages for people. Transgenic vegetables also pose disadvantages and potential dangers for people.)*

Strategy Text Structure Review the definition of the strategy. Remind students to identify the order in which ideas and events are presented as they read the rest of *The Mystery of Saint Matthew Island.* During reading, use the Extend Thinking questions and the During Reading Differentiated Instruction for additional support.

Revisit *The Mystery of Saint Matthew Island* on pp. 350–355. As students begin reading, remind them to apply the comprehension skill and strategy.

• The author mentions details about the lack of predators, how remote the island is, and how hunters don't use the island. What main idea about the reindeer deaths can you imply from these details? *(Possible answer: There were no obvious causes to account for so many deaths in such a short time.)*

• What details allowed Dr. Klein to rule out disease or parasites in the death of the reindeer on Saint Matthew Island? *(He had seen few signs of disease or parasites on earlier visits and the island was too remote for an infected animal to have reached it.)*

Critical Thinking Encourage students to think critically as they read *The Mystery of Saint Matthew Island.*

• What factors might have been overlooked by the scientists who introduced the reindeer?

• What other causes can you think of that might account for the reindeer deaths?

Objectives

• Summarize main ideas in a text in ways that maintain meaning.
• Analyze how the organizational pattern of a text influences the relationships among the ideas.

 A *Advanced* **DAY 3**

Extend Vocabulary

◉ **Endings -s, -es/Word Structure** Write the following sentence from *Mixed-Up Vegetables*: "Many farmers use pesticides to kill insects." How do you know whether the word *pesticides* is singular or plural? *(The base word is* pesticide, *"a chemical that kills insects and other pests." The ending* -s *makes the word plural, meaning "more than one chemical that kills insects and other pests.")*

Write the following words on the board. Have students add *-es* or *-s* to make the words plural.

promise *(promise + -s = promises)*
carcass *(carcass + -es = carcasses)*
shore *(shore + -s = shores)*
tundra *(tundra + -s = tundras)*
box *(box + -es = boxes)*
disaster *(disaster + -s = disasters)*

- Based on these words, what general rule can you infer about when to use the *-es* or *-s* ending to make words plural? *(Most words, including those that end in* e, *take the* -s *ending to become plural. Words that end in* x *or double* s *take the* -es *ending.)*

■ **Revisit** *The Mystery of Saint Matthew Island* on pp. 356–359. As students finish reading the selection, remind them to use the strategy.

■ **Critical Thinking** Then have students recall what happened in the selection. Encourage them to think critically.

- What lesson does the event teach us about introducing animals into an environment? *(We must look at a broader, more long-term picture that balances resources, population, and impact on other species in the environment.)*

- If scientists wanted to reintroduce reindeer to the island, what would you advise them to do? *(Possible answer: Keep population numbers in check by including a predator such as bears or wolves or by removing some reindeer occasionally to reduce the population.)*

Objectives
- Recognize an ending on a base word.

More Reading
Use additional Leveled Readers or other texts at students' instructional levels to reinforce this week's skills and strategies. For text suggestions, see the Leveled Reader Database or the Leveled Readers Skills Chart on pp. CL 24–CL 29.

Small Group Time

Genre Focus

"City Hawks"

■ **Before Reading or Revisiting** "City Hawks" on pp. 364–367, read the sidebar information on expository text on p. 364. Ask students to use the text features to preview the selection and then set a purpose for reading on their own.

■ **During Reading or Revisiting** Have students read independently. Encourage students to notice how the author presents information objectively. Make a T-chart on the board and label one column *Effects of People on Hawks* and the other *Effects of Hawks on People.* List both positive and negative effects in both columns. Point out that expository text often tries to provide all the relevant facts so that readers can make up their own minds about a topic. Ask: Which group of effects do you think is more important to address? Explain.

■ **After Reading or Revisiting** Have students discuss Reading Across Texts. Then have them do Writing Across Texts independently.

Objectives
• Synthesize ideas across two or three texts representing similar or different genres.

■ **Reread For Fluency** Have students silently reread passages from *Mixed-Up Vegetables.* Then have them reread aloud with a partner or individually. As students read, monitor fluency and provide corrective feedback. If students read fluently on the first reading, they do not need to reread three to four times. Assess the fluency of students in this group using p. 369j.

■ **Retell** Have students summarize the main idea and important supporting details from the Advanced Reader *Mixed-Up Vegetables.*

■ **Now Try This** Have students complete their projects. You may wish to review their work before they share the finished projects with classmates.

Mixed-Up Vegetables

Objectives
• Read aloud grade-level stories with fluency.

 English Language Learners

The ELL lessons are organized by strands. Use them to scaffold the weekly curriculum of lessons or during small group time instruction.

Academic Language

Students will hear or read the following academic language in this week's core instruction. As students encounter the vocabulary, provide a simple definition or concrete example. Then ask students to suggest an example or synonym of the word and identify available cognates.

Skill Words	main idea (idea)	paraphrase
	supporting	(parafrasear)
	detail (detalle)	conjunction
	cause (causa)	(conjunción)
	effect (efecto)	
Concept Words	balance	humans
	nature (naturaleza)	(humanos)
		upset

*Spanish cognates in parentheses

Concept Development

What unexpected effects can humans have on nature?

■ **Preteach Concept**

- **Prior Knowledge** Have students turn to pp. 344–345 in the Student Edition. Look at the picture of Mt. Rushmore. Tap into students' experiences with places where humans have altered nature. Who's faces are those? How they get on that mountain?

- **Discuss Concept** Elicit students' knowledge and experience of unexpected effects humans can have on nature. Sometimes people affect nature in good ways and sometimes in bad ways. Can you name both?

- **Poster Talk-Through** Read aloud the Poster Talk-Through on ELL Poster 27 and work through the Day 1 activities.

■ **Daily Concept and Vocabulary Development** Use the daily activities on ELL Poster 27 to build concept and vocabulary knowledge.

Objectives
• Use prior knowledge and experiences to understand meanings in English.

Content Objectives

- Use concept vocabulary related to effects humans have on nature.

Language Objectives

- Express ideas in response to art and discussion.

- Use prior experiences to understand ideas.

Daily Planner

DAY 1	• **Frontload Concept** • **Preteach** Comprehensio Skill, Vocabulary, Phonics Spelling, Conventions • **Writing**
DAY 2	• **Review Concept,** Vocabulary, Comprehension Skill • **Frontload Main Selectio** • **Practice** Phonics/Spellin Conventions/Writing
DAY 3	• **Review Concept,** Comprehension Skill, Vocabulary, Conventions Writing • **Reread Main Selection** • **Practice** Phonics/Spellin
DAY 4	• **Review Concept** • **Read ELL/ELD Readers** • **Practice** Phonics/Spellin Conventions/Writing
DAY 5	• **Review Concept,** Vocabulary, Comprehension Skill, Phonics/Spelling, Conventions • **Reread ELL/ELD Reade** • **Writing**

*See the ELL Handbook for ELL Workshops with targeted instruction.

Concept Talk Video

Use the Concept Talk Video Routine (*ELL Handbook,* p. 477) to build background about humans' unexpected effects.

Language Objectives

Learn and use high-frequency words.

Understand and use basic vocabulary.

Learn meanings of grade-level vocabulary.

Write using content-based vocabulary.

Language Opportunity: Writing

Have students write with the lesson words, which are content-based vocabulary. Have them write sentences to describe art in the selection or from the poster. They can share their sentences with partners to check for understanding.

Language Opportunity: Speaking

Have students use high-frequency words and lesson vocabulary to tell about the people, places, and things they might find on Saint Matthew Island. Students can tell about what a trip to the island might be like with each student giving feedback.

ELL — English Language Learners

Basic Vocabulary

■ **High-Frequency Words** Use the vocabulary routines and the high-frequency list on page 455 of the *ELL Handbook* to systematically teach newcomers the first 300 sight words in English. Students who began learning ten words per week at the beginning of the year are now learning words 261–270. Have students categorize high-frequency words from this week's list as people, objects, or other. They can choose high-frequency words to use in sentences.

Lesson Vocabulary

■ **Preteach** Introduce the Lesson Vocabulary using this routine:

1. Distribute copies of this week's Word Cards (*ELL Handbook,* p. 185).

2. Display ELL Poster 27 and reread the Poster Talk-Through.

3. Using the poster illustrations, model how a word's meaning can be expressed with other similar words: The deer is *scrawny,* or very skinny, from lack of food.

4. Use these sentences to reveal the meaning of the other words.

- The *carcasses* showed that many animals had died. (**bodies of dead animals**)

- The flat and wide open *tundra* covered a large area. (**frozen land**)

- The *parasites* fed off the carcass. (**organisms that live off of other organisms**)

- A dead animal will *decay*. (**rot**)

- Many animals face *starvation*. (**extreme hunger**)

- The sun *bleached* the rocks. (**removed the color from**)

- I had a *suspicion* that something was wrong. (**bad feeling**)

Objectives
- Use visual, contextual, and linguistic support to enhance and confirm understanding of increasingly complex and elaborated spoken language.
- Understand the general meaning, main points, and important details of spoken language ranging from situations in which topics, language, and contexts are familiar to unfamiliar.

ELL English Language Learners

Phonics and Spelling

■ **Final Syllable -ance, -ence**

- **Preteach** Write *dif/fer/ence,* dividing the word into syllables. Sound it out, pausing between each syllable. Then blend the syllables together. Review that each syllable has a vowel sound. Remind students to pay attention to syllables to help them spell and pronounce words.

- **Teach/Model** Write *absence* and *appearance*. Model identifying syllables and distinguishing intonation patterns when pronouncing the words. When I say *ab/sence* I hear two vowel sounds, so there are two syllables. *Ap/pear/ance* has three vowel sounds and syllables. Notice which syllable is stressed when I say each word. Have students repeat after you.

- **Practice** Write *evidence, clearance, insurance,* and *excellence.* Have students divide and identify the number of syllables. Then help students pronounce each word, considering intonation patterns.

Word Analysis: Homophones

■ **Preteach** Write the following riddle as you ask it: What is black and white and read all over? (a newspaper) Tell students that the question seems to be asking about colors (black, white, and red), but what sounds like the color *red* is actually *read*, a past tense form of the verb *read*. Explain that *read* and *red* are homophones—words that sound the same but mean completely different things. Invite students to share other homophones they know.

■ **Teach/Model** Write these homophone pairs on the board: *herd, heard; sea, see; male, mail; weight, wait; their, there.* Explain the meaning of each word and point out the different spellings.

■ **Practice** Copy and distribute p. 222. Read the directions aloud and help students answer the first item in each exercise.

Beginning/Intermediate Help students read the words, if necessary. Have students identify the letters that are different in each pair of homophones.
Advanced/Advanced High Challenge students to find homophones in the reading selection or in their first languages.

Content Objectives
- Identify homophones.
- Distinguish syllables in multi-syllabic words.
- Listen for vowel sounds in individual syllables.
- Learn academic vocabulary

Language Objectives
- Apply phonics and decoding skills to vocabulary.
- Discuss the pronunciation and meaning of homophones.
- Distinguish intonation patterns of English.
- Use contextual support to develop vocabulary.

Homophones and Context

Tell students they can figure which homophone is used with context. Write *heard* and *herd* and define them. Then say a sentence: *I heard some one talking.* Ask them which word you used. Have them tell the clues that helped them determine meaning.

Develop Academic Vocabulary

Follow up on the academic vocabulary by focusing on p. 349 of the Student Edition. Have students locate words in the selection that have homophones. Discuss the words' meanings. *(die/dye, road/rod whether/weather, through/ threw, their/there/they're)*

Content Objectives

Determine the main idea and identify details.

Identify main ideas and details that aid comprehension.

Language Objectives

Understand the main ideas in spoken language.

Give information using academic words.

Discuss how to identify the most important idea of a topic.

Identify details that support the main idea.

Use details from text to write a conclusion.

Ask for clarification as needed.

Language Opportunity: Listening

Have students listen for main ideas and supporting details. Read p. 355 of the Student Edition as students listen. Ask them for the main points. (reindeer died in late winter; no predators or people killed them)

ELL — English Language Learners

Comprehension
Main Idea and Details

■ **Preteach** The most important idea about a topic is called the main idea. You can find details in the text that will support the main idea. Have students turn to Envision It! on p. EI•12 in the Student Edition. Read the text aloud. Have students ask for clarification of the text before discussing the details if needed. Have students identify details of what they see on the page. (subway, bus, person on bicycle, person skating, car, truck) Ask students what these details illustrate. (many different ways to travel around a city) Have students state this idea as the main idea of the page. (There are many different ways to travel in a city.)

■ **Reteach** Distribute copies of the Picture It! (*ELL Handbook*, p. 186). Have students look at the picture and then read the passage aloud. Have them answer the questions using the academic expressions *main idea* and *details*. What is Stonehenge? (a circle with large stone slabs) Why was Stonehenge made? (no one knows why) (**Answers** 1. Stonehenge is a mysterious place. 2. Possible responses: the stones weigh up to 50 tons; they come from 240 miles away; nobody is sure why they were placed there.)

 Beginning/Intermediate Reread the passage aloud with students. Guide them to underline important details. Then have them read the details aloud. **Advanced/Advanced High** Have students reread the passage. Then have them underline details that support their answers. Invite students to share the main idea and three details.

MINI-LESSON

Environmental Print

Tell students that when people go places in a town or city, they use signs to help them know where to go. Refer students to the visual in Envision It! on p. EI•12. You want to take a bus downtown. How do you know that the bus in the picture is the right one to take? (The sign on the bus says "Downtown.") Have students point out other signs in the picture. With a partner take turns asking for information to various locations, using concrete vocabulary and key words.

Objectives

- Understand the general meaning, main points, and important details of spoken language ranging from situations in which topics, language, and contexts are familiar to unfamiliar.
- Demonstrate English comprehension and expand reading skills by employing basic reading skills such as demonstrating understanding of supporting ideas and details in text and graphic sources, summarizing text and distinguishing main ideas from details commensurate with content area needs.

ELL *English Language Learners*

Reading Comprehension
The Mystery of Saint Matthew Island

Student Edition pp. 350–351

■ **Frontloading** Have students look through *The Mystery of Saint Matthew Island,* pp. 350–359 in the Student Edition. Distribute copies of the English summary of *The Mystery of Saint Matthew Island* (*ELL Handbook,* p. 187). Have students read the summary aloud with you. Encourage them to use support from you or from peers to understand unfamiliar words. Preview the selection by having students look at the pictures.

Sheltered Reading Ask questions to guide students' comprehension.

- p. 352: How many years did it take for the reindeer to go from six thousand to just a few live animals? (two years)

- p. 354: What was the first clue Klein found? (The reindeer all died about the same time.)

- pp. 354–355: How did Klein know the remaining animals were not getting good food? (Plants were damaged; the reindeer had low weights.)

- p. 355: What was needed to keep the reindeer in check? (predators)

As students are able, have them read silently for longer periods and check their comprehension.

■ **Fluency: Read with Appropriate Phrasing Using Punctuation Cues** Remind students that reading with phrasing means to pay attention to punctuation. Read the last paragraph on p. 352, modeling phrasing. Then have pairs choose a paragraph on p. 353 to read with appropriate phrasing. Have students monitor their understanding of spoken language as they listen to partners. Have them pair up to read Student Edition p. 359. They can take turns reading aloud and restating the main points to monitor understanding.

After Reading Help students summarize the text with the Retelling Cards. Then have students turn to p. 369 in the Student Edition. Have students use the Interview Activity to follow directions and listen to their partners as they ask and answer questions.

Content Objectives
- Monitor and adjust comprehension.
- Make and adjust predictions.

Language Objectives
- Monitor understanding of spoken language.
- Read grade-level text with appropriate phrasing, using punctuation cues.
- Summarize text using visual support.
- Follow spoken directions.
- Use peer support to develop vocabulary.
- Read silently.

Graphic Organizer

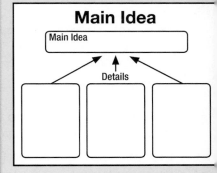

Main Idea

Main Idea

Details

Audio Support
Students can prepare for reading *The Mystery of Saint Matthew Island* by using the eSelection or the AudioText CD. See the AudioText CD Routine (*ELL Handbook,* p. 477) for suggestions on using these learning tools.

Objectives
- Understand the general meaning, main points, and important details of spoken language ranging from situations in which topics, language, and contexts are familiar to unfamiliar.
- Demonstrate comprehension of increasingly complex English by participating in shared reading, retelling or summarizing material, responding to questions, and taking notes commensurate with content area and grade level needs.

For additional leveled instruction, see the **ELL/ELD Reader Teaching Guide.**

Comprehension
All Things in Balance

ELD Reader   ELL Reader

■ **Before Reading** Distribute copies of the ELL and ELD Readers, *All Things in Balance,* to students at their reading level.

• **Preview** Read the title aloud with students and provide support to help students develop background knowledge. This is a nonfiction text about how nature is balanced and what can happen when it is out of balance. Invite students to look through the pictures and name what they see.

• **Set a Purpose for Reading** Let's read to find out how nature can be balanced or out of balance.

■ **During Reading** Follow the Reading Routine for both reading groups.

1. Read the entire Reader aloud slowly.

2. Reread pp. 2–4, pausing to build background or model comprehension. Use the questions in the chart to check students' comprehension.

3. Have students reread pages pp. 2–4 in pairs, taking turns reading alternate pages.

4. Repeat steps 2–3 for pp. 5–7.

■ **After Reading** Use the exercises on the inside back cover of each Reader and invite students to share their writing. In a whole-group discussion, ask students, What is needed for nature to be balanced? Record their answers on the board and invite them to point to pictures in the book to support their answers.

ELD Reader Beginning/Intermediate

■ **p. 2** Where do big plant-eaters live? (Africa)

■ **p. 7** How did pigs get to the Channel Islands? (People brought them.) Read aloud the sentences that tell you the answer. (Then humans came to the Channel Islands. They brought pigs.)

Writing What are two details that support the main idea that the balance of nature usually works well? Find and copy the details. Read them aloud to your partner.

ELL Reader Advanced/Advanced High

■ **p. 2** What do you call animals that eat only plants? (herbivores)

■ **p. 5** What happens if there are not enough plants for herbivores to eat? (They become thin and may die.)

Study Guide Distribute copies of the ELL Reader Study Guide (*ELL Handbook*, p. 190). Help students determine which plants and animals to draw and then write what is most important about each level. Review their responses together. (**Answers** See *ELL Handbook*, pp. 209–212.)

Objectives
• Read linguistically accomodated content area material with a decreasing need for linguistic accomodation as more English is learned.

 English Language Learners

Conventions
Conjunctions

- **Teach/Model** Display these sentences on the board: I saw lightning and heard thunder. I took my umbrella because it started to rain. Lourdas walks to school, but today she took the bus. I will give her the book now or after school. Have students identify the conjunction in each sentence (*and, because, but, or*). Remind students that conjunctions are words that connect or join words, phrases, and complete thoughts. Note that conjunctions can join two similar things (*and*), give a choice (*or*), join two different ideas (*but*), or give more information (*because*).

- **Practice** Have pairs use the conjunctions to create additional sentences. Ask pairs to share their sentences with the class. Invite the class to identify the conjunctions.

Reteach
Display the following conjunctions on the board: *and, because,* or, *but*. Write the following sentences:

He is smiling _____ he got a good grade.

Luc has to decide whether to stay home _____ go to the game.

I put peas _____ carrots in the soup.

Tito used to play baseball, _____ now he likes basketball.

- **Practice** Have students use the correct conjunctions to fill in each blank.

 Leveled Support

Beginning Have students go to the board and circle or point to the conjunction that completes each sentence (*because, or, and, but*).

Intermediate Have students read the conjunction that completes each sentence.

Advanced/Advanced High Have students write the conjunction that completes each sentence. Then have them read the sentences.

Content Objectives
- Identify conjunctions.
- Explain the purpose of coordinating and subordinating conjunctions

Language Objectives
- Speak using modifiers.
- Use conjunctions to connec ideas meaningfully.

 Transfer Skills

Conjunctions Speakers of Chinese and some other languages may build sentences using two conjunctions where English typically uses one: *Because the sun came up, so I could see the clock.* Help students practice English patterns.

Grammar Jammer

For more practice with conjunctions, use the Grammar Jammer for this target skill. See the Grammar Jammer Routine (*ELL Handbook*, p. 478) for suggestions on using this learning tool.

Objectives
- Speak using a variety of grammatical structures, sentence lengths, sentence types, and connecting words with increasing accuracy and ease as more English is acquired.

ELL English Language Learners

Writing a Paraphrase

■ **Introduce** Display the paraphrase model and read it aloud. Review that a paraphrase is explaining something in your own words. A paraphrase includes all of the author's ideas in the original text, but is simpler than the original. What is the mystery? (Honeybee colonies have died.) What clues did scientists look at? (bees from Australia, bee products from China, samples of colonies that died in the last three years) What did they find? (They found one kind of virus in all of the samples.) Tell students that a paraphrase would include of all these ideas, written in their own words. Point out that sentences in the writing model vary in length.

Writing Model
Why honeybees are dying is a mystery. Whole colonies have collapsed even though there is enough food. Scientists thought of many reasons. They took samples of bees from Australia and bee products from China. Then they looked at samples of colonies that had died in the last three years. One kind of virus was in all of the samples. The virus may be why the bees are dying.

■ **Practice** Work with students to paraphrase the model, using the following frame.
The mystery is _____. Scientists looked at _____. They found _____.

Be sure students vary sentence lengths for interest and fluency.

■ **Write** Have students write one or two paragraphs in which they describe a mystery and the clues that were found that reveal what happened, how it happened, and why. Suggest they write a scientific mystery similar to *The Mystery of Saint Matthew's Island.* Help with topics and writing as necessary. Then have students exchange papers with partners and have the partners paraphrase the mysteries. Remind them to include all of the author's ideas.

Beginning Have students create a picture to paraphrase their partner's mystery. Encourage them to include all of the clues. Then have them dictate a title starting with *The Mystery of* ____ for you to write on the picture.

Intermediate Have students use a frame similar to what was used in Practice to write their paraphrases.

Advanced/Advanced High Have students write their mysteries independently. Then have pairs exchange papers and write their paraphrases. Encourage partners to check to be sure that all important ideas are included.

Objectives
• Narrate, describe, and explain with increasing specificity and detail to fulfill content area writing needs as more English is acquired.
• Share information in cooperative learning interactions.

Content Objectives
Identify the features of a paraphrase.

Language Objectives
Write a paraphrase of a mystery, including clues to reveal what happened, how it happened, and why.

Share feedback for editing and revising.

Retell or summarize material.

Write using a variety of sentence lengths.

Language Opportunity: Listening and Speaking
Paraphrasing is like retelling. Have students retell information after they listen. Read p. 352 of the Student Edition and ask students to retell the information in their own words. Model as necessary.

This Week on Reading Street!

The Unexpected

Question of the Week

How can we learn from the results of our actions?

Daily Plan

Don't Wait Until Friday

Whole Group

- ◉ Compare and Contrast
- ◉ Affixes: Suffixes *-less, -ful*
- • Fluency/Rate
- • Research and Inquiry

MONITOR PROGRESS | **Success Predictor**

| Day 1 Check Oral Vocabulary | Days 2–3 Check Retelling | Day 4 Check Fluency | Day 5 Check Oral Vocabulary |

Small Group

Teacher-Led

- • Reading Support
- • Skill Support
- • Fluency Practice

Practice Stations

Independent Activities

Customize Literacy More support for a balanced literacy approach, see pp. CL•1–CL•47

Customize Writing More support for a customized writing approach, see pp. CW•1–CW•10

Whole Group

- • Writing: Parody
- • Conventions: Commas
- • Spelling: Latin Roots

Assessment

- • Weekly Tests
- • Day 5 Assessment
- • Fresh Reads

You Are Here! Unit 6 Week 3

This Week's Reading Selections

Main Selection Genre: **Myth**

Paired Selection Genre: **Origin Myth**

Leveled Readers

ELL and ELD Readers

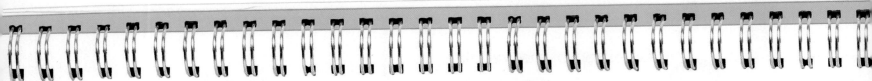

	Build Concepts	Comprehension
Whole Group	Let's Talk About pp. 370–371	Envision It! Skills/Strategies · Comprehension Skills Lesson pp. 372–373
**Go Digital**	• Concept Talk Video	• Envision It! Animations • eSelections
Small Group and Independent Practice	King Midas and the Golden Touch pp. 376–377 ELL and ELD Readers Leveled Readers	King Midas and the Golden Touch pp. 376–377 ELL and ELD Readers Leveled Readers Envision It! Skills/Strategies Reader's and Writer's Notebook · Practice Station Flip Chart
Go Digital	• eReaders • eSelections	• Envision It! Animations • eSelections • eReaders
Customize Literacy	• Leveled Readers	• Envision It! Skills and Strategies Handbook • Leveled Readers
**Go Digital**	• Concept Talk Video • Big Question Video • eReaders	• Envision It! Animations • eReaders

 Question of the Week

How can we learn from the results of our actions?

Vocabulary

Envision It!
Vocabulary
Cards

Vocabulary Skill Lesson
pp. 374–375

- Envision It! Vocabulary Cards
- Vocabulary Activities

Fluency

Let's Learn It!
pp. 400–401

- eSelections
- eReaders

Conventions and Writing

Let's Write It! pp. 396–397

- Grammar Jammer

Envision It!
Vocabulary
Cards

King Midas and
the Golden Touch
pp. 376–377

Practice
Station
Flip Chart

Words!

Reader's
and Writer's
Notebook

King Midas and
the Golden Touch
pp. 376–377

Practice
Station
Flip Chart

ELL and ELD
Readers

Leveled
Readers

Reader's
and Writer's
Notebook

King Midas and
the Golden Touch
pp. 376–377

Practice
Station
Flip Chart

- Envision It! Vocabulary Cards
- Vocabulary Activities
- eSelections

- eSelections
- eReaders

- Grammar Jammer

- Envision It! Vocabulary Cards

- Leveled Readers

- Reader's and Writer's Notebook

- Vocabulary Activities

- eReaders

- Grammar Jammer

You Are Here!
Unit 6
Week 3

My 5-Day Planner for Reading Street!

Don't Wait Until Friday
MONITOR PROGRESS

	Check Oral Vocabulary **Day 1** pages 370j–373f	**Check Retelling** **Day 2** pages 374a–383e

Get Ready to Read	**Concept Talk,** 370j
	Oral Vocabulary, 371a
	   specimen, valuable, geologist, rare
	Listening Comprehension, Read Aloud, 371b
		Concept Talk, 374a
		Oral Vocabulary, 374b
		   deplorable, outcome
		Word Analysis, 374c
		   Complex Spelling Patterns: *ci*/sh/, *ti*/sh/, *ous*/us/
		Literary Terms, 374d
		   Foreshadowing
		Story Structure, 374d
		   Conflict and Resolution

Read and Comprehend	**Comprehension Skill,**
	   ◉ Compare and Contrast, 371c
	Comprehension Strategy,
	   ◉ Story Structure, 371c
	READ Comprehension, 372–373
	Model Fluency, Rate, 372–373
	Introduce Lesson Vocabulary, 373a
	   adorn, cleanse, lifeless, precious, realm, spoonful
		Vocabulary Skill, ◉ Affixes: Suffixes *-less, -ful,* 374e
		Vocabulary Strategy, Word Structure, 374e
		Lesson Vocabulary, 374–375
		   adorn, cleanse, lifeless, precious, realm, spoonful
		READ Vocabulary, 374–375
		Model Fluency, Rate, 374–375
		READ Main Selection, *King Midas and the Golden Touch,* 376–383a

Language Arts	**Research and Inquiry,** Identify Questions, 373b **Spelling,** Latin Roots, 373c **Conventions,** Commas, 373d **Handwriting,** Cursive Letter *s* and *S*, 373d **Writing,** Parody, 373e–373f	**Research and Inquiry,** Navigate/Search, 383b **Conventions,** Commas, 383c **Spelling,** Latin Roots, 383c **Writing,** Parody, Plot, 383d

You Are Here!
Unit 6 Week 3

Question of the Week
How can we learn from the results of our actions?

Check Retelling	Check Fluency	Check Oral Vocabulary
Day 3 pages 384a–397c	**Day 4** pages 398a–401e	**Day 5** pages 401f–401q

Concept Talk, 384a
Oral Vocabulary, 384b
    victor, unforeseen
Comprehension Check, 384c
Check Retelling, 384d
	Concept Talk, 398a
	Oral Vocabulary, 398b
	    repercussion, penitence
	Genre,
	    Origin Myth: Characters, 398c
		Concept Wrap Up, 401f
		Check Oral Vocabulary, 401g
		    specimen, valuable, geologist,
		    rare, deplorable, outcome, victor,
		    unforeseen, repercussion,
		    penitence
		Amazing Ideas, 401g
		Review ◎ Compare and Contrast,
		    401h
		Review ◎ Affixes: Suffixes *-less,*
		    -ful, 401h
		Review ◎ Word Analysis, 401i
		Review ◎ Literary Terms, 401i

READ **Main Selection,** *King Midas and
    the Golden Touch,* 384–393a
Retelling, 394–395
Think Critically, 395a
Model Fluency, Rate, 395b
Research and Study Skills, Order
    Form/Application, 395c
	READ **Paired Selection,**
	    "Prometheus, the Fire-Bringer,"
	    398–399a
	Let's Learn It! 400–401a
	    Fluency: Rate
	    Vocabulary: Affixes: Suffixes
	    -less, -ful
	    Listening and Speaking:
	    Storytelling
		Fluency Assessment,
		    WCPM, 401j–401k
		Comprehension Assessment,
		    ◎ Compare and Contrast,
		    401l–401m

Research and Inquiry, Analyze, 395d
Conventions, Commas, 395e
Spelling, Latin Roots, 395e
Let's Write It! Parody, 396–397a
Writing, Parody, Voice, 397b–397c
	Research and Inquiry,
	    Synthesize, 401b
	Conventions, Commas, 401c
	Spelling, Latin Roots, 401c
	Writing, Parody, Revising,
	    401d–401e
		Research and Inquiry, Communicate,
		    401n
		Conventions, Commas, 401o
		Spelling Test, Latin Roots, 401o
		Writing, Parody, Commas, 401p
		Quick Write for Fluency, 401q

Grouping Options for Differentiated Instruction
Turn the page for the small group time lesson plan.

Planning Small Group Time on Reading Street!

SMALL GROUP TIME RESOURCES

Look for this Small Group Time box each day to help meet the individual needs of all your students. Differentiated Instruction lessons appear on the DI pages at the end of each week.

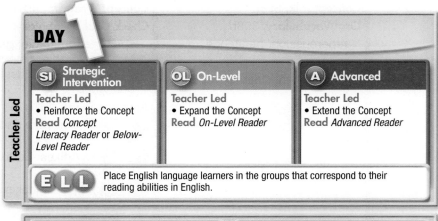

DAY 1

Teacher Led

SI Strategic Intervention	**OL** On-Level	**A** Advanced
Teacher Led	**Teacher Led**	**Teacher Led**
• Reinforce the Concept	• Expand the Concept	• Extend the Concept
Read *Concept Literacy Reader* or *Below-Level Reader*	**Read** *On-Level Reader*	**Read** *Advanced Reader*

ELL Place English language learners in the groups that correspond to their reading abilities in English.

Practice Stations
• Read for Meaning
• Get Fluent
• Word Work

Independent Activities
• Concept Talk Video
• *Reader's and Writer's Notebook*
• Research and Inquiry

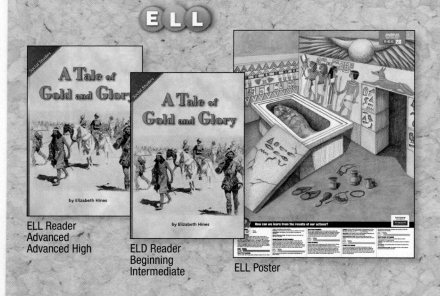

ELL

A Tale of Gold and Glory
by Elizabeth Hines

ELL Reader
Advanced
Advanced High

A Tale of Gold and Glory
by Elizabeth Hines

ELD Reader
Beginning
Intermediate

ELL Poster

You Are Here!
Unit 6
Week 3

Day 1

SI Strategic Intervention	**Reinforce the Concept,** DI•51–DI•52 **Read Concept Literacy Reader** or **Below-Level Reader**
OL On-Level	**Expand the Concept,** DI•57 **Read On-Level Reader**
A Advanced	**Extend the Concept,** DI•62 **Read Advanced Reader**
ELL English Language Learners	DI•66–DI•75 **Frontload Concept Preteach Skills Writing**

Reading Street Response
to Intervention Kit

Reading Street
Practice Stations Kit

How can we learn from the results of our actions?

SI Strategic Intervention

Below-Level
Reader

Concept Literacy Reader

King Midas and the Golden Touch pp. 376–377

OL On-Level

On-Level Reader

A Advanced

Advanced
Reader

Prometheus the Fire-Bringer pp. 398–399

Small Group Weekly Plan

Day 2	Day 3	Day 4	Day 5
Reinforce Comprehension, DI•53 Revisit **Main Selection**	**Reinforce Vocabulary,** DI•54 Read/Revisit **Main Selection**	**Reinforce Comprehension,** Practice Retelling DI•55 Genre Focus Read/Revisit **Paired Selection**	**Practice Fluency,** DI•56 Reread **Concept Literacy Reader** or **Below-Level Reader**
Expand Comprehension, DI•58 Revisit **Main Selection**	**Expand Vocabulary,** DI•59 Read/Revisit **Main Selection**	**Expand Comprehension,** Practice Retelling DI•60 Genre Focus Read/Revisit **Paired Selection**	**Practice Fluency,** DI•61 Reread **On-Level Reader**
Extend Comprehension, DI•63 Revisit **Main Selection**	**Extend Vocabulary,** DI•64 Read/Revisit **Main Selection**	**Extend Comprehension,** Genre Focus DI•65 Read/Revisit **Paired Selection**	**Practice Fluency,** DI•65 Reread **Advanced Reader**
DI•66–DI•75 **Review Concept/Skills** **Frontload Main Selection** **Practice**	DI•66–DI•75 **Review Concept/Skills** **Reread Main Selection** **Practice**	DI•66–DI•75 **Review Concept** **Read ELL/ELD Readers** **Practice**	DI•66–DI•75 **Review Concept/Skills** **Reread ELL/ELD Reader** **Writing**

Practice Stations for Everyone on Reading Street!

Word Wise
Final syllables -*ant*, -*ent*, -*ance*, and -*ence*

Objectives
- Spell words with final syllables -*ant*, -*ent*, -*ance*, and -*ence*.

Materials
- *Word Wise* Flip Chart Activity 28
- word cards
- paper • pencil

Differentiated Activities

⬤ Choose two word cards for each final syllable: -*ant*, -*ent*, -*ance*, and -*ence*. Write the words in a list. Write sentences using each of your words. Add other words with these final syllables to the list.

▲ Choose three word cards for each final syllable: -*ant*, -*ent*, -*ance*, and -*ence*. Write the words in a list. Write sentences using each of your words. Add other words to the list with these final syllables.

■ Choose four word cards for each final syllable: -*ant*, -*ent*, -*ance*, and -*ence*. Write the words in a list. Write sentences using each of your words. Add other words with these final syllables to the list.

Technology
- Online Dictionary

Word Work
Final syllables -*ant*, -*ent*, -*ance*, and -*ence*

Objectives
- Identify words with final syllables -*ant*, -*ent*, -*ance*, and -*ence*.

Materials
- *Word Work* Flip Chart Activity 28
- word cards
- paper • pencil

Differentiated Activities

⬤ Choose two word cards for each final syllable: -*ant*, -*ent*, -*ance*, and -*ence*. Quietly say each word aloud. Write the words in a list. Circle the final syllable in each word.

▲ Choose ten word cards. Quietly say each word aloud. Write the words in a list. Circle the final syllable in each word. Write sentences using six of the words.

■ Choose twelve word cards, and quietly say each word aloud. Write the words in a list. Circle the final syllable in each word. Write sentences using eight of the words.

Technology
- Modeled Pronunciation Audio CD

Words to Know
Endings -*s* and -*es*

Objectives
- Determine the meaning of words ending with -*s*, and -*es*.

Materials
- *Words to Know* Flip Chart Activity 28
- word cards
- paper • pencil

Differentiated Activities

⬤ Choose six word cards. Write the words in a list. Use the dictionary to check each word's part of speech. Next to the word, write its part of speech. Write sentences using your words.

▲ Choose eight word cards, and write the words in a list. Check each word's part of speech in the dictionary, and write it next to the word. Write sentences using your words.

■ Choose ten word cards, and write the words in a list. Check each word's part of speech in the dictionary, and write it next to the word. Write sentences using your words.

Technology
- Online Dictionary

You Are Here!
Unit 6 Week 3

Practice Station
Flip Chart

Use this week's materials from the Reading Street Leveled Practice Stations Kit to organize this week's stations.

Let's Write!
Mystery

Objectives
• Write a mystery.

Materials
• *Let's Write!* Flip Chart Activity 28
• paper • pencil

Differentiated Activities

● Think of mystery stories you have read. Write a mystery about a strange event. Explain what the mystery is. Write clues that reveal what happened. Tell how the mysterious event happened.

▲ Write a mystery about a strange event or occurrence. Explain what the mystery is, and write sentences with clues that reveal what happened. Include details providing an explanation to the mystery.

■ Write a mystery about a strange event or occurrence. Explain what the mystery is, and give clues that reveal what happened. Include details describing how and why the mystery happened.

Technology
• Online Graphic Organizers

Read for Meaning
Main idea and details

Objectives
• Identify the main idea and details in a nonfiction selection.

Materials
• *Read for Meaning* Flip Chart Activity 28
• Leveled Readers
• paper • pencil

Differentiated Activities

● Choose and read one of the books your teacher provided. Think about what the selection is mostly about. Write one sentence telling about the main idea. Write one sentence with a detail from the selection that tells more about this idea.

▲ Choose and read one of the books your teacher provided, and think about the selection's main idea. Write one sentence stating the main idea. Write two sentences that give details from the story and tell more about the main idea.

■ As you read the book you chose from those your teacher provided, think about the selection's main idea. Write a short paragraph stating the main idea. Include details from the selection that tell more about the main idea.

Technology
• Leveled Reader Database

Get Fluent
Practice fluent reading

Objectives
• Read aloud using punctuation clues to guide phrasing.

Materials
• *Get Fluent* Flip Chart Activity 28
• Leveled Readers

Differentiated Activities

● Work with a partner. Choose a Concept Literacy Reader or Below-Level Reader. Take turns reading a page from the book. Use the reader to practice appropriate phrasing. Provide feedback as needed.

▲ Work with a partner. Choose an On-Level Reader. Take turns reading a page from the book. Use the reader to practice appropriate phrasing. Provide feedback as needed.

■ Work with a partner. Choose an Advanced Reader. Take turns reading a page from the book. Use the reader to practice appropriate phrasing. Provide feedback as needed.

Technology
• Leveled Reader Database
• Reading Street Readers CD-ROM

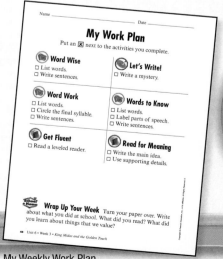

My Weekly Work Plan

Objectives
- Introduce the weekly concept.
- Develop oral vocabulary.

Today at a Glance

Oral Vocabulary
specimen, valuable, geologist, rare

Comprehension
- Compare and contrast
- Story structure

Reading
"Andrew's Wish"

Fluency
Rate

Lesson Vocabulary
Tested vocabulary

Research and Inquiry
Identify questions

Spelling
Latin roots

Conventions
Commas

Handwriting
Cursive letters *s* and *S*

Writing
Parody

Concept Talk

Question of the Week

What can we learn from the results of our actions?

Introduce the concept

To further explore the unit concept of The Unexpected, this week students will read, write, and talk about how our actions can have unexpected results. Write the Question of the Week on the board.

ROUTINE | **Activate Prior Knowledge** | **Team Talk**

① **Think** Have students think about the results, or consequences, that our actions might have.

② **Pair** Have pairs of students discuss the Question of the Week. Encourage students to consider each other's suggestions.

③ **Share** Call on a few students to share their ideas with the group. Guide the discussion and encourage elaboration with prompts such as:

- What did you discuss about our actions and their results?
- Tell me about a time when things didn't go the way you planned them.

Routines Flip Chart

Anchored Talk

Develop oral vocabulary

Have students turn to pp. 370–371 in their Student Editions. Look at each of the photos. Then, use the prompts to guide discussion and create the *What we can learn from the results of our actions* concept map.

- What is in the water with the swan? Why? (Garbage is in the water because people probably threw litter there.) Sometimes people do things without thinking about what will happen. The results are *unforeseen*. Let's put the word *unforeseen* on our concept map.
- Why is the team smiling? (Because they won the trophy.) This is the *outcome* of playing well. Let's add *outcome* to the concept map.

Student Edition pp. 370–371

Objectives
• Listen to and interpret a speaker's messages and ask questions.
• Identify the main ideas and supporting ideas in the speaker's message.

Oral Vocabulary

Let's Talk About

Unexpected Results of Our Actions

◉ Describe actions resulting in the unexpected.

◉ Listen to a classmate's messages about unexpected results.

◉ Determine classmates' main and supporting ideas about the unexpected.

READING STREET ONLINE
CONCEPT TALK VIDEO
www.ReadingStreet.com

• You've learned **2 7 0** Amazing Words ★ so far this year!

370 371

Amazing Words

You've learned **2 7 0** words so far.

You'll learn **0 1 0** words this week!

specimen	outcome
valuable	victor
geologist	unforeseen
rare	repercussion
deplorable	penitence

Writing on Demand

Writing Fluency
Ask students to respond to the photos on pp. 370–371 by writing as well as they can and as much as they can about learning from the results of people's actions.

• What is this archaeologist looking at? (An ancient work of art.) Many archaeologists look for *specimens* of things from another time. *Specimen* is another word to add to our map.

• After discussing the photos, ask: How can we learn from the results of our actions?

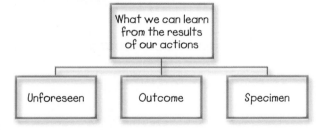

What we can learn from the results of our actions

Unforeseen | Outcome | Specimen

Connect to reading

Help students set purposes for reading by telling them that this week they will be reading about actions that have unexpected consequences. Encourage students to add concept-related words to this week's concept map.

ELL Preteach Concepts Use the Day 1 instruction on ELL Poster 28 to assess and build background knowledge, develop concepts, and build oral vocabulary.

ELL

English Language Learners

ELL support Additional ELL support and modified instruction is provided in the *ELL Handbook* and in the ELL Support lessons on pp. DI•66–DI•75.

Listening comprehension English learners will benefit from additional visual support to understand the key terms in the concept map. Use the pictures on pp. 370–371 to scaffold understanding.

Frontload for Read Aloud Use the modified Read Aloud on page DI•69 in the ELL Support lessons to prepare students to listen to "Valuables" (p. 371b).

ELL Poster 28

Objectives
- Develop listening comprehension.
- Develop oral vocabulary.

Check Oral Vocabulary
SUCCESS PREDICTOR

Oral Vocabulary
Amazing Words

Introduce Amazing Words

"Valuables" on p. 371b is about discovering the value of an object. Tell students to listen for this week's Amazing Words—*valuable, geologist, rare* and *specimen*—as you read.

Model fluency

As you read "Valuables," model appropriate rate by reading at a speed that is appropriate to the text and will improve the listener's comprehension.

Amazing Words Oral Vocabulary Routine

> valuable
> geologist
> rare
> specimen

Teach Amazing Words

1 Introduce Write the word *valuable* on the board. Have students say the word aloud. Relate the word *valuable* to the selection "Valuables." The narrator of the poem did not know if the fossil was *valuable*. What context clues help you understand the meaning of *valuable*? Supply a student-friendly definition. *Valuable* means "being worth money."

2 Demonstrate Break into groups. Have students consider suggestions from other group members to demonstrate understanding. Are diamonds and gold valuable? Can you name other valuable things?

3 Apply Ask students to provide a synonym or antonym for the word *valuable*.

See p. OV•3 to teach *geologist, rare,* and *specimen*.

Routines Flip Chart

Apply Amazing Words

To build oral language, lead a discussion about the Amazing Words.

Don't Wait Until Friday

MONITOR PROGRESS Check Oral Vocabulary

During discussion, listen for students' use of Amazing Words.

If... students are unable to use the Amazing Words to discuss the concept,

then... use Oral Vocabulary Routine in the Routines Flip Chart to demonstrate words in different contexts.

Day 1	**Days 2–3**	**Day 4**	**Day 5**
Check Oral Vocabulary	Check Retelling	Check Fluency	Check Oral Vocabulary

Success Predictor

Valuables

by X. J. Kennedy

I found a fossil in a rock:
The print of some lost fern
That died a million years or so
Ago. I had to learn

If it was valuable or not—
I rushed right off to show
Aunt Jessie the geologist—
Could it be rare? She'd know.

"A beauty of a specimen,"
She said. (Wow! how intense!
I'd struck it rich!) "It's common, though
Worth maybe eighty cents."

But now I keep it on my shelf,
Its stone leaves crisp and nice,
With things that matter to me, not
For sale at any price.

Oral Vocabulary

Succes
Predicto

Objectives
◎ Use comparing and contrasting to aid comprehension.
◎ Use story structure to aid comprehension.
• Read grade-level text with appropriate rate.

Skills Trace
◎ **Compare and Contrast**
Introduce U2W1D1; U2W3D1; U6W3D1
Practice U2W1D2; U2W1D3; U2W3D2; U2W3D3; U6W3D2; U6W3D3
Reteach/Review U2W1D5; U2W3D5; U2W4D2; U2W4D3; U6W3D5
Assess/Test Weekly Tests U2W1; U2W3; U6W3 Benchmark Tests U2

KEY:
U=Unit   W=Week   D=Day

Skill ↔ Strategy
Compare and Contrast
Story Structure

Student Edition p. EI•6

Introduce compare and contrast

Envision It!

When we compare and contrast things, we look for both similarities and differences. The first bullet gives us some words that clue us in to when the author is comparing and contrasting. What clue words would you use to show that two things are similar? (*same, also, like,* or *as*) What clue words would you use to show that two things are different? (*before, although, however, but,* or *unlike*) Have students turn to p. EI•6 in the Student Edition to review compare and contrast. Then read "Andrew's Wish" with students.

Model the skill

Think Aloud Today we are going to read a story about a boy who faces a difficult decision. After reading the first paragraph, I can compare and contrast Andrew and his friends. How are Andrew and his friends alike? (They love riding on trails.) How are they different? (Andrew does not have a mountain bike, but his friends do.)

Guide practice

Have students finish reading "Andrew's Wish" on their own. After they read, have them use a graphic organizer like the one on p. 372 to compare and contrast Andrew's "wishes" at the beginning and end of the story.

Strategy check

Story Structure Remind students that using the strategy of story structure can help them understand the events in "Andrew's Wish."

Model the strategy

Envision It!

Think Aloud Stories usually have some kind problem or conflict that needs to be resolved by the end of the story. Many times, certain incidents in the story foreshadow or give rise to what will happen next in the story. By paying careful attention to the incidents that lead up to the climax of the story, you can often predict how the story will end. Review the strategy of story structure on p. EI•22 of the Student Edition by having students tell what incidents in the story foreshadow or give rise to what happens at the end of "Andrew's Wish."

Student Edition p. EI•22

On their own

Use p. 407 in the *Reader's and Writer's Notebook* for additional practice with compare and contrast.

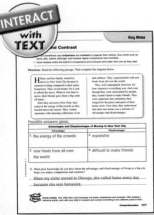

Reader's and Writer's Notebook p. 407

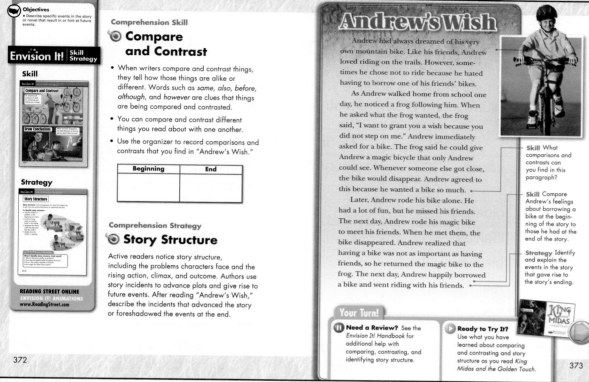

Objectives
- Describe specific events in the story or novel that result in or hint at future events.

Envision It! | Skill/Strategy

Skill

Compare and Contrast

Draw Conclusions

Strategy

Story Structure

READING STREET ONLINE
ENVISION IT! ANIMATIONS
www.ReadingStreet.com

372

Comprehension Skill

Compare and Contrast

- When writers compare and contrast things, they tell how those things are alike or different. Words such as *same*, *also*, *before*, *although*, and *however* are clues that things are being compared and contrasted.

- You can compare and contrast different things you read about with one another.

- Use the organizer to record comparisons and contrasts that you find in "Andrew's Wish."

Beginning	End

Comprehension Strategy

Story Structure

Active readers notice story structure, including the problems characters face and the rising action, climax, and outcome. Authors use story incidents to advance plots and give rise to future events. After reading "Andrew's Wish," describe the incidents that advanced the story or foreshadowed the events at the end.

Andrew's Wish

Andrew had always dreamed of his very own mountain bike. Like his friends, Andrew loved riding on the trails. However, sometimes he chose not to ride because he hated having to borrow one of his friends' bikes.

As Andrew walked home from school one day, he noticed a frog following him. When he asked what the frog wanted, the frog said, "I want to grant you a wish because you did not step on me." Andrew immediately asked for a bike. The frog said he could give Andrew a magic bicycle that only Andrew could see. Whenever someone else got close, the bike would disappear. Andrew agreed to this because he wanted a bike so much.

Later, Andrew rode his bike alone. He had a lot of fun, but he missed his friends. The next day, Andrew rode his magic bike to meet his friends. When he met them, the bike disappeared. Andrew realized that having a bike was not as important as having friends, so he returned the magic bike to the frog. The next day, Andrew happily borrowed a bike and went riding with his friends.

 Skill What comparisons and contrasts can you find in this paragraph?

 Skill Compare Andrew's feelings about borrowing a bike at the beginning of the story to those he had at the end of the story.

Strategy Identify and explain the events in the story that gave rise to the story's ending.

Your Turn!

⏸ **Need a Review?** See the *Envision It! Handbook* for additional help with comparing, contrasting, and identifying story structure.

▶ **Ready to Try It?** Use what you have learned about comparing and contrasting and story structure as you read *King Midas and the Golden Touch*.

 KING MIDAS

373

Student Edition pp. 372–373

Model Fluency
Rate

Model fluent reading

Have students listen as you read paragraph 1 of "Andrew's Wish," using a steady rate. Explain that you slow your rate as you read words or sentences that are more difficult to understand.

ROUTINE **Oral Rereading**

① **Read** Have students read paragraph 2 of "Andrew's Wish" orally.

② **Reread** To achieve optimal fluency and comprehension, students should reread aloud the text three to four times.

③ **Corrective Feedback** Have students read aloud without you. Provide feedback about their rate of speaking and encourage them to group words together to achieve a natural rhythm. Listen for appropriate rate of speech.

Routines Flip Chart

Skill Like his friends, Andrew loved to ride bikes. Unlike his friends, Andrew sometimes chose not to ride.

Skill At the beginning of the story, Andrew hated borrowing bikes. At the end, he does not mind it.

Strategy The problem is that Andrew feels uncomfortable borrowing a bike, so he sometimes does not ride. Andrew resolves it by realizing that it is better to borrow a bike and be with his friends.

Differentiated Instruction

SI Strategic Intervention

Compare and Contrast Have students work in pairs to find comparison clue words in "Andrew's Wish." Ask them to use a chart to show what things are compared in this story.

A Advanced

Compare and Contrast Ask students to write this story from the point of view of one of Andrew's friends. How would they compare Andrew's attitude at the beginning of the story with his attitude at the end?

ELL

English Language Learners

Compare and Contrast Write down the clue words *like, as, but,* and *unlike.* Create sentences that use a clue word to show comparison or contrast. As you say each sentence, have the student point to the clue word you are using and then say if you are comparing or contrasting.

Objectives
• Activate prior knowledge of words.
• Identify question for research.

Vocabulary
Tested Vocabulary

Lesson vocabulary

To help students acquire word knowledge, have students create a four-column chart showing pictures with captions of lesson words.

Word	Definition	Picture	Caption
adorn	to decorate	Draw a picture of outdoor lanterns.	<u>adorn</u> with lights
cleanse			
lifeless			
precious			
realm			
spoonful			

Activate prior knowledge

Guide students in using a print or electronic dictionary or glossary to find the definition of *adorn* that fits with the topic of decorating. They should also determine the syllabication, pronunciation, and part of speech of each word and then draw a picture and write a caption for each word.

Suffixes -less and -ful

Ask students which word ends with the suffix *-less* (*lifeless*). Explain that the suffix *-less* adds the meaning "without" to the root word. Ask how the suffix changes the meaning of the word *life.* Then ask students the same questions about the suffix *-ful.* By the end of the week, students should know the lesson words and have completed the chart. Use the Strategy for Meaningful Word Parts to help students read words with suffixes.

Preteach Academic Vocabulary

 Academic Vocabulary Write the following words on the board:

myth	commas in a series
parody	appositives
climax	rhythmic patterns of language

Have students share what they know about this week's Academic Vocabulary. Use the students' responses to assess their prior knowledge. Preteach the Academic Vocabulary by providing a student-friendly description, explanation, or example. Then ask students to define the Academic Vocabulary term in their own words.

Research and Inquiry
Identify Questions

INTERNET GUY
Don Leu

Teach

Discuss the Question of the Week: *How can we learn from the results of our actions?* Tell students they will research the way people in our country value gold. They can research how gold's value is determined, how it is mined, or how it is used. They will present their findings to the class as an oral presentation on Day 5.

Model

> **Think Aloud** Some people consider gold to be very valuable. During the Gold Rush in the mid-1800s, people moved across the country to mine gold. I would like to find out more about how people mine gold. Some possible questions are *How did people mine gold during the Gold Rush? How do they mine gold today?*

Guide practice

Ask students to pick a research topic about gold in the United States. They should formulate open-ended inquiry questions about their topic. Explain that tomorrow they will conduct research.

On their own

Have students come up with a plan for their research. Suggest that they search reference texts, nonfiction books, and online sources.

21st Century Skills
Weekly Inquiry Project
Day 1 Identify Questions
Day 2 Navigate/Search
Day 3 Analyze
Day 4 Synthesize
Day 5 Communicate

Small Group Time

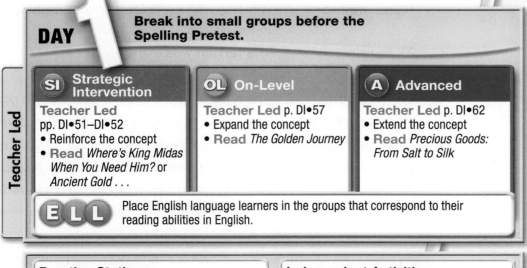

DAY 1

Break into small groups before the Spelling Pretest.

Teacher Led

SI Strategic Intervention	**OL On-Level**	**A Advanced**
Teacher Led pp. DI•51–DI•52 • Reinforce the concept • **Read** *Where's King Midas When You Need Him?* or *Ancient Gold . . .*	**Teacher Led** p. DI•57 • Expand the concept • **Read** *The Golden Journey*	**Teacher Led** p. DI•62 • Extend the concept • **Read** *Precious Goods: From Salt to Silk*

ELL Place English language learners in the groups that correspond to their reading abilities in English.

Practice Stations	**Independent Activities**
• Read for Meaning • Get Fluent • Word Work	• Concept Talk Video • *Reader's and Writer's Notebook* • Vocabulary Activities

ELL

English Language Learners
Multilingual vocabulary
Students can apply knowledge of their home languages to acquire new English vocabulary by using the Multilingual Vocabulary Lists (*ELL Handbook*, pp. 431–444).

King Midas and the Golden Touch **373b**

DAY 1

Language Arts
30–35 mins.

Objectives
- Spell words with Latin roots correctly.
- Use commas in compound sentences.
- Write cursive capital letter *S* and lowercase *s* in words.

Spelling Pretest
Latin Roots

Introduce

Remind students that words with Latin roots are words or parts of words that come from the Latin language. This week we will spell words with the Latin roots *port, aud, dec, terr,* and *dict.*

Pretest

Use these sentences to administer the spelling pretest. Say each word, read the sentence, and repeat the word.

1. portable	The parents brought the **portable** crib to the park.	
2. audience	The **audience** loved the play.	
3. decade	A **decade** is a ten-year period.	
4. territory	The **territory** was occupied by settlers.	
5. auditorium	All **auditorium** seats were taken.	
6. dictionary	Look up difficult words in a **dictionary.**	
7. terrace	No one ever sits on our **terrace.**	
8. reporter	The **reporter** quoted the mayor in the article.	
9. December	**December** is the twelfth month.	
10. contradict	Your opinion might **contradict** mine.	
11. export	China can **export** plenty of silk to other countries.	
12. decimal	Use a **decimal** point to write amounts of money.	
13. audit	They did an **audit** at the bank.	
14. transport	We need a refrigerated truck to **transport** the milk.	
15. audition	I want to **audition** for the lead role.	
16. prediction	Her **prediction** of good things to come was true.	
17. import	You must pay extra taxes to **import** those foods.	
18. jurisdiction	He only has **jurisdiction** over this county.	
19. decathlon	Athletes who participate in a **decathlon** are entered in ten events.	
20. terrain	The **terrain** was extremely rocky.	

Challenge words

21. terra cotta	The artist's studio is full of **terra cotta** pottery.
22. subterranean	I am afraid to explore **subterranean** caves.
23. valedictorian	This year's **valedictorian** made straight As.
24. supportiveness	The **supportiveness** of our fans is helpful.
25. inaudibly	I couldn't hear him when he spoke **inaudibly.**

Self-correct

After the pretest, you can either display the correctly spelled words or spell them orally. Have students self-correct their pretests by writing misspelled words.

On their own

For additional practice, use *Let's Practice It!* p. 324 on the *Teacher Resources DVD-ROM.*

Let's Practice It!
TR DVD•324

Conventions
Commas

Teach

Display Grammar Transparency 28, and read aloud the explanation and examples in the box. Point out that a comma has many different uses, but it always indicates a pause. Explain that a comma is always used before the conjunction in a compound sentence.

Model

Add commas where they are needed in items 1 and 2. Then show how you applied comma rules to determine the correct answer.

Guide practice

Guide students to complete the remaining items. Remind them to review the different uses for commas and apply the right one. Record the correct responses on the transparency.

Daily Fix-It

Use Daily Fix-It numbers 1 and 2 in the right margin.

Connect to oral language

Have students read sentences 3 to 5 on the transparency and explain where to place commas to correctly complete each sentence.

Grammar Transparency 28, TR DVD

Handwriting
Cursive Letter *s* and *S*

Model letter formation

Display the uppercase cursive letter *S* and the lowercase letter *s*. Follow the stroke instruction pictured to model letter formation.

Model spacing

Explain that writing can be hard to read if the spacing between letters is not consistent. In addition, spaces must be added between words so they do not all run together. Model writing this sentence with proper spacing between letters and words: *Sean used several short sentences in his speech.*

Guide practice

Have students write these sentences. *She has seven sisters. Sam says his scooter is speedy.* Circulate around the room, guiding students.

Academic Vocabulary

commas in a series the commas used after every item listed except the last

appositives noun phrases that describe other nouns

Daily Fix-It

1. The king keeped gold silver and jewels in the dungeon. *(kept; gold, silver, and)*
2. He didnt beleive anything wa more important than wealth. *(didn't believe)*

English Language Learners
Language Production: Joining simple sentences Model saying a sentence that describe your clothing: *I am wearing red.* Ask a student: *What color are you wearing?* When the student replies, join your two sentences: *I am wearing red, but you are wearing blue.* Write the compound sentence on the board, circling the comma and underlining the word *but.* Have pairs of students practice joinin simple sentences using differen sentence starters. For example. *My name is ____, but your nam is ____. I like to eat ____ for lunch, but you like to eat ____.* Offer corrective feedback when needed.

Writing—Parody
Introduce

MINI-LESSON

5 Day Planner
Guide to Mini-Lessons

DAY 1	Read Like a Writer
DAY 2	Building the Plot
DAY 3	Voice and Humor in Parody
DAY 4	Revising Strategy: Subtracting
DAY 5	Proofread for Commas

MINI-LESSON

Read Like a Writer

■ **Introduce** This week you will write an imaginative story that is a parody of *King Midas and the Golden Touch.* A parody imitates the work on which it is based, but it uses humor to poke fun at that work.

Prompt In *King Midas and the Golden Touch,* a greedy king wishes that everything he touches would turn into gold. Imagine if the king's touch had turned things into something other than gold. What would it be? Write a parody, telling this story.

Trait Voice

Mode Narrative

Reader's and Writer's Notebook p. 408

■ **Examine Model Text** Let's read an example of a parody written to **poke fun at the familiar story** "The Three Little Pigs." One thing that makes this story funny is the point of view of the person telling the story. According to this narrator, things happened a bit differently for the pigs. Have students read "The Three Pigs" on p. 408 of their *Reader's and Writer's Notebook.*

■ **Key Features** Parodies that make fun of stories must still contain all the story elements: **plot, style, and language.** Underline the events in the story that are similar to those in the original tale. Have students point out **details** that were **changed** purposely **for comic effect.**

Narratives have actions and events that build toward the **climax** of the story, the point of greatest tension. To show the **rising action** in the model, isolate the climax by circling the seventh paragraph. Discuss why this represents the point of greatest tension. Then have students start at the beginning of the story and number the events that lead up to the climax. Talk about how the remaining events in the story tie up loose ends.

Review key features

Review the key features of a parody with students. You may want to post the key features in the classroom for students to refer to as they work on their compositions.

Key Features of a Parody

- imitates a familiar story's plot, style, and language
- changes details of the original story for comic effect
- may include action that rises to a climax

ROUTINE — Quick Write for Fluency — Team Talk

1. **Talk** Have pairs take two or three minutes to discuss the features of a parody.

2. **Write** Each person writes a short paragraph describing how the plot of a parody works.

3. **Share** Partners read their paragraphs to one another.

Routines Flip Chart

Wrap Up Your Day

✔ **Build Concepts** What did you learn about the types of lessons that come from the results of our actions?

✔ **Oral Vocabulary** Have students use the Amazing Words they learned in context sentences.

✔ **Homework** Send home this week's Family Times newsletter in *Let's Practice It!* pp. 325–326 on the *Teacher Resources DVD-ROM*.

Let's Practice It!
TR DVD•325–326

Write Guy
Jeff Anderson

Details, Details

Ask children to notice details in mentor text. Rather than pointing out many details, select one that is beyond the obvious. *(It was hot* vs. *The sun melted my crayons that sat on the long window sill in the kitchen.)* What evocative description reveals something new to readers? With guidance, children can learn how to include *details that matter* rather than obvious ones or simply long lists.

Academic Vocabulary

A **parody** is a piece of writing that uses humor to poke fun and imitate another piece of writing. The **climax** of a story is the point at which it reaches its most exciting moment.

English Language Learners

Model Text Read the writing model, helping students understand the sequence of events. Talk about how one event leads to another, and how the story gets more exciting as you go along. Remind students that this genre is meant to entertain readers. Ask them what they like best about this story.

Preview DAY 2

Tell students that tomorrow they will read a myth about a king who has the power to turn everything he touches into gold.

Objectives
- Expand the weekly concept.
- Develop oral vocabulary.

Today at a Glance

Oral Vocabulary
eplorable, outcome

Word Analysis
omplex spelling patterns: *ci* /sh/,
/sh/, ous /us/

Literary Terms
oreshadowing

tory Structure
onflict and resolution

esson Vocabulary
 Suffixes: *-less, -ful*

Leading
Hospital for Wild Animals"
ing Midas and the Golden Touch

luency
ate

esearch and Inquiry
avigate/Search

pelling
atin roots

Conventions
ommas

Vriting
arody

Concept Talk

Question of the Week

 How can we learn from the results of our actions?

Expand the concept

Remind students of the weekly concept question. Tell students that today they will begin reading *King Midas and the Golden Touch.* As they read, encourage students to pay attention to the events that happen as a result of King Midas's actions.

Anchored Talk

Develop oral vocabulary

Have students look back at the photos on pages 370–371 and think about the Read Aloud, "Valuables" to talk about the Amazing Words: *valuable, geologist, rare,* and *specimen.* Add these and other concept-related words to the concept map to develop students' knowledge of the topic. Break into groups. Have students elicit suggestions from other group members in a discussion of the following questions:

- What would you do if you found a *specimen* of a new type of flower?
- What kinds of tools are most *valuable* to a *geologist?*
- Why are complete dinosaur skeletons so *rare?*

Oral Vocabulary
Amazing Words

Amazing Words

specimen	outcome
valuable	victor
geologist	unforeseen
rare	repercussion
deplorable	penitence

Teach Amazing Words

> **Amazing Words** **Oral Vocabulary Routine**
>
> **1 Introduce** Write the Amazing Word *outcome* on the board. Have students say it aloud with you. Relate the word *outcome* to the photo of the sports team. What was the *outcome* of the game? How can we determine the *outcome* in the photo? (The team in the photo won because they are holding up a trophy.) Have students use the context to determine the definition of the word. An *outcome* is the result of an event, such as a game or contest.
>
> **2 Demonstrate** Have students answer questions to demonstrate understanding. What *outcome* would you expect if you didn't study for a test? What can players do to affect the *outcome* of a soccer game?
>
> **3 Apply** Have students apply their understanding. Talk about the *outcome* of a game or other event you know about.
>
> See p. OV•3 to teach *deplorable.*

Routines Flip Chart

Apply Amazing Words

Before students read "Hospital for Wild Animals" on page 375, have them set their own purpose for reading. To set a purpose, students can think about the *deplorable* state of the owl and how the author created a better *outcome.*

Connect to reading

Explain that today students will read about a king whose actions have unexpected results. As they read, they should think about this week's concept question, *How can we learn from the results of our actions?* and the Amazing Words *outcome* and *deplorable,* apply to the king.

ELL **Reinforce Vocabulary** Use the Day 2 instruction on ELL Poster 28 to teach lesson vocabulary and discuss the lesson concept.

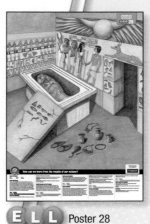

ELL Poster 28

Objectives
- Understand and practice complex spelling patterns.
- Understand foreshadowing in fiction.
- Understand story structure.

Word Analysis
Complex Spelling Patterns: *ci*/sh/, *ti*/sh/, *ous*/us/

Teach complex spelling patterns

Display the word *precious*. Ask students to read it aloud. Use vertical lines to separate the syllables: pre/cious. Have students identify the syllable in *precious* that combines the /sh/ and /us/ sounds. Write the following chart on the board.

Model

Think Aloud Many words contain complex spelling patterns, or unexpected and difficult combinations of letters. The word *precious* has two unexpected spelling patterns. The letters *ci* in the word sound like /sh/, and the *-ous* ending sounds like the word *us*.

	ci	*ti*	*ous*
precious			
action			
mysterious			
musicians			
enormous			
cautious			

Guide practice

Have students write an "X" underneath the column with the correct /*sh*/ or /*us*/ sound spelling. Remind them that some words may belong in more than one column. Tell students that the spelling pattern *ci* can be the result of a consonant change.

On their own

Say *music, musician* and *magic, magician*. Ask students to spell the words. Emphasize how the spelling and pronunciation of each word changes from *c*/k/ to *ci*/sh/ when the ending is added. Follow the Multisyllabic Word Strategy to teach the word *crucial*.

ROUTINE Multisyllabic Word Strategy

1. **Introduce the strategy** Display the word *crucial*. Underline *cial*. Explain that you will use sound spellings to read the word.

2. **Connect to sound-spellings** In the word *crucial*, the *c* combines with *i* to make a /*sh*/ sound, as in *special*.

3. **Read the word** Blend the syllables together to read the word *crucial*. Continue the Routine with the words *gracious* and *suspicion*.

Routines Flip Chart

Literary Terms
Foreshadowing

Teach foreshadowing

Tell students that authors use foreshadowing to give the reader hints about events that happen later in a story. Explain that foreshadowing is most often used in fiction, though it can also be used in nonfiction. Foreshadowing can create suspense or prepare the reader for unexpected plot turns.

Model foreshadowing

 If I look at "Hospital for Wild Animals" on page 375 I notice that the very first sentence talks about places where magic happens. Does this hint about something that will happen later in the story? (It hints that the "lifeless" owl will have a miraculous recovery.)

Guide practice

Tell students that today they will be reading a myth called *King Midas and the Golden Touch*. As they read, they should look for examples of foreshadowing.

On their own

Have students look for examples of foreshadowing in other selections from their Student Edition.

Story Structure
Conflict and Resolution

Teach story structure

Explain to students that most stories set up a conflict or goal that must be resolved by the characters through the events of the story. Each event gives rise to future events until the climax of the story. After that, the conflict is resolved.

Model the strategy

 When I read a story, I like to look for the central conflict or goal in the story. Knowing what the problem is helps me to focus on the story and characters. The easiest way for me to identify the conflict or goal is to look at what the main characters want. I then pay attention to what the characters do to get what they want, and how their actions give rise to future events.

Guide practice

Review "Andrew's Wish" with students and discuss the conflict and resolution in the story. Discuss the incidents that advance the story and lead to the climax and resolution.

On their own

Have students look for examples of conflict and resolution in other selections from their Student Edition.

Vocabulary Strategy for
⟲ Suffixes: -less, -ful

Student Edition p. W•6

Teach suffixes: -less, -ful

Envision It!

Tell students that when they encounter an unknown word, they should use the word structure strategy of dividing the word into syllables. Explain how dividing a word into syllables can help identify the suffixes and root or base words. Refer students to *Words!* on p. W•6 in the Student Edition for additional practice.

Model the strategy

Think Aloud

Write the word *armful* on the board. To help me understand this word, I'm going to start by breaking it into syllables. Use a line to divide the word into the syllables *arm* and *ful*. Now that I have made the word into two syllables, I can see that the second syllable is a suffix. Since I know that *-ful* can mean "the amount of," I add that meaning to the base word *arm* and get a word that means "the amount your arms can hold."

Guide practice

Write this sentence on the board. *The sheets hung lifeless on the clothesline.* Have students break the multisyllablic words into syllables. Then have them identify the word that contains a suffix *(lifeless)* and use the suffix to determine its meaning. For additional support, use *Envision It! Pictured Vocabulary Cards* or *Tested Vocabulary Cards*.

On their own

Read "Hospital for Wild Animals" on p. 375. Have students look for root words that can be changed by adding the suffix *-less* or *-ful*. Have them make a list of the words they create and their meanings. For additional practice, use *Reader's and Writer's Notebook* p. 409.

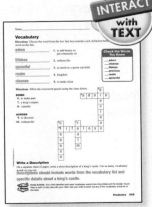

Reader's and Writer's Notebook p. 409

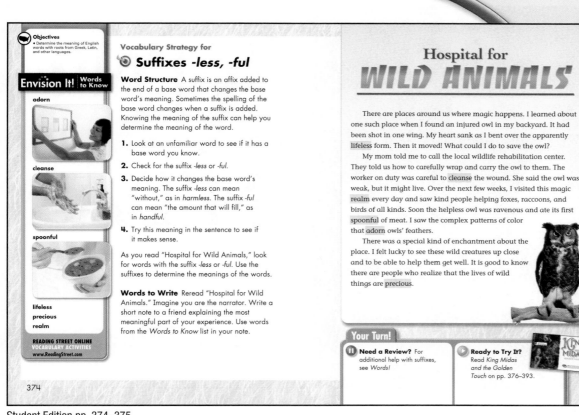

Student Edition pp. 374–375

Reread for Fluency
Rate

Model fluent reading

Read the first paragraph of "Hospital for Wild Animals" aloud, keeping your expression slow and steady as you speak the words. Explain to students that reading a passage slowly and accurately can help them to understand it.

ROUTINE — Oral Rereading — Team Talk

1. **Read** Have students read paragraph 1 of "Hospital for Wild Animals."

2. **Reread** To achieve optimal fluency, students should reread the text three to four times.

3. **Corrective Feedback** Have students read aloud without you. Provide feedback about their rate of speaking and encourage them to speak slowly and accurately. Listen for appropriate rate of speech.

Routines Flip Chart

Lesson Vocabulary

adorn add beauty to; decorate
cleanse make clean
lifeless without life
precious having great value
realm kingdom
spoonful as much as a spoon can hold

Differentiated Instruction

SI Strategic Intervention

Word Structure Have students work in pairs to divide these words into syllables: *cupful, wonderful, hopeless, endless, peaceful, sleepless.* Have them speak each word aloud, clapping for each syllable.

ELL

English Language Learners

Cognates Point out the Spanish cognates in this week's selection vocabulary: *adorn/adorne, and precious/precioso.*

Build Academic Vocabulary Use the lesson vocabulary pictured on p. 374 to teach the meanings of *adorn, cleanse, and spoonful.* Call on pairs to write the words on sticky notes and use them to label images of the words on the ELL Poster.

Objectives
- Understand the elements of a myth.
- Use illustrations to preview and predict.
- Set a purpose for reading.

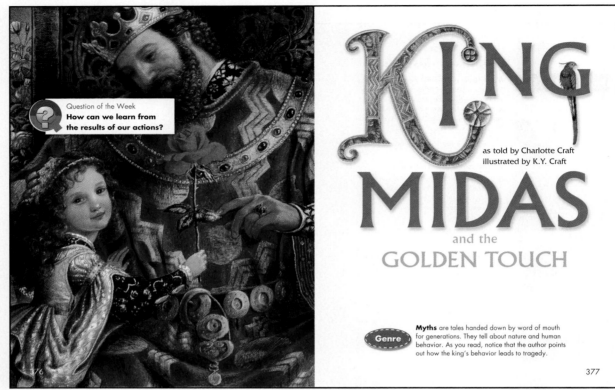

Student Edition pp. 376–377

Build Background

Discuss King Midas

Team Talk Have students turn to a partner and elicit and consider suggestions from each other about the Question of the Week and these questions about King Midas. Have students identify points of agreement and disagreement with their partner.

- Have you ever heard anything about King Midas?
- What makes a king different from other people?
- What kind of stories do kings often appear in?

Connect to selection

Have students consider each other's suggestions and discuss their answers with the class. Possible responses: King Midas could make things turn to gold. Kings are special because they rule other people, live in castles, are very rich, and wear nice clothes. Kings often appear in fairy tales or legends. For additional opportunities to build background, use the Background Building Audio.

Prereading Strategies

Genre

Explain that a **myth** is an old story passed by word of mouth from one generation to the next. Myths are often used to explain natural phenomena but can be used to tell important life lessons.

Preview and predict

Have students preview the title and illustrations for *King Midas and the Golden Touch*. Have them predict what they will find out as they read.

Prior to reading, have students set their own purposes for reading this selection. To help students set a purpose, ask them to think about ways in which their actions have had unintended consequences.

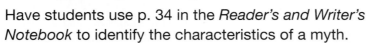

Strategy Response Log

Have students use p. 34 in the *Reader's and Writer's Notebook* to identify the characteristics of a myth.

INTERACT
with
TEXT

Small Group Time

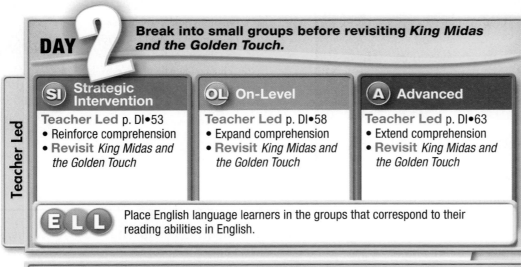

DAY 2 Break into small groups before revisiting *King Midas and the Golden Touch.*

Teacher Led

SI Strategic Intervention	**OL** On-Level	**A** Advanced
Teacher Led p. DI•53	Teacher Led p. DI•58	Teacher Led p. DI•63
• Reinforce comprehension	• Expand comprehension	• Extend comprehension
• **Revisit** *King Midas and the Golden Touch*	• **Revisit** *King Midas and the Golden Touch*	• **Revisit** *King Midas and the Golden Touch*

ELL Place English language learners in the groups that correspond to their reading abilities in English.

Practice Stations
• Words to Know
• Get Fluent
• Word Wise

Independent Activities
• Background Building Audio
• *Reader's and Writer's Notebook*
• Research and Inquiry

Differentiated Instruction

 SI **Strategic Intervention**

Work with students to set a purpose for reading, or if time permits, have students work with partners to set purposes.

 A **Advanced**

Ask students to compare this myth to other stories they have heard or read. What makes this story a myth?

Double Day Read Multidraft Reading

For **Whole Group** instruction, choose one of the reading options below. For each reading have students set the purpose indicated.

Option 1
Day 2 Read the selection. Use Guide Comprehension to monitor and clarify understanding.
Day 3 Reread the selection. Use Extend Thinking to develop higher-order thinking skills.

Option 2
Day 2 Read the first half of the selection, using both Guide Comprehension and Extend Thinking instruction.
Day 3 Read the second half of the selection, using both Guide Comprehension and Extend Thinking instruction.

 **ELL**

English Language Learners

Build background To build background, review the selection summary in English (*ELL Handbook* p. 193). Use the Retelling Cards to provide visual support for the summary.

OPTION 1 Guide Comprehension Skills and Strategies

Teach Compare and Contrast

Compare and Contrast Have students reread p. 378, paragraphs 3 and 4, and have them use a Venn diagram to compare and contrast King Midas and daughter Aurelia.

Corrective Feedback

If... students are unable to find similarities and differences between King Midas and Aurelia,

then... model guiding students in identify comparisons.

Let's Practice It!
TR DVD•327

Model the Skill

 Think Aloud To compare two characters, I need to find things that they have in common. What did both King Midas and Aurelia love? (They both love the roses.)

Student Edition pp. 378–379

OPTION 2 Extend Thinking Think Critically

Higher-Order Thinking Skills

Compare and Contrast • Analysis Look at the first paragraph on page 378. How does the author compare gold to music? Possible response: The writer compares the sound of gold clinking to musical notes played by the king's musicians.

There once lived a very rich king called Midas who believed that nothing was more precious than gold. He loved its soft yellow hue and comforting weight in the palm of his hand. The chink of gold coins dropped into a leather purse sounded sweeter to him than the songs of his finest musicians. There was only one thing that Midas loved more, and that was his daughter, Aurelia.

"Aurelia," he often told her as she played by the throne, "someday I shall bequeath to you the greatest treasury of gold in all the world."

There had been a time, however, when King Midas loved roses as much as he now loved gold. He had once called together the best gardeners in his realm, and the garden they created for him became renowned for the beauty and variety of its roses.

But in time the delicate fragrances and exquisite colors meant nothing to Midas. Only Aurelia still loved the garden. Every day she would pick a bouquet of the most perfect roses to adorn the king's breakfast table. But when Midas saw the flowers, he would think, *Their beauty lasts but a day. If they were gold, it would last forever!*

One day the king's guards found an old man asleep under the rosebushes and brought him before King Midas.

"Unbind him," Midas ordered. "Without my gold, I would be as poor as he. Tonight he shall dine with me!"

So that night the old man sat at the king's table, where he was well fed and entertained by the king himself. And after a good night's sleep, the old man went on his way.

378

Genre • Evaluation Compare King Midas to another king that you have read about in text of a different genre. How were their attitudes toward gold similar? How were they different? Answers will depend on students' prior reading. Many students may answer that other kings were more interested in ruling than collecting gold.

How did their feelings toward gold differ? (King Midas came to love gold more than the roses, but Aurelia did not.) Their love for roses is a way they are alike. Their different feelings about gold is a contrast between the two characters.

On Their Own

Have students use their own Venn Diagrams to compare and contrast King Midas with the old man on p. 378. For additional practice, use *Let's Practice It!* p. 327 on the *Teacher Resources DVD-ROM.*

Differentiated Instructio

 Advanced

Greek Myths Students may enjoy reading other myths like *King Midas* online. Have them use a student-friendly search engine and the keywords "Greek myths." Be sure to follow classroom guidelines for Internet use.

379

Infer • Synthesis What can you infer about King Midas's character from his decision to help the old man? What evidence from the text supports your inference? **Possible response: King Midas loves gold, but he is a good man. He is able to feel sympathy for people who have much less than he does.**

 ELL

English Language Learners
Activate Prior Knowledge King Midas's favorite thing was gold. Ask students to discuss what they know about gold. Why is gold valuable? How do people use gold? Can you think of something that would be more valuable than gold?

OPTION 1 Skills and Strategies, continued

Teach Draw Conclusions

Review **Draw Conclusions** Ask students: Based on the text, what can you conclude about how and why the young man appears to King Midas? (Possible response: He has appeared through magic. He is the old man from the rose garden who has come to reward King Midas for his good deeds.)

Corrective Feedback

If… students have difficulty answering the question,

then… model how to draw conclusions.

Let's Practice It!
TR DVD●328

Model the Skill

Think Aloud The mysterious stranger appears suddenly in the locked chamber, his figure glows and he now looks like a young man, so he must be a magical creature of some sort.

380

Student Edition pp. 380–381

OPTION 2 Think Critically, continued

Higher-Order Thinking Skills

Review **Draw Conclusions • Analysis** What details in the text led King Midas to conclude that he was in the presence of a magical being? Give specific examples from the text. The room "suddenly filled with light," the figure was "glowing," and the person was able to enter the room even though the door was locked.

Genre • Analysis Explain the function of the magical character's relationship with King Midas in the story. The magical character grants King Midas the wish that everything he touches will turn to gold. Since the genre of this story is a myth, the wish will probably cause King Midas to learn a valuable lesson.

He says he wants to reward King Midas for his kindness and asks what the king wants. I can draw the conclusion that the young man wants to reward King Midas because it is rare for a king to help a poor man.

That morning, as he often did, Midas went down into his dungeon. With a large brass key, he unlocked the door to the secret chamber where he kept his gold. After carefully locking the door behind him, he sat down to admire his precious wealth.

"Ah, I do love it so," he sighed, gazing at his riches. "No matter how hard I work, no matter how long I live, I will never have enough."

He was lost in these thoughts when the chamber suddenly filled with light. King Midas looked up and was amazed to behold the glowing figure of a young man. Since there was no way into the room but through the locked door, Midas knew that he was in the presence of magic.

"Do you not recognize me, friend?"

Midas shook his head. The mysterious stranger smiled at him, and it seemed that all the gold in the dungeon glittered even brighter.

"I am the old man from the rose garden. Instead of punishing me for trespassing, you entertained me at your table. I had thought to reward you for your kindness, but with so much gold, you must surely want for nothing."

"That's not true," cried Midas. "A man can never have enough gold."

The stranger's smile broadened. "Well, then, what would make you a happier man?"

Midas thought for only a moment. "Perhaps if everything I touched would turn to gold," he said.

381

Make Predictions • Evaluation Do you think that King Midas will be happier once his wish comes true? Explain your answer. Possible responses: King Midas may not be as happy as he thinks, because the wish might cause him problems.

On Their Own

Have students draw a conclusion about King Midas based on his wish. (Possible response: King Midas is greedy for more gold.) For additional practice, use *Let's Practice It!* p. 328 on the *Teacher Resources DVD-ROM.*

Differentiated Instruction

SI Strategic Intervention

Draw Conclusions Remind students that a conclusion is a decision or opinion that makes sense after thinking about the facts and details. Have students point to the details on this page that lead to the conclusion that the young man is magical.

Connect to Social Studies

The word *gold* is used frequently in English. Encourage students to share phrases or images they know that contain the word *gold*. For example, the phrase *good as gold* means something true and valuable. The phrase "the golden touch" has its origin in the King Midas myth, but it has also come to mean achieving success in almost anything one attempts.

ELL

English Language Learners

Monitor understanding Have students read aloud the third paragraph on p. 381. How does the young man get into the room? (by using magic) Have students look back at the text to clarify their understanding.

bjectives

Analyze story structure through character, setting, and events.

OPTION 1 Skills and Strategies, continued

Teach Story Structure

Story Structure Have students begin to fill out a Story Structure organizer with boxes for Characters, Setting, Events, Problem, and Solution. Tell them to fill in the characters box and the setting box.

Corrective Feedback

If... students are not able to identify the characters or setting,

then... model how to identify characters and setting in a story.

Model the Strategy

Think Aloud The characters are the people in the story. So, I need to look through the pages for names or descriptions of people. King Midas is one character. His daughter Aurelia is another.

hat is your wish?"

"Yes, for then it would always be at my fingertips," Midas assured him.

"Think carefully, my friend," cautioned the visitor.

"Yes," replied Midas. "The golden touch would bring me all the happiness I need."

"And so it shall be yours."

With that, the mysterious figure became brighter and brighter, until the light became so intense that Midas had to close his eyes. When he opened them, he was alone once again.

Had the enchantment worked?

Midas eagerly rubbed the great brass door key but was greatly disappointed. There was no gold in his hands. Bewildered, he looked around the dim room and wondered if perhaps he had been dreaming.

But when King Midas awoke the next day, he found his bedchamber bathed in golden light. Glistening in the morning sun, the plain linen bedcovers had been transformed into finely spun gold!

Jumping out of bed, he gasped with astonishment. The bedpost turned to gold as soon as he touched it. "It's true," he cried. "I have the golden touch!"

Midas pulled on his clothes. He was thrilled to find himself wearing a handsome suit of gold—never mind that it was a bit heavy. He slid his spectacles onto his nose. To his delight, they too turned to gold—never mind that he couldn't see through them. With a gift as great as this, he thought, no inconvenience could be too great.

382

Student Edition pp. 382–383

OPTION 2 Think Critically, continued

Higher-Order Thinking Skills

Story Structure • Analysis How does the author change the setting in the middle of page 382? The setting changes from King Midas's secret chamber to his bedroom. The author jumps from King Midas rubbing the door to the chamber to waking up the next morning in his bed.

Foreshadowing • Analysis Make an inference about why the visitor cautions King Midas by saying, "Think carefully, my friend." Possible response: The visitor knows that bad things may happen if King Midas gets his wish. He likes King Midas and does not want him to make a choice he will regret.

The magical young man is a third. To find the setting, I look for the places that the characters are in, such as King Midas's secret chamber or his bedroom.

On Their Own

Have students list a few events on their organizer, describing how each incident gives rise to or fore-shadows future events. Point out that the problem and solution boxes should remain blank, since the students haven't read about the problem or solution yet.

383

Background Knowledge • Evaluation • Text to Self How would you react if everything you touched turned to gold? Do you think you would have the same reaction as King Midas? Possible responses: Yes, I would be excited because the golden touch would make me rich, or no, because having such powers would be frightening.

Check Predictions Have students look back at the predictions they made earlier and discuss whether they were accurate. Then have students preview the rest of the selection and either adjust their predictions accordingly or make new predictions.

Differentiated Instruction

 Strategic Intervention

Answer Questions Ask students to identify at what point in the story King Midas realizes that he has the "golden touch," and describe how this changes him.

 Advanced

Critical Thinking Based on the text they've read so far, ask students what they think will happen now that King Midas has the "golden touch."

ELL

English Language Learners
Monitor comprehension With students, read aloud the paragraph beginning with "But when King Midas awoke…" What detail shows that King Midas's wish has come true? (The plain bedcovers have turned into gold.)

Story Structure If students have difficulty understanding the change in setting, have them use sensory details to visualize the secret chamber and King Midas's bedroom.

 If you want to teach this selection in two sessions, stop here.

King Midas and the Golden Touch **383a**

Objectives
- Find pertinent information from print and online sources.
- Recognize and correctly use commas.
- Practice correctly spelling words with Latin roots.

Research and Inquiry
Navigate/Search

Teach

Remind students about the inquiry questions they developed the previous day. Have them search reference texts and the Internet using keywords related to their questions.

Model

Think Aloud I used a student-friendly search engine and the keywords *gold mining* to begin my search. I learned that there are many ways to mine gold. During the Gold Rush, miners used techniques such as panning for gold and sluice boxes. Nowadays, people use metal detectors as well as special techniques to remove gold from hard rocks. I now have some new keywords to search: *gold panning, sluice box mining, hard rock mining,* and *gold metal detectors.* I will try to find more information about these techniques. There may be an entry in the encyclopedia. I will also look for photos of people doing each of these things so I can add visual aids to my oral presentation.

Guide practice

Have students continue to search online, and encourage them to consult reference texts such as print or electronic encyclopedias. Whether the source is online or in print, students should carefully evaluate the information for relevance, validity, and reliability. For example, an encyclopedia article about gold mining may be a better source than a novel about gold miners or a personal Web site about someone who went gold mining on a vacation. Ask students why it is important to cite sources that are valid and reliable.

On their own

To prepare for their Works Cited page, have students identify and write down bibliographic information for each source. Write a model bibliography entry on the board. Remind students that they will need to record the author, title, page number, publisher, and publication year or each print source. For each Web site, they should record the Web address, author, and date they accessed the Web site.

Conventions
Commas

Teach

Write this sentence on the board: *King Midas loved gold, but he loved Aurelia more.* Tell students that the comma and the conjunction *but* join two simple sentences to make this compound sentence. Use these sentences to review other uses of the comma: to separate items in a list, and to set apart an appositive, an introductory word or phrase, or a noun of direct address. *Midas went to his dungeon, unlocked the door, and admired his treasure. A stranger, a young man, wanted him to make a wish. Whenever Midas touched something, it turned to gold. I like reading, Chad, don't you?*

Guide practice

Write this sentence. Have students tell where commas belong and why. They should recognize three different uses for commas.

While we are decorating the tables Eva my niece is making soup sandwiches and salad for the party.

Daily Fix-It

Use Daily Fix-It numbers 3 and 4 in the right margin.

Connect to oral language

Have students look for and read aloud sentences showing different uses of commas on the first page of *King Midas and the Golden Touch.* (compound sentence, appositive, compound sentence, introductory phrase, introductory phrase)

On their own

For more practice, use the *Reader's and Writer's Notebook* p. 410.

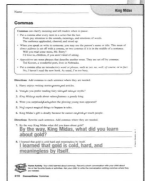
Reader's and Writer's Notebook p. 410

Spelling
Latin Roots

Teach

Write *portable* on the board. Underline *port* and explain that it is a Latin root meaning "to carry." Remind students that this week, they are learning words with five different Latin roots.

Guide practice

Write the remaining spelling words on the board. Help students underline and define the Latin root in each word.

On their own

For more practice, use the *Reader's and Writer's Notebook* p. 411.

Reader's and Writer's Notebook p. 411

Daily Fix-It

3. José drawed a picture of King Midas Aurelia and the young man. *(drew; Midas, Aurelia, and)*

4. The king was overcome with greif when the littel girl was turned to gold. *(grief; little)*

 **ELL**

English Language Learners
Conventions
To provide students with practice on commas, use the modified grammar lessons in the *ELL Handbook* and the Grammar Jammer! online at:
www.ReadingStreet.com

DAY 2 Language Arts

Objectives
- Map out plot events of a story to show how they build toward a climax.

Writing—Parody
Writing Trait: Plot

Introduce the prompt

Remind students that the selection they'll be reading this week, *King Midas and the Golden Touch,* is a myth. They will be writing an imaginative story, called a parody, which is meant to poke fun at this myth. Review the key features of a narrative composition. Remind students to think about these features as they plan their writing. Then explain that they will begin the writing process for a narrative composition today. Read aloud the writing prompt.

Writing Prompt

In *King Midas and the Golden Touch,* a greedy king wishes that everything he touches would turn into gold. Imagine if the king's touch had turned things into something other than gold. What would it be? Write a parody, telling this story.

Select the topic

 Think Aloud To help decide what things in our story might turn into besides gold, let's make a chart. We can list ideas on one side and suggest ways each one might be funny on the other side. **Display a T-chart.** I think we should consider things that people love and wish they had more of, just like King Midas always wanted more gold. I know one thing I love and seem to never get enough of is chocolate. What would be funny about having things turn to chocolate? One idea I have is that it would melt and make a mess. Ask students to suggest other ideas, and fill in the chart as they give examples. Talk about how humorous each idea might be.

Things Besides Gold	Why It Would Be Funny
chocolate	The chocolate things would melt.
diamonds	Everyone might be blinded by light from such big diamonds.
animals	Everything would be noisy and messy.

Corrective feedback

Circulate around the room as students use the chart to choose the thing they will feature in their stories. Conference briefly with students who are having problems making a choice. Ask each struggling student to consider which idea would become more and more exciting as the king touches things, which idea could help build a plot toward a climax, and how the scenes could be funny.

MINI-LESSON

Building the Plot

■ Thinking about how one event leads to the next helps you create a strong plot line. In my parody, I'm going to write about having things turn to chocolate. I want each new thing that is touched to become a funnier problem for the king. The first thing he touches should be something small that he can eat. However, once he eats it it is gone forever, so it should be something useful. **Write this information at the top of a chain of boxes.**

■ At the end of the chain of events should be the climax. What will be so funny and impossible for the king that he will beg for his touch to be taken away? I think it could be that he likes to take a hot bath. However, when he gets into the tub, it turns to chocolate and melts. He looks like he has been playing in mud! **Write this information in the bottom box of the chain.**

Have students begin their own chain of events using the form on p. 412 of their Reader's and Writer's Notebook.

ROUTINE — Quick Write for Fluency **Team Talk**

1. **Talk** Have pairs discuss the plot chains they have developed.
2. **Write** Each student describes the climax of their story.
3. **Share** Each partner reads the other's sentences. Then each partner asks the other one questions about the climax.

Routines Flip Chart

Wrap Up Your Day

✔ **Build Concepts** Have students discuss how King Midas felt about gold.

✔ **Compare and Contrast** Compare King Midas's love of roses with his love of gold.

✔ **Story Structure** Who are the major characters and events in "King Midas and the Golden Touch"?

Differentiated Instruction

 Advanced

Denouement Challenge students to consider the ending events of their story, thinking about any loose ends that can be tied up. Show them how to create a plot diagram that includes the events on the other side of the climax.

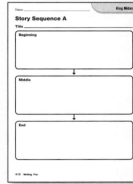

Reader's and Writer's Notebook p. 412

Teacher Tip

Point out that students are doing a quick write and should not worry about perfectly writing the climactic event of their stories. The idea is to know what will happen and why, not to write it as it will appear in the story.

Preview DAY 3

Tell students that tomorrow they will continue to read about King Midas, whose wish will have unexpected results.

Objectives
• Expand the weekly concept.
• Develop oral vocabulary.

Today at a Glance

Oral Vocabulary
unforeseen, victor

Comprehension Check/Retelling
Discuss questions

Reading
King Midas and the Golden Touch

Think Critically
Retelling

Fluency
Rate

Research and Study Skills
order form/application

Research and Inquiry
Analyze

Spelling
Latin roots

Conventions
Commas

Writing
Parody

Concept Talk

Question of the Week

How can we learn from the results of our actions?

Expand the concept

Remind students of the Question of the Week. Discuss how the question relates to the unexpected result of King Midas's kindness. Tell students that today they will read about the consequences of King Midas's wish. Encourage students to think about how the Amazing Words relate to *King Midas and the Golden Touch.*

Anchored Talk

Develop oral vocabulary

Use illustrations to review pp. 376–383 of *King Midas and the Golden Touch.* Discuss the Amazing Words *outcome* and *deplorable.* Add these and other concept-related words to the concept map. Have students break into groups. Then have them use the following questions to identify points of agreement among group members and develop their understanding of the concept.

• King Midas had an unexpectedly good *outcome* from his kindness. What outcome would you expect if you helped someone who needed it?

• Some people might find King Midas's love of gold *deplorable.* What attitudes do you find deplorable?

Oral Vocabulary
Amazing Words

Amazing Words
valuable	deplorable
geologist	unforeseen
rare	victor
specimen	repercussion
outcome	penitence

Teach Amazing Words

⭐Amazing Words⭐ Oral Vocabulary Routine

1) **Introduce** Write the word *unforeseen* on the board. Have students say it with you. Getting a wish granted was an unforeseen result of King Midas's kindness. Have students use the context to determine a definition of *unforeseen*. (When something is *unforeseen,* that means that no one predicted it would happen.)

2) **Demonstrate** Have students answer questions to demonstrate understanding. Have you ever encountered an unforeseen event in your life? (Answers will vary.)

3) **Apply** Have students apply their understanding. Is the weather tomorrow something that is unforeseen or can it be predicted? (Answers will vary.)

See p. OV•3 to teach *victor.*

Routines Flip Chart

Apply Amazing Words

Help students establish a purpose for reading. As students read pp. 384–393 of *King Midas and the Golden Touch,* have them think about the *unforeseen* outcome of King Midas's wish and whether the story has a *victor.*

Connect to reading

Explain that today students should read to discover the unexpected results of King Midas's wish. As they read, students should think about how the Question of the Week and the Amazing Words *unforeseen* and *victor* apply to the king.

ELL Expand Vocabulary Use the Day 3 instruction on ELL Poster 28 to help students expand vocabulary.

ELL Poster 28

King Midas and the Golden Touch **384b**

Objectives

- Use compare and contrast to aid understanding.
- Use the story structure strategy to aid comprehension.
- Use word structure to determine the meanings of words with suffixes.

Comprehension Check

Have students discuss each question with a partner. Ask several pairs to share their responses.

✓ **Genre • Analysis** What elements of this story indicate that it is a myth, rather than another type of story? Possible response: The story takes place long ago, and has larger-than-life characters, magic, and gods. It deals with a wish coming true for someone, which probably means that it will teach a moral lesson.

✓ **Compare and Contrast • Analysis** How are King Midas and Aurelia similar? How are they different? Possible responses: They are similar in loving things very strongly. They are different because King Midas loves gold and Aurelia loves roses.

✓ **Story Structure • Evaluation** Based on the events of the story so far, what future events do you think King Midas's wish might give rise to? Possible response: I think King Midas will find out that his golden touch is more of a burden than a blessing. The last paragraph on p. 382 suggests that not everything is better when it's made of gold, since he couldn't see through his eyeglasses and his clothes were too heavy, so probably he will turn something into gold by accident.

✓ **Suffixes • Synthesis** Use word structure to determine the meanings of *eventful* and *hopeless* in the following sentence: After the king's eventful day, sleep seems hopeless. Possible responses: I see the suffix *-ful* at the end of the base word *event*. Since I know that *-ful* can mean "full of," I think *eventful* means "full of events or happenings." I see the suffix *-less* at the end of the base word *hope*. Since I know that *-less* can mean "without," I think *hopeless* means "without hope."

✓ **Connect Text to Self** King Midas's wish was that everything he touched would turn to gold. If you were given one wish, what would it be? Possible response: I would wish that my homework would always get the highest marks.

Strategy Response Log

INTERACT with TEXT

Have students revisit p. 34 in the *Reader's and Writer's Notebook* to add additional information about myths.

Check Retelling

Have students retell what they have read of *King Midas and the Golden Touch,* paraphrasing information in the text in a way that maintains its meaning and logical order. Encourage students to use the text features in their retellings.

Corrective feedback

If... students leave out important details,

then... have students look back through the illustrations in the selection.

Small Group Time

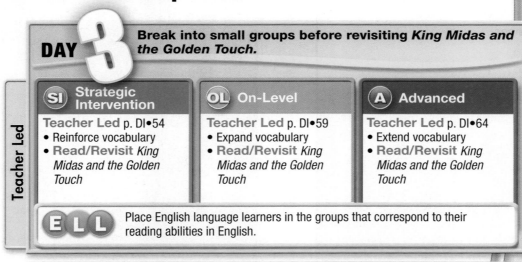

DAY 3

Break into small groups before revisiting *King Midas and the Golden Touch.*

Teacher Led

SI Strategic Intervention

Teacher Led p. DI•54
- Reinforce vocabulary
- **Read/Revisit** *King Midas and the Golden Touch*

OL On-Level

Teacher Led p. DI•59
- Expand vocabulary
- **Read/Revisit** *King Midas and the Golden Touch*

A Advanced

Teacher Led p. DI•64
- Extend vocabulary
- **Read/Revisit** *King Midas and the Golden Touch*

ELL Place English language learners in the groups that correspond to their reading abilities in English.

Practice Stations
- Let's Write
- Get Fluent
- Word Work

Independent Activities
- AudioText: *King Midas*
- *Reader's and Writer's Notebook*
- Research and Inquiry

ELL

English Language Learners

Check retelling To support retelling, review the multilingual summary for *King Midas and the Golden Touch* with the appropriate Retelling Cards to scaffold understanding.

Objectives
▸ Draw conclusions to aid comprehension.

OPTION 1 Skills and Strategies, continued

Teach Draw Conclusions

Review **Draw Conclusions** Ask students: What conclusions can you infer about why the king is in a hurry on pages 384–385? What evidence from the text supports your conclusion? (Possible response: He is in a hurry because he is excited about his golden touch and wants to use it in his garden. He may also be rushing because he is afraid that he'll lose his golden touch, and he wants to use it quickly.)

Corrective Feedback

If... students have difficulty answering the question,
then... model how to draw conclusions.

 **Multidraft Reading**

If you chose...

Option 1 Return to Extend Thinking instruction starting on p. 378–379.
Option 2 Read pp. 384–393.
Use the Guide Comprehension and Extend Thinking instruction.

Student Edition pp. 384–385

Model the Skill

Think Aloud When I read the text and study the picture on pages 384–385, I know that Midas is in a hurry to go outside to the garden. I conclude that he wants to use his golden touch there.

Without wasting another moment, Midas rushed out of

384

● **Compare and Contrast • Evaluation** Compare and contrast the left side and the right side of the illustration on pages 384–385. Which side looks better? Why? Possible response: The architecture is the same, but almost everything on the left side has turned to gold. The left side is golden but not very lively. The right side is colorful and full of life.

OPTION 2 Think Critically, continued

Higher-Order Thinking Skills

Review **Draw Conclusions • Analysis** Look at the illustration on pages 384–385 and draw a conclusion about whether or not King Midas has touched any people yet. Provide evidence to support your conclusion. Possible response: The people behind King Midas still have color in their hair, faces, and clothing, showing that they are not made of gold. Therefore, King Midas has not touched them.

Since the golden touch is magic, I can also conclude that King Midas is hurrying because he's afraid that it won't last.

the room, through the palace, and into the garden.

385

On Their Own

Have students look at the illustration on pp. 384–385 and infer a conclusion about what would happen if King Midas were to touch one of the plants or flowers. Encourage students to cite evidence from the text to support their conclusion.

Foreshadowing • Analysis How do the text and illustration foreshadow what may happen later in the story? **Possible response:** King Midas is hurrying toward the plants and flowers, which are living things that would turn into gold if he touched them. Perhaps he might touch some other living things later in the story.

Differentiated Instruction

 Advanced

Explore a topic Have students examine the illustrations to determine which country and time period provides the closest historical setting for this version of the myth. Students may use the Internet to find examples of costumes and architecture from various time periods and cultures.

ELL

English Language Learners
Monitor comprehension Have students read aloud the text on pp. 384–385 and look at the illustration. What is King Midas doing? (He is hurrying through the palace.) What information do you get from the illustration that you didn't get from the text? (He is touching everything in his path, because nearly everything behind him in the illustration has turned to gold.)

OPTION 1 Skills and Strategies, continued

Teach Compare and Contrast

Compare and Contrast Ask students to compare and contrast Aurelia's reaction to the golden roses with what King Midas expected her to feel. (Aurelia is saddened by the golden roses because she can no longer smell them. King Midas expected her to be happy because they would never fade.)

Corrective Feedback

If… students have difficulty comparing and contrasting,
then… model how to compare and contrast.

Student Edition pp. 386–387

Model the Skill

Think Aloud I will look at the difference between Aurelia's feelings about the golden roses and her father's expectations. Aurelia reacts by sobbing because the roses are now hard and yellow.

386

OPTION 2 Think Critically, continued

Higher-Order Thinking Skills

Compare and Contrast • Evaluation Compare the roses before and after King Midas touched them. Do you agree with King Midas or Aurelia about whether the roses were better red than gold? **Possible response:** Aurelia was right to be sad. The roses were prettier and more colorful before they were turned to gold. Now they are hard and heavy and have no scent.

Sensory Details • Evaluation Reread the first paragraph on page 387. Evaluate the impact of the sensory details the author uses to describe the roses. **Possible response:** The sensory details in the paragraph include the words "glistened," "morning dew," and "gently perfumed." These details create a pleasant, peaceful image of the living roses.

But King Midas had expected her to be happy because the roses will never fade.

On Their Own

Have students write an explanation of how King Midas's porridge differs from what he expected it to be like.

Connect to Social Studies

Gold has many uses in medicine. Discuss the various ways that gold is used to help people, such as dental fillings, pain relief for those with rheumatoid arthritis, and to coat lasers and thermometers.

The roses glistened with the morning dew, and their scent gently perfumed the air. Midas went from bush to bush, touching each of the blossoms.

"How happy Aurelia will be when she sees these roses of gold!" he exclaimed. He never noticed how the perfect golden blossoms drooped and pulled down the bushes with their weight.

Soon it was time for breakfast. Midas sat down just as Aurelia entered the room, clutching a golden rose, her face wet with tears.

"Father, Father, a horrible thing has happened," she said, sobbing. "I went to the garden to pick you a flower, but all of the roses have become hard and yellow."

"They are golden roses now, my love, and will never fade."

"But I miss their scent, Father," cried Aurelia.

"I am sorry, my dear. I thought only to please you. Now we can buy all the roses you could ever wish for." Midas smiled at his daughter to comfort her. "Please wipe your eyes, and we'll have our breakfast together."

Midas lifted a spoonful of porridge to his mouth, but as soon as the porridge touched his lips it turned into a hard golden lump.

387

Make Predictions • Analysis How do you think King Midas will end up feeling about his wish? Explain. Possible response: He will regret it, because it is making his daughter unhappy and because now he can't eat anything he touches.

ELL

English Language Learners
Extend language Tell students that *scent* refers to a smell or odor. Ask them to name a word that sounds the same but is spelled differently. *(sent)*

Objectives
⊃ Analyze suffixes to aid comprehension.

OPTION 1 Skills and Strategies, continued

Teach Suffixes -less, -ful

⊙ **Suffixes -less, -ful** Have students use their knowledge of suffixes to determine a meaning for the word *spoonful* in paragraph 1 on p. 388.

Corrective Feedback

If... students are unable to determine the meaning of the word,
then... model using suffixes to determine the meaning of a word.

Reader's and Writer's
Notebook p. 413

Model the Skill

Think Aloud When I see the *-ful* ending on a word, then I know that the meaning of the root word will change. The root word for *spoonful* is *spoon*. I know what a spoon is.

Perhaps if I eat quickly, he thought, puzzled, and snatched a fig from a bowl of fruit. It turned to solid gold before he could take a bite. He reached out for some bread, but his fingertips had no sooner brushed against the loaf than it, too, turned to gold. He tried cheese and even a spoonful of jam, but all to no avail. "How am I to eat?" he grumbled.

"What's wrong, Father?" asked Aurelia.

"Nothing," he answered, wishing not to worry her. "Nothing at all, my child."

But Midas began to wring his hands. If he was hungry now, he imagined how much more hungry he would be by dinner. And then he began to wonder: Will I ever eat again?

Aurelia, who had been anxiously watching her father all this time, slipped out of her chair and went to comfort him. "Please don't cry," she said. Midas smiled and took her hand in his. But suddenly he recoiled in horror.

His daughter stood before him, an expression of concern frozen on her face, a teardrop clinging to her golden cheek. His cursed touch had turned Aurelia into a lifeless statue.

388

Student Edition pp. 388–389

OPTION 2 Think Critically, continued

Higher-Order Thinking Skills

⊙ **Suffixes -less, -ful • Analysis** Use what you know about suffixes to determine the meaning of the word *lifeless* in the last paragraph on page 388. The suffix *-less* means "without," so *lifeless* means "without life."

Cause and Effect • Analysis What caused Aurelia to turn into a lifeless statue when King Midas touched her? How might King Midas have prevented this from happening? **King Midas wished for the golden touch, which turned Aurelia into gold. He could have prevented this by asking for a different, less dangerous wish.**

The suffix *-ful* means "full of," or "the amount of." So a *spoonful* is the amount of something that would fit in a spoon. When I see the word *spoonful,* I will remember to think of the "spoon being full."

389

Genre • Evaluation What important truth do you think King Midas will learn from the results of his actions? Possible response: He might learn to reconsider his greedy love of gold.

On Their Own

Have students identify the suffix and use it to determine the definition of the following words: *beautiful, cupful, plentiful, useless,* and *harmless.* For additional practice, use the *Reader's and Writer's Notebook* p. 413.

Differentiated Instruction

SI Strategic Intervention

Monitor comprehension Ask students to reread the early parts of the story and then reread p. 388 to help them identify how King Midas's life has changed.

ELL

English Language Learners

Extend language Read aloud the phrase *to no avail* on page 388, paragraph 1. Explain that it means "of no use" or "without benefit." Ask students why the king's attempts to eat were *to no avail.*

Objectives
◎ Compare and contrast to extend understanding of the text.

OPTION 1 Skills and Strategies, continued

Teach Compare and Contrast

◎ **Compare and Contrast** Ask students to compare and contrast King Midas's feelings about his wish on p. 391 with the way he felt earlier. (Now, King Midas considers his wish to be a curse, because it turned his daughter into a lifeless statue. Before, he thought it would make him a happy man.)

Corrective Feedback

If… students have difficulty answering the question,
then… model how to compare and contrast.

Model the Skill

 Think Aloud On page 391, King Midas says that the gift "is a curse to me now." The word *now* is a clue word that his attitude has changed.

Student Edition pp. 390–391

OPTION 2 Think Critically, continued

Higher-Order Thinking Skills

◎ **Compare and Contrast • Analysis** What other word does the author use on pages 390–391 to show comparison and contrast? Explain how the word is used and what it compares or contrasts.

Midas howled in anguish and tore at his hair. He couldn't bear to look at the statue, but neither could he bear to leave her side.

"Well, King Midas, are you not the happiest of men?" Midas wiped his eyes and saw the mysterious stranger standing before him once again.

"Oh, no, I am the most miserable of men!" he cried.

"What? Did I not grant your wish for the golden touch?"

390

Possible response: The author uses the word *but* twice to show contrast. The first use is on p. 390, paragraph 1, as King Midas's horror at the sight of the statue is contrasted with his love for his daughter. On p. 391, paragraph 1, the word *but* shows a contrast between King Midas's feelings toward the golden touch before and after his daughter was turned into a statue.

He now sees the golden touch as a curse. Before, he thought it would make him happier.

On Their Own

Remind students that other clue words that show comparison or contrast are *but, now, same, also, before, although,* and *however.* Have them use three of these words in sentences.

"Yes, but it is a curse to me now." Midas wept. "All that I truly loved is now lost to me."

"Do you mean to say," asked the young man, "that you would prefer a crust of bread or a cup of water to the gift of the golden touch?"

"Oh, yes!" Midas exclaimed. "I would give up all the gold in the world if only my daughter were restored to me."

391

Foreshadowing • Analysis Look back at the last two paragraphs on page 378. How does that passage foreshadow what King Midas learns on pages 390–391? **Possible response:** In the passage on page 378, King Midas pities the poor old man and feeds him a fancy dinner. But now King Midas would prefer a simple crust of bread and water if he could share it with his daughter.

Character • Evaluation Think about the role of the magical young man in this story and his relationship with King Midas. Why do you think he came to grant King Midas a wish? Possible response: Since the young man is magical, perhaps he is a god who wanted to teach the greedy King Midas a lesson.

ELL

English Language Learners
Access Content Read aloud p. 390. Point out that the word *bear* has two meanings. Explain that *bear* can mean "a large animal with thick fur." However, here *bear* means "to put up with" or "to be able to stand something." Ask students why they think King Midas couldn't bear to look at the statue of his daughter or bear to leave her side.

Objectives
◎ Analyze story structure.

OPTION 1

Skills and Strategies, continued

Teach Story Structure

◎ **Story Structure** Explain to students that in addition to a conflict/resolution structure, stories can also have a problem/solution structure. Have students complete their story chart organizers and then identify the problem and solution.

Corrective Feedback

If... students are not able to fill in the problem and solution in the story chart organizer,

then... model for students how to fill in their organizers.

Student Edition pp. 392–393

OPTION 2

Think Critically, continued

Higher-Order Thinking Skills

◎ **Story Structure • Synthesis** What was King Midas's major problem in this story? Describe how it gave rise to future events. Possible response: King Midas's major problem was his greediness because it gave rise to many other problems, such as the loss of his daughter.

Model the Strategy

Think Aloud Sometimes it's easier to identify the problem in a story by looking at the solution. The solution for King Midas was to cleanse himself in the river.

"Then make your way to the river that flows past the borders of your kingdom. Follow the river upstream until you reach its source. As you cleanse yourself in the foaming spring, the golden touch will be washed away. Take with you a vase so that you may sprinkle water over any object you wish to change back to its original form." With those words, the young man vanished.

As soon as Midas reached the spring, he plunged in without removing even his shoes. As the water washed the gold from his clothes, he noticed a pretty little violet growing wild along the banks and gently brushed his finger against it. When he saw that the delicate purple flower continued to bend with the breeze, he was overjoyed.

Midas made his way back to the palace, where the first thing he did was to sprinkle the water over his beloved Aurelia. No sooner did the water touch her cheek than she was restored, laughing at her father's game and remembering not a moment of being a golden statue.

Together, the two went out to the rose garden. Midas sprinkled each frozen rose with a little river water, and Aurelia clapped her hands when she saw them cured of their golden blight.

Joyfully, then, Midas restored all else he had transformed—except for a single rose, kept forever as a reminder of the golden touch.

392

Draw Conclusions • Evaluation Think about the last image of the story. Do you think it was wise for King Midas to keep a single golden rose as a reminder of his golden touch? Why or why not? Possible response: Yes, it was wise because he would always remember the lesson he learned about being greedy, and he would not repeat it.

What did he need to cleanse himself of? If I can answer that question, then I'll know what the major problem was in the story of King Midas.

On Their Own

Have students reread their story chart organizers and add any notes about characters, settings, or events that they are missing. Then have students describe how each event gives rise to the next.

Differentiated Instruction

 Strategic Intervention

Story Structure In pairs, have students ask and answer questions that will help them to identify how each event in the story gives rise to the next.

 Advanced

Extend Critical Thinking After reading *King Midas and the Golden Touch,* have students discuss how the illustrations complement the text.

393

 English Language Learners

Vocabulary Point out the phrase *golden blight* in paragraph 4 on p. 392. Explain that a *blight* is a disease that affects plants. Have students use the definition of the word to determine the meaning of the phrase *golden blight* in the context of the story.

Comprehension Check

Spiral Review

Literary Elements: Character and Plot • Synthesis How do you think King Midas's attitude toward gold will change now that he has learned his lesson? Possible response: He will be less interested in gold. He may even dislike gold since it will remind him of a painful time in his life.

Literary Elements: Theme • Evaluation Have you ever learned a lesson similar to King Midas's? Explain. Possible response: Answers will vary, but students should describe a time when they learned that other things are more valuable than money or material possessions.

Check Predictions Have students return to the predictions they made earlier and confirm whether they were accurate.

Objectives

◉ Use compare and contrast to aid comprehension.

◉ Use story structure to aid comprehension.

Check Retelling

SUCCESS PREDICTOR

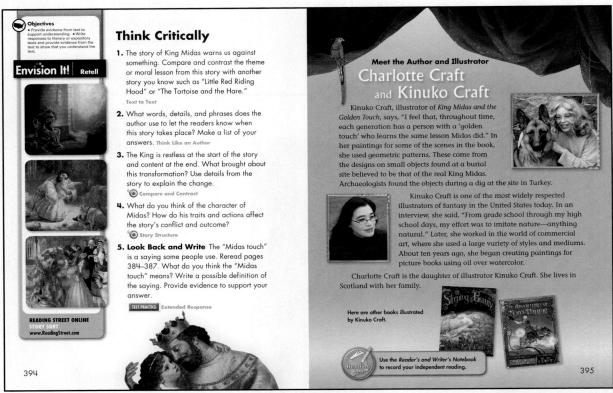

Objectives
• Provide evidence from text to support understanding. • Write responses to literary or expository texts and provide evidence from the text to show that you understand the text.

Envision It! Retell

Think Critically

1. The story of King Midas warns us against something. Compare and contrast the theme or moral lesson from this story with another story you know such as "Little Red Riding Hood" or "The Tortoise and the Hare." **Text to Text**

2. What words, details, and phrases does the author use to let the readers know when this story takes place? Make a list of your answers. **Think Like an Author**

3. The King is restless at the start of the story and content at the end. What brought about this transformation? Use details from the story to explain the change. **Compare and Contrast**

4. What do you think of the character of Midas? How do his traits and actions affect the story's conflict and outcome? **Story Structure**

5. **Look Back and Write** The "Midas touch" is a saying some people use. Reread pages 384–387. What do you think the "Midas touch" means? Write a possible definition of the saying. Provide evidence to support your answer.

TEST PRACTICE Extended Response

READING STREET ONLINE
STORY SORT
www.ReadingStreet.com

394

Meet the Author and Illustrator
Charlotte Craft
and Kinuko Craft

Kinuko Craft, illustrator of *King Midas and the Golden Touch*, says, "I feel that, throughout time, each generation has a person with a 'golden touch' who learns the same lesson Midas did." In her paintings for some of the scenes in the book, she used geometric patterns. These come from the designs on small objects found at a burial site believed to be that of the real King Midas. Archaeologists found the objects during a dig at the site in Turkey.

Kinuko Craft is one of the most widely respected illustrators of fantasy in the United States today. In an interview, she said, "From grade school through my high school days, my effort was to imitate nature—anything natural." Later, she worked in the world of commercial art, where she used a large variety of styles and mediums. About ten years ago, she began creating paintings for picture books using oil over watercolor.

Charlotte Craft is the daughter of illustrator Kinuko Craft. She lives in Scotland with her family.

Here are other books illustrated by Kinuko Craft.

Use the Reader's and Writer's Notebook to record your independent reading.

395

Student Edition pp. 394–395

Retelling

Envision It!

Have students work in pairs to retell the selection, using the Envision It! Retelling Cards as prompts. Remind students that they should accurately summarize the main topic and important ideas in a way that maintains meaning and logical order. Monitor students' retellings.

Scoring rubric

> **Top-Score Response** A top-score response makes connections beyond the text, describes the characters and plot, and draws conclusions from the text.

Plan to Assess Retelling

☑ **Week 1** Assess Strategic Intervention students.

☑ **Week 2** Assess Advanced students.

☑ **This week assess Strategic Intervention students.**

☐ **Week 4** Assess On-Level students.

☐ **Week 5** Assess any students you have not yet checked during this unit.

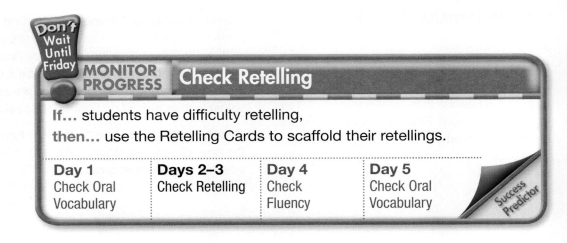

Don't Wait Until Friday

MONITOR PROGRESS Check Retelling

If... students have difficulty retelling,

then... use the Retelling Cards to scaffold their retellings.

Day 1 Check Oral Vocabulary	**Days 2–3** Check Retelling	**Day 4** Check Fluency	**Day 5** Check Oral Vocabulary

Success Predictor

Think Critically

Text to world

1. The myth warns against valuing wealth over living things. Answers will vary depending on what story the student chooses.

Think like an author

2. The phrase *There once lived;* King Midas keeps his money in a dungeon and eats porridge; he speaks very formally; the women wear long skirts and the king wears a robe; the food and dishes look like they are from old paintings.

Compare and contrast

3. King Midas is restless at the beginning because he wants more and more gold. He changes when his greed results in his daughter turning into a golden statue. He is content at the end because he has a different attitude. He values life instead of gold.

Story structure

4. King Midas is childish because he doesn't think about the consequences of his actions. His lack of foresight is central to the story's conflict because it results in him harming his daughter and himself, even though he doesn't mean to. By the end he has learned what to value in life. He has grown as a person.

5. **Look Back and Write** To build writing fluency, assign a 10–15 minute time limit.

Suggest that students use a prewriting strategy, such as brainstorming or using a graphic organizer, to organize their ideas. Remind them to establish a topic sentence about the meaning of this common idiom in the text and support it with facts, details, or explanations from the text. As students finish, encourage them to reread their responses, revise for organization and support, and proofread for errors in grammar and conventions.

Scoring rubric

Top-Score Response A top-score response compares the story of King Midas with the common use of the phrase "Midas touch."

A top-score response should include:

- The "Midas touch" is about creating wealth.
- King Midas was able to turn things into gold by touching them.
- An example of how the expression is used today.

Differentiated Instruction

 Strategic Intervention

Have students work with partners to brainstorm possible meanings of the phrase *Midas touch* and to share experiences when they have heard or read the phrase. Encourage students who are unfamiliar with the phrase to research its meaning.

Meet the Illustrator

Have students read about Kinuko Craft on p. 395. Ask them how Kinuko Craft found inspiration for her illustrations.

Independent Reading

After students enter their independent reading information into their Reading Logs or a journal, have them summarize what they have read. Remind students that a summary should be no more than a few sentences about the main idea of a text and should maintain the meaning and logical order of the text.

English Language Learners

Retelling Use the Retelling Cards to discuss the selection with students. Place the cards in an incorrect order and have volunteers correct the mistake. Then have students explain where each card should go as they describe the correct sequence of the selection.

Objectives
• Read grade-level text with rate.
• Reread for fluency.
• Understand order forms and applications.

Model Fluency
Rate

Model fluent reading

Have students turn to p. 390 of *King Midas and the Golden Touch.* Have students follow along as you read the pages. Tell them to listen to the rhythm and rate of your voice as you read the dialogue between King Midas and the stranger.

Guide practice

Have the students follow along as you read the page again. Then have them reread the page as a group without you until they read at the appropriate rate and rhythm and with no mistakes. Ask questions to be sure students comprehend the text. Continue in the same way on p. 391.

Reread for Fluency

Corrective feedback

If... students are having difficulty reading at the correct rate, **then...** prompt:

• Do you think you need to slow down or read more quickly?

• Read the sentence more quickly. Now read it more slowly. Which helps you understand what you are reading?

• Tell me the sentence. Read it at the rate that would help me understand it.

ROUTINE **Oral Rereading**

1. **Read** Have students read p. 390 of *King Midas and the Golden Touch* orally.

2. **Reread** To achieve optimal fluency, students should reread the text three to four times.

3. **Corrective Feedback** Have students read aloud without you. Provide feedback about their rate of speaking and encourage them to group words together to achieve a natural rhythm. Listen for appropriate rate of speech.

Routines Flip Chart

Research and Study Skills
Order Form/Application

Teach

Discuss with students what they would use to order something they would like to purchase or what they would use to apply for a job or special program. Then explain these definitions of order forms and applications.

- An order form is a chart a person uses to purchase something from a catalog or advertisement. By completing the form, the customer can purchase merchandise via the mail or electronically.

- An application form is a means by which a person can apply for a job or a special school or program to which they wish to be accepted.

- When filling out an order form or an application, you should always follow directions and record information accurately.

Provide groups with examples of different order forms or applications. Have each group show their forms to the class, telling what kind it is and describing the information it is requesting. Have students use the text features and graphics of the order form or application to help them gain an overview of the text and locate necessary information.

Guide practice

Discuss these questions:

What information do you need in order to fill out a job application? (Possible response: name, address, phone number, educational and employment history)

What is the purpose of an order form? (to tell a company what things you would like to buy from them)

After groups have described their forms, ask specific questions about the information requested on each form.

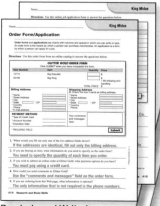

Reader's and Writer's Notebook pp. 414–415

On their own

Have students complete pp. 414–415 of the *Reader's and Writer's Notebook.*

Objectives
- Analyze data for usefulness.
- Review and explain comma rules.
- Spell frequently misspelled words.

Research and Inquiry
Analyze

Teach

Tell students that today they will analyze their research and focus on facts that are most relevant to their oral presentations. Have them ask themselves questions in order to narrow their focus and refine their inquiry topic.

Model

Think Aloud I ask myself, *What have I found?* I have found good, reliable information on a few techniques from the Gold Rush, including gold panning and sluice boxes. I also learned about a few techniques used today. Although I read about some other techniques, I didn't find as much information on those. So I will concentrate on the techniques I found the most information about. I'll add those techniques to my inquiry question. My new inquiry questions are *How do gold panning and sluice box mining work? How do modern techniques such as hard rock mining and metal detecting work?* These are more specific than my original questions.

Guide practice

Have students analyze their findings. They may need to rewrite their inquiry questions. Encourage them to think about the specific aspect of gold or gold mining that they wish to present.

On their own

Have students assess the information they have and do more research if necessary. Remind them that they will need photos or other visual aids for a poster, as well as quotes that can be used to support their conclusions. Tell students to look for primary sources (newspaper articles from the time or diary entries and letters from gold miners, for example) to find good quotes. They will need to use multiple sources for their oral presentation.

Conventions
Commas

Review

Remind students that this week they learned about the comma, a punctuation mark that tells readers to pause. Commas have many uses, including the following:

- A comma and a conjunction join two simple sentences to make a compound sentence.
- Commas separate items in a list.
- Commas set apart appositives, introductory words or phrases, and nouns of direct address.

Daily Fix-It

Use Daily Fix-It numbers 5 and 6 in the right margin.

Connect to oral language

Have students read the sentences, pausing at each comma. Ask them to explain why each comma is included.

> **Dad, could we have bacon, lettuce, and tomato sandwiches?**
>
> **We had them last week, but I want to eat them again.**

For additional practice, use *Let's Practice It!* p. 329 on the *Teacher Resources DVD-ROM.*

Let's Practice It!
TR DVD•339

Spelling
Latin Roots

Frequently misspelled words

The words *believe, friend, friends,* and *piece* are often mispelled. They follow the rule "*i* before *e* except after *c.*" I'm going to read a sentence. Choose the correct word to complete the sentence and then write it correctly.

1. **That jigsaw puzzle has a missing _____.** (piece)

2. **I went to the movie with three of my _____.** (friends)

3. **If you _____ in yourself, you can do anything.** (believe)

4. **My neighbor is also my best _____.** (friend)

Reader's and Writer's
Notebook p. 416

On their own

For more practice, use the *Reader's and Writer's Notebook* p. 416.

Differentiated Instruction

SI Strategic Intervention

Citation Check Check to see whether students have included quotations as part of the evidence supporting their topic sentences. Ask to see their citations. This is a perfect opportunity to review with students the difference between a direct quotation and a paraphrase and the need to cite sources in both situations.

Daily Fix-It

5. Grandpa always says that the bestest things in life are free? *(best; free.)*

6. Hes right a hug is free. *(He's right. A)*

Objective
• Understand the criteria for an effective narrative composition.

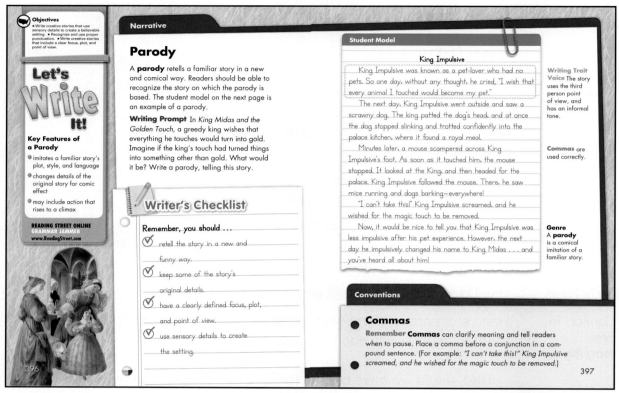

Student Edition pp. 396–397

Let's Write It!
Parody

Teach

Use pp. 396–397 in the Student Edition. Direct students to read the key features of a parody which appear on p. 396. Remind students that they can refer to the information in the Writer's Checklist as they write their own parody.

Read the student model on p. 397. Point out the ways that the humorous parody resembles the original King Midas myth.

Connect to conventions

Remind students that commas signal the reader to pause. Commas have several different uses within sentences. Point out the different correct uses of commas in the model.

Writing—Parody
Writing Trait: Voice

Display rubric

Display Scoring Rubric 28 from the *Teacher Resources DVD* and go over the criteria for each trait under each score. Then, using the model in the Student Edition, choose students to explain why the model should score a 4 for one of the traits. If a student offers that the model should score below 4 for a particular trait, the student should support that response. Remind students that this is the rubric that will be used to evaluate the imaginative story they write.

Scoring Rubric: Parody

	④	③	②	①
Focus/Ideas	Creative events used to create wonderful parody	Several humorous events used to create a sense of parody	Few events included that truly capture the sense of parody	No humor produced by including events that reflect parody
Organization	Clear sequence of events with excellent sense of action building toward climax	Understandable sequence of events, but somewhat lacking in sense of building action	Sequence of events not clear; little sense of building action	Incorrect or no sequence of events; no building action
Voice	Great mimicry of original myth's style, language, and point of view produced in a humorous parody	Some good mimicry of original myth's style, language and point of view with good use of humor	Little resemblance to original myth, which makes the humor mostly unsuccessful	No resemblance to original myth so little success with the humor of parody
Word Choice	Excellent word choice that reveals an attempt to closely match the style of the myth	Some good word choice that shows some attention was paid to the style of the myth	Lacks clear language or indication of attempts to match the style of the myth	Vague, dull, or misused words and no relationship to the original myth
Sentences	Well-crafted sentences with plenty of variety	Smooth sentences; not as much variety	Many short, choppy sentences; too many similar sentences	Many fragments and run-ons
Conventions	Excellent control and accuracy; confident and correct use of commas	Good control; commas used correctly, but not consistently	Errors that may prevent understanding; shows lack of understanding of how to use commas	Frequent errors that interfere with meaning; shows no understanding of how to use commas

Plot chain

Have students get out the plot chains that they worked on yesterday. If they have not completed mapping out the plot, have them work until they are satisfied with the action leading to the story's climax.

Write

You will be using your plot chains as you write the draft of your parody. When you are drafting, don't worry if your composition does not sound exactly as you want it. You will have a chance to revise it tomorrow.

Differentiated Instruction

 Advanced

Humor Have partners write their own definition of the type of humor that they see resulting from a parody. You might suggest some words to consider using in their definitions: *unexpected, ridiculous, impossible.*

English Language Learners

Have pairs of students concentrate on finding some of the story's original details as they look at the parody of *King Midas and the Golden Touch.* For example, explain that the story's point of view is the same. Ask students to find some things about the story line that remain the same.

Objectives
- Write a first draft of a parody.
- Understand the proper voice for a parody.
- Develop a style that matches what the author used in the original myth.

Writing, continued
Writing Trait: Voice

MINI-LESSON

Voice and Humor in Parody

■ **Introduce** Remind students that a parody is humorous. The humor comes from using the style of writing of the original piece, which was intended to be serious, to describe the events so ridiculous that readers can't help but laugh. Parody writers should think about the voice and style of the original. Display the Drafting Tips for students. Emphasize that while they write they should look at the myth, trying to match the style.

King Midas and the Chocolate Touch

There once lived a powerful King named Midas who believed he could never have enough of the thing he loved most in life. That thing was chocolate. King Midas ate chocolate for breakfast. He ate chocolate for lunch. He ate chocolate for dinner. Between meals King Midas drank chocolate milk and he had a cup of hot cocoa at bedtime.

Every single time King Midas tasted chocolate, you could count on hearing him say these words: "Chocolate, sweet chocolate, nothing is so wonderful. I wish everything I touched would turn into sweet chocolate!"

One morning the king's wish came true. When he touched the alarm clock to turn it off, the clock became chocolate. Delighted, the king ate the sweet time piece. Then he got ready for his first meeting of the day. His clothing turned into spun chocolate sugar! He could barely resist eating it. King Midas thought he was running late, but he had eaten his only clock, so he couldn't be sure.

"I must hurry," King Midas thought, licking the chocolate soap from his fingers.

Wherever Midas went, chocolate followed. When he wanted a snack, he just snapped off a piece of furniture or gobbled up whatever he was holding. When King Midas ate a law after signing it, his assistants watched in horror. Midas just licked his lips and smiled.

By the end of the day, King Midas was ready to relax in the royal tub. He was feeling especially sticky from his chocolate clothing. His servants prepared everything the way he liked it. The water was just hot enough, and there were lots of bubbles.

"Ahh," Midas breathed as he sank into the tub.

Within seconds he was sitting in warm, gooey chocolate syrup. "No!" he screamed. "I want to be clean! I wish I had never tasted chocolate! I don't want any more chocolate!"

The king's sobs filled his chocolate palace. His greed for chocolate was gone, but he would pay for it until the day his new wish might come true.

Unit 6 King Midas and the Golden Touch   Writing: Model **28A**

Writing Transparency 28A, TR DVD

Drafting Tips

✔ To get started, review your plot chain. Are the events funny, and do they build toward the climax?

✔ Make sure to use the language and style of the myth while describing your funny events.

✔ Decide whether to keep the myth's point of view. *King Midas and the Golden Touch* is told by a narrator who knows everything, even the characters' thoughts and feelings.

✔ Don't worry about grammar and mechanics when drafting. You'll focus on these things during the proofreading stage.

Think Aloud I'm going to write the opening paragraphs of my parody. I want to describe the setting and introduce the main characters. These will be similar to those elements of the original King Midas myth. However, since I am writing a parody, when I begin to describe the events, those will be different. They will be funny. I will refer to my plot chain to be sure I'm describing the events in the order I had planned.

Direct students to use the drafting tips to guide them in writing their drafts. Remind them to match the language, style, and point of view of the original myth as much as possible.

ROUTINE   Quick Write for Fluency   Team Talk

1. **Talk** Have pairs talk about what they've noticed about the original voice of the King Midas myth.

2. **Write** Each person writes a few sentences that mimic the voice of the King Midas myth, being sure to use commas in at least one sentence.

3. **Share** Partners read each other's sentences and check for proper use of commas.

Routines Flip Chart

 Advanced

Style Challenge students to write descriptions of the style of writing used in *King Midas and the Golden Touch*. Encourage them to consider the following elements of literary style: sentence structure; flowery, descriptive language vs. fast-paced depictions of action; use of dialogue; use of figurative language; mood; paragraph structure.

Wrap Up Your Day

✔ **Build Concepts** Have students discuss the unexpected results of King Midas's wish.

✔ **Compare and Contrast** How would you compare and contrast the king from the time he had the golden touch to after his touch was gone?

✔ **Story Structure** Describe the events that led to King Midas' realization that his daughter was more important than gold.

Preview DAY 4

Tell students that tomorrow they will read about Prometheus, a god who helped humans.

Objectives
- Develop the weekly concept.
- Develop oral vocabulary.

Today at a Glance

Oral Vocabulary
penitence, repercussion

Genre
Origin myth

Reading
"Prometheus the Fire-Bringer"

Let's Learn It!
Fluency: Rate
Vocabulary: Word structure
Listening/Speaking: Storytelling

Research and Inquiry
Synthesize

Spelling
Latin Roots

Conventions
Commas

Writing
Parody

Concept Talk

Question of the Week

What can we learn from the results of our actions?

Expand the concept

Remind students that this week they have read how people had unexpected results from their actions. Tell students that today they will read about the unexpected consequences for humans when the Greek gods became involved in a conflict.

Anchored Talk

Develop oral vocabulary

Use illustrations to review pp. 384–393 of *King Midas and the Golden Touch.* Discuss the Amazing Words *unforeseen* and *victor.* Add these and other concept-related words to the concept map. Then have them use the following questions to identify points of disagreement among group members, use context to determine or clarify the meaning of the unfamiliar Amazing Words, and develop their understanding of the concept.

- The trouble King Midas has is an *unforeseen* effect of his golden touch. Is it possible to plan for *unforeseen* results from your actions?

- King Midas feels like a *victor* when his wish was first granted. What would make you feel like a *victor?*

Strategy Response Log

Have students use p. 34 in the *Reader's and Writer's Notebook* to add information they learned to the "L" column of their KWL charts. Then have students summarize the selection.

INTERACT with TEXT

Oral Vocabulary
Amazing Words

Amazing Words

Amazing Words	
valuable	deplorable
geologist	unforeseen
rare	victor
specimen	repercussion
outcome	penitence

Teach Amazing Words

Amazing Words Oral Vocabulary Routine

1 Introduce Write the word *repercussion* on the board. Have students say it aloud with you. One repercussion of King Midas's wish was that he caused harm to his daughter. Have students use the context to determine a definition for the word. (A *repercussion* is usually a negative result from an event or action.)

2 Demonstrate Have students answer questions to demonstrate understanding. What might be a repercussion of robbing a bank? (going to jail)

3 Apply Have students apply their understanding. Give me an example of a *repercussion* that you heard about or read in the news lately.

See p. OV•3 to teach *penitence.*

Routines Flip Chart

Apply Amazing Words

As students read "Prometheus the Fire-Bringer" on pp. 398–399, have them think about the *repercussion* of Prometheus's decision to teach humans and whether he ever felt *penitence* for teaching them.

Connect to reading

Explain that today students should read to learn more about Prometheus, who stole fire from Mount Olympus. As they read, they should think about how the Question of the Week and the Amazing Words *penitence* and *repercussion* apply to his actions.

ELL **Produce Oral Language** Use the Day 4 instruction on ELL Poster 28 to extend and enrich language.

ELL Poster 28

King Midas and the Golden Touch **39**

Let's Think About Genre

Origin Myth: Characters

Introduce the genre

Explain to students that what we read is structured differently depending on the author's reasons for writing and what kind of information he or she wishes to convey. Different types of texts are called genres. Tell them that myth is one type of genre.

Discuss the genre

Remind students that origin myths are hundreds or thousands of years old. Myths include supernatural events involving gods, humans, and forces of nature. The origin myth, in particular, explains the beginnings of different natural phenomena. Usually, the natural phenomenon explained in an origin myth is the result of one or more character's actions or a conflict between characters.

On the board, draw a T-chart like the one below. Label the columns *Characters* and *What they did.* Activate prior knowledge by asking the following questions:

- What is the purpose of origin myths? Possible response: To explain things that would otherwise be puzzling or strange, such as why a mountain erupted or where the oceans came from.

- What type of characters usually appear in origin myths? Possible response: There are often gods or other supernatural beings. Sometimes the characters have names, and sometimes the characters represent universal concepts, such as man or woman.

- What are the roles and functions of characters in origin myths? Possible response: The powerful characters often change the natural order of things. A god might suddenly create a thunderstorm, an island, or a rivers as a result of a conflict. Sometimes a god might give the gift of an important technology to characters that he or she has a positive relationship with.

Characters	What they did
Athena	Gave people olive trees
Maui	Created Hawaiian islands

Guide practice

Have students work in small groups to create a T-chart showing other mythical characters and how they were said to have affected the world.

Connect to reading

Tell students that they will now read an ancient Greek myth about the discovery of fire. Have students recall "The Story of Phan Ku" and "Thunderbird and Killer Whale in Unit 2." While they read, ask them to compare and contrast the themes and moral lessons of these myths to "Prometheus the Fire-Bringer."

Small Group Time

DAY **4** **Break into small groups before reading or revisiting "Prometheus the Fire-Bringer."**

Teacher Led

SI Strategic Intervention	**OL** On-Level	**A** Advanced
Teacher Led p. DI•55 • Practice retelling • Genre focus • **Read/Revisit** "Prometheus the Fire-Bringer"	**Teacher Led** p. DI•60 • Practice retelling • Genre focus • **Read/Revisit** "Prometheus the Fire-Bringer"	**Teacher Led** p. DI•65 • Genre focus • **Read/Revisit** "Prometheus the Fire-Bringer"

 Place English language learners in the groups that correspond to their reading abilities in English.

Practice Stations
• Read for Meaning
• Get Fluent
• Words to Know

Independent Activities
• AudioText: "Prometheus the Fire-Bringer"
• *Reader's and Writer's Notebook*
• Research and Inquiry

objectives

- Understand the functions of characters in origin myths.
- Use compare and contrast to aid comprehension.
- Use story structure to aid comprehension.

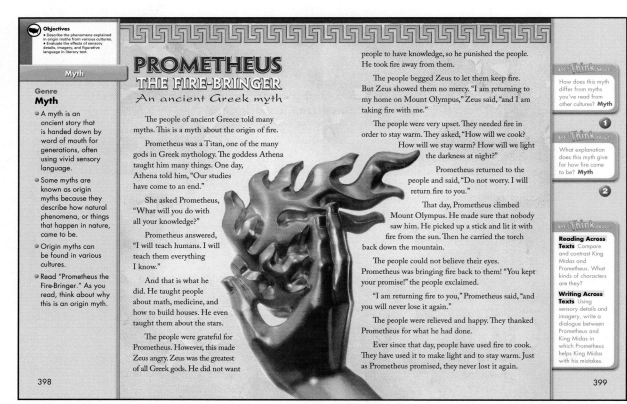

Objectives
- Describe the phenomena explained in origin myths from various cultures.
- Evaluate the effects of sensory details, imagery, and figurative language in literary text.

Myth

Genre
Myth

- A myth is an ancient story that is handed down by word of mouth for generations, often using vivid sensory language.
- Some myths are known as origin myths because they describe how natural phenomena, or things that happen in nature, came to be.
- Origin myths can be found in various cultures.
- Read "Prometheus the Fire-Bringer." As you read, think about why this is an origin myth.

PROMETHEUS
THE FIRE-BRINGER
An ancient Greek myth

The people of ancient Greece told many myths. This is a myth about the origin of fire.

Prometheus was a Titan, one of the many gods in Greek mythology. The goddess Athena taught him many things. One day, Athena told him, "Our studies have come to an end."

She asked Prometheus, "What will you do with all your knowledge?"

Prometheus answered, "I will teach humans. I will teach them everything I know."

And that is what he did. He taught people about math, medicine, and how to build houses. He even taught them about the stars.

The people were grateful for Prometheus. However, this made Zeus angry. Zeus was the greatest of all Greek gods. He did not want

people to have knowledge, so he punished the people. He took fire away from them.

The people begged Zeus to let them keep fire. But Zeus showed them no mercy. "I am returning to my home on Mount Olympus," Zeus said, "and I am taking fire with me."

The people were very upset. They needed fire in order to stay warm. They asked, "How will we cook? How will we stay warm? How will we light the darkness at night?"

Prometheus returned to the people and said, "Do not worry. I will return fire to you."

That day, Prometheus climbed Mount Olympus. He made sure that nobody saw him. He picked up a stick and lit it with fire from the sun. Then he carried the torch back down the mountain.

The people could not believe their eyes. Prometheus was bringing fire back to them! "You kept your promise!" the people exclaimed.

"I am returning fire to you," Prometheus said, "and you will never lose it again."

The people were relieved and happy. They thanked Prometheus for what he had done.

Ever since that day, people have used fire to cook. They have used it to make light and to stay warm. Just as Prometheus promised, they never lost it again.

398   399

Think How does this myth differ from myths you've read from other cultures? **Myth**

1

Think What explanation does this myth give for how fire came to be? **Myth**

2

Think **Reading Across Texts** Compare and contrast King Midas and Prometheus. What kinds of characters are they?

Writing Across Texts Using sensory details and imagery, write a dialogue between Prometheus and King Midas in which Prometheus helps King Midas with his mistakes.

Student Edition pp. 398–399

Guide Comprehension
Skills and Strategies

Teach the genre

Origin Myth: Characters Have students preview "Prometheus the Fire-Bringer" on pp. 398–399. Have them skim the story for names. Ask: What natural phenomenon is this myth about, and who are its major characters?

Corrective feedback

If... students are unable to identify the theme and major characters, **then...** use the model to guide students in identifying clues about theme and character.

Model the genre

Think Aloud When I read the title, I see that this must be about fire. Who are the characters? If I am trying to identify the major characters, I look for the parts where there is dialogue and look at who is speaking. Then I look for capitalized names. The names that I see are Prometheus, Athena, and Zeus. These must be the major characters in the story.

On their own

After reading the myth, have students write one or two paragraphs describing Prometheus and Zeus and how they affect the lives of the people.

Extend Thinking
Think Critically

Higher-order thinking skills

 Compare and Contrast • Evaluation How were the lives of people different before Zeus took fire away and afterwards? Possible response: After Zeus took away fire, the people couldn't cook their food, stay warm, or see in the darkness.

Story Structure • Analysis What is the conflict in this myth? Possible response: The major conflict is between Prometheus wanting to help humans and Zeus wanting to punish them.

Literary Elements: Character and Plot • Analysis What is the relationship between Athena and Prometheus? How does it advance the plot? Possible response: Athena was Prometheus's teacher. She taught him everything she knew, and he, in turn, taught everything he knew to the humans, which made Zeus angry.

Let's Think About...

1. In this myth, the characters are gods with humanlike qualities. In other myths, the characters are animals.

2. Prometheus climbed Mt. Olympus, lit a stick using the sun, and returned fire to the people after Zeus took it away.

Reading Across Texts

Have students use a T-chart to compare and contrast King Midas and Prometheus.

Writing Across Texts

Have students use a story map to plan their dialogue between Prometheus and King Midas. Have them create a problem from one of King Midas's mistakes and then write the resolution that Prometheus helps bring about.

Objectives

- Read with fluency and comprehension.
- Divide words into root words and suffixes.
- Present and listen to storytelling presentations.

Check Fluency
SUCCESS PREDICTOR

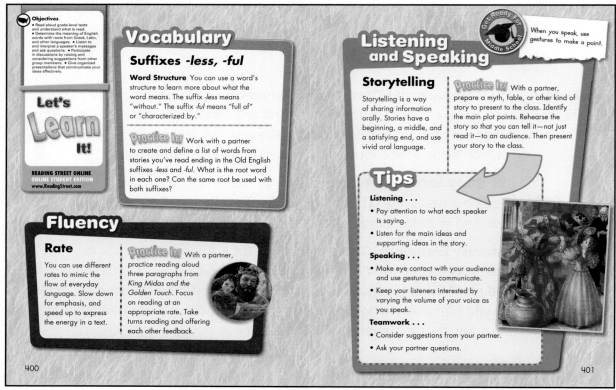

Objectives
- Read aloud grade-level texts and understand what is read. • Determine the meaning of English words with roots from Greek, Latin, and other languages. • Listen to and interpret a speaker's messages and ask questions. • Participate in discussions by raising and considering suggestions from other group members. • Give organized presentations that communicate your ideas effectively.

Vocabulary

Suffixes -less, -ful

Word Structure You can use a word's structure to learn more about what the word means. The suffix -less means "without." The suffix -ful means "full of" or "characterized by."

Practice It! Work with a partner to create and define a list of words from stories you've read ending in the Old English suffixes -less and -ful. What is the root word in each one? Can the same root be used with both suffixes?

Let's Learn It!

READING STREET ONLINE
ONLINE STUDENT EDITION
www.ReadingStreet.com

Fluency

Rate

You can use different rates to mimic the flow of everyday language. Slow down for emphasis, and speed up to express the energy in a text.

Practice It! With a partner, practice reading aloud three paragraphs from *King Midas and the Golden Touch*. Focus on reading at an appropriate rate. Take turns reading and offering each other feedback.

Listening and Speaking

When you speak, use gestures to make a point.

Storytelling

Storytelling is a way of sharing information orally. Stories have a beginning, a middle, and a satisfying end, and use vivid oral language.

Practice It! With a partner, prepare a myth, fable, or other kind of story to present to the class. Identify the main plot points. Rehearse the story so that you can tell it—not just read it—to an audience. Then present your story to the class.

Tips

Listening . . .
- Pay attention to what each speaker is saying.
- Listen for the main ideas and supporting ideas in the story.

Speaking . . .
- Make eye contact with your audience and use gestures to communicate.
- Keep your listeners interested by varying the volume of your voice as you speak.

Teamwork . . .
- Consider suggestions from your partner.
- Ask your partner questions.

400

401

Student Edition pp. 400–401

Fluency
Rate

Guide Practice

Use the Student Edition activity as an assessment tool. Make sure the reading passage is at least 200 words in length. As students read aloud with partners, walk around to make sure their rate of speech is appropriate and that it follows natural rhythms of speech.

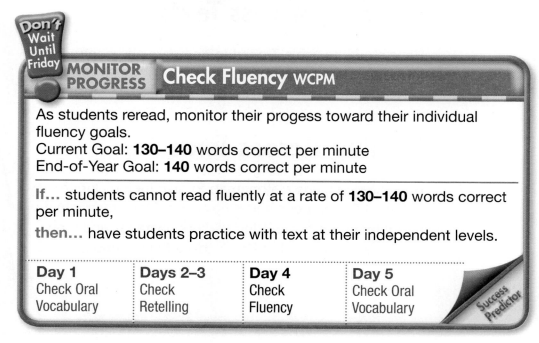

Don't Wait Until Friday

MONITOR PROGRESS **Check Fluency** WCPM

As students reread, monitor their progess toward their individual fluency goals.
Current Goal: **130–140** words correct per minute
End-of-Year Goal: **140** words correct per minute

If... students cannot read fluently at a rate of **130–140** words correct per minute,

then... have students practice with text at their independent levels.

Day 1 Check Oral Vocabulary	Days 2–3 Check Retelling	Day 4 Check Fluency	Day 5 Check Oral Vocabulary	Success Predictor

Vocabulary
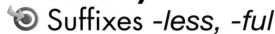 Suffixes *-less, -ful*

Teach word structure

Word Structure Write these words on the board:

**spoonful   lifeless   cheerful   fearless   wonderful
careless**

Draw a line between the root *spoon* and the suffix *-ful.* Explain to students that dividing a word into the root and suffix can help in determining the meaning of the word.

Guide practice

Ask student volunteers to identify the root and suffix, and then use the suffix to determine the definition of each word.

On their own

Walk around the room as students work with partners to make sure the words they have listed have correct suffixes. Check to make sure partners know the meanings of the words they are listing.

Listening and Speaking
Storytelling

Teach

Tell students that in preparing and practicing their stories, they will need to make sure that they are prepared to present their stories in an organized manner, probably using a chronological format. Using a chronological format will help students tell the story, rather than just read it to the audience.

Guide practice

Encourage the student pairs to give each other feedback about their stories as they practice. Remind students that good speakers maintain eye contact with listeners, speak at an appropriate rate and volume with clear enunciation, make natural gestures with their hands and body, and use proper conventions of language while speaking. Also remind the students to listen attentively to the speaker and to take notes to help them accurately interpret the speaker's verbal and nonverbal messages.

On their own

Have students present their stories to the class.

Storytelling

Remind students to maintain an appropriate posture and to use eye contact and natural gestures to communicate their stories effectively. Tell students that preparing and practicing w help them in their presentations

E L L

English Language Learners
Storytelling Suggest to students that they write down on a note card any English words from their stories that they find difficult to remember. Have them refer to the note cards, if needed, during their presentations.

401a

Objectives
- Prepare an oral presentation.
- Review commas.
- Spell words with Latin roots correctly.

Research and Inquiry
Synthesize

Teach

Have students synthesize their research findings into an oral presentation that summarizes their findings about the influence of gold in American history. They should create a poster or a short electronic slide show to support their presentation. Give students the following tips as they prepare their oral presentation.

- Create a topic sentence that sums up your most important points and answers your inquiry question. Write it down so you can show it to the audience.

- Draw a conclusion about the role of gold in American history. Support your conclusion with evidence.

- Use quotes from primary sources or newspaper articles to support your ideas. It may be helpful to write some of these quotes on your poster or in a presentation slide. Make sure you copy quotes word-for-word. Always write down who said the quote and where you found it.

- Find appropriate photos and illustrations and integrate them into your presentation.

- Use information from multiple sources, and make sure each source is reliable.

- Create a Works Cited page or slide with bibliographic information for each source.

- Organize your presentation logically. Make sure it flows together and does not include unnecessary details.

Guide practice

Discuss the differences between plagiarism and paraphrasing. Make sure students understand that plagiarism means copying someone else's ideas and passing them off as your own. They should paraphrase facts only by putting them in their own words and making sure to credit their sources.

On their own

Encourage students to rehearse their presentation with a partner. Make sure students are complimenting each other on good things as well as giving constructive advice.

Conventions
Commas

Test practice

Remind students that grammar skills, such as using commas correctly, are often assessed on important tests. Remind students that commas indicate a pause and can have different uses in sentences:

- A comma plus a conjunction joins two simple sentences to form a compound sentence.
- Commas separate items in a list.
- Commas set apart appositives, introductory words or phrases, and nouns of direct address.

Daily Fix-It

Use Daily Fix-It numbers 7 and 8 in the right margin.

On their own

For additional practice, use the *Reader's and Writer's Notebook* p. 417.

Reader's and Writer's Notebook p. 417

Spelling
Latin Roots

Practice spelling strategy

Work with a partner. Write the list words on note cards and sort them according to the Latin root each word has. Compare the way you have sorted the words, and explain why you sorted them in this way. Then, take turns with your partner naming and spelling a word that is an additional example of each Latin root.

On their own

For additional practice, use *Let's Practice It!* p. 330 on the *Teacher Resources DVD-ROM*.

Let's Practice It!
TR DVD•330

Daily Fix-It

7. This story is more funnier then that one. *(is funnier than)*

8. My neice loves to write stories songs and poems. *(niece; stories, songs, and)*

Objectives
- Revise draft of a narrative composition.
- Apply revising strategy Subtracting.
- Include plot events that build toward the climax.

Writing—Parody
Revising Strategy

MINI-LESSON

Revising Strategy: Subtracting

- Yesterday we wrote a parody of King Midas. Today we will revise our drafts. The goal is to make it clearer, interesting, and informative.

- Display Writing Transparency 28B. Remind students that revising does not include corrections of grammar and mechanics. Then introduce the revising strategy Subtracting.

Writing Transparency 28B, TR DVD

- When we revise, we ask ourselves, *Have I removed details that are redundant or repetitive?* The revising strategy **Subtracting** is the process by which we delete words and sentences to improve the flow of our writing. In the first paragraph, I have used three sentences in a row that are repetitive. *(sentences 3, 4, and 5)* I could combine these sentences into one sentence. The first sentence in my second paragraph is wordy. I don't need to use the word *single* after the word *Every*. I can also reword *count on hearing him* so that it is less wordy.

Tell students that as they revise they should look for ways to tighten up wordy sentences and delete any repetitive information.

Revising Tips

✔ Subtract redundant details to make sentences less wordy.

✔ Vary your sentences by using a mix of shorter and longer sentences.

Peer conferencing

Peer Revision Have students exchange papers for peer revision. Have them write three comments about the partner's writing. The first one should be a compliment. The second should focus on how the partner could revise by deleting redundancies or tightening up words. Refer to *First Stop* for more about peer conferencing.

Have students revise their compositions using the suggestions their partners wrote during Peer Revision as well as the key features of narrative composition to guide them. They should be especially focused on building the plot toward the climax. Be sure that students are using the revising strategy Subtracting.

Corrective feedback

Circulate around the room to monitor students as they revise. If you notice students correcting errors, remind them that they will have time to edit tomorrow. They should be working on content and organization today.

ROUTINE **Quick Write for Fluency** **Team Talk**

1. **Talk** Pairs discuss what they learned about Aurelia from reading *King Midas and the Golden Touch.* What kind of person was she?

2. **Write** Each person writes a brief paragraph that describes Aurelia. The paragraph should be viewed as the way in which she is introduced to readers.

3. **Share** Partners check each other's paragraphs for the use of detail that would help to bring the character to life in a story.

Routines Flip Chart

Wrap Up Your Day

✔ **Build Concepts** Have students discuss how Prometheus's decision to teach humans had unexpected results.

✔ **Oral Vocabulary** Monitor students' use of oral vocabulary as they respond: What were the repercussions of Zeus's actions?

✔ **Story Structure** Describe the events that gave rise to Zeus taking fire away from humans.

Write Guy
Jeff Anderson

Show Off-in a Good Way

Post students' successful sentences or short paragraphs. Celebrate them as writers. Select a sentence of the week, and write it large. Display it as a poster inside or outside the classroom door. Students learn from each other's successes.

E L L

English Language Learners
Modify the prompt Allow beginning English speakers to work with a partner, dictating their composition as a series of events that build in excitement. In the revising step, have students delete events that are the least exciting or the least humorous.

Differentiated Instruction If students have trouble writing their compositions, remind them that they have already mapped out the events. Now they just need to put those events together. Suggest that they list the events and add transition words to more clearly link the events together. Once this is done, students should have more confidence in turning the list into the paragraphs of a story.

Preview DAY 5

Remind students to think about what Prometheus learned from the results of his actions.

Objectives
- Review the weekly concept.
- Review oral vocabulary.

Today at a Glance

Oral Vocabulary

Comprehension
- Compare and contrast

Lesson Vocabulary
- Suffixes -less, -ful

Word Analysis
Complex spelling patterns: ci/sh/, ti/sh/, ous/us/

Literary Terms
Foreshadowing

Assessment
Fluency
Comprehension

Research and Inquiry
Communicate

Spelling
Latin roots

Conventions
Commas

Writing
Parody

Check Oral Vocabulary
SUCCESS PREDICTOR

Concept Wrap Up

Question of the Week
How can we learn from the results of our actions?

Review the concept   Have students look back at the reading selections to find examples of characters learning from their actions.

Review Amazing Words   Display and review this week's concept map. Remind students that this week they have learned ten Amazing Words related to unexpected results. Have students use the Amazing Words and the concept map to answer the question *How can we learn from the results of our actions?*

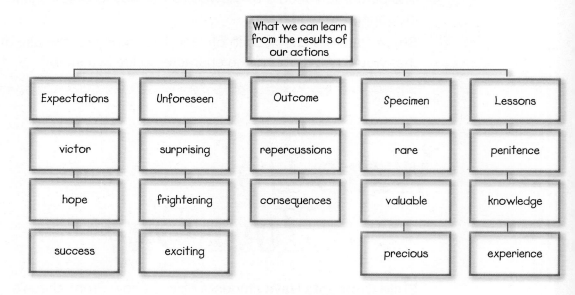

What we can learn from the results of our actions

Expectations	Unforeseen	Outcome	Specimen	Lessons
victor	surprising	repercussions	rare	penitence
hope	frightening	consequences	valuable	knowledge
success	exciting		precious	experience

ELL **Check Concepts and Language** Use the Day 5 instruction on ELL Poster 28 of poster to monitor students' understanding of the lesson concept.

ELL Poster 28

Amazing Ideas

Amazing Words

valuable	deplorable
geologist	unforeseen
rare	victor
specimen	repercussion
outcome	penitence

Connect to the Big Question

Have pairs of students discuss how the Question of the Week connects to the Big Question: *What can we learn from encounters with the unexpected?* Tell students to use the concept map and what they have learned from this week's Anchored Talks and reading selections to form an Amazing Idea—a realization or "big idea" about The Unexpected. Then ask pairs to share their Amazing Ideas with the class. Have students consider each other's suggestions and identify points of agreement and disagreement.

Amazing Ideas might include these key concepts:

- When the unexpected occurs, we might be surprised at our own actions.
- It's how we react to unexpected events that determines our character.
- We can plan for new events by learning from our reactions to the unexpected.

Write about it

Have students write a few sentences about their Amazing Idea, beginning with "This week I learned...."

It's Friday

MONITOR PROGRESS   **Check Oral Vocabulary**

Have individuals use this week's Amazing Words to describe unexpected consequences. Monitor students' abilities to use the Amazing Words and note which words you need to reteach.

If... students have difficulty using the Amazing Words,

then... reteach using the Oral Vocabulary Routine, pp. 371a, 374b, 384b, 398b, OV•3.

Day 1	**Days 2–3**	**Day 4**	**Day 5**
Check Oral Vocabulary	Check Retelling	Check Fluency	Check Oral Vocabulary

Success Predictor

ELL

English Language Learners
Concept map Work with students to add new words to the concept map.

Oral Vocabulary Success Predictor

Objectives
- Review compare and contrast.
- Review suffixes *-less* and *-ful*.
- Review complex spelling patterns: *ci/sh/, ti/sh/, ous/us/*.
- Review foreshadowing.

Comprehension Review
Compare and Contrast

Student Edition p. EI•6

Teach compare and contrast

Envision It!

Review the definition of compare and contrast on p. 372. Remind students that clue words such as *like, as, but,* and *unlike* may be used to compare and contrast. For additional support have students review p. EI•6 on comparing and contrasting.

Guide practice

Have student pairs find an example of comparing and contrasting in *King Midas and the Golden Touch.* Then have pairs explain how and why the author compares two different things.

On their own

For additional practice with compare and contrast have students use *Let's Practice It!* p. 331 on the *Teacher Resources DVD-ROM.*

Let's Practice It!
TR DVD•331

Vocabulary Review
Suffixes *-less, -ful*

Teach suffixes: *-less, -ful*

Remind students to divide words into word parts using their word structure to help them identify suffixes and determine the meaning of the word.

Guide practice

Review with students how to determine the correct meaning of *spoonful* by dividing the word into the root wood *spoon* and the suffix *-ful*.

On their own

Have students create context sentences for the words *spoonful* and *life-less* after they have determined the meaning of each word with the help of their suffixes.

Word Analysis Review
Complex Spelling Patterns: *ci*/sh/, *ti*/sh/, *ous*/us/

Teach complex spelling patterns

Review the pronunciation of the spelling patterns *ci*/sh/, *ti*/sh/, and *ous*/us/ with students. Discuss the pronunciation of these words: *special, question,* and *gracious.*

Guide practice

Display the following words: *election, spacious, cautious, malicious,* and *essential.* Use the Multisyllabic Word Strategy to teach word *election.*

ROUTINE **Multisyllabic Word Strategy**

① **Look for syllables** Display the word *election.* Underline the syllable *tion.*

② **Connect to meaning** I see the word *election* and I feel as though the *t* should be pronounced /t/. But *t* combines with *i* to make a /sh/ sound as in *creation.*

③ **Blend** Blend the syllables together to read the word *election.*

Routines Flip Chart

On their own

Have students work in pairs to underline the *ci, ti,* and *ous* patterns in the displayed words. Then have students spell other words with these consonant changes.

Literary Terms Review
Foreshadowing

Teach foreshadowing

Have students reread pp. 376–383 of *King Midas and the Golden Touch.* Remind students that foreshadowing is a way that authors hint at events that happen later in a story.

Guide practice

Find an example of foreshadowing from pp. 376–383 of the story. Have students describe what later events were foreshadowed and how previous incidents gave rise to later incidents in the story.

On their own

Have students write a short story, using foreshadowing to hint at an event that takes place later in the piece.

Objectives
- Read grade-level text with fluency.

Plan to Assess Fluency

☑ **Week 1** Assess Advanced students.

☑ **Week 2** Assess Strategic Intervention students.

☑ **This week assess On-Level students.**

☐ **Week 4** Assess Strategic Intervention students.

☐ **Week 5** Assess any students you have not yet checked during this unit.

Set individual goals for students to enable them to reach the year-end goal.

Current Goal: 130–140 WCPM

Year-End Goal: 140 WCPM

Assessment

Check words correct per minute

Fluency Make two copies of the fluency passage on p. 401k. As the student reads the text aloud, mark mistakes on your copy. Also mark where the student is at the end of one minute. To figure words correct per minute (WCPM), subtract the number of mistakes from the total number of words read in one minute. To check the student's comprehension of the passage, have him or her retell you what was read.

Corrective Feedback

If… students cannot read fluently at a rate of 130–140 WCPM,
then… make sure they practice with text at their independent reading level. Provide additional fluency practice by pairing nonfluent readers with fluent readers.

If… students already read at 140 WCPM,
then… they do not need to reread three or four times.

Small Group Time

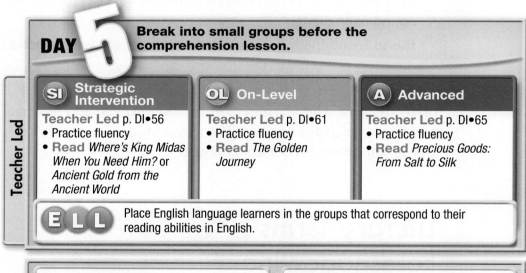

DAY 5 Break into small groups before the comprehension lesson.

Teacher Led

SI Strategic Intervention
Teacher Led p. DI•56
- Practice fluency
- Read *Where's King Midas When You Need Him?* or *Ancient Gold from the Ancient World*

OL On-Level
Teacher Led p. DI•61
- Practice fluency
- Read *The Golden Journey*

A Advanced
Teacher Led p. DI•65
- Practice fluency
- Read *Precious Goods: From Salt to Silk*

ELL Place English language learners in the groups that correspond to their reading abilities in English.

Practice Stations
- Words to Know
- Get Fluent
- Read for Meaning

Independent Activities
- Grammar Jammer
- Concept Talk Video
- Vocabulary Activities

Judy's Wish

Judy was the receptionist at Mr. Knox's Box Factory. "If I had a nickel for   15
every time that phone rang I'd retire a very rich woman," she always said.   29

One day, a fairy came to her, right there in the factory lobby. "You're   43
on," said the fairy. "You get a nickel every time that phone rings."   56

"Mr. Knox's Boxes. How may I direct your call?" Judy said happily to the   70
next caller. The morning was as busy as ever. Her switchboard lit up. "Mr.   84
Knox's Boxes. Please hold," she told the next caller. She put them on hold and   99
pushed the next button.   103

By the time lunchtime rolled around, Judy was exhausted. She had even   115
forgotten about her wish until she saw the mound of nickels sitting on her desk.   130

"Maybe I can buy my lunch with that," she thought. But it took her the   145
entire lunch hour to tally up the coins. Lunchtime was over before she even left   160
her desk.   162

"Mr. Knox's Boxes," she started again sadly. "Please hold." By the time   174
the factory closed that day, Judy's desk had collapsed under the weight of the   188
nickels.   189

The next day, nickels rained down on the factory lobby. "Oh, what have I   203
done?" Judy said in despair.   208

Just then, the fairy appeared again. "You don't look like a satisfied   220
customer," said the fairy. "How about a refund?"   228

And suddenly, the nickels stopped falling. "But clean up this mess!" said   240
the fairy.   242

MONITOR PROGRESS   • **Check Fluency**

Objective

• Read grade-level text with comprehension.

Assessment

Check comprehension

Compare and Contrast Use "The Grass is Always Greener" on p. 401m to check students' understanding of compare and contrast.

1. What unforeseen problem did George discover about Guzman's yard? (Possible response: It is a lot of trouble to maintain a yard like Guzman's.)

2. How does Guzman's lawn compare to George's? (Possible response: Guzman's yard is much bigger, in better condition, and has trees and a vegetable garden. George's is small and dry with no trees or gardens.)

3. How do George's feelings about Guzman's lawn at the beginning of the passage compare with his feelings at the end of the passage? (Possible response: At first, he admires the lawn and wants one like it. Later, he is glad he doesn't have one.)

Corrective feedback

If... students are unable to answer the comprehension questions, **then...** use the Reteach lesson in the *First Stop* book.

The Grass is Always Greener

George had a tiny patch of grass for a backyard. There were no trees to give the yard shade, so there were plenty of brown patches of grass that got burned from too much sun. Whenever George went in his yard, he always found himself gazing over the fence into his next-door neighbor's pristine yard.

"Guzman has the best yard I've ever seen," he told his wife at dinner one night. "It's about three times bigger than ours, and it has beautiful trees for shade and a great little vegetable garden. He keeps it in such good condition too. It's much greener than ours."

"Well, why don't you tell him so yourself?" said his wife.

The next day, George told Guzman how much he admired his yard. "I would give anything to have a yard like that," said George.

"Be careful what you wish for," replied Guzman. "That yard drives me insane."

"What?" said George in surprise. He did not think that there could be unforeseen problems with something so beautiful. "Why wouldn't you want a yard like that?"

"Mowing is a definite chore because it's so big. It's unbearable in the middle of summer. Then fall rolls around and I'm out there raking leaves from those trees every weekend. And that vegetable garden is infested with pests. We'll be lucky if we get one tomato out of all of our efforts this year. And that lawn is so green because I spend a fortune on fertilizers. The outcome might be nice to look at, but I don't think it's worth my time."

"Wow!" said George. "Your yard actually doesn't look so good to me anymore."

MONITOR PROGRESS • Compare and Contrast

Objectives
- Communicate inquiry results.
- Take spelling test.
- Review commas.

Research and Inquiry
Communicate

Present ideas Have students share their inquiry results by giving an organized oral presentation about how gold has influenced American history. Ask students to tell what sources they used.

Listening and speaking Remind students how to be good speakers and how to communicate effectively with their audience.

- Emphasize your topic sentence and use it to catch the audience's attention.
- Make sure you draw a clear conclusion and use quotes and evidence to support it.
- Speak clearly and loudly.
- Keep eye contact with audience members.
- Speak at a comfortable rate, pronouncing words clearly.
- Use natural, appropriate gestures as you make your point. Point to your visual aids when appropriate.
- Use standard language so that the audience has no trouble understanding your conclusion.
- At the end of your presentation, talk briefly about the sources you used.

Remind students of these tips for being a good listener.

- Pay careful attention to the oral presentation. Listen to the conclusions and evidence and interpret the speaker's verbal and nonverbal messages.
- Make sure you understand the speaker's purpose and main conclusion. If you don't, ask about it at the end of the presentation.
- Ask questions to clarify the speaker's point of view.

Spelling Test
Latin Roots

Spelling test

To administer the spelling test, refer to the directions, words, and sentences on page 373c.

Conventions
Extra Practice

Teach

Remind students that a comma indicates a pause to the reader. Commas are used in sentences in different ways. A comma and a conjunction join two simple sentences into a compound sentence. Commas separate items in a list and set off appositives, introductory words or phrases, and nouns of direct address.

Guide practice

Have students work in pairs. Each partner should write two short statements about the other's interests. They should then trade papers and turn the two sentences into a compound sentence.

> **Juanita likes math. Juanita's favorite hobby is reading.**
>
> **Juanita likes math, but her favorite hobby is reading.**

Daily Fix-It

Use Daily Fix-It numbers 9 and 10 in the right margin.

On their own

Write these sentences from *King Midas and the Golden Touch*. Have students add commas where they belong. Students should complete *Let's Practice It!* p. 332 on the *Teacher Resources DVD-ROM*.

> **1. Without my gold, I would be as poor as he.**
>
> **2. Do you not recognize me, friend?**
>
> **3. Midas rushed out of the room, through the palace, and into the garden.**
>
> **4. I went to the garden to pick you a flower, but all of the roses have become hard and yellow.**
>
> **5. With those words, the young man vanished.**

Daily Fix-It

9. Losing the golden touch filled he with releif. *(him; relief)*

10. "Look father the roses are back! They are not hard and uglie." *(Look, Father,; ugly)*

Let's Practice It!
TR DVD•332

Objectives
- Proofread revised drafts of narrative composition, including correct use of commas.
- Create and present final drafts.

Writing—Parody
Writer's Craft: Commas

Review revising

Remind students that yesterday they revised their narrative compositions, paying particular attention to deleting redundant details and tightening sentences to eliminate wordiness. Today they will proofread their compositions.

MINI-LESSON

Proofread for Commas

Writing Transparency 28C, TR DVD

■ **Teach** When we proofread, we look closely at our work, searching for errors in mechanics such as spelling, capitalization, punctuation, and grammar. Today we will focus on making sure that commas are used correctly.

■ **Model** Let's look at a paragraph from the composition we started yesterday. Display Writing Transparency 28C. Explain that you will look for errors in the use of commas. I see a couple of problems in the last sentence of the paragraph. The sentence has an introductory phrase, *Between meals.* This should be followed by a comma. In addition, this sentence is a compound sentence. It needs a comma before the conjunction, *and.* Model returning to the beginning of the paragraph to look for other types of errors, such as the capitalization error in sentence 1. Explain to students that they should reread their story a number of times, each time looking for different types of errors: spelling, punctuation, capitalization, and grammar.

Proofread

Display the Proofreading Tips. Ask students to proofread their compositions, using the Proofreading Tips and paying particular attention to commas. Circulate around the room answering students' questions. When students have finished editing their own work, have pairs proofread one another's stories.

Proofreading Tips

✔ Be sure that the commas have been applied correctly.

✔ Check for correct use of other types of punctuation marks.

✔ Check for correct spelling, capitalization, and grammar.

Present

Have students incorporate revisions and proofreading edits into their stories to create a final draft.

Give students two options for presenting: An oral presentation to the class or an illustrated version of the story in book form. For oral presentations, students should remember the importance of voice in a parody. The parody might be more effective if their presentation style uses the seriousness of the original voice of the myth. Students creating an illustrated book should draw their own pictures, deciding how to divide page space between art and text. They should also create an illustration for the cover of the book. When students have finished, have each complete a Writing Self-Evaluation Guide.

ROUTINE Quick Write for Fluency Team Talk

1. **Talk** Pairs discuss what they learned about both myths and parodies this week.

2. **Write** Each person writes a paragraph that explains why you need to understand the original genre before you can do a parody of a work.

3. **Share** Partners read their paragraphs to one another.

Routines Flip Chart

Preview NEXT WEEK

How can unexpected encounters reveal hidden dangers? Tell students that next week they will read about the importance of safe travel.

Weekly Assessment

Use pp. 201–208 of *Weekly Tests* to check:

✔ **Word Analysis** Complex Spelling Patterns

✔ ⊚ **Comprehension Skill** Compare and Contrast

✔ Review **Comprehension Skill**
Draw Conclusions

✔ **Lesson Vocabulary**

adorn	precious
cleanse	realm
lifeless	spoonful

Weekly Tests

Advanced

On-Level

SI

Strategic
Intervention

Differentiated Assessment

Use pp. 163–168 of *Fresh Reads for Fluency and Comprehension*
to check:

✔ ⊚ **Comprehension Skill** Compare and Contrast

✔ Review **Comprehension Skill** Draw Conclusions

✔ **Fluency** Words Correct Per Minute

Fresh Reads for Fluency and Comprehension

Managing Assessment

Use *Assessment Handbook* for:

✔ **Weekly Assessment Blackline Masters for Monitoring Progress**

✔ **Observation Checklists**

✔ **Record-Keeping Forms**

✔ **Portfolio Assessment**

Assessment Handbook

Teacher Notes

Small Group Time

5-Day Plan

DAY 1
- Reinforce the concept
- Read Leveled Readers
  Concept Literacy
  Below Level

DAY 2
- ◉ Compare and
  Contrast
- ◉ Story Structure
- Revisit Student Edition
  pp. 376–383

DAY 3
- ◉ Suffixes
- Revisit Student Edition
  pp. 384–393

DAY 4
- Practice Retelling
- Read/Revisit Student
  Edition pp. 398–399

DAY 5
- Reread for fluency
- Reread Leveled
  Readers

3- or 4-Day Plan

DAY 1
- Reinforce the concept
- Read Leveled Readers

DAY 2
- ◉ Compare and
  Contrast
- ◉ Story Structure
- Revisit Student Edition
  pp. 376–383

DAY 3
- ◉ Suffixes
- Revisit Student Edition
  pp. 384–393

DAY 4
- Practice Retelling
- Read/Revisit Student
  Edition pp. 398–399
- Reread for fluency
- Reread Leveled
  Readers

3-Day Plan: Eliminate the shaded box.

DAY 1

Build Background

■ **Reinforce the Concept** Discuss the weekly question *How can we learn from the results of our actions?* Ask students to talk about a time when they tried something and got an unexpected result, such as banging a jar on the table to loosen the lid and having the jar break. What did they learn from their experiences? Not everything that we do in life will lead to the results we want. The challenge is to learn from our actions. That way, we can change how we act in the future and get different results. Discuss the words on the concept map on p. 370–371 in the Teacher Edition.

■ **Connect to Reading** This week you will read about people who got unexpected results from actions they took. Often, when we have something we value, we think that having more of it will make us happier. But our actions can lead to very different results. For instance, in the Read Aloud "Valuables," the narrator thinks that digging up fossils will make him rich. What was the result instead? *(He learns that he has dug up a common fossil, but he comes to treasure it and won't sell it for any price.)*

Objectives
- Interpret a speaker's messages (both verbal and nonverbal).

For a complete literacy instructional plan and additional practice with this week's target skills and strategies, see the **Leveled Reader Teaching Guide.**

Concept Literacy Reader

- **Read** *Where's King Midas When You Need Him?*

- **Before Reading** Preview the selection with students, focusing on key concepts and vocabulary. Then have them set a purpose for reading.

- **During Reading** Read the first two pages of the selection aloud while students track the print. Then have students finish reading the selection with a partner.

- **After Reading** After students finish reading the selection, connect it to the weekly question *How can we learn from the results of our actions?*

Below-Level Reader

- **Read** *Ancient Gold from the Ancient World*

- **Before Reading** Have students preview the selection, using the illustrations. Then have students set a purpose for reading.

- **During Reading** Do a choral reading of the first four pages of the selection. If students are able, have them read and discuss the remainder of the book with a partner. Have partners discuss the following questions:

- Why is gold so valuable? *(It's rare and beautiful; it can take many shapes but remains strong.)*

- What are some of the things that ancient people made out of gold? *(jewelry, ornaments, masks)*

- **After Reading** Have students look at and discuss the concept map. Connect the Below-Level Reader to the weekly question *How can we learn from the results of our actions?* What happened to cultures that used gold to decorate their kingdoms? *(Others came to loot them and melt down their gold treasures.)*

MONITOR PROGRESS

If... students have difficulty reading the selection with a partner,
then... have them follow along as they listen to the Leveled Readers DVD-ROM.

If... students have trouble understanding how gold was used in the ancient world,
then... reread the relevant pages and discuss the photos and illustrations together.

Success Predictor

Objectives
- Interpret a speaker's messages (both verbal and nonverbal).

lent Edition p. EI•6

ore Reading

e additional Leveled
eaders or other texts at
udents' instructional levels
reinforce this week's skills
d strategies. For text sug-
stions, see the Leveled
ader Database or the
veled Readers Skills Chart
pp. CL24–CL29.

DAY **2**

Reinforce Comprehension

Skill Compare and Contrast Review with
students *Envision It!* on p. EI•6. Then use
p. 372 to review the definitions of compare and
contrast. Write this sentence on the board:
"Gold and silver are both precious metals, but
gold usually costs more." This statement tells
one way gold and silver are alike (precious
metals), and one way they are different (gold
costs more). The word *both* helps you compare
gold and silver. The word *but* helps you contrast them.

Strategy Story Structure Review the definition of story structure. Encourage
students to think about how the beginning of the story sets up the problem and
the rising actions. For additional support, refer students to *Envision It!* p. EI•22.

Revisit *King Midas and the Golden Touch* on pp. 376–383. Have students begin
reading the selection aloud with a partner. As they read, have them apply the
comprehension skill and strategy.

- What is the main problem in the story? *(King Midas wants more and more gold.)*

- How are King Midas and his daughter alike? *(They both appreciate beautiful
things.)*

- How are they different? *(Aurelia prefers roses to gold.)*

- What is the difference between King Midas before and after the stranger grants
his wish? *(Before: King Midas had wealth and power but longed for more gold;
After: he had a magical power to turn everything into gold.)*

Use the During Reading Differentiated Instruction for additional support for
struggling readers.

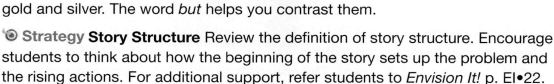

MONITOR PROGRESS

If... students have difficulty reading along with the group,
then... have them follow along as they listen to the AudioText.

Objectives
- Compare and contrast ideas and information.
- Describe incidents that advance the story or novel, explaining how each incident gives rise to or foreshadows
future events.

SI Strategic Intervention

DAY 3

Reinforce Vocabulary

Suffixes *-less*, *-ful*/Word Structure Write the words *handful* and *worthless* on the board and circle the suffixes. Ask volunteers to use them in sentences, such as "I ate a handful of walnuts" or "The torn shirt was worthless."

- What are the base words? *(hand, worth)*

- The suffix *-less* means "without." The suffix *-ful* in this case means "the amount that will fill." What is the meaning of *handful* and *worthless*? *("something that fills the hand" and "something without value or worth")*

Revisit *King Midas and the Golden Touch* on pp. 384–393. Review *Words!* on p. W•6. As students finish reading the selection, encourage them to pay attention to word structure in order to identify the suffixes *–less* and *-ful* in vocabulary. Write the words *spoon* and *life* on the board.

- How does the suffix *-ful* change the meaning of the word *spoon*? *(The word changes to mean "an amount that fills the spoon.")*

- How does the suffix *-less* change the meaning of the word *life*? *(The word changes to mean "without life, or dead.")*

Write these words on the board: *child, glass*

- What suffix would I add to make a word that means "being without children"? *(-less; childless)*

- What suffix would I add to make a word that means "amount that fills a glass"? *(-ful; glassful)*

Use the During Reading Differentiated Instruction for additional support for struggling readers.

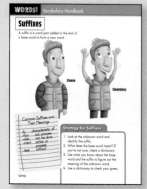

Student Edition p. W•6

More Reading

Use additional Leveled Readers or other texts at students' instructional levels to reinforce this week's skills and strategies. For text suggestions, see the Leveled Reader Database or the Leveled Readers Skills Chart on pp. CL24–CL29.

MONITOR PROGRESS

If... students need more practice with the lesson vocabulary, **then...** use *Envision It! Pictured Vocabulary Cards*.

Objectives
- Determine the meaning of grade-level academic English words derived from other linguistic affixes.

SI *Strategic Intervention*

Practice Retelling

■ **Retell** Have students work in pairs and use the Retelling Cards to retell *King Midas and the Golden Touch.* Monitor retelling and prompt students as needed. For example, ask:

- Where and when does this story take place?

- What is the problem in the story and how is it solved?

If students struggle, model a fluent retelling.

Genre Focus

■ **Before Reading or Revisiting** "Prometheus the Fire-Bringer" on pp. 398–399, read aloud the genre information about myths on p. 398. Explain to students that myths are passed down from one generation to the next. "Origin" means beginning, so origin myths tell how things came to be. "Prometheus the Fire-Bringer" is an origin myth about how humans came to have fire.

Then have students preview "Prometheus the Fire-Bringer."

- What features do you see on the page? *(a border design, the title telling me it's a Greek myth, artwork)*

- What origin do you think this myth explains? *(fire's origin)*

■ **During Reading or Revisiting** Have students read along with you while tracking the print. Stop to discuss any unfamiliar words or phrases, such as *mythology* and *mercy.*

■ **After Reading or Revisiting** Have students share their reactions to the myth. Then guide them through the Reading Across Texts and Writing Across Texts activities.

MONITOR PROGRESS

If... students have difficulty retelling the selection,
then... have them review the story using the illustrations.

Objectives
- Describe phenomena explained in origin myths from various cultures.

English Language Learners

The ELL lessons are organized by strands. Use them to scaffold the weekly curriculum of lessons or during small group time instruction.

Academic Language

Students will hear or read the following academic language in this week's core instruction. As students encounter the vocabulary, provide a simple definition or concrete example. Then ask students to suggest an example or synonym of the word and identify available cognates.

Skill Words	rhyme (*rima*)	series (*serie*)
	commas (*comas*)	compare (*comparar*)
	compound sentences	contrast (*contraste*)
Concept Words	actions (*acciones*)	results (*resultados*)
	fossil (*fósil*)	king

Spanish cognates in parentheses

Concept Development

How can we learn from the results of our actions?

■ **Preteach Concept**

- **Prior Knowledge** Have students turn to pp. 370–371 in the Student Edition. Call attention to the picture of the garbage in the water and tap into students' knowledge of pollution. Have you ever seen anything like this before? How did it make you feel? What should we do if we see garbage where it doesn't belong?

- **Discuss Concept** Elicit students' knowledge and experience of learning from our actions. What do you think the children on the softball team have learned from getting a trophy? How will it make a difference the next time they play? Supply background information as needed.

- **Poster Talk-Through** Read aloud the Poster Talk-Through on ELL Poster 28 and work through the Day 1 activities.

■ **Daily Concept and Vocabulary Development** Use the daily activities on ELL Poster 28 to build concept and vocabulary knowledge.

Objectives
- Internalize new academic language by using and reusing it in meaningful ways in speaking activities that build concept and language attainment.

Content Objectives
- Use concept vocabulary related to actions and their results.

Language Objectives
- Express ideas in response to art and discussion.

Daily Planner

DAY 1	• **Frontload Concept** • **Preteach** Comprehension Skill, Vocabulary, Phonics Spelling, Conventions • **Writing**
DAY 2	• **Review Concept,** Vocabulary, Comprehension Skill • **Frontload Main Selection** • **Practice** Phonics/Spelling Conventions/Writing
DAY 3	• **Review Concept,** Comprehension Skill, Vocabulary, Conventions/ Writing • **Reread Main Selection** • **Practice** Phonics/Spelling
DAY 4	• **Review Concept** • **Read ELL/ELD Readers** • **Practice** Phonics/Spelling Conventions/Writing
DAY 5	• **Review Concept,** Vocabulary, Comprehension Skill, Phonics/Spelling, Conventions • **Reread ELL/ELD Reader** • **Writing**

*See the ELL Handbook for ELL Workshops with targeted instruction.

Concept Talk Video

Use the Concept Talk Video Routine (*ELL Handbook*, p. 477) to build background knowledge about learning from results.

Language Objectives

Understand and use basic vocabulary.

Learn meanings of grade-level vocabulary.

Internalize new basic language.

Language Opportunity: Writing

Have students write to internalize the high-frequency words. They can use the words *complete, act, experience,* and *direct* to write an announcement about a school play. They can use *sense, mind,* and *art* to write about a painting or photograph.

ELL — English Language Learners

Basic Vocabulary

■ **High-Frequency Words** Use the vocabulary routines and the high-frequency word list on p. 456 of the *ELL Handbook* to systematically teach newcomers the first 300 sight words in English. Students who began learning ten words per week at the beginning of the year are now learning words 271–280.

Lesson Vocabulary

■ **Preteach** Introduce the Lesson Vocabulary using this routine:

1. Distribute copies of this week's Word Cards (*ELL Handbook,* p. 191).

2. Display ELL Poster 28 and reread the Poster Talk-Through.

3. Using the poster illustrations, model how a word's meaning can be expressed with other similar words: The *lifeless* mummy laid in the tomb. (without life, dead)

4. Use these sentences to reveal the meaning of the other words.

   • She *adorned* her hair with flowers. (decorated, put ornaments on)

   • The hiker jumped in the river to *cleanse* himself. (make clean)

   • My grandmother's ring is *precious* to me. (having great value)

   • The king ruled his *realm.* (kingdom)

   • He put a *spoonful* of cereal in his mouth. (the amount a spoon will hold)

Objectives
• Expand and internalize initial English vocabulary by learning and using high-frequency English words necessary for identifying and describing people, places, and objects, by retelling simple stories and basic information represented or supported by pictures, and by learning and using routine language needed for classroom communication.

ELL *English Language Learners*

■ **Reteach** Distribute a copy of the Word Cards to each student. Have students write a clue on each card to help them understand the words. Ask students the following questions about the Lesson Vocabulary to check understanding. Have them hold up the appropriate Word Card when they answer each question.

- If you *adorn* your clothes, are you decorating them? **(yes)**

- If something is *precious*, does it have little value or a great deal of value? **(a great deal of value)**

- When you *cleanse* your hands, are you cleaning them or dirtying them? **(cleaning them)**

- Does something that is *lifeless* make movements? **(no)**

- Is *realm* another word for a royal kingdom? **(yes)**

- Is a *spoonful* a large or small amount? **(a small amount)**

■ **Writing** Divide students into small groups. Give each group one or two Word Cards and the same number of blank cards. Ask students to write a riddle, or question, for each of the words. They can model it on the questions they just answered. When all groups have completed their cards, have them take turns asking their questions for other groups to answer. You may want to shuffle all the cards together and invite students to use them to play a match game.

LS Leveled Support

Beginning Help students read aloud the words on their cards. Have them use gestures or movement to show what the words mean. Then have them write the Lesson Vocabulary words.

Intermediate Have students read the words on their cards and tell what they mean. Reread some questions from the Reteach activity for students to use as models. Encourage them to seek clarification as needed. Have them read their questions to other groups.

Advanced/Advanced High Ask students to write questions about the vocabulary. Then have them share their questions with other groups. Encourage advanced students to listen carefully to the questions asked by other groups and answer them.

Language Objectives
- Produce drawings, phrase and short sentences to show understanding of Lesson Vocabulary.

ELL Teacher Tip
Research shows that it is best to "group and regroup [students] according to the specific goals at hand." Give English learners the opportunity to work with peers who can effectively model good speaking and reading skills. At the same time, allow students to take responsibilit for the tasks that they are able to handle.

Language Opportunity: Listening
Have students listen to a text using the lesson vocabulary. Turn to p. 375 in the Student Edition. Read the page aloud and ask questions to be sure that students understand the general meaning of the text and the way in which the words are used in the passage.

Use pp. 392 and 393 in the Student Edition to focus on listening for important details. Have students examine the illustrations on both pages as you read aloud from p. 392. Ask students to name important details, including how the word *cleanse* is used in the selection.

Content Objectives

- Monitor and adjust oral comprehension.

Language Objectives

- Ask for information in academic contexts.
- Discuss oral passages.
- Use a graphic organizer to take notes.

Graphic Organizer

Know	I Want to Know	I Learned

ELL Teacher Tip

Recognizing the sound of rhyming words in English can be challenging for English learners. As you read the poem, emphasize the words that rhyme. After reading the poem, ask students to name the rhyming words in each verse.

ELL Workshop

Encourage students to demonstrate listening comprehension of the Read Aloud and other spoken messages. Provide *Retell or Summarize* (*ELL Handbook,* pp. 408–409) for practice.

ELL English Language Learners

Listening Comprehension

A Precious Fossil

I found a fossil / Of a very old fern. / It was a million years old / I was to learn. Was it valuable?

I had to know. / I'd ask Aunt Jessie. / She'd say "yes" or "no." / "It's a beauty!" she said.

Wow! / How intense! / It's common, though / Only worth eighty cents.

Now I keep it on my shelf, / And it looks really nice. / It's valuable to me, / Not for sale at any price.

Prepare for the Read Aloud The modified Read Aloud above prepares students for listening to the oral reading "Valuables" on p. 371b.

- **First Listening: Listen to Understand** Write the title of the Read Aloud on the board. This is about a child who finds a fossil. Let's listen to find out if the fossil is valuable. How much is the fossil worth? Afterward, ask questions about the academic context, focusing on the idea of finding a fossil of a fern.

- **Second Listening: Listen to Check Understanding** Using a K-W-L chart (*ELL Handbook,* p. 480), work with students to list what they know about fossils and what questions they have. Record their ideas in the K and W columns. Now listen again to check your facts and get answers for your questions. After reading, complete the L column of the chart together.

Objectives

- Understand implicit ideas and information in increasingly complex spoken language commensurate with grade-level learning expectations.

ELL *English Language Learners*

Phonics and Spelling

■ **Words with Latin Roots**

- **Preteach** Write the following words on the board: *animal, animation, animated.* These all have the word part *anima. Anima* comes from Latin. It means "living." Many words in English have Latin roots. Learning these roots can help you learn more words.

- **Teach/Model** Write *aud* on the board. Write *auditorium* and *audience* beside it. Tell students that the Latin root *aud* means "to hear." So *auditorium* is a place where people go to hear something. Elicit that *audience* is a group of people gathered to hear something. Provide contextual support for these spoken words, show pictures or discribe both an auditorium and an audience.

- **Assess** Write the following words on the board: *decade, decimal, decathalon.* Tell students that *dec* is a Latin root meaning "ten." Ask students to write a sentence with one of these words.

Word Analysis: Complex Spelling Patterns *ous*/us/, *ci*/sh/, *ti*/sh/

■ **Teach/Model** Explain to students that in English, the suffix *-ous* means "having the quality of" or "relating to." Relate the spellings to elements of the English sound system. Even though it is spelled *-ous*, the suffix is pronounced /us/. Then write *precious* and say it aloud. Ask a student to underline the letters that make the /sh/ sound. Repeat this with *fictitious*.

■ **Practice** Display the following words: *adventure, courage, mountain.* Add the *-ous* ending to each word and have students pronounce them with you. Underline each *-ous* ending. Guide students in giving a definition of each word.

Leveled LS Support

Beginning/Intermediate Guide students in pronouncing, defining, and then writing the following words: *famous, humorous, fictitious.*

Advanced/Advanced High After students have learned the pronunciation and spelling of each word, have them use each word in a sentence.

Objectives
- Learn relationships between sounds and letters of the English language to represent sounds when writing in English.
- Learn relationships between sounds and letters of the English language and decode (sound out) words using a combination of skills such as recognizing sound-letter relationships and identifying cognates, affixes, roots and base words.

Content Objectives
- Spell words with complex spelling patterns.
- Recognize words with Lati roots.
- Use knowledge of Latin roots to determine word meanings.

Language Objectives
- Use context to understand spoken language.
- Pronounce words with complex spelling patterns.
- Discuss the meaning of words with the ending *-ous.*
- Recognize elements of the English sound system.

Transfer Skills
Words with Latin Roots Tell Spanish speakers that the Spanish language comes from Latin, so many of the Latin roots will already be familiar to them.

Practice
To provide students with additional instruction and practice for words with Latin roots, use the lessons in the ELL Handbook (pp. 300, 305).

Comprehension
Compare and Contrast

- **Preteach** Preteach the routine classroom words *compare* and *contrast*. When we compare things, we talk about how they are alike. When we contrast things, we talk about how they are different. Have students turn to Envision It! on p. EI•6 in the Student Edition to reinforce understanding of the classroom vocabulary. Read aloud the text together. Have students compare and contrast the bicycles, telling how they are alike and how they are different.

- **Reteach** Distribute copies of the Picture It! (*ELL Handbook,* p. 192). Ask students to describe the illustration. Prepare students for the first reading by asking them to listen for ways in which the author and Simon are alike. For the second reading, done chorally, have students listen for ways in which the author and Simon are different. Guide students in completing the practice exercises at their language proficiency level. (Simon: a lot of freckles, messy hair, not good at math; Author: no freckles, neat hair, good at math; Both: same height, love to play soccer, like pizza more than any other food)

Beginning Have students draw pictures to show how the author and Simon are alike and how they are different.

Intermediate Ask students to use phrases from the reading selection to complete the exercise.

Advanced/Advanced High Have students complete the graphic organizer with information from the story. Challenge them to use the graphic organizer to guide them in retelling how Simon and the author are alike and different. Provide language as needed.

MINI-LESSON

Similarities and Differences

When two things are alike, we say they have similarities. When they are different, we say they have differences. Look at Envision It! on p. EI•6 of the Student Edition. Use the following sentences frames to talk about the similarities and differences between the two bicycles: *They have similarities. They are both _____. They have differences. One _____; the other, _____.*

Objectives
- Learn new language structures, expressions, and basic and academic vocabulary heard during classroom instruction and interactions.
- Develop basic sight vocabulary, derive meaning of environmental print, and comprehend English vocabulary and language structures used routinely in written classroom materials.

ntent Objectives
Compare and contrast people and things.

Use a Venn diagram to map similarities and differences.

anguage Objectives
Derive meaning from environmental print.

Comprehend routine classroom English.

Talk and write about similarities and differences.

nvironmental Print
Focus on the environmental print on page EI•6. Point out he price tags on the items. This environmental print shows us how much items cost in stores. Tags usually nclude information about he items. Have students tell what kind of information they find on item labels in stores and why it's important to be able to read them.

 English Language Learners

Reading Comprehension
King Midas and the Golden Touch

■ **Frontloading** Read aloud the title. Have students brainstorm ideas about the meaning of a golden touch. A golden touch refers to someone for whom things turn to gold after touching them. Do you think this would turn out to be a good thing or a bad thing? Why? Guide students on a picture walk through *King Midas and the Golden Touch.* Ask students to predict what can happen to a king with a golden touch and record their predictions. During reading, pause and invite students to adjust their predictions. Provide students with a T-Chart to complete as they read the selection.

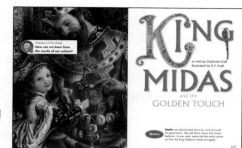
Student Edition pp. 376–377

Sheltered Reading Ask questions to guide comprehension. Support students as you read aloud so that they understand the challenging language of this text. Consider restating difficult passages.

- p. 378: What did King Midas believe was the most precious thing in the world? (gold) What was the only thing King Midas loved more? (his daughter)

- p. 381: What does King Midas wish? (that everything he touches will turn to gold)

- pp. 382–383: What happened when Midas pulled on his clothes? (They turned to gold.) What happened to everything he touched? (It turned to gold.)

- pp. 390–391: Was King Midas happy with the results of his action, or wish? (no) What would he trade all the gold in the world for? (his daughter)

- p. 392: Does King Midas get his wish? (yes) What do you think he learned from the results of his actions?

■ **Fluency: Read at the Appropriate Rate** Read the first paragraph on p. 378 at an appropriate rate. Have pairs of students read the paragraph aloud to each other. Partners should listen and offer feedback.

After Reading Have students use the Retelling Cards to summarize the text. Give one card to each group. Have them line up in story order and take turns retelling their section of the story.

Content Objectives
- Monitor and adjust comprehension.
- Make and adjust predictions.

Language Objectives
- Read grade-level text at the appropriate rate.
- Summarize text using visual support.
- Adapt language for informal purposes.
- Get support to read increasingly challenging language.

Audio Support
Students can prepare for reading *King Midas and the Golden Touch* by using the eSelection or the AudioText CD. See the AudioText CD Routine (*ELL Handbook,* p. 477).

Language Opportunity: Informal Language
Tell students that storytellers often use informal language when they tell stories. Have students retell *King Midas and the Golden Touch* to classmates, using the informal language of storytelling.

Objectives
- Understand the general meaning, main points, and important details of spoken language ranging from situations in which topics, language, and contexts are familiar to unfamiliar.

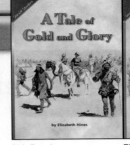 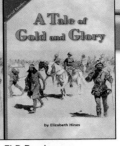

ELL Reader   ELD Reader

For additional leveled instruction, see the **ELL/ELD Reader Teaching Guide.**

Comprehension
A Tale of Gold and Glory

■ **Before Reading** Distribute copies of the ELL and ELD Readers, *A Tale of Gold and Glory.* Have students reed with linguistic accomodation, moving from the ELD to the ELL Readers as more English is acquired.

- **Preview** Read the title aloud with students: This is a nonfiction text about Spanish conquerors searching for gold. Invite students to look at the pictures to predict if the conquerors will find gold.

- **Set a Purpose for Reading** Let's read to find out if the Spanish conquerors find gold.

■ **During Reading** Follow the Reading Routine for both reading groups.

1. Read the entire Reader aloud slowly.

2. Reread pp. 2–7, pausing to build background or model comprehension. Use the questions in the chart to check students' comprehension.

3. Have students chorally read pp. 2–7.

4. Repeat steps 2–3 for pp. 8–12.

■ **After Reading** Use the exercises on the inside back cover of each Reader and invite students to share their writing. Ask: Do you think the Seven Cities of Gold existed? Why do you think Marcos de Niza said he saw the city? Record their answers on the board and invite them to point to pictures in the book to support their answers.

ELD Reader   Beginning/Intermediate

■ **pp. 2–3** What did the King and Queen of Spain want Christopher Columbus to find? (an easy route to India and China, and gold) Read aloud the sentences that give you the answer. (p. 3)

■ **p. 4** Which Native American nations had gold objects? (Incas and Aztecs)

■ **p. 5** What were the Spanish conquerors searching for? (Cibola, a land of gold)

Writing What fact about the Spanish conquerors is most interesting to you? Find the sentence in the book that tells about that fact. Copy the sentence. Then read it aloud to your partner.

ELL Reader   Advanced/Advanced High

■ **pp. 2–3** What did the King and Queen of Spain want Christopher Columbus to find? (an easy route to India and China, and gold) Did he find them? (no)

■ **pp. 8–9** What did Marcos de Niza say he found? (a large city full of riches) Who did the Spaniards send to conquer Cibola? (Francisco Vasquez de Coronado)

Study Guide Distribute copies of the ELL Reader Study Guide (*ELL Handbook,* p. 196). Scaffold comprehension of comparing and contrasting by helping students look back through the Reader to complete the graphic organizer. Review their responses together. (**Answers** See *ELL Handbook,* pp. 209–212.)

Objectives
- Understand the general meaning, main points, and important details of spoken language ranging from situations in which topics, language, and contexts are familiar to unfamiliar.
- Read linguistically accomodated context area material with a decreasing need for lingustic accomodations as more English is acquired.

English Language Learners

Conventions
Commas

■ **Teach/Model** Remind students that commas are used to separate groups of items in sentences in order to make the sentences easier to read. Display these sentences:

> Red white and blue are the colors of the United States flag.

> The sandwich was made of turkey lettuce mustard and tomatoes.

> Hockey baseball and soccer are three of my favorite sports.

Guide students in properly inserting commas between the items in each series.

■ **Practice** Have students call out three items in each of the following categories: fruits, cars, book titles, items on a menu. List the categories and the words students suggest on the board.

Leveled LS Support

Beginning Have pairs of students orally generate a sentence that contains one of the series of items. Write the complete sentence without commas. Ask students to help you put commas between each of the items in the series.

Intermediate Have students orally generate a sentence that contains one of the series of items. Ask them to write their sentence, putting commas between each of the items in the series.

Advanced Have students orally generate sentences that contain a series of items in each category. Have them write the sentences, putting commas between each of the items in the series.

Advanced High Have students orally generate questions that contain a series of items in each category. Have them write the questions, putting commas between each of the items in the series.

Content Objectives
• Use commas in a series.
• Name items in a category.

Language Objectives
• Speak using sentences that contain commas in a series.
• Ask questions that contain commas in a series.

Grammar Jammer
For more practice with punctuation, use the Grammar Jammer for this target skill. See the Grammar Jammer Routine (*ELL Handbook*, p. 478) for suggestions on using this learning tool.

Objectives
• Speak using a variety of grammatical structures, sentence lengths, sentence types, and connecting words with increasing accuracy and ease as more English is acquired.

Content Objectives

Identify the point of view from which a story is told.

Language Objectives

Write a paragraph telling what they can learn from the results of their actions.

Share feedback for editing and revising.

Use complex grammatical structures in writing.

ELL Teaching Routine

For practice spelling words related to results of actions, use the Spelling Routine (*ELL Handbook,* p. 476).

ELL Workshop

Students can collaborate with peers to discuss their writing. *Discuss with Classmates* (*ELL Handbook,* pp. 418–419) provides assistance with discussion.

ELL Workshop

Discuss that authors often express feelings in writing. Give students the opportunity to express feelings about the selection. *Express Feelings* (*ELL Handbook,* pp. 416–417) provides extra support.

ELL — English Language Learners

Point of View

■ **Introduce** Display the paragraph model and read it aloud. Review that a paragraph tells a story from the point of view of the narrator. Who is telling this story? (King Midas) How can you tell? (because he speaks of himself as "I." He speaks as King Midas would.)

Writing Model

I love gold more than anything in the world. I love its soft yellow color. I love how it feels when I hold it. I love my roses too. I wish they were gold, so they would last forever!

■ **Practice** Write the following paragraph on the board. Have students work with you to retell the story from the point of view of Aurelia. Have them think about what Aurelia might say about her father's love for gold.

My father loves _____ more than anything in the world. Sometimes, I think he loves gold more than he loves _____. He would even turn our beautiful _____ into gold. They would last forever, but they would not have their natural _____.

■ **Write** Have students write a paragraph about what they can learn from the results of their actions. Remind them that the paragraph should be written from their own point of view. For ideas, they can use *King Midas and the Golden Touch* or *A Tale of Gold.* Remind students to correctly use grammar structures. Have them focus on verb tenses. Because they are writing about an event in the part, they should past tense verbs. Have them check verb tense throughout their writing.

Beginning Guide students in writing one sentence about what they can learn from the results of their actions.

Intermediate Guide students in writing two sentences about what they can learn from the results of their actions.

Advanced Have students write a short paragraph about what they can learn from the results of their actions. Remind them that the paragraph should clearly reflect their point of view.

Advanced High Have students write a paragraph about what they can learn from the results of their actions. Encourage them to include a sentence with serial commas. Have partners exchange papers and provide feedback for revising and editing.

Objectives

• Share information in cooperative learning interactions.
• Write using newly acquired basic vocabulary and content-based grade-level vocabulary.

Customize Your Writing

Weekly Writing Focus
Writing Forms and Patterns

- Instruction focuses on a different **product** each week.
- Mini-lessons and models help students learn key features and **organizational patterns**.

Grade 5 Products tall tale, personal narrative, historical fiction, persuasive essay, poetry, expository composition, and so on

Grade 5 Organization Patterns letter, sequence, poetic forms, main idea and details, narrative, and so on

Daily Writing Focus
Quick Writes for Fluency

- **Writing on Demand** 🕐 Use the Quick Write routine for **writing on demand**.
- The Quick Write **prompt and routine** extend skills and strategies from daily writing lessons.

Unit Writing Focus
Writing Process ①②③

- Six **writing process** lessons pro___ structure to move students thr___ the steps of the writing process
- One-week and two-week pacin___ allows lessons to be used in **Writing Workshop**.

Steps of the Writing Process Plan ___ Prewrite, Draft, Revise, Edit, Pub___ and Present

Grade 5 Writing Process Products personal narrative, comic book, compare and contrast essay, cau___ and-effect essay, persuasive essa___ research report

Writing on Reading STREET

Write Guy
Jeff Anderson
Need Writing Advice?

Writing instruction is all about creat___ing effective writers. We don't want___ to crush the inner writer in a child___ by over-correcting and over-editing___ What makes effective writing instru___tion? Children need to write, write,___ write! But is that enough? Prob-ably not. All kinds of instruction and___ guidance go into making an effectiv___ writer.

The Write Guy offers advice on teacher and peer conferencing, focusing on writing traits, revising strategies, editing strategies, and much, much more.

MINI-LESSON

- Daily 10-minute mini-lessons focus instruction on the **traits** and **craft** of good writing.
- Instruction focuses on one writing trait and one writer's craft skill every week.

Traits focus/ideas, organization, voice, word choice, sentences, conventions

Craft drafting strategies, revising strategies, editing strategies

Read Like a Writer

- Use **mentor text** every week as a model to exemplify the traits of good writing.
- **Interact with text** every week to learn the key features of good writing.

Mentor Text Examine literature in the Student Edition.

INTERACT with TEXT Underline, circle, and highlight model text in the *Reader's and Writer's Notebook.*

stomize Your Writing

lternate Pacing Plan
or Unit Writing Projects

ometimes you want to spend more time on writing—perhaps you do a **Writing Workshop**.
his one- or two-week plan for the unit level writing projects can help.

1 Week Plan	Day 1	Day 2	Day 3	Day 4	Day 5
1 Plan and Prewrite	██	██			
2 Draft			██		
3 Revise				██	
4 Edit					██
5 Publish					██

2 Week Plan	Day 1	Day 2	Day 3	Day 4	Day 5	Day 6	Day 7	Day 8	Day 9	Day 10
1 Plan and Prewrite	██	██	██	██						
2 Draft					██	██	██			
3 Revise								██		
4 Edit									██	
5 Publish										██

rade 5 Unit Writing Projects

Internet Guy
Don Leu

Unit Writing Project I–21st Century Project

Unit 1 Podcasting

Unit 2 E-Newsletter

Unit 3 Story Exchange

Unit 4 E-Pen Pals

Unit 5 Community Interviews

Unit 6 Photo Description

Unit Writing Project 2–Writing Process

Unit 1 Personal Narrative

Unit 2 Comic Book/Graphic Novel

Unit 3 Compare and Contrast Essay

Unit 4 Cause-and-Effect Essay

Unit 5 Persuasive Essay

Unit 6 Research Report

21st Century Writing Using the Virginia English Standards of Learning (SOLs) *and* Common Core State Standards

To excel in the 21st Century, students must:

- acquire new skills, tools, knowledge, and thinking skills
- develop these skills and habits that will serve them as lifelong learners
- engage technology to transform knowledge and skills into useful contributions within a wide array of learning and working communities

21ˢᵗ Century Writing and the Virginia English Standards of Learning (SOLs) *and* Common Core State Standards

In this unit's 21ˢᵗ Century Writing Project, students will apply the five steps of process writing. The chart below provides instructional tips for guiding students through each step. Discuss these tips with students before they begin writing.

Process Writing Steps	Virginia English Standards of Learning (SOLs) *and* Common Core State Standards for English Language Arts*	Tips for Unit 6 21ˢᵗ Century Writing
1 **Plan and Prewrite**	VA 5.7.a, VA 5.7.b; CCSS Writing 2.b., CCSS Writing 5.	As students **plan** a photo description, encourage them to capture notes on photo details in a chart. *See Brainstorming Paragraph Focus and Details* on page CW•4.
2 **Draft**	VA 5.7.c, VA 5.7.d, VA 5.7.e, VA 5.7.f, VA 5.7.g; CCSS Writing 2.a.	As students **draft,** encourage use of spatial order to organize ideas. See the *Draft the Body of a Descriptive Paragraph Mini-lesson* on page CW•6.
3 **Revise**	VA 5.7.h, VA 5.7.i; CCSS Writing 5.	As students **revise,** have them exchange their drafts for peer revision. Use the *Use Vivid, Imaginative Details Mini-lesson* on page CW•7.
4 **Edit**	VA 5.8; CCSS Writing 5., CCSS Language 2.	As students **edit,** note that spelling checkers will not identify homophone misuse. *See Using the Computer to Help Edit Drafts* on page CW•8.
5 **Publish**	VA 5.9.c; CCSS Writing 6.	When students **publish** their writing, have them display their photo descriptions. See *Options for Presenting* on page CW•10.

*© Copyright 2010. National Governors Association Center for Best Practices and Council of Chief State School Officers. All rights reserved.

Integrating 21ˢᵗ Century Skills and the Virginia Computer/Technology Standards of Learning (SOLs)

The chart below shows the skills taught in this unit's 21ˢᵗ Century Writing Project and the Virginia Computer/Technology Standards of Learning that correspond to these skills.

21st Century Skills in This Project	Virginia Computer/Technology Standards of Learning
Photographing or Researching Images with a Search Engine pages CW•3	VA C/T 3-5.6 The student will use technology to locate, evaluate, and collect information from a variety of sources.
Using Word Processing Tools pages CW•4–8	VA C/T 3-5.8.a Produce documents demonstrating the ability to edit, reformat, and integrate various software tools.
Designing Documents pages CW•9	VA C/T 3-5.8.a Produce documents demonstrating the ability to edit, reformat, and integrate various software tools.
Publishing Documents pages CW•10	VA C/T 3-5.8.b Use technology tools for individual and collaborative writing, communication, and publishing activities.

Virginia Writing Resources

A complete Composing Rubric, Written Expression Rubric, and Usage/Mechanics Rubric can be found in the Virginia Standards of Learning Test Prep Book Teacher's Manual. Use these resources to build writing skills during and after the teaching of Unit 6.

Reader's and Writer's Notebook

Grammar & Writing Book

Digital Resources
- Online Writing Transparencies

Teacher Resources DVD-ROM
- Reader's and Writer's Notebook
- Let's Practice It!
- Graphic Organizers
- Writing Transparencies

ISBN 13: 978-0-328-56592-4   ISBN 10: 0-328-56592-X

Photo Description

Writing Project Create a photo description of an image that reveals the unexpected.

Purpose Enhance skills in the use of a digital camera, the Internet, and computer applications for image and word processing and design.

Audience student, classmates, teacher, family

Introduce genre and key features

In this workshop, we will write a descriptive paragraph inspired by a photograph that shows something unexpected. We will use a digital camera to take pictures; a computer to draft, revise, and edit; and the Internet to publish our writing.

Key Features of a Photo Description

- focuses on an idea suggested by the image
- organizes details visually
- uses specific, vivid language
- may include figurative language and imagery

Academic Vocabular

Photo Description A photo description is a descriptive pa graph inspired by a photograp

Teacher Tip

Images of the Unexpected
Collect photographic images o surprising and unexpected phe nomena on a variety of subject Students can look through ther to get ideas for their own phote graphs or, if they cannot acces technology, to select the subjec for their photo description.

E L L

English Language Learners
Introduce Descriptive Writing
Explain that descriptions in English involve specific details. Display an object on a projector and provide a sentence frame for it:

A __ butterfly is resting ___.

Have students point out details of the image, and embellish the sentence frame to describe it. Point out typical placement for adjectives and adverbs in English sentences.

jectives

Understand and identify the features of a photo description.

Organize ideas to prepare for writing.

Plan and Prewrite

Read Like a Writer

■ **Examine Model Text** Display several images that capture unexpected phenomena, such as snow on a flower or a plant growing up from a crack in a sidewalk. To mesh with the 21st Century Transparency TC12, include a walking stick among the images. The world around us is full of surprising images. Discuss what is unexpected about each photo and what details make it special. You are going to take photos of something you find unexpected and write a paragraph describing the scene or object.

■ **Explore Model Text** Let's look at an example of a paragraph describing a walking stick that surprised the writer. This is the kind of text that you will write. Display and read aloud to students "The Stick That Isn't," 21st Century Transparency TC12. Have students refer to the photograph of a walking stick as you read the paragraph aloud. Have students identify details of the walking stick in the photo as they are described in the text.

21st Century Transparency TC12, TR DVD

Brainstorm unexpected images

If we look closely at the world, there are many sights that can amaze us. Let's think of subjects of photographs that could illustrate the unexpected and list some places we could look to take such pictures. Encourage students to list surprising things they have observed in accessible places such as the school grounds, a park, or their home. Guide students toward images of common scenes or objects such as insects, plants in unexpected places, or unique decorative touches. Write students' ideas on a chart on the board.

Surprising image	What makes it surprising	Where I could find it
dog and cat friends	dogs and cats sometimes do not get along	my neighbors
weird caterpillar	looks like a brush	in a garden
strange bugs	funny shapes	under a rock
collection of glass bottles	pretty colors, different shapes	grandma's house

Organize a field trip

Have students arrange to share to share the use of a digital camera during a photo expedition. Show students the proper use of the camera they will use. Set guidelines and rules for behavior on the expedition.

Photo expedition

Take the class on a walking field trip on your school playground or in the neighborhood around your school. Encourage them to take more than one photograph of a given subject and to consider the angle and point of view they want before they snap their pictures.

Corrective feedback

If... students have trouble brainstorming ideas for the unexpected,
then... point out unexpected things you notice in the room or outside the classroom window, and then ask students to look closely to find one thing unexpected or surprising around them.

Objectives
List a subject focus and details
for a descriptive paragraph.

 Plan and Prewrite

MINI-LESSON

Paragraph Focus and Details

■ We have taken pictures of the unexpected. Now we are going to write a paragraph of description to go with our photo. A writer begins a paragraph plan by deciding on the main idea or focus and listing vivid, specific details that support it. Display 21st Century Transparency TC14, the completed "Notes for Photo Description." Discuss the subject, date, and focus sections of the chart.

Photo Description Chart

Subject	walking stick on tree trunk
Date and Place Taken	April 5, on a tree in the school yard
Focus/surprise	a stick that started walking
What I noticed first	Greenish brown; bumpy and ridged like bark, slow-moving
Details about each part	
• head and eyes	• only can tell it's a head by the eyes; brown, like seeds, on sides of head
• body	• about four inches long, curved slightly
• legs	• legs like smaller branches off main twig, jointed, claws on the end
• tail	• long, skinny, two prongs on end

Unit 6 Photo Description   21st Century Writing **TC14**

21st Century Transparency
TC14, TR DVD

■ Place a hardcopy version of 21st Century Transparency TC13, the blank "Photo Description Chart," on students' desktops. Have them refer to their photograph and make notes in the first three boxes of the chart.

Photo Description Chart

Subject	
Date and Place Taken	
Focus/surprise	
What I noticed first	
Details about each part	

Unit 6 Photo Description   21st Century Writing **TC13**

21st Century Transparency
TC13, TR DVD

■ Display the photo of the walking stick as you model capturing details about the photo in the chart. Next, the writer lists all the details that are important to the surprising discovery. Looking at the photograph, I notice that the insect's body is about four inches long and curved slightly. Its legs look like tiny branches with joints. The round, brown things on each side of its head are eyes, but they look like seeds. The tail is long and skinny, with two prongs on the end. Point out the notes in the last box of the chart that list these details.

■ Have students complete their charts by entering details that describe their photograph. They can use these notes for reference as they draft their paragraphs.

Write a topic sentence

Students should use their hardcopy photo description charts to help them write a topic sentence for their descriptive paragraphs. Have students use a word processing program on the computer.

Writers begin their descriptive paragraph plan by writing a topic sentence that states the main idea or focus of the description. All the details about the walking stick explain how its parts look like stick parts. The writer stated the topic sentence this way: I discovered a walking stick, an insect that looks just like a stick.

Name and save file

Have students create and name a file for their photograph description and use their word processing application to write a topic sentence for their paragraph.

Include attention grabber

I notice that the topic sentence in the model is not the first sentence in the paragraph. The writer began the paragraph with sentences that catch your attention and explain how the unexpected discovery occurred. You may want to draw readers in to your paragraph by beginning with a similar introduction. **Have students insert one or two introductory sentences before their topic sentence if they wish.**

Objectives
- Organize paragraph details using spatial order.
- Write a descriptive paragraph from notes.

 **Draft**

MINI-LESSON

Body of a Descriptive Paragraph

■ **Use Spatial Order to Organize Ideas** Copy the following chart on the board. Often a writer describes things in the order in which the eye would see them. The details in a descriptive paragraph should be put in a logical order. Discuss why the chart examples might be described using the specified organization plans. Point out that the model description of the walking stick travels from the head to the tail.

Organization of Details	Example Description
from top to bottom (or bottom to top)	a person, a building
from left to right (or right to left)	a room
from near to far	a scene, a road

■ **Getting Started** Have students refer to their Photo Description Chart and decide on a logical plan for organizing their details. They can number the descriptive details in the last box of the chart. As they compose the body of their paragraph, have them write one or two sentences for each detail in the chosen order.

③ Revise

MINI-LESSON

Use Vivid, Imaginative Details

■ One way to revise descriptive writing is to replace general or clichéd language with precise nouns, vivid adjectives and adverbs, and colorful figures of speech. Explain that some figures of speech compare one thing to another in an original or striking way. Read these examples with students.

General Nouns bug, feeler, weird things

Specific Nouns insect, antenna, ridges and bumps

Unclear Adjectives and Adverbs cool, great, nicely

Vivid Adjectives and Adverbs jointed, clever, eerily

Cliché (overused phrase) I couldn't believe my eyes.

Colorful figure of speech Was it an enchanted stick from a fairy tale?

Discuss with students how more specific, vivid words create a crisper, clearer picture for readers.

Peer conferencing Pair students and have them exchange their drafts for revision. Ask partners to point out places in the paragraph that could be improved by more specific, vivid words.

Revise drafts Now we will revise our drafts of the paragraph that describes our photograph of the unexpected. As we revise, we make changes that will make our writing clearer and more vivid. We consider the changes suggested in peer conferencing. To be clear, descriptions need to have precise, vivid details and describe parts of the whole in a logical order.

Have students revise their drafts using the word processing application of their computer.

Corrective feedback If… students have difficulty making language more specific,
then… have them work with a partner to rank word sets like the following from general to specific and to explain their choices: *flower, plant, rosebud; boy, toddler, child; red, ruby, colorful; leisurely, slowly, at a snail's pace.*

Objectives
Edit a revised draft of a descriptive paragraph to correct errors in grammar, mechanics, and spelling.

4 Edit

Using the Computer to Edit

■ Review with students the grammar and spell-check function on their computer. Explain that they will need to proofread carefully to find errors the spell-check will miss.

■ The computer is programmed to find some common errors in language usage. However, it may miss errors. Sometimes, it suggests a change that will not improve your draft. Read each suggestion the spelling or grammar check makes carefully before you accept it. Type the following sentence in a word processing program and display it on an LCD projector or an interactive whiteboard:

It's body was about for inchs long with ridges and bumps just like a twig wood have.

Use the spelling and grammar check to check the sentence. The spell check missed several errors because words are spelled correctly but the wrong words are used. Which words need to be changed? Change *it's* to *its, for* to *four,* and *wood* to *would.* The spell check caught an error in spelling of a plural form. What is the correct way to spell the plural of *inch?* Change *inchs* to *inches.*

■ Have students practice editing the following sentences, first by using the grammar and spelling check and then by themselves.

The caterpillar looked like a fury pup.

Fuzy tufts of black, wide, and gold poked out of its bodie.

Edit drafts   Ask students to edit their own drafts. After they use the grammar and spelling check, have them print out the text of their paragraph and read it sentence by sentence to make further edits. Ask them to check their drafts for spelling, grammar, punctuation, and capitalization.

5 Publish and Present

MINI-LESSON

Combining Graphics and Text

▪ Display the walking stick photo you used to illustrate 21st Century Transparency TC12 using a page design or word processing application available to your class. Now that we have written our paragraphs describing our photographs, it is time to combine the text and picture. Demonstrate how to place, resize, and move the photo on the page and how to change text margins to create a page that looks neat and proportional.

▪ Demonstrate to students how to upload their photographs from the camera's memory card or scan their prints onto their desktop. Have students place their photos on the page with their paragraphs and design the page as they think appropriate. Circulate among students and give help as needed with formatting tasks, such as resizing photos and sizing and placing text.

Objectives
Give an oral presentation.
Evaluate text and graphics of photo descriptions.

 Publish and Present

Options for presenting

Offer students three options for presenting their photos and descriptive paragraphs:

Print a hard copies of their image and paragraph to share with families and classmates.	Convert the file to a Portable Document Format (PDF) and make it available via a class or school Web site.	Upload the file containing the text and photo to a class blog established at an educational blog site.

Sharing views of the unexpected

Invite students to share their photos and paragraphs in oral presentations. Encourage students to explain how they discovered the subject of their photograph and then read aloud their paragraph.

In a whole-class discussion, have students list lessons or surprising facts they learned through this workshop. Ask students to point out photo descriptions they especially liked and identify qualities or features that made them stand out.

Customize Literacy in Your Classroom

Table of Contents
for Customize Literacy

Customize Literacy is organized into different sections, each one designed to help you organize and carry out an effective literacy program. Each section contains strategies and support for teaching comprehension skills and strategies. *Customize Literacy* also shows how to use weekly text sets of readers in your literacy program.

Weekly Text Sets
to Customize Literacy

The following readers can be used to enhance your literacy instruction.

	Concept Literacy Reader	Below-Level Reader	On-Level Reader	Advanced Reader	ELD Reader	ELL Reader
Unit 6 WEEK 1	*Going Batty in Austin*	*A Happy Accident*	*Driven to Change*	*How the Wolves Saved Yellowstone*	*An Unexpected Friend*	*An Unexpected Friend*
Unit 6 WEEK 2	*Nature's Balance*	*Saving an American Symbol*	*The Kudzu Invasion*	*Mixed-Up Vegetables*	*All Things in Balance*	*All Things in Balance*
Unit 6 WEEK 3	*Where's King Midas When You Need Him?*	*Ancient Gold from the Ancient World*	*The Golden Journey*	*Precious Goods: From Salt to Silk*	*A Tale of Gold and Glory*	*A Tale of Gold and Glory*

Customize Literacy in Your Classroom

Instruction in comprehension skills and strategies provides readers with avenues to understanding a text. Through teacher modeling and guided, collaborative, and independent practice, students become independent thinkers who employ a variety of skills and strategies to help them make meaning as they read.

Mini-Lessons for Comprehension Skills and Strategies

Envision It!
A Comprehension Handbook

Unit 1	Literary Elements, Cause and Effect, Fact and Opinion, Summarize, Inferring, Text Structure
Unit 2	Compare and Contrast, Sequence, Author's Purpose, Visualize, Story Structure, Monitor and Clarify, Background Knowledge
Unit 3	Sequence, Main Idea and Supporting Details, Fact and Opinion, Graphic Sources, Predict and Set Purpose, Important Ideas
Unit 4	Draw Conclusions, Generalize, Graphic Sources, Questioning, Monitor and Clarify
Unit 5	Literary Elements, Graphic Sources, Author's Purpose, Cause and Effect, Generalize, Inferring, Summarize
Unit 6	Draw Conclusions, Main Idea and Supporting Details, Compare and Contrast, Fact and Opinion, Sequence, Text Structure, Questioning

Anchor Chart Anchor charts are provided with each strategy lesson. These charts incorporate the language of strategic thinkers. They help students make their thinking visible and permanent and provide students with a means to clarify their thinking about how and when to use each strategy. As students gain more experience with a strategy, the chart may undergo revision.

See pages 101–126 in the *First Stop on Reading Street* Teacher's Edition for additional support as you customize literacy in your classroom.

Good Readers DRA2 users will find additional resources in the *First Stop on Reading Street* Teacher's Edition on pages 104–105.

Contents

Pacing Guide

This chart shows the instructional sequence from *Scott Foresman Reading Street* for Grade 5. You can use this pacing guide as is to ensure you are following a comprehensive scope and sequence. Or, you can adjust the sequence to match your calendar, curriculum map, or testing schedule.

Grade 5

REVIEW WEEK

READING	UNIT 1					UNIT 2	
	Week 1	Week 2	Week 3	Week 4	Week 5	Week 1	Week 2
Comprehension Skill	Character and Plot	Cause and Effect	Theme and Setting	Fact and Opinion	Cause and Effect	Compare and Contrast	Sequence
Comprehension Strategy	Monitor and Clarify	Summarize	Inferring	Questioning	Text Structure	Visualize	Inferring
Vocabulary Strategy/Skill	Context Clues/ Homographs	Context Clues/ Homonyms	Dictionary/ Glossary/ Unknown Words	Context Clues/ Antonyms	Context Clues/ Multiple-Meaning Words	Context Clues/ Unfamiliar Words	Dictionary/ Glossary/ Unknown Words
Fluency	Expression	Rate	Expression	Phrasing/ Punctuation	Accuracy	Expression	Accuracy
Spelling/ Word Work	Short Vowel VCCV, VCV	Long Vowel VCV	Long Vowel Digraphs	Adding -ed, -ing	Contractions	Digraphs *th, sh, ch, ph*	Irregular Plurals

REVIEW WEEK

	UNIT 4					UNIT 5	
	Week 1	Week 2	Week 3	Week 4	Week 5	Week 1	Week 2
Comprehension Skill	Draw Conclusions	Generalize	Graphic Sources	Generalize	Draw Conclusions	Character and Plot	Graphic Sources
Comprehension Strategy	Questioning	Predict and Set Purpose	Important Ideas	Story Structure	Visualize	Background Knowledge	Inferring
Vocabulary Skill/ Strategy	Word Structure/ Endings	Context Clues/ Unfamiliar Words	Context Clues/ Synonyms	Context Clues/ Unfamiliar Words	Word Structure/ Suffixes	Word Structure/Greek and Latin Roots	Dictionary/ Glossary Unknown Words
Fluency	Phrasing	Accuracy	Rate	Expression	Phrasing	Expression	Expression
Spelling/ Word Work	Words from Many Cultures	Prefixes *sub-, over-, out-, under-, super-*	Homophones	Suffixes *-ible, -able*	Negative Prefixes	Multisyllabic Words	Related Words

Are you the adventurous type? Want to use some of your own ideas and materials in your teaching? But you worry you might be leaving out some critical instruction kids need? **Customize Literacy** *can help.* "

UNIT 3

REVIEW WEEK

REVIEW WEEK

Week 3	Week 4	Week 5	Week 1	Week 2	Week 3	Week 4	Week 5
Compare and Contrast	Author's Purpose	Author's Purpose	Sequence	Main Idea/ Details	Fact and Opinion	Main Idea/ Details	Graphic Sources
Story Structure	Monitor and Clarify	Background Knowledge	Summarize	Visualize	Predict and Set Purpose	Text Structure	Important Ideas
Word Structure/ Greek and Latin Roots	Context Clues/ Unfamiliar Words	Word Structure/ Endings -s, -ed, -ing	Context Clues/ Multiple-Meaning Words	Word Structure/ Greek and Latin Roots	Context Clues/ Homonyms	Context Clues/ Antonyms	Word Structure/ Prefixes
Expression	Phrasing	Rate	Expression	Rate	Phrasing	Rate	Accuracy
Vowel Sounds with r	Final Syllables -en, -an, -el, -le, -il	Final Syllables -er, -ar, -or	Words with Schwa	Compound Words	Consonant Sounds /j/, /ks/, /sk/, and /s/	One Consonant or Two	Prefixes un-, de-, dis-

UNIT 6

REVIEW WEEK

REVIEW WEEK

Week 3	Week 4	Week 5	Week 1	Week 2	Week 3	Week 4	Week 5
Author's Purpose	Cause and Effect	Generalize	Draw Conclusions	Main Idea/ Details	Compare and Contrast	Fact and Opinion	Sequence
Monitor and Clarify	Summarize	Questioning	Important Ideas	Text Structure	Story Structure	Predict and Set Purpose	Background Knowledge
Context Clues/ Multiple-Meaning Words	Context Clues/ Unfamiliar Words	Word Structure/ Prefixes	Dictionary/ Glossary/ Unknown Words	Word Structure/ Endings	Word Structure/ Suffixes	Word Structure/ Unfamiliar Words	Context Clues/ Homographs
Accuracy	Phrasing	Rate	Accuracy	Phrasing/ Punctuation Clues	Rate	Phrasing	Expression
Greek Word Parts	Latin Roots	Greek Word Parts	Suffixes -ous, -sion, -ion, -ation	Final Syllable -ant, -ent, -ance, -ence	Latin Roots	Related Words	Easily Confused Words

Section 1 Planning

Pacing Guide

Grade 5 LANGUAGE ARTS

UNIT 1 — REVIEW WEEK

	Week 1	Week 2	Week 3	Week 4	Week 5
Speaking and Listening	Interview	Storytelling	How-to Demonstration	Sportscast	Job Ad
Grammar	Four Kinds of Sentences	Subjects and Predicates	Independent and Dependent Clauses	Compound and Complex Sentences	Common, Proper, and Collective Nouns
Weekly Writing	Directions	Tall Tale	Invitation	Newsletter Article	Expository Composition
Trait of the Week	Organization	Voice	Focus/Ideas	Word Choice	Organization/ Paragraphs
Writing	Podcast/Personal Narrative				

UNIT 2

	Week 1	Week 2
Speaking and Listening	Talk Show	Informational Speech
Grammar	Regular and Irregular Plural Nouns	Possessive Nouns
Weekly Writing	Description	Informal Letter
Trait of the Week	Sentences	Voice

UNIT 4 — REVIEW WEEK

	Week 1	Week 2	Week 3	Week 4	Week 5
Speaking and Listening	How-to Demonstration	Persuasive Speech	Description	Give Advice	Interview
Grammar	Subject and Object Pronouns	Pronouns and Antecedents	Possessive Pronouns	Indefinite and Reflexive Pronouns	Using *Who* and *Whom*
Weekly Writing	Picture Book	Friendly Letter	Formal Letter	Narrative Poetry	Autobiographical Sketch
Trait of the Week	Focus/Ideas	Sentences	Conventions	Word Choice	Voice
Writing	E-Pen Pals/Cause-and-Effect Essay				

UNIT 5

	Week 1	Week 2
Speaking and Listening	Dramatization	Newscast
Grammar	Contractions and Negatives	Adjectives and Articles
Weekly Writing	Rhyming Poem	Notes
Trait of the Week	Word Choice	Focus/Ideas

UNIT 3

Week 3	Week 4	Week 5	Week 1	Week 2	Week 3	Week 4	Week 5
Readers' Theater	Panel Discussion	Documentary	Play Review	Newscast	Introducing a Special Person	Give Directions	Advertisement
Action and Linking Verbs	Main and Helping Verbs	Subject-Verb Agreement	Past, Present, and Future Tenses	Principal Parts of Regular Verbs	Principal Parts of Irregular Verbs	Troublesome Verbs	Prepositions and Prepositional Phrases
Poem	Personal Narrative	Historical Fiction	Play	Persuasive Speech	Ad Brochure	Description	Expository Text
Organization/ Poetic Structure	Word Choice	Word Choice	Word Choice	Focus/Ideas	Word Choice	Word Choice	Organization

E-Newsletter/Comic Book Graphic Novel

Story Exchange/Compare and Contrast Essay

UNIT 6

Week 3	Week 4	Week 5	Week 1	Week 2	Week 3	Week 4	Week 5
Storytelling	Discussion	Debate	Debate	Interview	Storytelling	Newscast	Readers' Theater
This, That, These, and *Those*	Comparative and Superlative Adjectives	Adverbs	Modifiers	Conjunctions	Commas	Quotations and Quotation Marks	Punctuation
Biographical Sketch	Letter to the Editor	Summary	Journal Entry	Mystery	Parody	Review	Personal Narrative
Sentences	Voice	Focus/Ideas	Voice	Focus/Ideas	Voice	Organization/ Paragraphs	Voice

Interview/Persuasive Essay

Photo Description/Research Report

Teaching Record Chart

This chart shows the critical comprehension skills and strategies you need to cover. Check off each one as you provide instruction.

Reading/Comprehension	DATES OF INSTRUCTION		
Compare and contrast the themes or moral lessons of several works of fiction from various cultures.			
Describe the phenomena explained in origin myths from various cultures.			
Explain the effect of a historical event or movement on the theme of a work of literature.			
Analyze how poets use sound effects (e.g., alliteration, internal rhyme, onomatopoeia, rhyme scheme) to reinforce meaning in poems.			
Analyze the similarities and differences between an original text and its dramatic adaptation.			
Describe incidents that advance the story or novel, explaining how each incident gives rise to or foreshadows future events.			
Explain the roles and functions of characters in various plots, including their relationships and conflicts.			
Explain the different forms of third-person points of view in stories.			
Identify the literary language and devices used in biographies and autobiographies, including how authors present major events in a person's life.			
Evaluate the impact of sensory details, imagery, and figurative language in literary text.			
Read independently for a sustained period of time and summarize or paraphrase what the reading was about, maintaining meaning and logical order (e.g., generate a reading log or journal; participate in book talks).			
Draw conclusions from the information presented by an author and evaluate how well the author's purpose was achieved.			
Summarize the main ideas and supporting details in a text in ways that maintain meaning and logical order.			

Tired of using slips of paper or stickies to make sure you teach everything you need to? Need an easier way to keep track of what you have taught, and what you still need to cover? **Customize Literacy** can help.

Reading/Comprehension	DATES OF INSTRUCTION		
Determine the facts in a text and verify them through established methods.			
Analyze how the organizational pattern of a text (e.g., cause-and-effect, compare-and-contrast, sequential order, logical order, classification schemes) influences the relationships among the ideas.			
Use multiple text features and graphics to gain an overview of the contents of text and to locate information.			
Synthesize and make logical connections between ideas within a text and across two or three texts representing similar or different genres.			
Identify the author's viewpoint or position and explain the basic relationships among ideas (e.g., parallelism, comparison, causality) in the argument.			
Recognize exaggerated, contradictory, or misleading statements in text.			
Interpret details from procedural text to complete a task, solve a problem, or perform procedures.			
Interpret factual or quantitative information presented in maps, charts, illustrations, graphs, timelines, tables, and diagrams.			
Establish purposes for reading a text based on what students hope to accomplish by reading the text.			
Ask literal, interpretive, and evaluative questions of a text.			
Monitor and adjust comprehension using a variety of strategies.			
Make inferences about a text and use evidence from the text to support understanding.			
Summarize and paraphrase information in a text, maintaining meaning and logical order.			
Make connections between and among texts.			

Student Edition p. El•6

Draw Conclusions

Objectives:
- Students draw conclusions about characters, events, or information in their reading.
- Students use their prior knowledge and evidence from text to support conclusions.
- Students evaluate a conclusion to see if it makes sense.

What is it? A **conclusion** is a decision a person makes after thinking about some facts and details. Drawing conclusions means figuring out something by thinking about it. Drawing conclusions allows readers to go beyond the literal meaning of a text and put information together in order to make decisions about what they are reading. At Grade 5, students are drawing conclusions about fiction and nonfiction texts. They are using evidence and prior knowledge to support their conclusions and evaluating them to see if they are valid.

How Good Readers Use the Skill Drawing conclusions, also called making inferences, is fundamental in reading and listening comprehension. When readers draw conclusions, they synthesize and evaluate information from stories and informational articles as they bring their own life experiences and prior knowledge to the text. The result is a deeper understanding of what they are reading.

Texts for Teaching

Student Edition
- *Weslandia,* 5.2, pages 26–37
- *The Gymnast,* 5.2, pages 142–151
- *The Truth About Austin's Amazing Bats,* 5.2, pages 324–335

Leveled Readers
- See pages 24–29 for a list of Leveled Readers.

Mini-Lesson 1

Teach the Skill

Use the **Envision It!** lesson on page El•6 to visually review draw conclusions.

Remind students that:
- a **conclusion** is a decision you reach that makes sense after you think about details or facts in what you read.
- to **draw a conclusion** think about what you know and make a decision about details in the text.
- a conclusion should make sense.

Practice

Model drawing a conclusion with a think-aloud:

The smell of peanuts and cotton candy filled the air. I heard clapping. I even heard the bellows of a really big animal. I knew a circus was going on.

Talk with students how you combined what you already knew about a circus with details to draw a conclusion. Next, show a few photographs or illustrations and have students practice identifying details and adding personal knowledge to draw conclusions. Have students tell why their conclusions make sense.

If... students have difficulty drawing conclusions from sets of details, **then...** focus on one or two details at a time.

Apply

As students read on their own, have them think about what they already know and add it to details in text.

Writing

Have students list details they could use to draw conclusions about their classroom.

 **Mini-Lesson 2**

Teach the Skill

Use the **Envision It!** lesson on page EI•6 to visually review draw conclusions.

Remind students that:

- a **conclusion** is a decision you reach that makes sense after you think about details or facts in what you read.
- to **draw a conclusion** think about what you know and make a decision about details in the text.
- a conclusion should make sense.

Practice

Supply students with a familiar piece of text. Model using details in the text to draw a conclusion about a character or main idea. *It says here that the character wipes tears from his eyes. I know that people sometimes cry when they are happy, but since this character has just lost a big soccer match, I think this character is sad.* Begin a chart and list details and conclusions you make from them.

Details	What I Already Know	My Conclusion
• Player has tears in his eyes. • Player has lost a big game.	People cry when they are sad.	Player is sad.

If... students have difficulty using details to draw conclusions, **then...** have students identify a detail and say how it relates to the character or main idea.

Apply

As students read on their own, have them use what they already know to draw conclusions.

Writing

Students can write sets of details and conclusions about a person or event.

 **Mini-Lesson 3**

Teach the Skill

Use the **Envision It!** lesson on page EI•6 to visually review draw conclusions.

Remind students that:

- a **conclusion** is a decision you reach that makes sense after you think about details or facts in what you read.
- to **draw a conclusion** think about what you know and make a decision about details in the text.
- a conclusion should make sense.

Practice

Emphasize that a conclusion should be valid; that is, it should make sense. Conclusions may change as more details are identified. Say: *We may draw conclusions about a character at the beginning of a story, based on our prior knowledge, and we may draw different ones at the end, based on what he or she does during the story. Think of a tale such as "Beauty and the Beast." Our conclusions about the beast change as we learn more about him.*

Have students add a column to their details/conclusions chart, one for recording why they think their conclusions are valid.

If... students have difficulty evaluating a conclusion, **then...** tell them to ask: *Is my conclusion based on an experience I have had or something I know about?* If they can answer "yes," their conclusion may be valid.

Apply

As students read, have them see if some of their conclusions change.

Writing

Students can write a letter to an author stating some conclusions.

Student Edition p. EI•12

Main Idea and Details

Objectives:
- Students identify main ideas in nonfiction passages and articles.
- Students use a graphic organizer to record ideas.
- Students express main ideas in their own words in ways that maintain meaning.
- Students give details to support main ideas.

What is it? The **main idea** of a piece of writing is what the piece is mostly about. At Grade 5, students are reading nonfiction that may have several main ideas and they are finding the main ideas of an article or a longer passage. They see parallels between main idea and theme. Sometimes a main idea is stated in a single sentence within a paragraph or article; at other times, readers must infer the main ideas and put them in their own words. Students learn to locate details that support the main idea.

How Good Readers Use the Skill Identifying and stating main ideas is a critical skill for readers because it helps them determine the important information in a text. At first, students think about what the selection is mostly about. They go on to select a statement of main idea, from a choice of statements or from the selection itself. They begin to identify details as pieces of information that enlarge on the main idea, help clarify the main idea, or give examples. Older readers are able to identify main ideas, stated or implied, and are able to frame main ideas in their own words.

Texts for Teaching

Student Edition
- *Leonardo's Horse,* 5.1, pages 360–377
- *Mahalia Jackson,* 5.1, pages 430–437
- *The Mystery of Saint Matthew Island,* 5.2, pages 350–359

Leveled Readers
- See pages 24–29 for a list of Leveled Readers.

Mini-Lesson 1

Teach the Skill

Use the **Envision It!** lesson on page EI•12 to visually review main idea.

Remind students that:
- the **topic** is what a paragraph or article is about.
- the **main ideas** are the most important ideas of the topic.
- **details** tell more about the main ideas.

Practice

Read the following and have students identify the topic (Franklin D. Roosevelt) and the stated main idea. Discuss with students how all the other sentences are details.

Franklin D. Roosevelt was a well-known President of the United States. He helped our country get through the Great Depression. Many people had lost their jobs and did not have enough money. As President, he began the New Deal program to make new jobs. These jobs put many people back to work. Roosevelt was also in charge of the way the United States fought in World War II.

If... students have difficulty identifying the stated main idea,
then... have students choose between two sentences, one of which states the main idea.

Apply

As students read the assigned text, have them first identify the topic and then the main idea.

Writing

Students can list topics they would like to write or read about.

Mini-Lesson 2

Teach the Skill

Use the **Envision It!** lesson on page EI•12 to visually review main idea.

Remind students that:

- the **main ideas** are the most important ideas of the topic.
- the **main idea** is often stated in a paragraph or article.
- **details** tell more about the main ideas.

Practice

Supply students with a nonfiction article that has subheads. Model using a main idea/details chart to organize the information in each section of the text. Think aloud as you figure out the main idea. For example: The subhead tells me what this section will be about. I will look for a sentence that states a main idea—it's often the first or last sentence in a paragraph or section. Some of these details are interesting, but not that important. Which details support the main idea?

If... students have difficulty identifying main ideas and details, **then...** provide a main idea and have students locate details for it and explain how they tell more about the main idea.

Apply

As students read the assigned text, have them use a main idea/details chart to organize information. They can use it to identify or state the main ideas of the article.

Writing

Give students a main idea and have them write a paragraph about it.

Mini-Lesson 3

Teach the Skill

Use the **Envision It!** lesson on page EI•12 to visually review main idea.

Remind students that:

- the **main ideas** are the most important ideas of the topic.
- the **main idea** may be implied in a paragraph or article and not stated directly.
- **details** tell more about the main ideas.

Practice

Supply students with a nonfiction article. (If it has subheads, you might choose one with fanciful rather than instructional subheads.) Choose a piece with an implied main idea. Reread a section aloud and use a main idea/details chart. Then think aloud as you figure out the main idea. For example: I don't see a sentence that states the main idea. When I look at the chart I made, it tells me what this section is all about. I will use my own words to write a sentence that tells what this section is all about.

Write a sentence of the main idea and then ask: What do you think? Does this make sense? Do the details support my main idea? Or do I need to rewrite it?

If... students have difficulty writing a main idea statement, **then...** tell them to finish this sentence: *The most important idea is that _____.*

Apply

As students read the assigned text, have them use a main idea/details chart to organize information.

Writing

Students can put the main idea of the selection in their own words.

Compare and Contrast

Student Edition p. EI•6

Objectives:
- Students define *compare* and *contrast*.
- Students identify some clue words that can help them see comparisons.
- Students can identify comparisons even when clue words are not used.
- Students make comparisons between text and prior knowledge and ideas.

What is it? **Comparing** and **contrasting** means finding likenesses and/or differences between two or more people, places, things, or ideas. At Grade 5, students are using clue words such as *like, but, unlike,* and *as* to help identify likenesses and differences in text, but they are also seeing likenesses and differences in text without clue words. They understand that looking for comparisons can help them remember what they read. They begin to compare text with their own prior knowledge and ideas.

How Good Readers Use the Skill Comparing and contrasting are basic reasoning devices. We try to understand an unknown using the known—i.e., a likeness or difference. At first, students notice likenesses and differences. Older students begin to use clue words as signals for comparisons. They learn about similes and metaphors, which are literary comparisons. Students also learn that authors sometimes use comparison and contrast as a way to organize their writing.

Texts for Teaching

Student Edition
- *At the Beach: Abuelito's Story,* 5.1, pages 182–193
- *The Ch'i-lin Purse,* 5.1, pages 236–249
- *King Midas and the Golden Touch,* 5.2, pages 376–393

Leveled Readers
- See pages 24–29 for a list of Leveled Readers.

Mini-Lesson 1

Teach the Skill

Use the **Envision It!** lesson on page EI•6 to visually review compare and contrast.

Remind students that:
- to **compare** means to tell how things are the same or almost the same.
- to **contrast** means to tell how things are different.
- they can group things by comparing and contrasting.

Practice
Have students visualize two vehicles, such as a bicycle and a bus. Draw a Venn diagram (two overlapping circles) on the board with these labels: *Bicycle, Both Vehicles, Bus.* Work together to list qualities that are unique to each and then list the qualities the two vehicles share. Help get students started by asking: How are the two vehicles alike? How are they different? Students can name shape, size, number of wheels, purpose, and so on.
If... students have difficulty identifying likenesses and differences of two vehicles in their mind,
then... show pictures and have them begin with color, shape, and size.

Apply
As students read on their own, have them think about how places and people they read about are alike and different.

Writing
Students can write a compare/contrast paragraph using the information in the diagram.

Teach the Skill

Use the **Envision It!** lesson on page EI•6 to visually review compare and contrast.

Remind students that:
- to **compare** means to tell how things are the same or almost the same.
- to **contrast** means to tell how things are different.
- some comparison/contrast texts have no clue words and you need to figure out the comparison on your own.
- they can compare what they read to their own experiences.

Practice

Write the following paragraph on the board and read it with students. Juan and Jamie are in the same grade. Juan goes to North School, but Jamie goes to West School. They like sports, although neither plays on a team yet. Juan likes baseball and hopes to make the team in the spring, while Jamie prefers soccer. Unlike Juan, however, Jamie practices every day. Circle the words *but, neither, while,* and *unlike.* Explain that these are clues to comparisons. Reread the sentences together and then complete a Venn diagram. Ask: Did you find other likenesses and differences that weren't preceded by clue words? How did you figure it out? (reading carefully)

If... students have difficulty identifying likenesses,

then... have them ask themselves: *Are they alike in this way? Are they different?*

Apply

As students read on their own, have them compare what they read to what they already know.

Writing

Students can write a paragraph comparing two people using some clue words.

Teach the Skill

Use the **Envision It!** lesson on page EI•6 to visually review compare and contrast.

Remind students that:
- to **compare** means to tell how things are the same or almost the same.
- to **contrast** means to tell how things are different.
- clue words in text can help them see when an author is comparing or contrasting people, places, things, or ideas.
- some comparison/contrast texts have no clue words and you need to figure out the comparison on your own.

Practice

Think of two things to compare, for example, two characters from a story. As a class, create a Venn diagram, deciding on the specific qualities and the qualities they share. Have partners write sentences using the qualities. Review the clue words that will help their readers see comparisons.

Words for Comparing	Words for Contrasting
like alike similarly also in addition same as well as	unlike on the other hand but however different instead of

Have partners share their sentences. Talk about how finding likenesses and differences (comparisons and contrasts) as they read will help them better understand what they read.

If... students have difficulty writing sentences with clue words,

then... provide sentence starters, for example, *The king loved gold, but the queen loved _____.*

Apply

As students read on their own, have them make charts or diagrams to note comparisons and contrasts.

Writing

Students can turn their sentences into a paragraph or short story.

Text Structure

Mini-Lesson

Student Edition p. EI•24

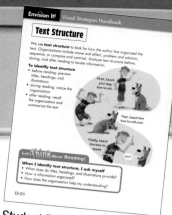

Understand the Strategy

Text structure refers to how a nonfiction article is organized. Externally, nonfiction articles include titles, subheads, graphics, and so on. Internally, a nonfiction article is organized in a way that best presents the content. This organization may be sequential, comparative, explanatory (cause-effect), or descriptive. Recognizing text structure helps readers understand and recall ideas.

Teach

Use the **Envision It!** lesson on page EI•24 to visually review text structure with students.

Remind students that authors organize information in various ways. Provide examples of the following organizational patterns for students.

Organization Patterns of Text

Pattern	Word Clues	Text Features
Sequence	dates; times; *first, then, before*	time lines, flow charts, maps
Comparison/Contrast	*however, as well as, similarly*	comparison charts
Cause-Effect	*because, since, as a result*	diagrams
Description	*for example, most important*	photos, captions

Practice

Supply students with a short piece of nonfiction, such as a biographical sketch. Read the selection together and call attention to the text features, clue words, and any other evidence to support its organization pattern (sequential). Then have students reread the piece and work in pairs to locate these features on their own. Bring the group together and summarize the piece, using sequential order. On subsequent occasions, use a different nonfiction piece, such as a science article that explains a process. Over time, have them work with all the patterns listed in the chart.

If... students have difficulty recognizing sequential text structure,

then... chunk the text for them and have them look for clue words. They can put chunks together to see more examples of clue words for sequence.

Apply

Ask students to think about possible text structure as they preview and get ready to read. Then have them revise or confirm their ideas after reading.

Anchor Chart

Anchor charts help students make their thinking visible and permanent. With an anchor chart, the group can clarify their thinking about how to use a strategy. Display anchor charts so readers can use them and add to them as they read. Here is a sample chart for figuring out text structure.

Objectives:

- Students recognize that texts can be organized in sequential order, by description, comparison/contrast, or cause-effect.
- Students use clue words and other text features that signal a text's organization.
- Students ask questions to help them determine text structure.

Texts for Teaching

Student Edition

- *Ten Mile Day,* 5.1, pages 146–159
- *The Mystery of Saint Matthew Island,* 5.2, pages 350–359

Leveled Readers

- See pages 24–29 for a list of Leveled Readers.

Text Structure

1. Look over the article before you start to read. Ask: *What is the topic? What text features are there? Can they help me figure out text structure?*

2. Read the subheads. They can be clues to text structure.

3. Look for clue words as you read.
   Sequence clue words: *before, after, first, next, last*
   Compare/contrast clue words: *both, neither, on the other hand, likewise*
   Cause-effect clue words: *because, consequently, as a result, this led to*
   Description clue words: *most important, also, for example*

4. Look for patterns as you read.
   Sequence: Information is told in time order.
   Compare/contrast: The author tells how things or places or people are the same and/or different.
   Cause-effect: The author explains how things work or what happens and why.
   Description: The author tells all about one thing, person, or place.

Anchor Chart

5. If you know the structure, use a graphic organizer that fits. Take notes to remember what you read.

6. Write a summary of what you read. Try to put it in the same text structure.

Using Multiple Strategies

Good readers use multiple strategies as they read. You can encourage students to read strategically through good classroom questioning. Use questions such as these to help students apply strategies during reading.

Answer Questions

- Who or what is this question about?
- Where can you look to find the answer to this question?

Ask Questions

- What do you want to know about _____?
- What questions do you have about the _____ in this selection? Use the words *who, what, when, where, why,* and *how* to ask your questions.
- Do you have any questions after reading?

Graphic Organizers

- What kind of graphic organizer could you use to help you keep track of the information in this selection?

Monitor and Clarify

- Does the story or article make sense?
- What don't you understand about what you read?
- Do you need to reread, review, read on, or check a reference source?
- Do you need to read more slowly or more quickly?
- What is a _____? Where could you look to find out?

Predict/Confirm Predictions

- What do you think this story or article will be about? Why do you think as you do?
- What do you think you will learn from this selection?
- Do the text features help you predict what will happen?
- Based on what has happened so far, what do you think will happen next?
- Is this what you thought would happen?
- How does _____ change what you thought would happen?

Preview

- What do the photographs, illustrations, or graphic sources tell about the selection?
- What do you want to find out? What do you want to learn?

Background Knowledge

- What do you already know about _____?

- Have you read stories or articles by this author before?

- How is this selection like others that you have read?

- What does this remind you of?

- How does your background knowledge help you understand _____?

- Did the text match what you already knew? What new information did you learn?

Story Structure

- Who are the characters in this story? the setting?

- What is the problem in this story? How does the problem get solved?

- What is the point of this story?

Summarize

- What two or three important ideas have you read so far?

- How do the text features relate to the important ideas?

- Is there a graphic organizer that can help you organize the information before you summarize?

Text Structure

- How has the author organized the writing?

- What clues tell you that the text is structured _____?

Visualize

- When you read this, what do you picture in your mind?

- What do you hear, see, or smell?

- What do you think _____ looks like? Why do you think as you do?

> **❝** You know explicit strategy instruction is a must! But you also want students to use strategies every time they read. **Customize Literacy** shows you how to help them do this. **❞**

Glossary of Literacy Terms

This glossary lists academic language terms that are related to literacy.
They are provided for your information and professional use.

A

alliteration	the repetition of a consonant sound in a group of words, especially in poetry
allusion	a word or phrase that refers to something else the reader already knows from history, experience, or reading
animal fantasy	a story about animals that talk and act like people
answer questions	a reading strategy in which readers use the text and prior knowledge to answer questions about what they are reading
antonym	a word that means the opposite of another word
ask questions	a reading strategy in which readers ask themselves questions about the text to help make sense of what they read
author's point of view	the author's opinion on the subject he or she is writing about
author's purpose	the reason the author wrote the text
autobiography	the story of a real person's life written by that person

B

background knowledge	the information and experience that a reader brings to a text
biography	the story of a real person's life written by another person

C

cause	why something happens
character	a person, an animal, or a personified object in a story
chronological order	events in a selection, presented in the order in which they occurred
classify and categorize	put things, such as pictures or words, into groups
climax	the point in a story at which conflict is confronted
compare	tell how things are the same
comprehension	understanding of text being read—the ultimate goal of reading
comprehension strategy	a conscious plan used by a reader to gain understanding of text. Comprehension strategies may be used before, during, or after reading.
conclusion	a decision or opinion arrived at after thinking about facts and details and using prior knowledge
conflict	the problem or struggle in a story
context clue	the words, phrases, or sentences near an unfamiliar word that give the reader clues to the word's meaning
contrast	tell how things are different

details small pieces of information

dialect form of a language spoken in a certain region or by a certain group of people that differs from the standard form of that language

dialogue written conversation

diary a day-to-day record of one's activities and thoughts

draw conclusions arrive at decisions or opinions after thinking about facts and details and using prior knowledge

D

effect what happens as the result of a cause

etymology an explanation of the origin and history of a word and its meaning

exaggeration a statement that makes something seem larger or greater than it actually is

expository text text that contains facts and information. Also called *informational text*.

E

fable a story, usually with animal characters, that is written to teach a moral, or lesson

fact piece of information that can be proved to be true

fairy tale a folk story with magical characters and events

fantasy a story that could not really happen

fiction writing that tells about imaginary people, things, and events

figurative language the use of language that gives words a meaning beyond their usual definitions in order to add beauty or force

flashback an interruption in the sequence of events of a narrative to include an event that happened earlier

folk tale a story that has been passed down by word of mouth

foreshadowing the use of hints or clues about what will happen later in a story

F

generalize make a broad statement or rule after examining particular facts

graphic organizer a drawing, chart, or web that illustrates concepts or shows how ideas relate to each other. Readers use graphic organizers to help them keep track of and understand important information and ideas as they read. Story maps, word webs, Venn diagrams, and KWL charts are graphic organizers.

graphic source a chart, diagram, or map within a text that adds to readers' understanding of the text

G

H

historical fiction	realistic fiction that takes place in the past. It is an imaginary story based on historical events and characters.
humor	writing or speech that has a funny or amusing quality
hyperbole	an exaggerated statement not meant to be taken literally, such as *I'm so hungry I could eat a horse.*

I

idiom	a phrase whose meaning differs from the ordinary meaning of the words. *A stone's throw* is an idiom meaning "a short distance."
imagery	the use of language to create beautiful or forceful pictures in the reader's mind
inference	conclusion reached on the basis of evidence and reasoning
inform	give knowledge, facts, or news to someone
informational text	writing that contains facts and information. Also called *expository text.*
interview	a face-to-face conversation in which someone responds to questions
irony	a way of speaking or writing in which the ordinary meaning of the words is the opposite of what the speaker or writer is thinking; a contrast between what is expected and what actually happens

J

jargon	the language of a special group or profession

L

legend	a story coming down from the past about the great deeds of a hero. Although a legend may be based on historical people and events, it is not regarded as historically true.
literary elements	the characters, setting, plot, and theme of a narrative text

main idea	the big idea that tells what a paragraph or a selection is mainly about; the most important idea of a text
metacognition	an awareness of one's own thinking processes and the ability to monitor and direct them to a desired goal. Good readers use metacognition to monitor their reading and adjust their reading strategies.
metaphor	a comparison that does not use *like* or *as*, such as *a heart of stone*
meter	the pattern of beats or accents in poetry
monitor and clarify	a comprehension strategy by which readers actively think about understanding their reading and know when they understand and when they do not. Readers use appropriate strategies to make sense of difficult words, ideas, or passages.
mood	the atmosphere or feeling of a written work
moral	the lesson or teaching of a fable or story
motive	the reason a character in a narrative does or says something
mystery	a story about mysterious events that are not explained until the end, so as to keep the reader in suspense
myth	a story that attempts to explain something in nature

M

narrative	a story, made up or true, that someone tells or narrates
narrator	the character in a selection who tells the story
nonfiction	writing that tells about real things, real people, and real events

N

onomatopoeia	the use of words that sound like their meanings, such as *buzz* and *hum*
opinion	someone's judgment, belief, or way of thinking
oral vocabulary	the words needed for speaking and listening
outcome	the resolution of the conflict in a story

O

paraphrase	retell the meaning of a passage in one's own words
personification	a figure of speech in which human traits or actions are given to animals or inanimate objects, as in *The sunbeam danced on the waves.*
persuade	convince someone to do or to believe something
photo essay	a collection of photographs on one theme, accompanied by text
play	a story that is written to be acted out for an audience

P

P

plot	a series of related events at the beginning, middle, and end of a story; the action of a story
poem	an expressive, imaginative piece of writing often arranged in lines having rhythm and rhyme. In a poem, the patterns made by the sounds of the words have special importance.
pourquoi tale	a type of folk story that explains why things in nature came to be. *Pourquoi* is a French word meaning "why."
predict	tell what a selection might be about or what might happen in a text. Readers use text features and information to predict. They confirm or revise their predictions as they read.
preview	look over a text before reading it
prior knowledge	the information and experience that a reader brings to a text. Readers use prior knowledge to help them understand what they read.
prop	an item, such as an object, picture, or chart, used in a performance or presentation

R

reading vocabulary	the words we recognize or use in print
realistic fiction	a story about imaginary people and events that could happen in real life
repetition	the repeated use of some aspect of language
resolution	the point in a story where the conflict is resolved
rhyme	to end in the same sound(s)
rhythm	a pattern of strong beats in speech or writing, especially poetry
rising action	the buildup of conflicts and complications in a story

S

science fiction	a story based on science that often tells what life in the future might be like
semantic map	a graphic organizer, often a web, used to display words or concepts that are meaningfully related
sensory language	the use of words that help the reader understand how things look, sound, smell, taste, or feel
sequence	the order of events in a selection or the order of the steps in which something is completed
sequence words	clue words such as *first*, *next*, *then*, and *finally* that signal the order of events in a selection

setting	where and when a story takes place
simile	a comparison that uses *like* or *as*, as in *as busy as a bee*
speech	a public talk to a group of people made for a specific purpose
stanza	a group of lines in a poem
steps in a process	the order of the steps in which something is completed
story map	a graphic organizer used to record the literary elements and the sequence of events in a narrative text
story structure	how the characters, setting, and events of a story are organized into a plot
summarize	give the most important ideas of what was read. Readers summarize important information in the selection to keep track of what they are reading.
supporting detail	piece of information that tells about the main idea
symbolism	the use of one thing to suggest something else; often the use of something concrete to stand for an abstract idea

S

tall tale	a humorous story that uses exaggeration to describe impossible happenings
text structure	the organization of a piece of nonfiction writing. Text structures of informational text include cause/effect, chronological, compare/contrast, description, problem/solution, proposition/support, and ask/answer questions.
theme	the big idea or author's message in a story
think aloud	an instructional strategy in which a teacher verbalizes his or her thinking to model the process of comprehension or the application of a skill
tone	author's attitude toward the subject or toward the reader
topic	the subject of a discussion, conversation, or piece of text

T

visualize	picture in one's mind what is happening in the text. Visualizing helps readers imagine the things they read about.

V

Leveled Readers Skills Chart

Scott Foresman Reading Street provides more than six hundred leveled readers.
Each one is designed to:

- Practice critical skills and strategies
- Build fluency
- Build vocabulary and concepts
- Develop a lifelong love of reading

Grade 5

Title	Level*	DRA Level	Genre	Comprehension Strategy	
Jenna and the High Dive	N	30	Realistic Fiction	Monitor and Clarify	
Dangerous Storms	N	30	Expository Nonfiction	Summarize	
Our Village	N	30	Historical Fiction	Inferring	
Rube Foster and the Chicago American Giants	N	30	Nonfiction	Questioning	
The Golden Spike	O	34	Expository Nonfiction	Text Structure	
The Ocean's Treasures	O	34	Expository Nonfiction	Visualize	
From Slave to Soldier	O	34	Historical Fiction	Inferring	
China: Today and Yesterday	O	34	Expository Nonfiction	Story Structure	
A Visit to the Navajo Nation	O	34	Expository Nonfiction	Monitor and Clarify	
Paul Revere's Ride	P	38	Narrative Nonfiction	Background Knowledge	
George Ferris's Wheel	P	38	Expository Nonfiction	Summarize	
The Designs of Da Vinci	P	38	Biography	Visualize	
Paleontology: Digging for Dinosaurs and More	P	38	Nonfiction	Predict and Set Purpose	
The Root of the Blues	P	38	Narrative Nonfiction	Text Structure	
The Magic of Makeup	P	38	Expository Nonfiction	Important Ideas	
The Long Trip Home	Q	40	Realistic Fiction	Monitor and Clarify	
Storm Chasing Challenges	Q	40	Expository Nonfiction	Summarize	
Toby's California Vacation	Q	40	Realistic Fiction	Inferring	
Famous Women in Sports	Q	40	Biography	Questioning	
Playing the Game	Q	40	Realistic Fiction	Questioning	
The Land of Plenty	Q	40	Historical Fiction	Predict and Set Purpose	
Surviving the Elements	Q	40	Expository Nonfiction	Important Ideas	
Moving	Q	40	Realistic Fiction	Story Structure	
Let the Games Begin	Q	40	Expository Nonfiction	Visualize	
Giant Pumpkin on the Loose	Q	40	Fiction	Background Knowledge	
A Railroad Over the Sierra	R	40	Expository Nonfiction	Text Structure	
Sea Life	R	40	Expository Nonfiction	Visualize	
A Spy in Disguise	R	40	Nonfiction	Inferring	
Abuela's Gift	R	40	Realistic Fiction	Story Structure	
Helping Others	R	40	Nonfiction	Monitor and Clarify	

* Suggested Guided Reading Level. Use your knowledge of students' abilities to adjust levels as needed.

The chart here and on the next few pages lists titles of leveled readers appropriate for students in Grade 5. Use the chart to find titles that meet your students' interest and instructional needs. The books in this list were leveled using the criteria suggested in *Matching Books to Readers* and *Leveled Books for Readers, Grades 3–6* by Irene C. Fountas and Gay Su Pinnell. For more on leveling, see the *Reading Street Leveled Readers Leveling Guide*.

Target Comprehension Skill	Additional Comprehension Instruction	Vocabulary
Character and Plot	Graphic Sources	Homographs/Context Clues
Cause and Effect	Draw Conclusions	Context Clues/Homonyms
Setting and Theme	Author's Purpose	Dictionary/Glossary/Unfamiliar Words
Fact and Opinion	Generalize	Context Clues/Antonyms
Cause and Effect	Graphic Sources	Context Clues/Multiple Meanings
Compare and Contrast	Graphic Sources	Unfamiliar Words/Context Clues
Sequence	Draw Conclusions	Dictionary/Glossary/Unfamiliar Words
Compare and Contrast	Draw Conclusions	Word Structure/Greek and Latin Roots
Author's Purpose	Main Idea and Details	Context Clues/Unfamiliar Words
Author's Purpose	Draw Conclusions	Word Structure/Endings
Sequence	Generalize	Context Clues/Multiple Meanings
Main Idea and Details	Compare and Contrast	Word Structure/Greek and Latin Roots
Fact and Opinion	Cause and Effect	Context Clues/Homonyms
Main Idea and Details	Author's Purpose	Context Clues/Antonyms
Graphic Sources	Main Idea and Details	Word Structure/Prefixes
Character and Plot	Problem and Solution	Word Structure/Suffixes
Cause and Effect	Draw Conclusions	Context Clues/Homonyms
Setting and Theme	Generalize	Dictionary/Glossary/Unfamiliar Words
Fact and Opinion	Compare and Contrast	Context Clues/Antonyms
Draw Conclusions	Theme	Word Structure/Endings
Generalize	Plot	Context Clues/Unfamiliar Words
Graphic Sources	Main Idea and Details	Context Clues/Synonyms
Generalize	Theme	Context Clues/Unfamiliar Words
Draw Conclusions	Graphic Sources	Word Structure/Suffixes
Character and Plot	Author's Purpose	Word Structure/Greek and Latin Roots
Cause and Effect	Draw Conclusions	Context Clues/Multiple Meanings
Compare and Contrast	Main Idea and Details	Unfamiliar Words/Context Clues
Sequence	Generalize	Dictionary/Glossary/Unfamiliar Words
Compare and Contrast	Theme	Word Structure/Greek and Latin Roots
Author's Purpose	Main Idea and Details	Context Clues/Unfamiliar Words

Leveled Readers Skills Chart *Continued*

Grade 5

Title	Level*	DRA Level	Genre	Comprehension Strategy
Titanic: The "Unsinkable" Ship	R	40	Narrative Nonfiction	Inferring
Aim High: Astronaut Training	R	40	Expository Nonfiction	Monitor and Clarify
The Inside Story of Earth	R	40	Expository Nonfiction	Summarize
The California Gold Rush	R	40	Expository Nonfiction	Questioning
A Happy Accident	R	40	Realistic Fiction	Important Ideas
Paul Revere/American Revolutionary War	S	40	Narrative Nonfiction	Background Knowledge
Build a Perpetual Motion Machine	S	40	Expository Nonfiction	Summarize
The Italian Renaissance and Its Artists	S	40	Expository Nonfiction	Visualize
Searching for Dinosaurs	S	40	Expository Nonfiction	Predict and Set Purpose
Blues Legends	S	40	Biography	Text Structure
Computers in Filmmaking	S	40	Nonfiction	Important Ideas
Saving an American Symbol	S	40	Expository Nonfiction	Text Structure
Ancient Gold from the Ancient World	S	40	Expository Nonfiction	Story Structure
The Flight Over the Ocean	S	40	Narrative Nonfiction	Predict and Set Purpose
Jazz, Jazz, Jazz	S	40	Narrative Nonfiction	Background Knowledge
Journey to the New World	T	50	Historical Fiction	Questioning
Wilma Rudolph: Running to Win	T	50	Biography	Predict and Set Purpose
Changing for Survival: Bird Adaptations	T	50	Expository Nonfiction	Important Ideas
The New Kid at School	T	50	Narrative Nonfiction	Story Structure
Strange Sports with Weird Gear	T	50	Expository Nonfiction	Visualize
Bill Lucks Out	T	50	Realistic Fiction	Background Knowledge
Explore with Science	U	50	Expository Nonfiction	Inferring
Sailing the Stars	U	50	Expository Nonfiction	Monitor and Clarify
The Journey Through the Earth	U	50	Science Fiction	Summarize
The United States Moves West	U	50	Expository Nonfiction	Questioning
Driven to Change	U	50	Expository Nonfiction	Important Ideas
The Kudzu Invasion	U	50	Expository Nonfiction	Text Structure
The Signs	V	50	Realistic Fiction	Monitor and Clarify
Weather Forecasting	V	50	Expository Nonfiction	Summarize
The Medicine Harvest	V	50	Historical Fiction	Inferring

* Suggested Guided Reading Level. Use your knowledge of students' abilities to adjust levels as needed.

You know the theory behind leveled books: they let you match books with the interest and instructional levels of your students. You can find the right reader for every student with this chart. 99

Target Comprehension Skill	Additional Comprehension Instruction	Vocabulary
Graphic Sources	Cause and Effect	Dictionary/Glossary/Unfamiliar Words
Author's Purpose	Graphic Sources	Context Clues/Multiple Meanings
Cause and Effect	Fact and Opinion	Context Clues/Unfamiliar Words
Generalize	Main Idea and Details	Word Structure/Prefixes
Draw Conclusions	Graphic Sources	Dictionary/Glossary/Unfamiliar Words
Author's Purpose	Cause and Effect	Word Structure/Endings
Sequence	Draw Conclusions	Context Clues/Multiple Meanings
Main Idea and Details	Generalize	Word Structure/Greek and Latin Roots
Fact and Opinion	Compare and Contrast	Context Clues/Homonyms
Main Idea and Details	Author's Purpose	Context Clues/Antonyms
Graphic Sources	Main Idea and Details	Word Structure/Prefixes
Main Idea and Details	Cause and Effect	Word Structure/Endings
Compare and Contrast	Draw Conclusions	Word Structure/Suffixes
Fact and Opinion	Graphic Sources	Context Clues/Unfamiliar Words
Sequence	Fact and Opinion	Context Clues/Homographs
Draw Conclusions	Plot	Word Structure/Endings
Generalize	Author's Purpose	Context Clues/Unfamiliar Words
Graphic Sources	Main Idea and Details	Context Clues/Synonyms
Generalize	Cause and Effect	Context Clues/Unfamiliar Words
Draw Conclusions	Compare and Contrast	Word Structure/Suffixes
Character and Plot	Cause and Effect	Word Structure/Greek and Latin Roots
Graphic Sources	Cause and Effect	Dictionary/Glossary/Unfamiliar Words
Author's Purpose	Sequence	Context Clues /Multiple Meanings
Cause and Effect	Character and Plot	Context Clues/Unfamiliar Words
Generalize	Fact and Opinion	Word Structure/Prefixes
Draw Conclusions	Main Idea and Details	Dictionary/Glossary/Unfamiliar Words
Main Idea and Details	Generalize	Word Structure/Endings
Character and Plot	Author's Purpose	Homographs/Context Clues
Cause and Effect	Author's Purpose	Context Clues/Homonyms
Theme and Setting	Draw Conclusions	Dictionary/Glossary/Unfamiliar Words

Leveled Readers Skills Chart Continued

Grade 5 Title	Level*	DRA Level	Genre	Comprehension Strategy
The Journey of African American Athletes	V	50	Biography	Questioning
The Land of Opportunity	V	50	Narrative Nonfiction	Summarize
Our Essential Oceans	V	50	Expository Nonfiction	Visualize
The Golden Journey	V	50	Historical Fiction	Story Structure
Stop That Train!	V	50	Narrative Nonfiction	Predict and Set Purpose
Grandma Betty's Banjo	V	50	Realistic Fiction	Background Knowledge
The Most Dangerous Woman in America	W	60	Nonfiction	Inferring
Moving to Mali	W	60	Realistic Fiction	Story Structure
The Talker	W	60	Nonfiction	Ask Questions
The National Guard: Today's Minutemen	W	60	Expository Nonfiction	Background Knowledge
Philo and His Invention	W	60	Nonfiction	Summarize
Art's Inspiration	W	60	Expository Nonfiction	Visualize
What's New With Dinosaur Fossils?	W	60	Expository Nonfiction	Predict and Set Purpose
The Blues Evolution	X	60	Narrative Nonfiction	Text Structure
Special Effects in Hollywood	X	60	Expository Nonfiction	Important Ideas
Cheaper, Faster, and Better	X	60	Expository Nonfiction	Questioning
Operation Inspiration	X	60	Realistic Fiction	Predict and Set Purpose
Can Humans Make a Home in Outer Space?	X	60	Expository Nonfiction	Important Ideas
Nathaniel Comes to Town	X	60	Realistic Fiction	Story Structure
What Makes Great Athletes?	X	60	Expository Nonfiction	Visualize
The Sandwich Brigade	X	60	Realistic Fiction	Background Knowledge
Space Travel Inventions	X	60	Expository Nonfiction	Inferring
Astronauts and Cosmonauts	Y	60	Expository Nonfiction	Monitor and Clarify
The Shaping of the Continents	Y	60	Expository Nonfiction	Summarize
From Territory to Statehood	Y	60	Expository Nonfiction	Questioning
How the Wolves Saved Yellowstone	Y	60	Expository Nonfiction	Important Ideas
Mixed-Up Vegetables	Y	60	Expository Nonfiction	Text Structure
Precious Goods: From Salt to Silk	Y	60	Expository Nonfiction	Story Structure
Traveling by Plane	Y	60	Narrative Nonfiction	Predict and Set Purpose
Unexpected Music	Y	60	Expository Nonfiction	Background Knowledge

* Suggested Guided Reading Level. Use your knowledge of students' abilities to adjust levels as needed.

You know the theory behind leveled books: they let you match books with the interest and instructional levels of your students. You can find the right reader for every student with this chart.

Target Comprehension Skill	Additional Comprehension Instruction	Vocabulary
Fact and Opinion	Fact and Opinion	Context Clues/Antonyms
Cause and Effect	Generalize	Context Clues/Multiple Meanings
Compare and Contrast	Author's Purpose	Unfamiliar Words/Context Clues
Compare and Contrast	Character	Word Structure/Suffixes
Fact and Opinion	Generalize	Context Clues/Unfamiliar Words
Sequence	Compare and Contrast	Context Clues/Homographs
Sequence	Graphic Sources	Dictionary/Glossary/Unfamiliar Words
Compare and Contrast	Character and Setting	Word Structure/Greek and Latin Roots
Fact and Opinion	Main Idea and Details	Context Clues/Unfamiliar Words
Author's Purpose	Main Idea and Details	Word Structure/Endings
Sequence	Generalize	Context Clues/Multiple Meanings
Main Idea and Details	Draw Conclusions	Word Structure/Greek and Latin Roots
Fact and Opinion	Draw Conclusions	Context Clues/Homonyms
Main Idea and Details	Cause and Effect	Context Clues/Antonyms
Graphic Sources	Sequence	Word Structure/Prefixes
Draw Conclusions	Cause and Effect	Word Structure/Endings
Generalize	Compare and Contrast	Context Clues/Unfamiliar Words
Graphic Sources	Main Idea and Details	Context Clues/Synonyms
Generalize	Theme and Plot	Context Clues/Unfamiliar Words
Draw Conclusions	Sequence	Word Structure/Suffixes
Character and Plot	Theme	Word Structure/Greek and Latin Roots
Graphic Sources	Generalize	Dictionary/Glossary/Unfamiliar Words
Author's Purpose	Compare and Contrast	Context Clues/Multiple Meanings
Cause and Effect	Graphic Sources	Context Clues/Unfamiliar Words
Generalize	Sequence	Word Structure/Prefixes
Draw Conclusions	Author's Purpose	Dictionary/Glossary/Unfamiliar Words
Main Idea and Details	Compare and Contrast	Word Structure Endings
Compare and Contrast	Draw Conclusions	Word Structure/Suffixes
Fact and Opinion	Setting	Context Clues/Unfamiliar Words
Sequence	Draw Conclusions	Context Clues/Homographs

What Good Readers Do

You can use the characteristics and behaviors of good readers to help all your students read better. But what are these characteristics and behaviors? And how can you use them to foster good reading behaviors for all your students? Here are some helpful tips.

Good Readers enjoy reading! They have favorite books, authors, and genres. Good readers often have a preference about where and when they read. They talk about books and recommend their favorites.

Develop this behavior by giving students opportunities to respond in different ways to what they read. Get them talking about what they read, and why they like or dislike it.

This behavior is important because book sharing alerts you to students who are somewhat passive about reading or have limited literacy experiences. Book sharing also helps you when you select books for the class.

Good Readers select books they can read.

Develop this behavior by providing a range of three or four texts appropriate for the student and then letting the student choose.

This behavior is important because students gain control over reading when they can choose from books they can read. This helps them become more independent in the classroom.

Good Readers read independently for longer periods of time.

Develop this behavior by taking note of the level of support students need during guided reading. Use this information to gauge independent reading time accordingly.

This behavior is important because students become better readers when they spend time reading many texts at their independent level.

Good Readers use text features to help them preview and set purposes.

Develop this behavior by having students use the title and illustrations in fiction texts or the title, contents, headings, and other graphic features in nonfiction texts to make predictions about what they will be reading.

This behavior is important because previewing actually makes reading easier! Looking at features and sampling the text enables readers to predict and set expectations for reading.

Good Readers predict and ask questions before and while they read.

Develop this behavior by asking questions. After reading a passage, ask students what they think will happen next in a fiction text. Have them ask a question they think will be answered in a nonfiction text and read on to see if it is.

This behavior is important because when students predict and ask questions as they read, they are engaged. They have a purpose for reading and a basis for monitoring their comprehension.

Good Readers read meaningful phrases aloud with appropriate expression.

Develop this behavior by giving students lots of opportunities to read orally. As they read, note students' phrasing, intonation, and attention to punctuation and give help as needed.

This behavior is important because reading fluently in longer, meaningful phrases supports comprehension and ease in reading longer, more complex texts.

Good Readers read aloud at an appropriate reading rate with a high percent of accuracy.

Develop this behavior by timing students' oral reading to calculate their reading rates. You can also record students' miscues to determine a percent of accuracy. This will help identify problems.

This behavior is important because when students read fluently texts that are "just right," they find reading more enjoyable. A fluent reader is able to focus more on constructing meaning and is more likely to develop a positive attitude toward reading.

~~Good Readers~~ use effective strategies and sources of information to figure out unknown words.

CH-
QU-
ST-

Develop this behavior by teaching specific strategies for figuring out unknown words, such as sounding out clusters of letters, using context, reading on, and using references.

This behavior is important because when readers have a variety of strategies to use, they are more able to decode and self-correct quickly. Readers who do these things view themselves as good readers.

~~Good Readers~~ construct meaning as they read and then share or demonstrate their understanding.

Develop this behavior by having students retell what they read or write a summary of what they read in their own words.

This behavior is important because the ability to retell or write a summary is essential for success in reading. It shows how well a student has constructed meaning.

~~Good Readers~~ locate and use what is explicitly stated in a text.

Develop this behavior by asking questions that require students to go back into the text to find explicitly stated information.

This behavior is important because the ability to recall, locate, and use specific information stated in a text enables readers to respond to literal questions as well as to support opinions and justify their responses.

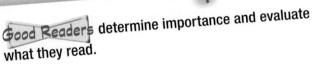 make connections.

Develop this behavior by asking questions to help students make connections: *What does this remind you of? Have you ever read or experienced anything like this?*

This behavior is important because making connections helps readers understand and appreciate a text. Making connections to self, the world, and other texts supports higher-level thinking.

Good Readers interpret what they read by making inferences.

Develop this behavior by asking questions to help students tell or write about what they think was implied in the text: *Why do you think that happened? What helped you come to that conclusion?*

This behavior is important because the ability to go beyond the literal meaning of a text enables readers to gain a deeper understanding. When students make inferences, they use background knowledge, their personal knowledge, and the text to grasp the meaning of what is implied by the author.

Good Readers determine importance and evaluate what they read.

Develop this behavior by always having students identify what they think is the most important message, event, or information in a text.

This behavior is important because readers must be able to sort out important from interesting information. The ability to establish and/or use criteria and provide support when making judgments is an important critical-thinking skill.

Good Readers support their responses using information from a text and/or their own background knowledge.

Develop this behavior by always asking students to give the reason(s) they identified an event, message, or idea as most important.

This behavior is important because the ability to justify one's response is important for all learners. It enables others to know the basis for a decision and provides an opening for further discussion.

Conversation Starters

Asking Good Questions When students read interesting and thought-provoking books, they want to share! You can encourage students to think critically about what they read. Use questions such as the following to assess comprehension as well as evoke good class/group discussions.

Author's Purpose

- Why did the author write this piece?

- How does figuring out the author's purpose help you decide how to read the text?

Cause and Effect

- Why did these events happen? How might they have been different if the causes had been different?

- Are there several causes that result in a single effect?

- Is there a single cause that has several effects?

Compare and Contrast

- What clue words show the author is comparing and/or contrasting in this article?

- How are the fictional characters and events in this story like and/or different from real people and events you know of?

Draw Conclusions

- Based on what you have read, seen, or experienced, what can you conclude about this event in the selection?

- This story seems to be a fantasy. Why might you conclude this?

- What words help you draw conclusions about the relationship between the characters?

Fact and Opinion

- What clue word or words signal that this is a statement of opinion?

- How could this statement of fact be proved true or false?

Generalize

- What generalization can you make about the story or the characters in it? What examples lead to that generalization?

- What details, facts, and logic does the author use to support this generalization?

- Is this a valid or a faulty generalization? Explain your ideas.

Graphic Sources

- How does the author use graphic sources (chart, maps, illustrations, time lines, and so on) to support ideas and opinions?

- This selection has many graphic sources. Which one or ones best help you understand the events or ideas in the selection? Why?

Literary Elements: Character, Setting, Plot, Theme

- Describe the main character at the beginning of the story and at the end of the story. How and why does this change take place?

- How is the setting important to the story? How might the story be different if its time or its place were different?

- What does the main character want at the beginning of the story? How does the main character go about trying to achieve this?

- A plot has a conflict, but the conflict isn't always between two characters. What is the conflict in this story? How is it resolved?

- In a few sentences, what is the plot of the story?

- What is the theme of the story? Use details from the story to support your statement.

Main Idea and Details

- What is the main idea of this paragraph or article? What are some details?

- The author makes this particular statement in the article. What details does the author provide to support that statement?

Sequence

- How is the sequence of events important in the text?

- Is the order of events important in this story? Why or why not?

- Based on what has already happened, what will most likely happen next?

Connecting Science and Social Studies

Scott Foresman Reading Street Leveled Readers are perfect for covering, supporting, or enriching science and social studies content. Using these books ensures that all students can access important concepts.

Grade 5 Leveled Readers

Science

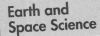

Earth and Space Science

Nonfiction Books

- Aim High: Astronaut Training
- Astronauts and Cosmonauts
- Can Humans Make a Home in Outer Space?
- Cheaper, Faster, and Better
- Dangerous Storms
- Explore with Science
- The Inside Story of Earth
- Sailing the Stars
- The Shaping of the Continents
- Space Travel Inventions
- Storm Chasing Challenges
- Traveling by Plane
- Weather Forecasting

Fiction Books

- The Journey Through the Earth
- The Signs

Life Science

Nonfiction Books

- Changing for Survival: Bird Adaptations
- Driven to Change
- How the Wolves Saved Yellowstone
- The Kudzu Invasion
- Mixed-Up Vegetables
- Our Essential Oceans
- Paleontology: Digging for Dinosaurs and More
- Sea Life
- Searching for Dinosaurs
- Surviving the Elements: Animals and Their Environments
- What's New with Dinosaur Fossils?

Fiction Books

- The Long Trip Home
- Toby's California Vacation

Physical Science

Nonfiction Books

- George Ferris's Wheel
- The Magic of Makeup: Going Behind the Mask
- Philo and His Invention
- The Search to Build a Perpetual Motion Machine

Fiction Books

- A Happy Accident
- Jenna and the High Dive

Grade 5 Leveled Readers

Social Studies

Citizenship

Nonfiction Books

- Helping Others
- The National Guard: Today's Minutemen
- The New Kid at School

Fiction Books

- Bill Lucks Out
- Giant Pumpkin on the Loose
- The Sandwich Brigade

Culture

Nonfiction Books

- Art's Inspiration
- China: Today and Yesterday
- Computers in Filmmaking: Very Special Effects
- The Root of the Blues
- Special Effects in Hollywood
- Strange Sports with Weird Gear
- The Talker
- Unexpected Music
- A Visit to the Navajo Nation

Fiction Books

- Abuela's Gift
- Grandma Betty's Banjo
- The Medicine Harvest
- Moving
- Moving to Mali

Culture

- Nathaniel Comes to Town
- Operation Inspiration
- Our Village
- Playing the Game

Economics

Nonfiction Books

- Ancient Gold from the Ancient World
- The Oceans' Treasures
- Precious Goods: From Salt to Silk

History

Nonfiction Books

- The Blues Evolution
- The California Gold Rush
- The Flight Over the Ocean: Yesterday and Today
- From Territory to Statehood
- The Golden Spike
- The Italian Renaissance and Its Artists
- Jazz, Jazz, Jazz
- The Land of Opportunity
- Let the Games Begin: History of the Olympics
- The Most Dangerous Woman in America

History

- Paul Revere and the American Revolutionary War
- Paul Revere's Ride
- A Railroad Over the Sierra
- Rube Foster and the Chicago American Giants
- Saving an American Symbol
- A Spy in Disguise
- Stop That Train!
- Titanic: The "Unsinkable" Ship
- The United States Moves West
- What Makes Great Athletes?

Fiction Books

- From Slave to Soldier
- The Golden Journey
- Journey to the New World
- The Land of Plenty

More Great Titles

Biography

- Blues Legends
- The Designs of Da Vinci
- Famous Women in Sports
- The Journey of African American Athletes
- Wilma Rudolph: Running to Win

Connecting Science and Social Studies

Need more choices? Look back to Grade 4.

Grade 4 Leveled Readers

Science

Earth and Space Science

Nonfiction Books

- *Danger: The World Is Getting Hot!*
- *Darkness Into Light*
- *Day for Night*
- *Earth's Closest Neighbor*
- *Let's Explore Antarctica!*
- *Looking For Changes*
- *The Mysteries of Space*
- *One Giant Leap*
- *Orbiting the Sun*
- *Putting a Stop to Wildfires*
- *Severe Weather: Storms*
- *Storm Chasers*
- *Wondrously Wild Weather*

Fiction Books

- *Exploring the Moon*
- *Flash Flood*
- *Life on Mars: The Real Story*
- *Stuart's Moon Suit*
- *Surviving Hurricane Andrew*
- *To the Moon!*

Life Science

Nonfiction Books

- *Birds Take Flight*
- *Come Learn About Dolphins*
- *Dolphins: Mammals of the Sea*
- *Florida Everglades: Its Plants and Animals*
- *The Gray Whale*
- *How Does Echolocation Work?*
- *Migration Relocation*
- *Mini Microbes*
- *Mysterious Monsters*
- *Plants and Animals in Antarctica*
- *Saving Trees Using Science*
- *Sharing Our Planet*
- *What in the World Is That?*

Life Science

Fiction Books

- *The Missing Iguana Mystery*
- *Protecting Wild Animals*
- *The Salamander Stumper*
- *Top Hat Tompkins, the Detective*

Grade 4 Leveled Readers

Social Studies

Citizenship

Nonfiction Books
- *Equality in American Schools*
- *Danger! Children at Work*
- *Dogs on the Job*

Fiction Books
- *Mountain Rescue*
- *The Super Secret Surprise Society*

Culture

Nonfiction Books
- *The Black Ensemble Theater*
- *The Diné*
- *From Spain to America*
- *What It Takes to Stage a Play*

Fiction Books
- *A Book of Their Own*
- *A New Home*
- *Birthday Surprise*
- *Cheers for the Cheetahs*
- *The Grizzly Bear Hotshots*
- *Living with Grandpa Joseph*
- *The Show Must Go On!*
- *Something to Do*
- *To Be a Star*

Economics

Nonfiction Books
- *The Alaskan Pipeline*
- *Ranches in the Southwest*
- *Ranching in the Great American Desert*
- *Two Powerful Rivers*

Fiction Books
- *The Seahaven Squids Host a Pet Wash*

History

Nonfiction Books
- *Becoming a Melting Pot*
- *The Civil Rights Movement*
- *Code Breakers: Uncovering German Messages*
- *Let's Get to Know the Incas*
- *The Long Journey West*
- *Meet the Maya*
- *The Navajo Code Talkers*
- *Pompeii, the Lost City*
- *The Rosetta Stone: The Key to Ancient Writing*
- *The Sauk and Fox Native Americans*
- *Speaking in Code*
- *The Story of Libraries*
- *Thor Heyerdahl's Incredible Raft*
- *We Shall Overcome*
- *The Women's Movement*

History

Fiction Books
- *Bessie Coleman*
- *The Incredible Alexander Graham Bell*

Geography

Nonfiction Books
- *America's National Parks*
- *Maine, Now and Then*
- *A Trip to Capital Hill*
- *The Wonders of Western Geography*

Fiction Books
- *From Sea to Shining Sea*

Government

Nonfiction Books
- *The Power of the People*
- *The United States Government*

More Great Titles

Biography
- *Amazing Female Athletes*
- *Jim Thorpe*
- *John Muir*
- *The Legacy of César Chávez*
- *Lewis and Clark and the Corps of Discovery*

Connecting Science and Social Studies

Need more choices? Look ahead to Grade 6.

Grade 6 Leveled Readers

Science

Earth and Space Science

Nonfiction Books

- *Earth and Its Place in Space*
- *Electricity*
- *Elements in Our Universe*
- *Exploring Mars*
- *Exploring the World Below*
- *Global Warming*
- *The Hidden Worlds of Caves*
- *The History of Green Power*
- *It's About Time!*
- *Living Greener*
- *Riches from Our Earth*
- *Swimming Safely in the Ocean*
- *Wonders Down Under*

Earth and Space Science

Fiction Books

- *The Domes on Mars*
- *Moon Kids, Earth Kids*
- *Moonman Markie*
- *The Rip Current Rescue*
- *Rock Canyon Challenge*
- *Sea's Visit: A Tale From Nigeria*
- *Tom Rides Out the Quake*

Life Science

Nonfiction Books

- *Animals of the Arctic*
- *Archaeology in China*
- *The Battle over the Rain Forests*
- *A Biome of the World: The Taiga*
- *The Debate over Zoos: Captive or Free?*
- *Ecosystems of Rain Forests*
- *Faithful Four-Footed Friends*
- *The Great Apes*
- *Life in the Arctic Circle*
- *Speaking for Wolves*
- *The Price of Knowledge: The Interaction of Animals and Scientists*
- *Saving Feathered Friends*

Fiction Books

- *Egg Watching*
- *Twilight of the Wolves*
- *The Very Special Gift*

Grade 6 Leveled Readers

Social Studies

Citizenship

Fiction Books

- The Best Community Service Project Ever

Culture

Nonfiction Books

- Armchair Archaeology
- Cuban Americans
- From China to America: My Story
- Living and Growing in China
- Tribes of the Amazon Rain Forest
- Viva America! Cubans in the United States

Fiction Books

- Adams's Hippo Lesson
- Chess Is for Fun
- How Anansi Captured the Story of the Rain
- Jeff and Jack
- Jenna the Scatterbrain
- Lady Red Rose and the Woods
- Monkey Tales
- Our New Life in the Big City
- Pedro's Flute
- Sally's Summer with Her Grandparents
- A Small-Town Summer
- When Julie Got Lost

History

Nonfiction Books

- Ancient Greece, Modern Culture
- Ancient Life Along the Nile
- The Aztec Empire
- The Chinese Struggle to America: An Immigration History
- Colonization and Native Peoples
- Defying Death and Time: Mummies
- Discovering Classical Athens
- The Freedoms of Speech and Assembly in the United States
- Greetings from the Four Corners!
- How Did Ancient Greece Become So Great?
- Immigrants of Yesterday and Today
- A Migrant Music: Jazz
- The Movements of Citizens
- Pulling Down the Walls: The Struggle of African American Performers
- The Race to the Bottom of the World
- Restless Humanity
- Robert Abbott's Dream: The Chicago Defender and the Great Migration
- The Secrets of the Past
- Spanish Conquests of the Americas
- The Struggle for Higher Education

History

- Uncovering the Secrets of Ancient Egypt

Fiction Books

- The Doaks of Montana
- From Youngsters to Old Timers
- Grizzled Bill's New Life
- Lucky Chuck and His Least Favorite Cousin
- The Noble Boy and the Brick Maker
- Sir Tom
- Sleepyville Wakes Up
- Timmy Finds His Home

Geography

Nonfiction Books

- The Mining Debate
- Mystery of the Ancient Pueblo
- The Quests for Gold

Fiction Books

- The Adventures in Matunaland

More Great Titles

Biography

- 20th Century African American Singers
- From Oscar Micheaux to the Oscars
- Inventors at Work

Planning Teacher Study Groups

Adventurous teachers often have good ideas for lessons. A teacher study group is a great way to share ideas and get feedback on the best way to connect content and students. Working with other teachers can provide you with the support and motivation you need to implement new teaching strategies. A teacher study group offers many opportunities to collaborate, support each other's work, share insights, and get feedback.

Think About It

A weekly or monthly teacher study group can help support you in developing your expertise in the classroom. You and a group of like-minded teachers can form your own study group. What can this group accomplish?

- Read and discuss professional articles by researchers in the field of education.

- Meet to share teaching tips, collaborate on multi-grade lessons, and share resources.

- Develop lessons to try out new teaching strategies. Meet to share experiences and discuss how to further improve your teaching approach.

Let's Meet!

Forming a study group is easy. Just follow these four steps:

1. **Decide on the size of the group.** A small group has the advantage of making each member feel accountable, but make sure that all people have the ability to make the same commitment!

2. **Choose teachers to invite to join your group.** Think about who you want to invite. Should they all teach the same grade? Can you invite teachers from other schools? Remember that the more diverse the group, the more it benefits from new perspectives.

3. **Set goals for the group.** In order to succeed, know what you want the group to do. Meet to set goals. Rank goals in order of importance and refer often to the goals to keep the group on track.

4. **Make logistical decisions.** This is often the most difficult. Decide where and when you will meet. Consider an online meeting place where group members can post discussion questions and replies if people are not able to meet.

What Will We Study? Use the goals you set to help determine what your group will study. Consider what materials are needed to reach your goals, and how long you think you will need to prepare for each meeting.

How Will It Work? Think about how you structure groups in your classroom. Then use some of the same strategies.

- **Assign a group facilitator.** This person is responsible for guiding the meeting. This person comes prepared with discussion questions and leads the meeting. This could be a rotating responsibility dependent on experience with various topics. This person might be responsible for providing the materials.

- **Assign a recorder.** Have someone take notes during the meeting and record group decisions.

- **Use the jigsaw method.** Not everyone has time to be a facilitator. In this case, divide the text and assign each portion to a different person. Each person is responsible for leading the discussion on that particular part.

Meet Again Make a commitment to meet for a minimum number of times. After that, the group can reevaluate and decide whether or not to continue.

> " Have some great teaching tips to share? Want to exchange ideas with your colleagues? Build your own professional community of teachers. **Customize Literacy** gets you started. "

Trial Lessons

Use your colleagues' experiences to help as you think about new ways to connect content and students. Use the following plan to create a mini-lesson. It should last twenty minutes. Get the support of your colleagues as you try something new and then reflect on what happened.

Be Creative! As you develop a plan for a mini-lesson, use these four words to guide planning: *purpose*, *text*, *resources*, and *routine*.

- **Purpose:** Decide on a skill or strategy to teach. Define your purpose for teaching the lesson.

- **Text:** Develop a list of the materials you could use. Ask your colleagues for suggestions.

- **Resources:** Make a list of the available resources, and consider how to use those resources most effectively. Consider using the leveled readers listed on pages CL24–CL29 and CL36–CL41 of Customize Literacy.

- **Routine:** Choose an instructional routine to structure your mini-lesson. See the mini-lessons in Customize Literacy for suggestions.

Try It! Try out your lesson! Consider audio- or videotaping the lesson for later review. You may wish to invite a colleague to sit in as you teach. Make notes on how the lesson went.

How Did It Go? Use the self-evaluation checklist on page CL45 as you reflect on your trial lesson. This provides a framework for later discussion.

Discuss, Reflect, Repeat Solicit feedback from your teacher study group. Explain the lesson and share your reflections. Ask for suggestions on ways to improve the lesson. Take some time to reflect on the feedback. Modify your lesson to reflect what you have learned. Then try teaching the lesson again.

Checklist for Teacher Self-Evaluation

How Well Did I ...	Very Well	Satisfactory	Not Very Well
Plan the lesson?			
Select the appropriate level of text?			
Introduce the lesson and explain its objectives?			
Review previously taught skills?			
Directly explain the new skills being taught?			
Model the new skills?			
Break the material down into small steps?			
Integrate guided practice into the lesson?			
Monitor guided practice for student understanding?			
Provide feedback on independent practice?			
Maintain an appropriate pace?			
Assess student understanding of the material?			
Stress the importance of applying the skill as they read?			
Maintain students' interest?			
Ask questions?			
Handle student questions and responses?			
Respond to the range of abilities?			

Books for Teachers

Students aren't the only ones who need to read to grow. Here is a brief list of books that you may find useful to fill your reading teacher basket and learn new things.

A Professional Bibliography

Afflerbach, P. "Teaching Reading Self-Assessment Strategies." *Comprehension Instruction: Research-Based Best Practices.* The Guilford Press, 2002.

Bear, D. R., M. Invernizzi, S. Templeton, and F. Johnston. *Words Their Way.* Merrill Prentice Hall, 2004.

Beck, I. L. and M. G. McKeown. *Improving Comprehension with Questioning the Author: A Fresh and Expanded View of a Powerful Approach.* Scholastic, 2006.

Beck, I., M. G. McKeown, and L. Kucan. *Bringing Words to Life: Robust Vocabulary Instruction.* The Guilford Press, 2002.

Blachowicz, C. and P. Fisher. "Vocabulary Instruction." *Handbook of Reading Research,* vol. III. Lawrence Erlbaum Associates, 2000.

Blachowicz, C. and D. Ogle. *Reading Comprehension: Strategies for Independent Learners.* The Guilford Press, 2008.

Block, C. C. and M. Pressley. "Best Practices in Comprehension Instruction." *Best Practices in Literacy Instruction.* The Guilford Press, 2003.

Daniels, H. *Literature Circles.* 2nd ed. Stenhouse Publishers, 2002.

Dickson, S. V., D. C. Simmons, and E. J. Kame'enui. "Text Organization: Instructional and Curricular Basics and Implications." *What Reading Research Tells Us About Children with Diverse Learning Needs: Bases and Basics.* Lawrence Erlbaum Associates, 1998.

Diller, D. *Making the Most of Small Groups: Differentiation for All.* Stenhouse Publishers, 2007.

Duke, N. and P. D. Pearson. "Effective Practices for Developing Reading Comprehension." *What Research Has to Say About Reading Instruction,* 3rd ed. Newark, DE: International Reading Association, 2002.

Fillmore, L. W. and C. E. Snow. *What Teachers Need to Know About Language.* Office of Educational Research and Improvement, U.S. Department of Education, 2000.

Fountas, I. C. and G. S. Pinnell. *Guiding Readers and Writers Grades 3–6: Teaching Comprehension, Genre, and Content Literacy.* Heinemann, 2001.

Guthrie, J. and E. Anderson. "Engagement in Reading: Processes of Motivated Strategic, Knowledgeable, Social Readers." *Engaged Reading: Processes, Practices, and Policy Implications.* Teachers College Press, 1999.

Harvey, S. and A. Goudvis. *Strategies That Work: Teaching Comprehension to Enhance Understanding.* 2nd ed. Stenhouse Publishers, 2007.

Keene, E. O. and S. Zimmerman. *Mosaic of Thought.* 2nd ed. Heinemann, 2007.

Leu Jr., D. J. "The New Literacies: Research on Reading Instruction with the Internet and Other Digital Technologies." *What Research Has to Say About Reading Instruction,* 3rd ed. International Reading Association, 2002.

McKeown, M. G. and I. L. Beck. "Direct and Rich Vocabulary Instruction." *Vocabulary Instruction: Research to Practice.* The Guilford Press, 2004.

McTighe, J. and K. O'Conner. "Seven Practices for Effective Learning." *Educational Leadership,* vol. 63, no. 3 (November 2005).

Nagy, W. E. *Teaching Vocabulary to Improve Reading Comprehension.* International Reading Association, 1998.

National Reading Panel. *Teaching Children to Read.* National Institute of Child Health and Human Development, 1999.

Ogle, D. and C. Blachowicz. "Beyond Literature Circles: Helping Students Comprehend Information Texts." *Comprehension Instruction: Research-Based Practices.* The Guilford Press, 2001.

Pressley, M. *Reading Instruction That Works: The Case for Balanced Teaching,* 3rd ed. The Guilford Press, 2005.

Stahl, S. A. "What Do We Know About Fluency?" *The Voice of Evidence in Reading Research.* Paul H. Brookes, 2004.

Taylor, B. M., P. D. Pearson, D. S. Peterson, and M. C. Rodriguez. "The CIERA School Change Framework: An Evidence-Based Approach to Professional Development and School Reading Improvement." *Reading Research Quarterly,* vol. 40, no. 1 (January/February/March 2005).

Valencia, S. W. and M. Y. Lipson. "Thematic Instruction: A Quest for Challenging Ideas and Meaningful Learning." *Literature-Based Instruction: Reshaping the Curriculum.* Christopher-Gordon Publishers, 1998.

Oral Vocabulary for

Let's Learn
Amazing Words

Amazing Bats

Amazing Words Oral Vocabulary Routine

fortuitous

1. **Introduce** *Fortuitous* means happening by chance; accidental.
2. **Demonstrate** It was *fortuitous* that I won the raffle.
3. **Apply** Have students name something in their lives that was *fortuitous.*

advantageous

1. **Introduce** *Advantageous* means giving a favorable benefit.
2. **Demonstrate** The agreement was *advantageous* to both groups.
3. **Apply** Have students name an *advantageous* event from the school year.

potential

1. **Introduce** *Potential* means an ability or skill that may develop in the future.
2. **Demonstrate** His teachers knew he had the *potential* to be an A student.
3. **Apply** Have students list something they have the *potential* for doing.

perspective

1. **Introduce** *Perspective* is a particular way of seeing or understanding something.
2. **Demonstrate** When viewed from his *perspective,* it doesn't look so bad.
3. **Apply** Ask students how *perspective* can help them in school.

happenstance

1. **Introduce** *Happenstance* is a chance occurrence or accident.
2. **Demonstrate** By *happenstance,* it started to rain just as the game finished.
3. **Apply** Have students name a *happenstance* event from their lives.

perceptive

1. **Introduce** A *perceptive* person is someone who has insight or understanding.
2. **Demonstrate** She is *perceptive.* She narrowed the choices to the right answer.
3. **Apply** Ask students how being *perceptive* can help them in life.

Saint Matthew Island

Amazing Words Oral Vocabulary Routine

refuge

1. **Introduce** A *refuge* is a shelter or protection from danger.

2. **Demonstrate** They took *refuge* in an abandoned cabin during the storm.

3. **Apply** Ask students to list places where they might find *refuge* during a storm.

domesticated

1. **Introduce** *Domesticated* is a change from a wild to a tame state.

2. **Demonstrate** People have *domesticated* many animals.

3. **Apply** Have students name some animals that have been *domesticated.*

contaminated

1. **Introduce** *Contaminated* means to make impure or polluted by contact.

2. **Demonstrate** The factory *contaminated* the water.

3. **Apply** Have students name ways that water can become *contaminated.*

prune

1. **Introduce** *Prune* means to cut off or out.

2. **Demonstrate** He had to *prune* a few unnecessary words from his essay.

3. **Apply** Have students give examples of when they might need to *prune* something.

composition

1. **Introduce** An objects *composition* is the way in which it is made up.

2. **Demonstrate** The *composition* of paper mache is glue, water, and paper.

3. **Apply** Ask students to list the *composition* of their favorite candy bar.

aggravate

1. **Introduce** To *aggravate* is to make worse or more severe.

2. **Demonstrate** Scratching can *aggravate* chicken pox.

3. **Apply** Have student name ways they can *aggravate* an injury.

King Midas

Amazing Words Oral Vocabulary Routine

DAY 1

geologist

① **Introduce** A *geologist* is a scientist who studies the earth and the process that formed it.

② **Demonstrate** The *geologist* studied the rock formations in the Grand Canyon.

③ **Apply** Have students name other things that a *geologist* might study.

rare

① **Introduce** *Rare* means something that is not often seen or found.

② **Demonstrate** My grandfather's coins are very *rare.*

③ **Apply** Have students name a place that has *rare* things.

specimen

① **Introduce** A *specimen* is a representative of the whole group.

② **Demonstrate** The scientist looked at a *specimen* he collected in the desert.

③ **Apply** Have students name a *specimen* from nature.

DAY 2

deplorable

① **Introduce** *Deplorable* means very bad in quality.

② **Demonstrate** The house was in *deplorable* condition when he bought it.

③ **Apply** Have students list things that might become *deplorable* if not cared for.

DAY 3

victor

① **Introduce** A *victor* is a winner.

② **Demonstrate** The *victor* of the debate won a free trip to Washington D.C.

③ **Apply** Have students tell about a time when they were a *victor* or felt like one.

DAY 4

penitence

① **Introduce** *Penitence* means feeling of sorrow for doing something wrong.

② **Demonstrate** *Penitence* caused me to apologize for lying to her.

③ **Apply** Have students name acts for which they might feel *penitence.*

UNIT 6 Acknowledgments

Text

Grateful acknowledgment is made to the following for copyrighted material:

Arnold Adoff Revocable Living Trust

"Under the Back Porch" from *Home* by Virginia Hamilton. Copyright 1992, 2008 by Virginia Hamilton. © 2010 by the Arnold Adoff Revocable Living Trust.

Atheneum Books for Young Readers an imprint of Simon & Schuster Children's Publishing Division

Reprinted with the permission of Atheneum Books for Young Readers, an imprint of Simon & Schuster Children's Publishing Division from *Desert Voices* by Byrd Baylor. Text copyright © 1981 Byrd Baylor.

Antheneum Books for Young Readers an imprint of Simon & Schuster Children's Publishing Divison & Joanne Settel & Columbia Literary Associates, Inc.

"Exploding Ants" by Joanne Settel, PH.D. Text copyright © 1999 Joanne Settel. Used by permission.

Barry Goldblatt Literary, LLC

"Tripping Over the Lunch Lady" by Angela Johnson. From *Tripping Over The Lunch Lady And Other School Stories.* Copyright © 2004 by Angela Johnson. Used by permission of Barry Goldblatt Literary LLC, as agent for the author.

Candlewick Press, Inc

"Weslandia" by Paul Fleischman. Text copyright © 1999 by Paul Fleischman. Illustrations copyright © 1999 by Kevin Hawkes. Reprinted by permission of the publisher Candlewick Press, Inc., Somerville, MA.

Caroline House an imprint of Boyds Mills Press

"The Mystery of Saint Matthew Island" from *The Case of the Mummified Pigs and Other Mysteries in Nature* by Susan E. Quinlan. Publishing by Caroline House, an imprint of Boyds Mills Press. Reprinted by permission.

Clairon Books an imprint of Houghton Mifflin Harcourt Publishing Company

"Which Lunch Table?" from *Swimming Upstream: Middle Grade Poems* by Kristine O'Connell George. Text copyright © 2002 by Kristine O'Connell George. Reprinted by permission of Clarion Books, an imprint of Houghton Mifflin Harcourt Publishing Company. All rights reserved.

Columbia University Press

"All About Gymnastics" from *The Columbia Electronic Encyclopedia, 6th ed.* Copyright © 2003. Used by permission of Columbia University Press.

Curtis Brown Ltd

"Share the Adventure" by Patricia and Fredrick McKissack. Copyright © 1993 by Patricia and Fredrick McKissack. First appeared in National Children's Book Week Poem, published by The Children's Book Council. Reprinted by permission of Curtis Brown, Ltd.

Doubleday a div of Random House, Inc & Faber & Faber

"The Bat" from the *Collected Poems of Theodore Roethke* by Theodore Roethke, copyright 1938.

Edward Blishen

Excerpt from "Journey to the Center of the Earth" by Jules Verne from *Science Fiction Stories,* chosen by Edward Blishen.

Estate of bp Nichol

"A Path to the Moon" from *Giants, Moosequakes and Other Disasters* by bp Nichol, 1985, Black Moss Press. Used by permission of The Estate of bp Nichol.

Farrar, Straus & Giroux, LLC

"The drum" from *Spin A Soft Black Song,* Revised Edition by Nikki Giovanni, illustrated by George Martins. Copyright © 1971, 1985 by Nikki Giovanni. Caution: Users are warned that this work is protected under copyright laws and downloading is strictly prohibited. The right to reproduce or transfer the work via any medium must be secured with FSG.

HarperCollins Publishers

"Keziah" from *Bronzeville Boys and Girls* by Gwendolyn Brooks. Copyright © 1956 by Gwendolyn Brooks Blakely. "King Midas and the Golden Touch" as told by Charlotte Craft, illustrated by K.Y. Craft. Text copyright © 1999 by Charlotte Craft. Illustrations copyright © 1999 by Kinuko Y. Craft. "Sunflakes" from *Country Pie* by Frank Asch. Copyright © 1979 Frank Asch. Used by permission of HarperCollins Publishers.

Henry Holt & Company, LLC

Adaptation of "The Hindenburg" by Patrick O'Brien. Copyright © 2000 by Patrick O'Brien. "The Skunk Ladder" from *The Grasshopper Trap* by Patrick F. McManus. Copyright © 1985 by Patrick F. McManus. Reprint by permission of Henry Holt and Company, LLC.

Houghton Mifflin Harcourt Publishing Company

Text and photographs from *Ghost Towns Of The American West* by Raymond Bial. Copyright © 2001 by Raymond Bial. From *Shipwreck Season* by Donna Hill. Copyright © 2008 by Donna Hill. Reprinted by permission of Houghton Mifflin Harcourt

Publishing Company. All rights reserved.

Lee & Low Books, Inc

"Colors Crackle, Colors Roar" from *Confetti: Poems For Children* by Pat Mora. Text copyright © 1996 by Pat Mora. Illustrations copyright © 1996 by Enrique O. Sanchez. "Sweet Music in Harlem and Author's Note" from *Sweet Music In Harlem* by Debbie Taylor. Text copyright © 2004 by Debbie A Taylor. Illustrations copyright © 2004 by Frank Morrison. Permission arranged with Lee & Low Books Inc., New York, NY 10016.

Lillian M. Fisher

"Camel" from *Camel* by Lillian M. Fisher. All other rights reserved, © Lillian M. Fisher 2004. Used my permission of the author, Lillian M. Fisher.

Madison Press Books & Robert Ballard

From *Ghost Liners: Exploring The World's Greatest Lost Ships* by Robert D. Ballard. Text © 1998 Odyssey Corporation and Rick Archbold. Used by permission.

Scholastic, Inc

"Talk with an Astronaut" from *Meet Famous Latinos, Ellen Ochoa from scholastic.com.* Copyright © 2004 by Scholastic Inc. Reproduced by permission of Scholastic Inc.

Thomson Learning Global Rights Group

"Your World" from *The Selected Works of Georgia Douglas Johnson, (African-American Women Writers, 1910-1940)* by Georgia Douglas Camp Johnson (Author), Claudia Tate (Introduction).1996. Revised edition copyright © 1974 by the Estate of Arna Bontemps. First edition copyright © 1963 by Arna Bontemps. Used by permission.

University Press of New England

Gary Soto. "The Gymnast" in *A Summer Life.* © 1990 by University Press of New England, Lebanon, NH. Reprinted with permission.

Note: Every effort has been made to locate the copyright owner of material reproduced on this component. Omissions brought to our attention will be corrected in subsequent editions.

Illustrations

Cover: Greg Newbold; **EI2–EI25** Dan Santat; **42** Jui Ishida; **52–70** Matt Faulkner; **83–91**Robert Mancini; **110–124** Gregory Christie; **162–164** Bob Dacey; **174–186** Richard Johnson; **220–224** Francis Livingston; **262–270** Marc Sasso; **307–308** Robert Barrett; **312–314** Shelly Hehenberger; **352–357** Tom McNeely; **W2–W15** Dean MacAdam.

Photographs

Every effort has been made to secure permission and provide appropriate credit for photographic material. The publisher deeply regrets any omission and pledges to correct errors called to its attention in subsequent editions.

Unless otherwise acknowledged, all photographs are the property of Pearson Education, Inc.

Photo locators denoted as follows: Top (T), Center (C), Bottom (B), Left (L), Right (R), Background (Bkgd)

18 (C) ©Piotr Naskrecki/Minden Pictures; **20** (B) ©Amos Nachoum/Corbis, (TL) ©Frank Lukasseck/Corbis, (CC) ©image100/Corbis; **24** (B) ©Adam Jones/Getty Images, (C) ©Jetta Productions/Dana Neely/Getty Images, (T) ©Roger Ressmeyer/Corbis; **46** (B) ©David Brooks/Corbis, (BR) ©Galen Rowell/Corbis; **47** (BC) ©Liba Taylor/Corbis; **49** (BR) ©Kevin Cooley/Getty Images, (T) ©Michael Krasowitz/Getty Images; **50** (C) ©Gwendolyn Plath/Getty Images, (B) ©PCL/Alamy Images, (T) PhotoLibrary; **51** (BR) ©Colin Hawkins/Getty Images; **76** (B) ©Keren Su/Corbis; **77** (CC) ©Frans Lanting/Corbis, (CR) ©Steven Hunt/Getty Images; **80** (B) ©Dan Saelinger/Getty Images, (T) ©Fancy/Veer/Corbis, (C) ©Peter Beck/Corbis; **82** (TR) ©Oliver Strewe/Getty Images, (BL) ©Steven Hunt/Getty Images; **83** (TR) ©Bob Elsdale/Getty Images, (TL) ©Fred Bavendam/Minden Pictures; **84** (BL) ©Ant Photo Library/NHPA Limited, (CL) ©Tim Flach/Getty Images; **85** (BR) ©Studio Carlo Dani/Animals Animals/Earth Scenes; **86** (TL) ©Tim Flach/Getty Images, (TC) Premaphotos/Animals Animals/Earth Scenes; **87** (TR) ©Mitsuaki Iwago/Minden Pictures, (TL) Scott Camazine; **88** (BL) ©Art Wolfe/Getty Images, (BR) ©David Tipling/Photographer's Choice/Getty Images, (TL) ©Tim Flach/Getty Images; **90** (T) ©Joe McDonald/Corbis, (BL) ©Michael & Patricia Fogden/

Minden Pictures, (CL) ©Tim Flach/Getty Images; **91 (TR)** ©Michael & Patricia Fogden/Corbis; **98** ©Kevin Schafer/Corbis; **99** (B) ©Brandon Cole Marine Photography/Alamy Images, (TR) ©Corbis/Jupiter Images; **100** (T) ©blickwinkel/Alamy Images, (C) ©Dave Watts/Alamy Images, (B) ©Michael & Patricia Fogden/Corbis, (B) ©Michael A. Keller/Corbis; **101** ©Wayne Lawler/Ecoscene/Corbis; **104** (B) ©David Young-Wolff/PhotoEdit; **105** (BR) ©Nicholas Prior/Getty Images, (CC) ©Randy Faris/Corbis; **108** (C) ©FB-STUDIO/Alamy Images, (B) ©Jim Naughten/The Image Bank/Getty Images, (T) Corbis; **136** (B) ©JLP/Jose Luis Pelaez/zefa/Corbis; **137** (CC) ©David Young-Wolff/PhotoEdit, (BR) ©Thomas Fricke/Corbis; **140** (T) ©Ann Stevens/Alamy, (B) ©Blend Images/Alamy; **144** (CR) Jupiter Images; **147** (BR) Veer, Inc.; **156** (C) ©Don Mason/Corbis; **158** (BR) ©Caron P., (BC) ©Jon Feingersh Photography, (BL) Corbis; **159** (CR) ©Dave Black Photography; **166** (C) Jupiter Images; **168** (B) ©Simon D. Warren/Corbis; **169** (BR) ©Jochen Tack/Alamy Images, (TC) ©Moodboard/Corbis; **172** (B) ©DLILLC/Corbis, (T) ©Fabrice Bettex/Alamy Images, (C) Photolibrary; **198** (BL) ©Bill Ross/Corbis, (B) ©Stephen Frink/Corbis; **199** (BR) ©Michael DeYoung/Getty Images; **202** (T) ©Michael Brooke/PhotoLibrary Group, Ltd., (B) ©Tom Stoddart/Getty Images, (C) ©WidStock/Alamy; **204** (C) Paintings ©1998 Ken Marschall; **206** (T, BR, BL, BC) Paintings ©1998 Ken Marschall; **207** (BL, BC) Paintings ©1998 Ken Marschall, (CR) The Granger Collection, NY; **208** (TC) Paintings ©1998 Ken Marschall; **210** (TR) Paintings ©1998 Ken Marschall, (BR) Woods Hole Oceanographic Institution; **211** (BR, BL) Woods Hole Oceanographic Institution; **212** (C) Paintings ©1998 Ken Marschall, Inc.; **214** (T) Paintings ©1998 Ken Marschall, Inc.; **215** (Inset) ©Michael Freeman/Corbis, (TR, TL) Woods Hole Oceanographic Institution; **228** (TL) ©Roger Ressmeyer/Corbis, (CL) GRIN/NASA; **229** (BR) ©NASA/Corbis; **232** (T) ©Barry Austin Photography/Getty Images, (B) ©Monkey Business Images Ltd/Photolibrary, (C) Jupiter Images; **234** (C) ©World Perspectives/Getty Images; **236** (TL) Getty Images, (TL) NASA; **237** (B) ©Mark Lawrence Photo; **239** (C) Corbis; **240** (C) NASA; **243** (C) NASA; **244** (B) ©NASA/Corbis; **250** (CR) Corbis, (TC) Getty Images; **251** (CR) ©Premium Stock/Corbis; **252** (BL) ©Time Life Pictures/NASA/Getty Images; **253** (CR) ©NASA/Roger Ressmeyer/Corbis; **256** (BL) ©Dorling Kindersley/Getty Images, (B) ©Macduff Everton/Corbis; **257** (TR) ©John & Eliza Forder/Getty Images; **260** (C) ©Imageshop/Corbis, (T) ©Joel Sartore/Photolibrary, (B) Corbis; **284** (BC) ©Dan Johnson /Jupiter Images, (B) ©Dave G. Houser/Corbis; **288** (B) ©Dennis Gilbert/PhotoLibrary Group, Ltd., (T) ©FK PHOTO/Corbis, (C) Photolibrary; **290** (C) ©James Nazz/Corbis; **291** (C) ©Chris Collins/Corbis; **292** (C) ©Raymond Bial, (L) DK Images; **293** (BL) ©John Cancalosi/Peter Arnold, Inc.; **294** (TL) ©Bettmann/Corbis; **295** (B) ©Western History Department/Denver Public Library, Western History Collection; **296** (T) ©Museum of History & Industry/Corbis, (BL) ©Raymond Bial; **298** (BR) ©David Stoecklein/Corbis, (BL) ©Raymond Bial; **299** (T) ©Raymond Bial; **301** (T) ©Lynn Radeka/SuperStock, (BR) ©Western History Department/Denver Public Library; **316** (C) Jupiter Images; **318** (TL) ©Andersen Ross/Getty Images, (B) ©Roger Tidman/Corbis; **319** (CR) ©Somos/Jupiter Images; **321** (R) ©Wally Eberhart /Jupiter Images; **322** (C) ©Aspix/Alamy, (T) ©Frank Greenaway/Getty Images, (C) ©Jason Edwards/National Geographic/Getty Images; **323** (TR) ©James Hager/Robert Harding World Imagery/Getty Images, (TL) ©Marty Snyderman/Getty Images; **338** (Bkgd) ©Paul A. Souders/Corbis; **340** (TR) Digital Stock, (TC, B) Getty Images; **341** (CR) Getty Images; **344** (CL) ©Kennan Ward/Corbis; **345** (BC) ©Glowimages/Getty Images; **348** (T) ©Gunter Marx/Alamy Images, (C) ©SMC Images/The Image Bank/Getty Images, (B) Getty Images; **350** (C) ©Natalie Fobes/Corbis; **355** (TR) Dr. David R. Klein; **356** (TC) ©Darrell Gulin/Corbis, (TL) ©David Muench/Corbis, (CR) ©Steve Austin/Papilio/Corbis; **359** (TR) ©David Roseneau, (CL) Art Sowls/Dr. David R. Klein; **364** (TR) ©Adam Rountree/AP Images, (B) ©Lincoln Karim/AP Images, (CC) ©Mitchell Funk/Getty Images; **366** (BL) ©Dan Callister/Rex USA, (BR) ©Mike Segar/Reuters/Landov LLC; **367** (B) ©Dan Callister/Rex USA; **370** (BL) ©Daniel LeClair/Corbis, (B) Jupiter Images; **371** (TR) ©Justin Kase/Alamy; **374** (B) ©foodfolio/Alamy Images, (T) ©Teresa De Paul/Getty Images, (C) Getty Images; **398** (CR) ©joeysworld/Alamy Images; **402** (CL) ©David Deas/Getty Images, (B) Jupiter Images; **403** (BC) ©ERproductions Ltd/Getty Images; **406** (T) ©Travelshots/Alamy, (C) Alamy, (B) Photolibrary; **428** (T) ©Hulton Archive/Getty Images; **430** (B) ©Hulton Archive/Getty Images; **431** (CL) ©AFP/Getty Images, (CR) ©Hulton Archive/Getty Images; **432** (C) ©James Quine/Alamy Images, (B) ©Matthias Clamer/Getty Images, (T) Getty Images; **434** (BC) ©Blend

Images/Jupiter Images, (B) ©Jeff Mitchell/Corbis; **435** (BC) ©Will & Deni McIntyre/Corbis; **464** (T) ©Art Kane Archives; **472** ©Peter Steiner/Alamy; **473** Getty Images; **474** (BL) ©FogStock/Index Open, (TR) Getty Images; **475** ©Everett Johnson/Index Open; **476** Digital Vision; **477** (T) ©Elmer Frederick Fischer/Corbis, (BR) Tracy Morgan/©DK Images; **479** (R) ©Image Source/Getty Images, (L) Getty Images; **480** ©Patrik Giardino/Corbis; **481** Getty Images; **482** (R) ©photolibrary/Index Open, (L) ©Tetra Images/Alamy; **483** (R) ©Blend Images/Alamy, (L) Paul Springett/©DK Images; **484** (L) ©Image Source (R) Susanna Price/©DK Images; **485** Getty Images; **584** (CL) ©Richard T. Nowitz/Corbis.

Teacher's Edition

Text

Grateful acknowledgment is made t the following for copyrighted materi

Caroline House an imprint of Boyds Mills Press, Inc

From *All the King's Animals: The Return of Endangered Wildlife to Swaziland* by Cristina Kessler. (Caroline House, an imprint of Boyd Mills Press, 1995.) Reprinted with th permission of Boyds Mills Press, Inc Text copyright © 1995 by Cristina Kessler.

Curtis Brown, Ltd

"Valuables" by X.J. Kennedy as first appeared in *The Kite That Braved Old Orchard Beach,* published by McElderry Books. Copyright © 1991 by X.J. Kennedy. Used by permissior of Curtis Brown, Ltd.

Note: Every effort has been made to locate the copyright owner of material reproduced on this component. Omissions brought to our attention wil be corrected in subsequent editions.

KWL Strategy: The KWL Interactive Reading Strategy was developed and is used by permission of Donna Ogle, National-Louis University, Skokie, Illinois, co-author of *Reading Today and Tomorrow,* Holt, Rinehart & Winston Publishers, 1988. (See also the *Reading Teacher,* February 1986, pp. 564–570.)

Understanding by Design quotes: Wiggins, G. & McTighe, J. (2005). *Understanding by Design.* Alexandria, VA: Association for Supervision and Curriculum Development.

Illustrations

Cover Greg Newbold

Running Head Linda Bronson

Photographs

Every effort has been made to secure permission and provide appropriate credit for photographic material. The publisher deeply regrets any omission and pledges to correct errors called to its attention in subsequent editions.

Unless otherwise acknowledged, all photographs are the property of Pearson Education, Inc.

Teacher Notes

Teacher Resources

Looking for Teacher Resources and other important information?

In the **First Stop** on Reading Street

- **Dear Fifth Grade Teacher**
- **Research into Practice on Reading Street**
- **Guide to Reading Street**
- **Assessment on Reading Street**
- **Customize Writing on Reading Street**
- **Differentiate Instruction on Reading Street**

- **ELL on Reading Street**
- **Customize Literacy on Reading Street**
- **Digital Products on Reading Street**
- **Teacher Resources for Grade 5**
- **Index**

Teacher Resources

Looking for Teacher Resources and other important information?

In the **First Stop** on Reading Street